T0367600

I Was Born
GAY
I Was Born
AGAIN

JonPual McLurék

ARCHWAY
PUBLISHING

Archway Publishing books may be ordered through booksellers or by contacting:

Archway Publishing
1663 Liberty Drive
Bloomington, IN 47403
www.archwaypublishing.com
844-669-3957

Scripture taken from the King James Version of the Bible.

ISBN: 978-1-4808-8839-5 (sc)
ISBN: 978-1-4808-8838-8 (hc)
ISBN: 978-1-4808-8840-1 (e)

Library of Congress Control Number: 2020907605

Print information available on the last page.

Archway Publishing rev. date: 12/23/2020

Dedicated

To my mother, Lula Bell Hill, 1960s Mississippi sharecropper, full of faith toward God, and who celebrated ninety-two years old on February 18, 2020. You have set a good example for all of your eleven children by bringing us up in the Lord's church. Years of shepherding a house full of tots and teens off to Sunday school is no small feat. You have been a perfect example of long suffering, forgiveness, love, patience, and inspiration. With an abundance of love and appreciation, this book is for you.

Contents

Acknowledgments

I thank God for giving me the spirit that moved me to write this book. It has been said that there are as many opinions as there are noses—everybody has one. With that in mind, I've allowed this saying to be my guidepost for what I have to say. I've backed every sentence and thought with scripture. Every truth in my writing is from the word of God.

Thank you to God for all the great Church of Christ gospel ministers and teachers from whom I have received tutelage over these fifty-plus years as a member of the body of Christ, and whom God has allowed to cross my path in "The Way." Thank you to Herbert Moore of Atlanta, Georgia, for his inspiring expression "This is getting good right here" as his eyes twinkle and face lights up with a big smile while he explains the gospel. I saw in him what the scripture means when it says, "Taste the word of God."

Special thanks to Barbara and Don Scott. Out of all the individuals from whom I requested help for the initial funds to get my book self-published, they were the first to back me and gave me four times more than the amount I had requested. And before others, whom I had asked before them, this gift was a boost of encouragement to me. Thank you to Wy and Jim Bowman and Carrie and Bryan Armour for their investment in me and my book.

May God's word not go out void, and may this book inspire readers to make the necessary changes that will save their souls, putting them on the right side of history.

Preface

I remember my first encounter with the notion of boys behaving like girls. A young male transferred to my small Mississippi high school in my tenth-grade year from a school in New York. Some forty years later, I could not have ever imagined (in my young mind back then), that this would have been the status of such a notion as it has become today—the twenty first century. Over the past decades, as early as the nineties (for me), I have observed this movement, from fledgling rainbow-flag-waving parades in Atlanta, GA and across the country to skillfully maneuverings; making inroads into the fabric of our American society (sports, entertainment, and TV: sitcoms and movies). But it wasn't until the election of the first black president of these United States that brought this somewhat sleeping giant to a screeching halt for me.

It was the gay and lesbian community's proclamation of civil rights on behalf of their cause and their attempts to identify their struggles with black America's civil rights movement, hitching a ride on the first black president's coattail. They have positioned themselves as a group to be reckoned with, politically speaking, in the voting polls. Americans forced upon, in the election ballots, concerning gay marriage in a Taser-like or jolting effect. It was a "while America slept" moment for this country. This became a wakeup call to which I am willing to respond. The LGBT community wants to be heard and because I have been a student of the bible since childhood, I am writing to challenge that notion, allowing the readers to see both sides: what the Gays are saying and what the Bible is saying about the subject of marriage and being born gay. Being a student of the Bible, I understand that these are not just people going to hell. Guess what? If I fail to warn the wicked, I go to hell, too—say what!

It is my hope and prayer that the purchasers of this book will view both perspectives (in the raw/nonpolitically correctness and unapologetic way it is meant to be) in a way they have not been challenged before, and make a non-sugarcoated, intelligent decision about the matter. The Gays are out there and the Bible is out there. It seems that the Gays claim to hold a dirty little secret that not even God (Who has all knowledge) is privy to. You can choose: truth or lie.

It is my prayer that the reader will leave with a better understanding of the following:

➢ The ill-rationalization and non-sequitur of the LGBT argument
➢ The deceitfulness in their messages
➢ The non-sustainability in their cause
➢ The irrevocable damage in their cause

Because this book provides biblical proof of God's expectation, it will inspire the readers and honest hearts to consider the following:

➢ Challenge the readers to examine what is being asked of them by the LGBT community.
➢ Help believers and non-believers realize the numerous scriptures that support God's view of the matter and none for the effeminate.
➢ Show it is not a question of freedom and rights which are already freely given by God to every man, but it is a battle of good vs. evil.
➢ Give readers an understanding that the real problem is not homosexuality, but the ones who allow it to permeate our society.

All have sinned and all stand at a guilty distance from God. It was God who initiated "Come Out." Everyone has to come out from darkness and unto the marvelous light of Jesus Christ. Come out and separate (sanctify yourself/set apart) from evil deeds and worldly lust and walk in the newness of life in Jesus Christ. All are called upon to make the necessary change: make your election sure. This book challenges judges, religious leaders, politicians, effeminate, atheists, and this nation of God-fearing citizens to make a change for the better. In the past, evil was visited upon good. It was done in the past with the Jim Crow Laws, Bloody Sunday, Trail of Tears, and Women Suffrages, but this country made the necessary changes for the betterment by advancing to a better place in history and in the sight of God: such were some of you. But this is not the time to digress to calling evil, good and good, evil. God is the one who calls effeminate (homosexuality: men with men/women with women) an abomination in His sight. This book's main theme (focus) is on 1 Corinthians 6, addressing the state that all men find themselves at some degree or another: "as such were some of you, but you have been washed." The solution in 1 Corinthians chapter six is our solution—21st Century solution. The heterosexual, homosexual, and the man or woman that see himself or herself as the good person will have to consider that all have sinned and come short of the glory of God. All three groups: (A) heterosexual, (B) homosexual, and (C) the 'good' person will have to make the necessary changes to align him/herself with the will of God: hear, believe, repent, confess, and be baptized. It may be as simple as one that stops sinning and or another that starts speaking out against sin, taking into consideration the sins of omission and commission.

It is my hope that this book will be an eye opener to the unlearned in scripture and an encourager to those who need to be reminded and have the scriptural support to not keep silence but stand in the gap; not straying from the old path and save a soul, which could very well be their own in not failing to warn the wicked.

Introduction

And Such Were Some of You

> Know you not that the unrighteous shall not inherit the kingdom of God? Be not deceived: neither fornicators, or idolaters, or adulterers, nor effeminate, nor abuser of themselves with mankind, nor thieves, nor covetous, nor drunkards, nor revilers nor extortioners, shall inherit the kingdom of God. And such were some of you: but you are washed, but you are sanctified, but you are justified in the name of the Lord Jesus, and by the Spirit of our God.
>
> —1 Corinthians 6:9–11

Native Americans, white settlers from England (Europeans), and natives of Africa in one facet or another all changed this wilderness of a country into the America we know and love. In spite of what each group used to be, because of the dynamics of change—forced, welcomed, or assimilated—they can all say, in an Americanized way, "We are not the people we were in the pioneering days of this great country." We made the necessary changes for the betterment of the whole. Wars were fought and won, blood and tears were shed for rights and freedoms, and treaties were made for land and territories. In our early American experience, we endured and embraced some of the movements and revolutions that define who we are today, including the Boston Tea Party, the Bill of Rights, the U.S. Constitution, the Declaration of Independence, Jim Crow, Bloody Sunday, the Trail of Tears, Wounded Knee, women's suffrage, Title IX, trees bearing "strange fruits" in the South, and the Emancipation Proclamation. Towns and cities went up. Railroads and automobiles were built. Business enterprises, industries, and corporations made inroads in our economy. Banks and financial institutions were woven into the fabric of the nation. From horses and stagecoaches to airplanes flown continent to continent and spaceships bound for the moon, from the telephone switchboard and rotary-dialed phones to cell phones, smartphones, and the Internet, our quest to conquer and create a better future in science and technology for America hasn't been quenched by centuries of time or their immense challenges.

While I examined the common denominator among the American Indians, European settlers, and enslaved Africans, Native Americans were in oneness with nature, and they had respect for the land and the Creator of the spirit of man and beast. Settlers or pilgrims from Europe came seeking freedom of religion, and Africans held strong beliefs (faith) and reverenced the power in the God of heaven. No matter how horrific ("hellrific") and dark this union meant to some, God was in the plan. Joseph's brothers put him in a dark pit, and he was later sold into slavery, but God was in the plan. See Genesis 45:7–8.

Late president Ronald Ragan recognized the hand of God, the Providence of God in the formation of this great nation. In his autobiography, *An American Life*, he wrote,

> I was raised to believe that God has a plan for everyone and that seemingly random twists of fate are all a part of His plan. My mother—a small woman with auburn hair and a sense of optimism that ran as deep as the cosmos—told me that everything in life happened for a purpose. She said all things were part of God's Plan, even the most disheartening setbacks, and in the end, everything worked out for the best. If something went wrong, she said, you didn't let it get you down: You stepped away from it, stepped over it, and moved on. Later on, she added, something good will happen and you'll find yourself thinking—"If I hadn't had that problem back then, then this better thing that did happen wouldn't have happened to me."[1]

---

[1] Ronald Reagan, *An American Life* (New York: Simon and Schuster, 1990), 20–21.

God and the fear of God as the source of love, life, and powerful protector in all that is good for man, plants, animals, and the universe were their (native Americans, European or pilgrim settlers, and kidnapped and enslaved Africans) common denominators. This union, almighty God being its common denominator, worked according to His plan and allowed this country to stand out as the envy of all nations in the world in its power, might, and allegiance to God. America built its strength on the motto "In God We Trust." As a country, we are still experiencing an abundance of blessings in wealth and progress, in technology and military might, and in humanitarian and global recognition as a great power.

Unfortunately, though, America has taken a detour and is heading the opposite way, down a dark path, and removing God at an unprecedented rate from the fabric of America. God was in the plan at the Tower of Babel. When man became proud and arrogant and trusted in his own strength and power, God stepped in, spreading the people over the face of the earth. From them languages, nationalities, and ethnicities were formed (Genesis 11). Man did evil and increased in wickedness and idolatry before God, but God found a nation of people in the Israelites, who kept His word. God favors the nation of people who call on His name and trust in Him.

This providence worked according to God's purpose. The American Indians, white settlers, Europeans, and Africans (African Americans) from across the face of the earth, with different cultures and languages, were brought together through God's divine plan and purpose to create a country, a Christian nation that called on the true God (In God We Trust). "All the inhabitants of the earth are accounted as nothing, and He does according to His will among the host of heaven and among the inhabitants of the earth; and none can stop His hand or say to Him, 'What have you done?'" (Daniel 4:35).

Presently, in this country, we have switched gears. Our hearts are full of arrogance, strength, power, and knowledge; we are turning away from God, and this is not good for the betterment of the people of this nation. God's warning is, "The wicked shall be turned into hell and all the nations that forget God" (Psalm 9:17). Our former president, Barack Obama, delivered his commencement address to the US Military Academy at West Point's class of 2014 on Wednesday, May 28, 2014. Mr. Obama recognized the role America should and must play as a nation that trusts in the almighty God of heaven. "America must always lead on the world stage. If we don't, no one else will…

But U.S. military action cannot be the only—or even primary—component of our leadership in every instance."[2]

The president spoke of a strategy for foreign policy, weighing in on isolationism and interventionism. Mr. Obama touched on the *legitimacy* of power, which will be addressed in chapter one of this book. He said, "When we cannot explain our efforts clearly and publicly, we face terrorist propaganda and international suspicion; we erode legitimacy with our partners and our people; and we reduce accountability in our own government.[3] The scripture tells us that God cannot lie. "In My Father's house are many mansions: if it were not so, I would have told you" (John 14:2). Although there are many who try to interpret (erode the truth with propaganda) the Bible, the scripture clearly speaks of one doctrine—*one* Lord, *one* God, and *one* faith—despite thirty-two-hundred-plus faiths in the world. "Knowing this first, that no prophecy of the scripture is of any private interpretation" (2 Peter 1:20). The scripture supports the legitimacy of God's word and His authority over man's affairs.

Some might feel that America is too big to fail; well, that is exactly what the Father of Lies wants us to believe. Those who built the Tower of Babel, Adam and Eve, and Satan suffered because of the lust of the eye, the lust of the flesh, and the pride of life. Has America become too smart, powerful, and disobedient to God?

America's document (held out and followed), its bible, is the US Constitution. Besides the Holy Bible, it is the cornerstone of how America governs its people. The men who wrote the Constitution were Bible-believing men, and their faith in God strongly influenced the construction of this document and the lives of the people who accepted it as their country's constitution; it wasn't written by someone coming to America with a former country's ideas and constitution.

Right before our eyes, we are watching an attack on America (from within) and on the beliefs of its people in God, the institution of marriage, the church, and whatever else has the name God in it, including Christian practices, as its moral guideline for operation. For example, consider the Boy Scouts of America. The Boy Scouts organization is being disannulled of value, purpose, and morals; and characters of evil intent are devouring it. We are a

---

[2] Carrie Dann, "Obama Offers Foreign Policy Vision at West Point," NBC News.com, May 28, 2014.
https://www.nbcnews.com/politics/first-read/obama-offers-foreign-policy-vision-west-point-n116306 (updated 11/23/19)
[3] Ibid

country that boasts we are built on immigrants. We have foreigners who do all they can to become nationalized American citizens and afterward attack our Constitution, our Pledge of Allegiance, prayer in schools, and anything that mentions God. It won't be long before people seeking to become citizens of this great nation will challenge "In God We Trust" on our currency. America isn't an atheistic country, and our founding fathers (drafters of the US Constitution) weren't atheists. If America allows people who had nothing to do with building this great nation to dictate to God-fearing citizens how not to acknowledge God, will there be an America in the next century? If it is in God we trust, when God is removed from America, will there be an America? If He isn't in America, how can we have the audacity to ask God to bless America? Why would He?

In our early history as a country, we weren't where we wanted to be, but we kept moving toward a higher goal and trusting God to bless us and place us where we needed and should be. We are recognized as a strong military might and humanitarian nation, a nation that trusts in the almighty God. Our history isn't squeaky clean or without fault. We wear the shame and still have the scars and stench of slavery in pockets of America. Even today a disproportionate segment of our society still seeks to be treated fairly in housing, education, employment, wages, health insurance, health care, businesses, home loans, and police protection. As a nation that boasts of being a Christian nation, thank God we aren't the people we once were (in other words, "And such were some of you"). And it will take God to help us continue on the path of becoming more of who we need and should to be in His sight and in the sight of other nations.

As Americans, we should and can feel good about ourselves as a nation that supports Christian missionary works and the spreading of the gospel of Christ to many pagan worshippers around the globe, where many enslave and use their women, girls, and children for live blood sacrifice in dehumanizing rituals and cultural traditions. Once Christ is taught and accepted, one is free from the tradition and rudiments (or nonessential thoughts) of this world. "If the Son therefore shall make you free, you shall be free indeed" (John 8:36).

Let America take heed and not be deceived by what is happening in this nation today. Let us not be like those destroyed in Sodom and Gomorrah because we, the *righteous* found, fail to speak out against the evil that is upon us and fail to repent of our course (Amos 4:11). We fought for what was right in the dark days of our past: Jim Crow and slavery; in other words, the suffrage of black people or African Americans, women, and Indians. We shouldn't fail to do the right thing today. "And whosoever shall not receive you, nor hear your words, when you depart out of that house or city, shake off the dust of your feet. Verily I say to you, It shall be more tolerable for the land of Sodom and Gomorrah in the Day of Judgment than for that city" (Matthew 10:14–15; also see Luke 10:12; 17:28–30; 2 Peter 2:4–10; Jude 1:7).

Let's take a moment and examine how mighty and great America really is. "Except the Lord build the house, they labor in vain that build it: except the Lord keep the city, the watchman wakes but in vain" (Psalm 127:1). Now, do we know how great and mighty we are? The stench or odorous lifestyle of homosexuality in the nostrils of God destroyed Sodom and Gomorrah. Is America the next Sodom and Gomorrah? *Those who fail to learn the lesson of history are doomed to repeat it.* The scriptures tell us that things we read in God's holy word were written for our admonition, upon whom the ends of the world have come (1 Corinthians 10:11). When we take the time to study history, we will come to know that mighty nations have succumbed to less mighty nations. Let us not give God a reason to withdraw His blessings and protection from America. It's not our military might but God who keeps the city.

"And such were some of you." God is still calling people (man) to make a change that is in line with His plan for them—taking them out of the pit of sin and putting them in high places. Joseph, who found himself in a pit, ended up serving as ruler over half of Pharaoh's kingdom; as vizier of Egypt, he was second in command to Pharaoh. In Christ, people who are enslaved to sin and death can inherit a mansion—home in heaven and life eternally with God through their obedience to the gospel of Jesus Christ.

> His lord said to him, Well done, good and faithful servant; you have been faithful over a few things, I will make you ruler over many things: enter you into the joy of your lord. (Matthew 25:23)
>
> In My Father's house are many mansions: if it were not so, I would have told you. I go to prepare a place for you. And if I go and prepare a place for you, I will come again, and receive you to Myself; that where I am, there you may be also. (John 14:2–3)

It doesn't matter what kind of a 'pit of a lifestyle' you find yourself in in this life; Jesus has a wonderful and marvelous plan for you. He is there to lift you out of sin and set you on the right path to obtain salvation, and you also can proclaim as the effeminates, fornicators, adulterers, thieves, drunkards, and so forth in 1 Corinthians 6 that such were some are you, but you are washed, sanctified, and justified in the Lord Jesus.

Let us in America change course and turn back toward God. Let us truly put our trust in God so He will continue to bless us. In return, we will give Him no reason not to.

As mentioned in the preface, the only reason this book was even conceived is that I thought it was very interesting, while observing the 2008 presidential campaign and election, how the gay agenda positioned itself as a force to be recognized. What was interesting to observe was how the issue of homosexuality played out in the media as far as being a political sect holding some voting power of persuasion in the polls. My thoughts were these: Now who are these people? What exactly is their importance in what is happening with the first black president? Was Mr. Obama an easy target to ride on or piggyback on the civil rights issue: black people in America struggles, suffrages and landmark cases? This notion of boys wanting to be girls, I recall from my high school days over forty-five years ago, had advanced to a far cry from a confused teenager from up north, coming to live in a small southern town. Today's gay rights individuals certainly aren't victims or subjected to homosexual codes or Jim Crow, poll taxes, or gerrymandering for being homosexuals; they don't even stand in jeopardy of having any freedom denied by the Voting Rights Acts of 1965. They aren't forced to ride in the back of buses, drink from separate water fountains, use separate public bathrooms, or eat at separate lunch counters. In their hellrific struggles in America, black people just wanted to be treated like human beings through God's inalienable rights. The gays and lesbians want to have intercourse (unnatural or inhuman) with a man or woman of the same sex. God has deemed this activity an abomination (Leviticus 18:22). The two "civil" rights movements aren't equal causes in any stretch of the imagination. Men who get sex-change operations are still men because there's no new Creator around making or creating new beings. They want to share the same bathroom or restroom with your young daughters at the malls, restaurants, and other public places in defiance of nature and contempt and hate toward God.

Motivated by these thoughts, I began to take a look in the Bible and search the scriptures. Surprisingly, I observed that no other sinners from "the list" fought so hard to have his or her way or challenged God, even though they were called out for their ungodly deeds. This stimulated my curiosity even more to find out just what has been said about homosexuality in scripture, in light of what is currently happening in this country. I purposefully centered this book on a few issues chronologically happening between 2013 and 2016. I began a diligent search, following local and national news, the Internet, and the Supreme Court.

In 1 Corinthians 6:9–11, which I hereafter refer to as "the list," we find,

"Know you not that the unrighteous shall not inherit the kingdom of God? Be not deceived: neither fornicators, or idolaters, or adulterers, nor *effeminate*, nor abuser of themselves with mankind, nor thieves, nor covetous, nor drunkards, nor revilers nor extortioners, shall inherit the Kingdom of God. And such were some of you: but you are washed, but you are sanctified, but you are justified in the name of the Lord Jesus and by the Spirit of our God" (emphasis added). Also see Romans 1:21–32.

Why are we having this debate at this point in man's history on the face of this earth? Didn't God say being effeminate **is** an abomination in His sight? (Leviticus 18:22, Romans 1: 25-32). Who wants to debate with God? No, seriously, really, who? Who is wiser than God? Who is stronger and more powerful than God? Did man give God His sight, or did God give man his sight? Does God not know what is abominable or not abominable in His sight? Can you believe we are searching for a gay gene and trying to prove God wrong? I discovered while researching the subject that many of today's authors, in support of the gay lifestyle, seek to reinterpret the Bible, looking for scriptures to trip God up on what He has said or to help God out by explaining to God and man what God really meant when He said what He said, not realizing it is to their own destruction (Deuteronomy 4:2; 18:18–20; Galatians 1:8; Revelation 22:19). "Add you not to His words, less He reprove you, and you be found a liar" (Proverbs 30:6).

Why are there no other offenders on "the list" saying they are predisposed to a lifestyle because of some genetic problem—a lying gene, a thieving gene, an adultery gene, a fornicator gene, or an alcoholic (drunkard) gene? Are they not on "the list" too? I wanted to know why and in particular why the effeminates are the ones coming out into the light, while the others are ashamed of their acts and prefer to not let anyone else, if possible, know what they do behind closed doors, in darkness, or out of the light. Effeminates aren't the only ones on "the list," although they are the sinners labeled as an abomination. Is that why they are so upset with God and anyone else who calls them out? It is the author's intention to bring what the Scripture has to say about homosexuality and Sodom and Gomorrah out front just as the gays have come out front in this country, the USA. The gays want to be heard, and it is only fair that the Scriptures are heard, too. Taking the time (making a concerted effort) to examine the subject of homosexuality and scripture, one can make an intelligent assessment of the two: both of their claims. Not that we really need to, because God has already said, "Let God be true and every man a liar." Hear what thus says the Lord. Nevertheless, come let us take this walk through the pages of inspiration together.

And Such Were Some of You

DESTRUCTION OF THE TEA CARGOES.

The Townshend Acts and Tea Act placed tax on goods (paper, glass, sugar, and tea); these were merchandise the colonies needed. Anger from these acts led to boycotts, killings, and the dumping of tea into the Boston Harbor, called the "Boston Tea Party" (1773).

The Boston Tea Party was the result of taxation without representation and eventually led to the American Revolutionary War, US independence from British rule, and the Declaration of Independence.

MANIFESTATIONS DES SUFFRAGETTES A LONDRES
Une sortie de prison triomphale

Voting at the time was restricted to white males. Because of sexism and the racism from white suffragists, black women continued to experience difficulties in their rights to vote from the 1920s and continuing into the 1960s. The black women activists' role in the era of women suffrages was extremely influential in the success of the women's suffrage movement. A few noted leaders were black women like Harriet Tubman, Sojourner Truth, Ida B. Wells, Mary Church Terrell, Annie Sims Banks, Ella Baker, Angela Davis, and Rosa Parks.[4]

The United States forced and removed many tribes of Indians, including the Chickasaws Indians, from their Mississippi homes and territories in the mid-1800s. This act of forcing Indians off their lands and placing them on reservations came to be known in history as the Trail of Tears. Many Indians died en route to reservations from illness, diseases, and exposure to the harsh elements. Bodies of Lakota Indians were piled into a mass grave in the frozen, hard soil of South Dakota. After the massacre, it became known as the Battle of Wounded Knee or Wounded Knee Massacre (December 1890).

In 1987, Congress designated the original 2,422-mile Trail of Tears National Historic Trail, commemorating the two main routes used during

---

[4] Wikipedia, s.v. "Marginalizing African American Women," African American Woman Suffrage, accessed May 9, 2014. https://en.wikipedia.org/wiki/African-American_women%27s_suffrage_movement, last modified November 20, 2019, 21:40

the forced removal. At that time, many of the side routes used during the removal weren't well documented, including important round-up routes from the forts, to which the Cherokee had originally been taken in North Carolina, Georgia, Tennessee, and Alabama; as well as unique routes taken by detachments led by pro-treaty leader John Bell and Cherokee Captain John Benge. Subsequent research has identified those routes, and in 2006, Congress directed the National Park Service to determine whether more routes of the Cherokee removal would be eligible to be added to the existing National Historic Trail.

Taking a stroll back to a not-so-distant time, we see that slavery in the United States and property played a big part in voting rights, which were restricted to the white male. When this requirement was abolished, the nation became more democratic in its laws. The North abandoned any hold on the slave as property, but Southern states' slave owners fought to keep slavery legal and to maintain the privilege to the lifestyle they had become accustomed to through the servitude (human trafficking or kidnapping) of African slaves. When Abraham Lincoln became president, several Southern states and their land owners feared the end of that lifestyle, with ownership of people (other human beings) to do with at their pleasure. They decided to secede from the United States, form their own military, and elect their own president, thus creating the Confederate States of America. President Lincoln counteracted, calling the action illegal, thus setting off the American Civil War (1861–1865). The Union won the battle, with Robert E. Lee (Confederate soldier/general) surrendering to Ulysses S. Grant (Union soldier/general) in 1865.

President Lincoln was assassinated in 1865, but the piece of legislation for which he fought during his administration was the Emancipation Proclamation, which outlawed slavery. The Republican Party carried out his wishes. Black people, by US law, were then equal (due to inalienable rights by God) and unrestricted. This legislation granted the black male voting rights via constitutional amendments, but he still faced opposition from his oppressors. After the act, it took a century later, after the civil rights movement and nonviolent protests against discrimination, for full citizenship to improve the lives of black people in America. The Civil Rights Act and the Voting Rights Act were passed in 1964.

Pictorial Illustrations of Historic Events

- European whites were granted freedom from British rule. The Treaty of Paris (1783) ended the American Revolutionary War (1775–1783) between Great Britain and the United States of America. The war started because of taxes imposed on Americans from the British Parliament.
- Declaration of Independence (July 4, 1776); the thirteen colonies (and newly sovereign states) were no longer under British rule; they formed a new nation, the United States of America. The Declaration was signed on July 2 and celebrated on July 4.
- Emancipation Proclamation: End of Slavery January 1, 1863
- Women's Voting Rights 1920: Nineteenth Amendment
- The Voting Right Act of 1965
- Indian Civil Rights Act of 1968

It is clear that God, the creator, cares for mankind and his rights to exist in a peaceful, happy, prosperous, and free status within the framework of what He deems good for male and female. The founding fathers of the Declaration of Independence (1776) demonstrated a showing of support of these common human desires that are providentially purported in this country and wrote the following sentiment:

"We hold these truths to be self-evident that all men are created equal. That they are endowed by their creator with certain unalienable Rights, that among these are life, liberty and the pursuit of happiness."

Chapter 1
The Authority of the Bible

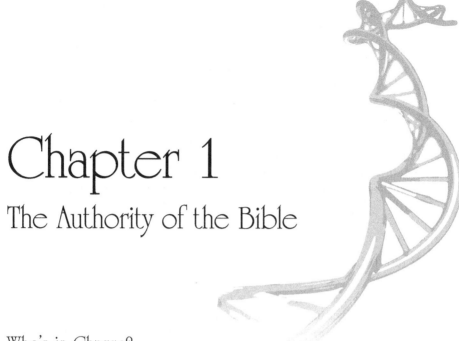

Who's in Charge?

"AND WHEN HE was come into the temple, the chief priests and the elders of the people came to Him as He was teaching, and said, By what authority do You these things? And who gave you this authority?" (Matthew 21:23).

No doubt they observed Jesus on many occasions healing the blind and the lame (v. 14). He cast the money changers out of the temple (v. 12). The multitudes (of people) sang praises to Him. "Hosanna to the son of David: Blessed is He that comes in the name of the Lord, Hosanna in the highest" (v. 9). And He stood in the temple and synagogue and taught, not as the scribes but as one with *authority* (Matthew 7:29).

We all want to know and ask these questions daily: Who's in charge? May I speak with your boss? Who is the owner of this business and/or property? We also want to know and ask (when things occur, especially when they affect us in a personal way), by what authority or who put the person making plans that affect our lives in charge? Who hasn't been the recipient of flippant comments like, "Who died and made you God?" or "Who put you in charge?" Jesus affected the influence the priests, scribes, and religious leaders had on the people, and they were quite disturbed by it—the changes.

No one would disagree that for the most part, and for all practical purposes and intents, the scribes asked a legitimate question. Also, any rational human being would agree that the authorization of regulatory processes in conduct and exchange in a society deemed civilized is necessary to abate chaos. In a society of people (who has the propensity to do as they please without taking into consideration how their actions could have a negative impact on others), how devastating it would be without submission to legitimate authority and rules. This submission is a necessary characteristic in a civilized nation, be it in government, judicial and local courts, the home, the school, and religion. For example, in the Catholic denomination, the pope is recognized as *head* of the Catholic Church. Many can identify with this analogy of power and authority. As you continue to read, you will discover that Christ claims to be the *head* of His Church while having all authority both in heaven and in earth.

What Is Authority?

Authority by definition means having the legal right to exercise power or to command or act in a manner of domination and jurisdiction over others. When that authority is lawful, it is understood that it must be obeyed, ignorance of the fact or not.

Wikipedia, the free encyclopedia, states that "authority" is the legitimate or socially approved use of power. "It is the legitimate power one person or a group holds over another." What I found very intriguing from Wikipedia's definition of power is the following statement: "The element of legitimacy is vital to the notion of authority and is the main means by which authority is distinguished from the more general concept of power. Power can be exerted by the use of force or violence. Authority, by contrast, depends on the acceptance by subordinates of the right of those above them to give the orders or directives."[5]

Jesus, who has all power, does not exert it or force it on mankind. He extends the latter—acceptance by subordinates of His rights to authority over their lives and their destiny. One accepts Jesus's authority over his or her life and accepts His offer of salvation and eternal life. "Whosoever will come after Me, let him deny himself, and take up his cross, and follow Me" (Mark 8:34).

Jesus's authority is legitimate; it comes from God and is not forced. No one is going to drag you kicking and screaming into heaven. It's only after you realize your undone condition without Christ that you will come running in flight to Him like a bat out of hell, asking the hills, rocks, and mountains to fall on you and hide you from the wrath of God (Revelation 6:16). But it will

---

[5] https://en.wikipedia.org/wiki/Authority_(sociology)

be too late. The thought of skilled climbers scaling the walls of the pearly gate or door to the kingdom is like believing other master shipbuilders could have built a better ship than Noah's ark and survived the biblical flood. The rain came down on the inhabitants in the days of Noah, and God shut the door to the ark. The fires of hell will overtake man, and there is a gulf that separates him from those on the other side. The Scriptures said there was a great gulf between the rich man and Lazarus.

There is no reaching heaven's gates if one allows himself or herself to be called into judgment without obedience to *God's plan of salvation*. It's through the door that you will have to enter (Matthew 7:13; Luke 13:24–25). We have already been told in Scripture that one cannot go over or under the gate (implicitly), but should strive to enter straight. Now that you are on the other side of life and at the Gate—heaven's gate, I don't think at this point there are still disbelievers: atheists and agnostics. Unfortunately, this may be the only cure for the atheist—oh well. The only way in is *straight* through the gate—[no pun intended]. God is omnipotent; the Creator of the world and that includes the creature, man. If you somehow made it here to this planet on your own and aren't a creature of God, this message is not for you; and by the way, you are an alien squatter big time!

God Gives Jesus Authority

Jesus is the only one who has told mankind, "All power is given to Me [Him] in heaven and in earth" (Matthew 28:18). Jesus said God is Lord of heaven and earth. Jesus declared that He has been from the beginning of the world; and not only that, but He was there during the creation of man. The apostle Paul declared that God made the world and everything in it; without Jesus, nothing was made.

Jesus declared that God had given Him all authority, and God testified to the fact that Jesus was His Son (Matthew 16–17). And again, at the Transfiguration in Matthew 17:1–5, God said, "This is my beloved Son, in whom I Am well pleased; hear you Him."

While Jesus was on earth over some two thousand years ago, He spoke only of having authority or, as we would say, being "put in charge" by God, His Father. Because of that fact, Jesus was able to speak or teach with authority (Matthew 7:28–29). One can hear Jesus in the Bible, the four Gospels (Matthew, Mark, Luke, and John), saying He didn't speak by His own authority, but what He said came from the Father. "He that loves Me not keeps not My sayings: and the word which you hear is not Mine, but the Father's which sent Me" (John 14:24).

The Apostles' Authority

In the continuum of who is in charge, when Jesus ascended into the heavens, He left some in charge of spreading or teaching the gospel, the word of God. "Go you therefore, and teach all nations, baptizing them in the name of the Father, and of the Son, and of the Holy Ghost; Teaching them to observe all things whatsoever I have commanded you and, lo, I am with you always even to the end of the world" (Matthew 28:19–20). The apostle Paul said the words the apostles spoke or taught were not their own (from man), but were from God through Jesus Christ. Paul, an apostle (not of men, neither by man, but by Jesus Christ and God the Father, who raised Him from the dead) wrote, "But I certify you, brethren that the gospel which was preached of me is not after man. For I neither received it of man, neither was I taught it, but by the revelation of Jesus Christ" (Galatians 1:11–12). Paul made this claim because of his life-changing encounter on the road to Damascus.

Since Jesus no longer walks in the physical body on earth and the apostles no longer walk in physical bodies on earth, the questions (spiritually speaking) beg to be answered. Who has the authority or who is in charge of telling mankind about right, wrong, good, bad, hell, heaven, morals, and immorality? And what is not sinful and what is sinful or abominable in the sight of God? Better yet, who has the authority to interpret what God and Jesus said about salvation for the soul of man?

We know from the 28 chapter of Matthew's account that Jesus commanded the apostles to go unto *all* the world [all nations] and preach the gospel (death, burial, and resurrection). By Jesus Christ's authority, the apostles were, through the working of the Holy Ghost, bringing into their memory the things Jesus had taught them and were able to record the truth of the gospel. The apostle Paul said by revelation He (the Holy Ghost) made known to him (Paul) the mystery, which he wrote about; and others are able to read and understand his knowledge in the mystery of Christ, which in other ages was not known to the sons of men as it has now been revealed by the Holy Ghost (Ephesians 3:3–4). This mystery is how Jesus died and was buried, and rose again the third day according to Scripture. And through His death, He broke down the middle wall of partition, and salvation is for all. There are no Jews and Greeks (Gentiles); all are one in Christ Jesus. He conquered death, never to die again. And all those who believe and obey will live eternally with Him. "For he that is dead is freed from sin. Now if we be dead with Christ, we believe that we shall also live with Him: Knowing that Christ being raised from the dead dies no more; death has no more dominion over Him. For in that He died, He died to sin once; but in that He lives, He lives to God" (Romans 6:7–10).

No doubt if the Jews (flaunting/bragging to be God's chosen people and privileged ones) had been privy to this mystery (plan), they wouldn't have been bent on crucifying Jesus, who had to die, shedding innocent blood to purchase man's soul (1 Corinthians 2:8). If Christ had not died, been crucified, or shed atoning blood for the sins of all mankind and all nations of people on the earth, the Jews would have remained the only people able to claim a legitimate relationship. Through Adam all died, and through Christ all have an opportunity for eternal life.

In summary, in Christ, those who obey Him are spiritual Jews and spiritual Israel. It's the circumcision of the heart and not the flesh (Jewish covenant with God under the Mosaic Law, a tradition of the people of God) that makes "man" a special people to God. There are no more Jews only but also Gentiles—both are one in Christ Jesus through the shedding of His blood on the cross. Scriptures say that the middle wall of partition between God's chosen people (Jews) and other nations of people ended with Christ's crucifixion; death, burial, and resurrection. And all have access to God and a home in heaven upon obedience to Jesus Christ. God says, "Hear ye Him— His Son."

Gospel Preachers' Authority

The New Testament is the apostles' writings and references to prophecies of the prophets. *The New Testament is the Old Testament revealed, and the Old Testament is the New Testament concealed.* The New Testament is the teaching of inspired men (apostles) and our *only* authority in matters of religion. The Holy Bible tells the righteous man of God to continue in the things he has learned and has been assured of, knowing of whom he has learned them. This would be the teaching/writing of the apostles and the preaching of gospel ministers today, who preach without addition to or subtraction from the word of God; that the scriptures are able to make us wise to salvation through Christ Jesus. "All scripture is given by inspiration of God and is profitable for doctrine, for reproof, for correction, for instruction in righteousness that the man of God may be perfect, thoroughly furnished to all good works" (2 Timothy 3:14–17).

It's important to know that there are many claiming to follow Christ and His teaching or doctrine while they add and subtract from the Scripture but have no authority to do so. Paul warned that following the tradition of men leads to vain and useless worship. There is a way that seems right to a man, but the end thereof is death (Proverbs 14:12). Many will stand before God at the judgment, having spent their time in unauthorized service in "will-worship." They will be among the ones who will hear, "Depart from me I never knew you" (Matthew 7:23; Colossians 2:23).

Would you not agree that there are a lot of "will worshippers," seeing that there are over thirty-five-hundred-plus denominational churches? The Bible, the word of God, still says *one* Lord, *one* faith, *one* baptism, and *one* God and Father of all. Contrary to religious and popular belief, the pope has no authority in New Testament teaching because of this one fact, Christ claims to be the *head* of "The Church" or "The Way") and is High Priest. Christians are part of the priesthood (1 Peter 2:9), and God is the Holy Father. Christians pray to God in the name of Christ to forgive them of their sins. No one is a middleman between God and man—not the pope or Catholic priests—but Christ Jesus and Jesus only. Christ named the Church and followers of Christ were first called "Christians" at Antioch (Acts 11:26). See where I'm going; no church in scripture is called the "Catholic Church" and no one following Christ was called a "Catholic." This holds true of any other denomination not mentioned in Scripture.

The Catholic Church is an example of traditions and teaching for *doctrines* the commandments of men talked about in Matthew 15:9. When one is baptized into Christ, he or she becomes a saint; the person is set aside (sanctified) and separate (set apart) from the world. The old man is dead, and he is a new creature in Christ. To become a saint in the Catholic Church, one must be canonized; this is some huge non-scripturally supported process or ritual. Christ, who knew no sins, forgives sins, but in the Catholic Church, there is a man (a sinner) who gets old and dies (the pope); he claims to forgive or offers up forgiveness for your sins. Where am I going with this? My question is where are you going with this pope forgiving you of your sins? Is it to heaven? Christ promised you that. The pope can't promise you something he doesn't have the power to give—mainly the absolution of sins. "Blessed are they whose iniquities are forgiven and whose sins are covered" (Romans 4:7; Psalm 32:1). "Bless me, 'holy father,' for I have sinned." —WHAT? REALLY! Can he do that? Confess your faults one to another in the church, where Christ is the head and where the effectual fervent prayers of the righteous man avails much (James 5:16).

Riddle me this: If God were a tolerant being, would He have bothered to send Christ down to show mankind the one way, the only way to live? God is patient, not tolerant. Let that thought sink in. He is waiting and willing for all to take advantage of the opportunity provided to repent before it is everlastingly too late. We are witnessing a deathly agenda in this nation (a Nineveh with violence and immorality); there is tolerance for what God calls an abomination in His sight (Jonah 1:2, Matthew 12:41, and Luke 11:32). We must understand that today, Christ is our Savior. But tomorrow, Christ is our judge. If one refuses to believe the Bible is the word of God, there is no continued need to establish arguments, assertions or hypotheses to conclude otherwise in conversation with this individual anyway. Eat, drink, and be merry. "If in this life only we have hope in Christ, we are of all men most miserable" (1 Corinthians 15:19).

The following scriptures explain the importance of the gospel. The gospel was preached by the apostles and continues to be preached today as God's plan of salvation. Let's examine what the apostle Paul had to say about the gospel. "Now if Christ be preached that He rose from the dead, how say some among you that there is no resurrection of the dead? But if there be no resurrection of the dead, then is Christ not risen? And if Christ be not risen, then is our preaching in vain, and your faith is also vain. Yea, and we are found false witnesses of God; because we have testified of God that He raised up Christ whom He raised not up, if so be that the dead rise not. For if the dead rise not, then is not Christ raised. And if Christ be not raised, your faith is vain and you are yet in your sins" (1 Corinthians 15:12–17).

Paul continued, "But now is Christ risen from the dead, and become the firstfruits of them that slept. For since by man came death, by man came also the resurrection of the dead. For as in Adam all died, even so in Christ shall all be made alive. But every man in his own order: Christ the firstfruits; afterward they that are Christ's at His coming. Then comes the end when He shall have delivered up obedient believers, the church [kingdom] to God, even the Father, when He shall have put down all rule and all authority and power" (1 Corinthians 15:20–24).

For the sake of argument, let's look into the area of reasonable deduction. Jesus is the only "spiritual" leader in the history of man (among many, including Buddha, Confucius, Gandhi, Mohammad, and so forth, whom people accept as spiritual leaders), who *has made promises* to man and backed them up by dying on the cross. Suffering a cruel death shows He understands the condition and dilemma or state of the soul of man far more than man himself. Jesus called the Old Testament the word of God (John 10:34–35). Name a spiritual leader other than Jesus who has claimed to be God's only begotten Son, who has claimed to have died for our sins, and who has claimed to have inspired men to write the scriptures, the word of God. Those men (apostles) wrote through the Holy Spirit so man can have a guide to instruct in all righteousness. What spiritual leader other than Jesus has claimed to have built a mansion for you (man) in heaven, thus, instructing that "Where I go, you too maybe also"? Name one thing Buddha, Confucius, Gandhi, Mohammad, and so forth went out of their way to do for you. Did they secure a home in heaven for you? Rarely for a good man would one dare to die (Romans 5:7–10). They have ears but don't hear, they have mouths but cannot speak, and they have eyes but cannot see (Psalm 115:5–8, 135:16–18). The others promise you nothing, and rightfully so; they cannot give you anything.

We have established that legitimate authority is complex and has written rules. The Bible is the written word of God. It comprises commands, instructions, and examples of what is acceptable and unacceptable. What is great is that there is no private interpretation (2Peter 1:20). Don't bother with a debate; God has already said there is no private interpretation. Of course, man over the centuries has tried to add and subtract for personal gain as it suits his purposes.

Distinguishing the many books that claim to be divine comes down to reasonable deduction. What are they claiming? Let's remember the Jews in Berea; the scriptures say they were more noble than those Jews at Thessalonica because they searched the scriptures daily to see what things the apostle Paul said were true/so (Acts 17:11-13). We are commanded to "work out our own [soul's] salvation with trembling and fear" (Philippians 2:12). There is something for us to do: read and study the Bible for ourselves. If we don't care to do that—well, that poses another problem for us individually. We can deal with that individually on the Day of Judgment, if we want to take that chance of being right in our own unscriptural convictions. The Bible claims to be the written word of God, given to man by inspired men. Forty men contributed to the sixty-six books we view as the Holy Bible. Over a span of sixteen hundred years, they wrote independently of each other without contradiction to the purpose, thought pattern, and plan of God for man's instruction in righteousness, salvation, and redemption. Their writings contributed to restoring man back to a proper relationship with God—a relationship that was severed by Adam's sin, but restored in Jesus Christ. As such, it would behoove us in the twenty-first century to be as noble or honest hearted as the Bereans of the early century and search the scriptures, identifying its claims to be such. After all, even the firmament declares His handiwork.

The fact is, out of all the religions in the world (over three thousand and counting), only two claim to have the word of God. Let's briefly compare the two, the Holy Bible and the Koran. The men who wrote the Bible claimed that these were not their words but that they had received the message of the Son of God. Jesus, the Son of God, claimed that the words He spoke were not His but that He had received them from God, the Father on high. God declares that Jesus is His Son that we should "hear ye Him." The Holy Ghost confirms the word and brought to the remembrance of the apostles the things Jesus had taught them. Out of the mouth of two or three witnesses shall every word be confirmed or established (2 Corinthians 13:1). We have the word given to us by God, Jesus Christ, and the Holy Ghost. The apostles were commanded to go into the world to preach and teach the word, making disciples of all men.

The Koran is Mohammed's teaching and his teaching only. Note also that Buddha's teaching is Buddha's teaching, and the same is true of Confucius and other religious leaders. Jesus said that the Father bore witness of Him and that they were one. The Holy Ghost confirms the word. Where did Mohammed get his backup for what he was saying? Where were his witnesses to confirm what he claimed to be from God?

The Order of Spiritual Authority

God the Father is the source of all authority. Jesus Christ, the Son of God, to whom the Father gave all authority claimed it, and no other spiritual leader refuted Him (1 Corinthians 15:28). Jesus personally taught the apostles, His hand-picked men. To the apostles: Christ gave authority to the apostles, New Testament disciples, to take the gospel to the entire world. To the gospel preachers: Apostle Paul told Timothy to imitate him. Let us use the New Testament as our authority to spread the gospel. To Christians: Disciples of Christ are commanded to share the gospel and to save souls. Christians are in the soul-saving business. Winning souls is a commandment from God.

Christians *won't* and *cannot* be silenced when it comes to the homosexual agenda or any other agenda that doesn't fall in line with God's plan of salvation, the spreading of the gospel. Christians are commanded to preach and teach the gospel. The scriptures ask, "Is it better to obey man, rather than God?" Furthermore, if Christians fail to warn the wicked, their blood will be on the Christians' hands. Besides, Christians know it's God's world and that He is in control, not the homosexuals. What isn't of God will come to naught. Peaching may seem like foolishness to man, but Christians are still commanded to go and preach. Preaching is the vehicle by which God has authorized and chosen to spread His word, His message of salvation (1Corinthians 1:18–25).

The Rulers of This World Authority

The word *authority* has its origin in Latin—*auctoritas*. In English, the word *authority* (*disambiguation*) can be used to mean power given by the state (in the form of members of Parliament, judges, police officers, and so forth) or by academic knowledge of an area (someone who is an authority on a subject). Max Weber on authority: The word *Authority* with a capital *A* refers to the governing body upon which such authority (with lower case *a*) is vested. In government, authority is used interchangeably often with power. A dictionary definition of *authority*: [6]

> (n) au.thor.i.ty (ə tháwrətee) 1). right to command: the right of power to enforce rules or give orders, 2). Holder of power: somebody or something with official power, and 3). Power given to somebody: power to act on behalf of somebody else, or official permission to do something.

People with power or the powerful can persuade or influence, by force and charisma, others to do what they wouldn't have done, be it spiritual and of a religious nature or by a ruling party (kings, queens, or bureaucratic powers); whereas people with authority hold claims to having a legitimate right to exercise power. A vigilante mob has the power to take the life of someone for hurting innocent people but no authority to take that life; whereas a judge of the court of law has the authority to sentence a person to death row. The courts and people of the land recognize a legitimate claim to that authority and are willing to justify and be subject to its power of authority as citizens.

Max Weber on Power vs. Authority

Maximilian Karl Emil "Max" Weber is a German sociologist, philosopher, and political economist, whose ideas influenced society. Max Weber divided legitimate authority into three types:[7]

---

[6] https://en.wikipedia.org/wiki/Authority_(sociology) last edited on 7 December 2019, at 05:41

[7] https://en.wikipedia.org/wiki/Tripartite_classification_of_authority ; Indes, "Authority" http://en.wikipedia.org/w/indes.pbb Title=Authority_(sociology) oblid=552913324

1. Rational-legal authority—a constitution type of authority, what is written and complex. Its legitimacy depends on formal rules and established law of the state.
2. Traditional authority—the right of hereditary monarchs, where power is passed on from one generation to another from long-established customs and social structures
3. Charismatic authority—the leader plays an important role and claims his or her authority comes from a divine or higher power (for example, God or natural law or rights).

In rational-legal authority, also known as a bureaucratic authority, power is legitimized by legally enacted rules and regulations such as in governments. In traditional authority, power is legitimized by respect for long-established cultural patterns. In charismatic authority, power is legitimized by extraordinary personal abilities that inspire devotion and obedience.

Weber states that what distinguishes authority from coercion, force, and power on one hand and leadership, persuasion, and influence on the other hand is legitimacy. Scripturally speaking, Jesus is legit in His authority. He does not force heaven on anyone, and His power of authority comes from God, the Creator of man.

What I found interesting about some views I gathered while researching a few philosophers' and scientists' hypotheses and philosophies about authority were two ideologies: capacity to coerced and exert power and the belief that some other factors could involve a mutually established relationship that benefits both parties in some fashion or another—one party submitting voluntarily to render service for protection from harm from a greater threat.

Jesus has been given all power and seeks a relationship with man, extending as far back as the Garden of Eden. The authority Jesus holds is what was given to Him by God is not to *exert* power by calling down angels at any time to destroy man. This authority as Lord over man's salvation is to accept and forgive when man willingly accepts Him as his Savior. This is how authority makes its connection with God and man—it's a relationship. The husband is the head of the wife, Christ is the head of the church, and children are commanded to obey their parents in the Lord. The husband should love his wife like Christ loved the church and laid down His life for the church. Man is to love the Lord God with all his heart, soul, strength, and mind; and his neighbor as himself. The church is the bride of Christ, baptized and obedient believers. Christ adds to the church; they become children of God, children of the kingdom, thus forming a relationship in submission to

Christ's authority. Christ has the authority to tell man how to conduct his life so he will be fit for eternality with Him in heaven

The Bible in History

There are many books written on the historical evidence of the Bible in history, science, archaeology, paleontology, geology, and theories of creation and evolution. As I ponder this, including cited materials referenced in this book from published works, what comes to mind is the story of the rich man and Lazarus. Once the rich man woke up in hell, he wanted Father Abraham, a biblical patriarch, to send Lazarus back from his well-rewarded position in Abraham's bosom to warn his brothers about the place he had found himself. Discerningly, Abraham said they (the rich man's brothers) had the prophets. Let them hear them. This was an opportunity the rich man let slip away. He allowed death to catch him unprepared to meet God in peace. Abraham continued, "If his brothers would not hear the prophets ... [God's preachers or ministers in like fashion we have today], neither will they hear someone from the dead." Look at us today in the twenty-first century. Jesus rose from the dead, but who is listening?

After listening to a video/DVD lecture series on *Rock-Solid Faith: How to Build It* by Bert Thompson, PhD, which was introduced to my congregation in 2016, I decided to cite the source. I had the opportunity to view on screen, take notes, and listen to Bert Thompson's lecture (thirteen-week series) on this work at several six o'clock evening services.[8] I later discovered his work on ApologeticsPress.org. I was also very pleased to discover that Apologetics Press (AP) has a staff of scientists and writers who are versed in the Holy Scriptures. I believe, as my readers will discover from this website, that AP[9] is an excellent source that will provide scientifically and biblically accurate information defending the truthfulness of New Testament Christianity and the authority of the Bible. For readers who are interested in further research (books, articles, or publications on creation, evolution, the authority of the Bible, God in creation and design, the origin of the university and earth), I know they have come to the right source, as I have discovered.

---

[8] https://store.apologeticspress.org/products/apdvdbt0022
[9] Auxiliary writers, "About A.P.—Apologetic Press," ApologeticsPress.org, accessed May 5, 2014, http://espanol.apologeticspress.org/apinfo/writers.

Purposeful Designer

In the beginning, God was in control and still is. The firmament declares His handiwork. Reading the books of Psalms, Job, Isaiah, and Leviticus, one will discover a vast amount of knowledge revealed in the Bible, knowledge that has taken scientists, historians, astronomers, and archeologists decades upon decades to catch up with and discover. Geological locations, kings or rulers, and events in history can be found accurately cited in the Bible; these are things that took man centuries to unearth. God required the Jews to circumcise the male child on the eighth day. "It took centuries before scientists understood how vitamin K played a role in this command from God."[10] Man originally thought the earth was flat. Isaiah spoke of the earth as a circle in chapter 40:22. "It is He that sits upon the circle of the earth." Job and Moses (Genesis) spoke of a great void, a place where no stars shine. And Job spoke of the planet earth in the solar system. "He stretches out the north over the empty place, and hangs the earth upon nothing" (Job 26:7). It wasn't until the invention of the electronic telescopes that man observed, experienced, and sought to understand the void in the universe where no stars shine (dark matter and dark galaxy). In the pig, an animal God commanded the Jews not to consume, scientists discovered the roundworm (*Trichinella spiralis*, trichinosis or parasitic disease). If not cooked properly, pork can cause illnesses.

There are so many things about this universe, revealed with such accuracy from forty different men who wrote over a space of sixteen hundred years (1500 BC to AD 50–100); that time spans three languages and two or three continents. There are also Bible lands and people, including rivers like the Pison River, the Gihon River that compasses the whole land of Ethiopia, and a third and fourth river, respectively, Hiddekel and Euphrates in Genesis 2:11-14). One can find places and people like Assyria, Africa, Egypt, Jerusalem, Babylonia, judges and kings (for example, King Nebuchadnezzar).

In 586 BC, Nebuchadnezzar destroyed Jerusalem and placed Israelites in Babylonian captivity. The book of Ezekiel describes events in history. Nineveh, destroyed in 612 BC (ancient capital of the Assyrian Empire), was established by Nimrod (Genesis 10:8–10). British archeologist A. H. Layard excavated the city (1845–1856) and unearthed the palace of King Sargon. Nineveh has its prophecy in the biblical accounts in the books of Genesis,

---

[10] Thompson, Bert. *Rock-Solid Faith: How to Build It.* Apologetics Press. https://www.bing.com/shop?q=bert+thompson+apologetics+press&FORM=SHOPPA&originIGUID=490269BA40964EF3B39CF03A74B9CACF

2 Kings, Isaiah, Jonah, Nahum, Zephaniah, and Matthew. "In the year that Tartan came to Ashdod, (when Sargon the king of Assyria sent him), and fought against Ashdod, and took it" (Isaiah 20:1).

The Bible in the Big Bang Theory

When certain individuals tried to tempt Jesus and trap Him in conversation with stupid questions, He stooped down and wrote in the sand, ignoring them to the Nth degree (John 8:6). Sometimes when people present nonsensical things to us, it's worth ignoring; simply (in your mind) just write in the sand (2 Timothy 2:23). The Bible has nothing to say about man's big bang theory or evolution. But the firmament does declare His glory and His handiwork! Nothing blew up, but there are scriptures that say something will burn up! Who do you think is lying? We weren't there for the alleged blowup or big bang, but rest assured that we all will be present for the "burn up." "But the day of the Lord will come as a thief in the night; in the which the heavens shall pass away with a great noise, and the elements shall melt with fervent heat, the earth also and the works that are therein shall be burned up" (2 Peter 3:10).

Sir Fred Hoyle coined the term "big bang." In the mid-1950s, Hoyle became the leader of a group of very talented experimental and theoretical physicists, who met in Cambridge. The group included William Alfred Fowler, Margaret Burbidge, and Geoffrey Burbidge. This group systematized basic ideas of how all the chemical elements in our universe were manufactured, thus beginning a field called "nucleosynthesis." The group produced the B2FH paper (known for the initials of the four authors). Hoyle, an atheist, presented in 1982 "Evolution from Space" for the Royal Institution's Omni Lecture. After considering what he thought of as a very remote probability of earth-based abiogenesis, he concluded, "If one proceeds directly and straightforwardly in this matter, without being deflected by a fear of incurring the wrath of scientific opinion, one arrives at the conclusion that biomaterials with their amazing measure or order must be the outcome of intelligent design. No other possibility I have been able to think of."[11]

Hoyle, an English astronomer noted primarily for the theory of stellar nucleosynthesis and his often-controversial stance on the cosmological and scientific matter, died in 2001, never accepting the big bang theory.

---

[11] Wikipedia, s.v. "Fred Hoyle," last modified May 13, 2019, http://en.wikipeida.org/wiki/Fred_Hoyle

Science, God, and the Universe

Evolutionists, cosmologists, scientists, physicists, astrophysicists, physiologists, paleontologists, geologists, and so on have much to say about the formation or evolution of man, the earth, and the universe. It is a costly, time-consuming, and somewhat painstaking process to prove or disprove the creation of man, the creation of the earth, and the creation of the universe or the heavens. Libraries are filled with volumes of research, books, and journals on the subject. The irony is that one needs only to lift his or her finger(s) and turn to Genesis 1 to get all the answers man has spent centuries trying to get to the bottom of—what an awesome God!

God isn't trying to pull the wool over man's eyes. If man has a piece of wool or veil over his eyes, he needs only to take the same finger(s) and lift it off, and then proceed with turning the pages of inspiration for instructions from the word of God. Unlike Satan, the Father of Lies, God cannot lie. If man fails to seek and study the word of God, he has only himself to blame.

Science leans heavily on observation and reproducibility (repeatability), based on the identical circumstances or happenings as they relate to matter and energy involvement on each other. The results should be the same if the process is to be considered to have any veracity (accuracy or true statement). Here in the above statement, scientists attempt to demonstrate by developing a hypothesis and the proof that if the exact or identical something occurs, the results are the same at any time of its occurrence. Scientists, in their attempt to prove the formation of the universe, equipped only with a man-made instrument (telescope) for observation and man-made formulations, calculations, and hypothesis to explain likely repeatability of occurrences in the cosmos, only illuminate man's limited knowledge—the distance as far as the heavens are from the earth.

We have one universe that did not just happen by chance at some point and time. If scientists' calculations were correct about when the next occurrence takes place for no particular reason, then we will have two universes coexisting and then three and on and on throughout eternity. How absurd. There will be universes on top of universes, worlds on top of worlds, or one canceling out the other endlessly for those of the persuasion that matter and energy remain the same. The earth, the universe, and man have a designer and Creator, and He would be God. Science makes a hypothesis and theorizes that matter and energy cannot be created or destroyed.

Our little knowledge is limited to what we can see and observe; this speaks nothing to our ability to know and fully understand or comprehend what we cannot physically observe. There lies the problem with those who set out to prove or disprove the existence of God. God has His witnesses already: the firmament declares His handiwork. Science wants to prove or disprove that the universe (as far as our eyes can see with or without the aid of telescopes and spaceships) is eternal. God said the world (our world will be folded up like a rag and that the earth will be burned up. Who's listening? God speaks of a beginning and an ending of the world we live in. Still, who's listening?

Could God Possibly Agree with the Whole Panel of "Ists"?

Maybe if all the "ists" were to step back and stop trying to prove or disprove something, to one-up on each other, they may realize they are saying the same thing. And surprisingly, God agrees with them.

The most common understanding is that the word *void* means or represents nothing. Science deduces existence down to two elements: mind and matter. It was the interaction of the mind of God (spirit and energy) and matter (body of water) that brought about man's and earth's existence we know today. Yes, the book of Genesis says God stepped out from beyond and created the heavens and universe through the black hole where time and space do not exist to create a world. This is a universe that contains earth, which includes man, the sun, the moon, stars, seas, fish, birds, cattle, vegetation, and other living creatures. Genesis speaks of this creation where everything came in its mature form. And man was created last. "Through faith, we understand that the worlds were framed by the word of God so that things which are seen were not made of things which do appear" (Hebrews 11:3).

Can you imagine being around when God spoke things into existence? God spoke, and it was so. I'm sure we would classify this mighty phenomenal as a "big bang," with things popping up all over the place. Today when thunder roars in the heavens, buildings shake. This shaking can be felt miles away like some implosion at a construction site. The dry land (matter) rose up out of the waters (matter) and separated at the command of God's mind (spirit and energy). There were earthquakes and erupting volcanoes on land and from the deep, slicing and creating mountains, valleys, and landscapes as the earth plates slid and scraped against each other. "Let there be a firmament in the midst of the waters, and let it divide the waters from the waters" (Genesis 1:6). The earth in creation could easily have been rumblings, and it may have been very volatile and combustible in many instances where a variety of first-time occurrences in nature and in some instances, happening spontaneously throughout in various places in the universe. Can you imagine Adam standing on a spot where a huge tree popped up out of the ground? Not a seedling but a huge tree. A man could get seriously hurt! It wouldn't be hard to imagine this occurrence could be summarized as a "big bang." Everything was exploding on to the scene all over the planet and into its own unique adult and mature existence with the ability of reproducibility (producing seed after its own kind), the work of an intelligent designer. This one-time phenomenon, the chance of happening, was purpose driven. God decided to make the world and place man in it. "Let Us make man."

Did the universe evolve from nothing? The scripture says the earth was void and without form. For the "ists," that says nothing from nothing produces nothing; well, there was God [*Spirit/energy*], and there was water [*matter*]. It was something of a nothing (void), dark and lifeless, and God moved upon it (interaction between mind and spirit or energy and matter or water and dry land). There was darkness upon the face of the deep. Apparently, time stood still within this darkness, and it wasn't until God called upon light to appear and caused a separation of the two that time began on earth: the beginning of day and night. "And the evening and the morning were the first day" (Genesis 1:4—5). Just darkness—there is your black hole. God stepped out from beyond the heavens, space, and time and came on the scene (the deep) to create a world. The earth was void; there is your nothing. Things popping up in their mature stage all over the planet; there is your big bang.

Science attempts at "logical" analysis—in other words, man's wisdom to prove or disprove the creation of man—is just as futile as proving some happen-by-chance spontaneous combustion, the big bang theory, without any other explanation than that it just happened by chance. The only "by chance" was that God decided to make it happen—He created a world. Man's preexistence is the God-breathed relationship on His creation. There is a part of man created from the dust of the ground that will return upon his demise, and there is part of man that cannot die because it is not from earth; that part existed before the earth, the sun, the moon, the stars, and the cosmos.

Any concept of quanta interactions existing in creation can be understood as the energy created by God's being (Spirit), and it is that Spirit that moved upon and had interaction with, matter (water). Those things had forcefully come forth with a bit of chaotic appearing as only man could conceptualize in his limited imagination. God saw fit and necessary to spare man, creating him last. God put His special touch on the creature man. Of all things God created, the man was His hands-on work. Man is the jewel and crown of His creation, more precious than earth, the things in earth, and his terrestrial life form. No one knows how the bones form in the womb (Ecclesiastes 11:5).

The body is such a great machine. God, the designer, and the Holy Ghost (energy) worked on the earthly matter or mortal man—in other words, the ghost in the machine. When the Spirit departs, the matter or mortal man collapses into decay. The body returns back to the earth. Yes, if you haven't yet been told, you are more than bones and skin heading to the grave; there is the other part of you, the part that cannot ever die. Unfortunately, because of disbelief and disobedience, many will not make it back to the original status; they will face the grim reality of "Where I am you cannot come." They will live eternally in some other place (hell), which is prepared for the devil and his angels.

The theory that matter and energy cannot be created or destroyed aligns with the knowledge that God (energy/spirit) is in everything and that there is water (matter) under the heavens and above the heavens; therein nothing changed. There is the spirit and the water: energy and matter. Jesus said He is the living water (John 4:13, 14; 7:38; Isaiah 12:3). God will remain forever. Man will die, and creation will fade away. Man is 92 percent water, and his spirit from God is temporarily housed in a fleshly matter. We recognize cycles of increase and decrease by the hands of God. The world is set by God, who cannot be understood, and only He knows the time of the world's demise; not even the angels know that time (Matthew 24:36). We can search from here throughout eternality. The body God created cannot be understood or reproduced. The details of its DNA and genetic codes are so vast. One single cell masses in detail the amount of information compiled in the world's libraries combined. The whole duty of man is to fear God and keep His commandments. If man understood this simple command, it would make him a very wise being on the face of this earth. It makes one wonder why there aren't many volumes of research and books on how to fear God and keep His commandments, but there are many on why there is no God; the universe just happened by chance, and man (as a species) evolved to the intellectual being he is.

It is Jesus who tells mankind, as He did with doubting Thomas, that it's faith that lights (no human eyes) the way to human intellect and will give man the ability to observe beyond the clouds, cosmos, and the other realms outside of our universe. The Holy Spirit will allow man to see and understand what one needs to know and believe about the eternal existence of God and the preexistence of man. "Let Us make man in Our own image," and "They have become like Us to know good and evil." All knowledge is from God. God remains eternal in the heavens and is not contingent upon man. "If I were hungry, I would not tell you: for the world is Mine, and the fullness thereof" (Psalm 50:12).

By now (this point in your existence on earth), you have rationalized that you exist. If you are reading this sentence, you can make an accurate conclusion that you exist based on this particular evidence. From this logical reasoning in deduction, you realize that the ball is in your court, and it is your decision or move. Now, what do you plan to do about your knowledge of your existence? Let's examine the Bible to see what it says. Are you listening now? "Save yourself from this untoward generation and seek out your salvation with trembling and fear" (Philippians 2:12). This should be every bit of an act to make your election sure. Note that Satan trembled. Will that be your reaction to the knowledge of God, or will you take action to secure your salvation, to make it back to your preexistent status with God? Satan was there and lost out; he is going about like a roaring lion, seeking whom he can destroy. He doesn't want that part of you that was with God back with God. He can't be there, and he has made it his mission to make sure you aren't either.

God told Moses to tell Israel that I AM sent me [him] to you—Exodus 3:14. The fact that each of us can exclaim "I am" whoever and so and so—"I am a man," "I am a person," "I am a human being"—demonstrates that the "I am" in each of us is the God who breathes life into man. Man is as much an I AM as God is the great I AM THAT I AM. This is your most true and concrete evidence of God; you exist because God exits. Without God, man (you) cannot exist. "In Him was life; and the life was the light of men. (John 1:3–4). Do you believe you exist? Does one need more logic or evidence other than this fact?

The universe operates like a well-oiled machine with great synchrony, timeliness, and precision. The orderliness isn't disputed by the panel of "ists" or atheists or agonists. Without this precision, any malfunction would be detrimental to the existence of man. Planets in our galaxy, including the sun and moon, are located or orbited at the accurate distance away from earth to sustain life as we know it. If the earth rotated off its axis too close or too far from the sun, life as we know it on planet earth would cease to exist. It would become harsh and inhabitable, meaning we would all burn up or plunge into a horrific ice age. We would freeze to death. The moon affects ocean tides. The dry land God allowed to appear (Genesis 1:9) would now again be under the waters, depending on how whacked out the moon became with its cycles. It is due to this orderliness that scientists have been able to go to the moon, understand or observe solar and lunar eclipses, and understand natural laws of the universe—including gravity.

The earth and universe started with water. And God made the firmament, and divided the waters which were under the firmament from the waters which were above the firmament: and it was so.

And God called the firmament Heaven and the evening and the morning were the second day (Genesis 1:7–8).
Let the waters under the heaven be gathered together to one place, and let the dry land appear—and it was so. (Genesis 1:9)

Water is life sustaining. Our bodies are more than 90 percent water. Our salvation is water: baptism. Many don't want to work with water when it pertains to the saving of the soul, but there you have it. Out came blood and water. The Spirit of God moved upon the face of the waters. Water has always been in the plan. Water controls the temperature on earth. From these bodies of waters, we get rain for drinking water and growing crops for food. We get oxygen from plant life in the oceans and seas. Without the oceans and other bodies of water, we would not have enough oxygen to breathe. Approximately four-fifths of the earth is covered with water.

Many who confess to be atheists and agnostics want others to believe they believe that the planet and life, including human life, happened by accident and that there is no God, no Creator and intelligent designer of the universe. There will be many who will continue to try to persuade the alleged (atheist folks) that there is a God. If what Jesus had to say to doubting Thomas about faith isn't enough, certainly piles on top of piles of evidence to convince the unrepentant and unbeliever of God won't be enough. God did not honor the rich man's request to send Lazarus back to warn his brothers about the reality of God and heaven or Satan and hell. The reply was that they had the prophets. And of course, we have the gospel ministers and preachers of the gospel. The rich man in hell recognized his unwise decision, and Lazarus in Abraham's bosom was satisfied with his wise decision. The atheist will recognize, and the obedient believer will be satisfied because it is certainly not by sight but by faith. "For I am not ashamed of the gospel of Christ: for it is the power of God to salvation to everyone that believes; to the Jew first, and also to the Greek" (Romans 1:16).

Finding an Atheist vs. Individuals Who Confess to Being Atheists

In the first covenant God made with Israel (Hebrew nation), God wrote His commandments on tables of stone. But now in spiritual Israel (obedient believers), not the physical nation of Israel, God has put His law in their minds and hearts.

> For finding fault with them, He says Behold, the days come, says the Lord, when I will make a new covenant with the house of Israel and with the house of Judah: Not according to the covenant that I made with their fathers in the day when I took them by the hand to lead them out of Egypt; because they continued not in My covenant, *and I regarded them not*, says the Lord. For this is the covenant that I will make with the house of Israel after those days, says the Lord; I will put My laws into their mind, and write them in their hearts: and I will be to them a God, and they shall be to Me a people: And they shall not teach every man his neighbor, and every man his brother, saying, know the Lord: for all shall know Me, from the least to the greatest. (Hebrews 8:7–11; Hebrews 10:16, emphasis added)

One cannot disbelieve in God, even if he or she wanted to. True, one may not know Him (who He is) or understand or acknowledge Him. Look at Acts 17:23. The apostle Paul encountered individuals who understood that there were spiritual forces or beings higher than man. "For as I passed by and beheld your devotions, I found an altar with this inscription, TO THE UNKNOWN GOD, whom therefore you ignorantly worship, Him declare I to you."

Men (individuals; male and female) have to put forth a concerted effort to force God out of their minds. "And even as they did not like to retain God in their knowledge, God gave them over to a reprobate mind, to those things which are not convenient [natural]" (Romans 1:26-32). Being without God means being without understanding of the direction one should go, with ethics and morals. Some find themselves without natural affection, and even when knowing (homosexual or not) the judgment of God, they which commit such things (knowing right from wrong) are worthy of death; not only do they do the same but have pleasure in them that do them.

The wise almighty God fixed it so no one is without excuse. From the cave man to the astronaut and all between, everyone understands the concept of right and wrong (good and evil), and knows there is a supreme being. God gave man a guideline to morals and ethics from the Old Testament books to the New Testament books. "O Lord, I know that the way of man is not in himself: it is not in man that walks to direct his steps" (Jeremiah 10:23).

Without God anything goes in the sense or morals and ethics. Even though man tries to act that way, God didn't leave it up to man to make that choice. Man will surely suffer the consequences of his bad choices. If it were left up to man, his sense of right and wrong (good and evil, morals and ethics) would be ruled by the times of the century, cultures, opinions, majority rules, and so forth. God has made known what is acceptable in His sight and says to let every man be a liar but God be true. Man's opinion of what is right or wrong outside of what God commands is unacceptable and leads to his own personal, spiritual, and physical demise. If our value system is derived from our individual cultures, then who is to say whether cultural differences in opinion of right and wrong and what is acceptable or unacceptable are relevant in determining what is moral or ethical in the universe. Universally speaking, lying is lying everywhere, stealing is stealing everywhere, and murder is murder everywhere. It is only when one is trying to get away with something he or she knows to be wrong that the absolute or absolutism of the matter, the reality, and the relativisms get murky.

"Wherefore gird up the loins of your *mind*, be sober, and hope to the end for the grace that is to be brought to you at the revelation of Jesus Christ; as obedient children, not fashioning yourselves according to the former lusts in your ignorance: But as He which has called you is holy, so be you holy in all manner of conversation [behavior]; because it is written, be you holy; for I am holy" (1 Peter 1:13–16, emphasis added).

Centuries ago, homosexuality and bestiality were sins and abominable acts against God and nature. Culturally, homosexuality and bestiality were sins and abominable acts against God and nature. Hiding in the closet (acts unexposed) demonstrates that in the opinion of the masses, homosexuality is a sin, and God said homosexuality and bestiality are sins (1 Corinthians 6:9; Leviticus 18:22–23). Centuries have passed since the demise of Sodom and Gomorrah, and now it is the opinion and language of the culture (twenty-first century) in the United States of America that homosexuality is now acceptable. In essence, everybody is doing his or her own thing, and it's okay to be tolerant of behaviors that will land one in a devil's hell: you are okay, and I'm okay. There are no right or wrong ways to behave. To show our "goodness" by the acceptance of other people's poor behaviors and abominable acts, we feel we must put on our tolerance hats. News flash: God's word hasn't changed, and He has already told man He cannot lie. "And the Lord said, because the cry of Sodom and Gomorrah is great, and because their sin is very grievous..." (Genesis 18:20). Read about God's visit and personal assessment of these wicked cities.

📖 Book Corner Excerpt

"The Bible Always Passes the Test" by Wayne Jackson, MA (reprinted by permission)[12]

Q.
Critics have claimed that the Bible contains all kinds of factual errors. Is the Bible trustworthy when it speaks of historical matters?

A.
The Bible contains two kinds of information. Some of it can be checked; some of it cannot. For example, it is not possible to "check" scientifically the accuracy of Genesis 1:1—"In the beginning God created the heavens and the earth." While the affirmation is not in any way inconsistent with available scientific data, at the same time the statement is one of prehuman history and therefore does not lend itself to empirical investigation.

On the other hand, the Scriptures contain hundreds of references that arise out of the background of human history. These may be tested for accuracy. If it is the case that the Bible is demonstrated to be precise in thousands of historical details, it is not unreasonable to conclude that its information in other matters is equally correct.
In fact, one of the most amazing features of the Bible is its uncanny reliability in the smallest of details. Let us note a few examples of biblical precision.

---

[12] Wayne Jackson, M.A. "The Bible Always Passes the Test," Apologetics Press. http://www.apologeticspress.org/APContent.aspx?caegory=13&article=1087

During His personal ministry, Jesus once passed through the region of Samaria. Near Sychar, the Lord stopped for a brief rest at Jacob's well. He engaged a Samaritan woman in conversation, during which He suggested that He could provide the woman with water that could perpetually quench her thirst. Misunderstanding the nature of the Master's instruction, the woman, alluding to Jacob's well, declared: "Sir, you have nothing to draw with, and the well is deep" (John 4:11). The statement is quite correct, for even now, some twenty centuries later, Jacob's well is approximately 80 feet deep—the equivalent of an eight-story building!

Reflect upon another example. In Acts 10 there is the account of Peter's visit in the city of Joppa. Luke declared that Peter was staying in the home of Simon, a tanner of animal hides. Then the historian said, almost as an afterthought, "whose house is by the seaside" (Acts 10:6). Hugh J. Schonfield, author of the infamous book, *The Passover Plot* (and certainly no friend of Christianity), has commented on this passage as follows: "This is an interesting factual detail, because the tanners used sea water in the process of converting hides into leather. The skins were soaked in the sea and then treated with lime before the hair was scraped off."

Consider another interesting case of Bible precision. When Paul was en route to Rome for trial, the ship upon which he sailed became involved in a terrible storm. When it eventually became apparent that the vessel was in a very dangerous circumstance, the crew cast the ship's anchors into the water. At the same time, they "loosed the rudder bands, hoisted up the foresail, and aimed the ship towards the beach" (Acts 27:40). There is an interesting and subtle point in the Greek text that is not apparent in the King James Version. The original language actually says that they "loosed the bands of the rudders" (plural). This is amazingly precise, for in ancient times, ships actually possessed two paddle-rudders, not a single rudder as with modern vessels. In 1969, a submerged ancient ship was discovered in the Mediterranean Sea off the coast of Cyprus. An examination of the ruins gave evidence of dual rudder-oars by which the boat was steered (see *National Geographic,* November 1974), thus demonstrating the remarkable accuracy of Luke's record.

The Bible can be tested—historically, geographically, scientifically, etc. And it always passes the test. Its incredible accuracy can be explained only in light of its divine inspiration. **http://www.apologeticspress.org**

Understanding the Times

"And of the children of Issachar, which were men that had understanding of the times, to know what Israel ought to do" (1 Chronicles 12:32). It is when man understands that he can never be smarter or more righteous than his Creator, and that he cannot direct his own steps, that he moves forward in a positive direction and communication as it relates to his eternal salvation.

A few years ago, I was privileged to hear a sermon titled "Understanding the Times." It was my first time hearing the phrase "Speaking the language of Ashdod." The minister elaborated on its meaning. God's people adopted the lifestyle and language of people to whom they lived and intermarried. The youths, because of this cultural adaptation, understood only what they were exposed to and never knew or understood their native Hebrew tongue, the language of the people of God (Nehemiah 13:23–25). The sermon pointed out that three things have to occur to influence a culture or sustain a society: language, reasoning, and behavior. In our language, we communicate by what things mean. What would happen if one opened the dictionary and discovered all words had changed their meanings? It would change the culture and the way society communicated. In our reasoning or the way we think, we justify what is acceptable, tolerable, and moral. In our behavior, we act out of what we understand to be acceptable, moral, and ethical. Language drives a nation.

Today many have rejected God and don't want to retain him in their knowledge (Romans 1:21-32), and this is reflected in our language, reasoning, and behavior. Lying is softly described as perjury, theft as embezzlement, and homosexuality and lesbian as an alternative or gay lifestyle. Hear the unchanging language or the word of God and its meaning. The abominable and all liars shall have their part in the lake which burns with fire and brimstone (Revelation 21:8). "Lay not up for yourselves treasures on earth where thieves break in and steal" (Matthew 6:19). We can conclude from these few verses that abominable (effeminate and bestiality acts), liars, and thieves will not be in heaven. Inclusion is the language of today—anything or everything goes. But God still communicates to man that he needs to separate (come out from the evildoers of the world) and sanctify himself to God. The youth of today who knows nothing of an earlier culture in the USA, which displayed and communicated high moral behavior, is being influenced by another language as this country adapts and accepts the homosexual and lesbian lifestyle. Men in defiance of the will of God and not wanting to identify with creation—God made male and female—speak the language of the gender neutral, unisex, bisexuals, and transvestites.

This country, the USA, has left its native tongue of speaking Christian values and morals. What is heard in the streets now is an unfamiliar language that's not from God. Marriage is no longer the union between a male and female (opposite sex) but between same-sex couples. This country's religious communities are speaking the language of Ashdod. Many people are lost and totally confused about what is going on. As rainbow flags are flown, protesters rally to be heard, police and citizen assault each other; there are more mass shootings and more and more senseless violence. Hatred and confusion are on the rise in a nation that has forgotten God. Many will be voicing the lyrics of Motown's artist Marvin Gaye: "What's Going On?" It is still the responsibility and command from God to the church to preach the gospel, the word and language of God. It is God's will that all men (mankind) be saved.

Ethics and Morals and Absolute Truth

A lack of ethics and morals can exist only outside of God. If man continued to eat from the tree in the midst of the Garden of Eden, he would live forever and he would be as gods, knowing good and evil. Man didn't and cannot set the standard for good and evil, right and wrong. Good is what God says it is, and wrong is what God says it is. Man doesn't get to call the shots on what is good and what is evil (ethics, morals, and truth). If God says a behavior is an abomination in His sight, the debate is over.

The other black hole and para universe (with its own gravitational forces) exist outside of time and space and continually draws and pulls one (our minds) into a deep, spiritually dark and physical death, if one allows himself or herself to linger there. It thrives and is nourished by selfishness; this is the total opposite of "Love your neighbor as yourself" and "Esteem others higher than self." In selfishness, where the only right and wrong that exist or that matter are what directly or indirectly affect the continuum of happiness and prosperity of self. It is God's command that Christians seek the mind of God and stay connected with the life-giving source of their existence. It is God's will that all men be saved, get connected, and stay connected through obedience to Christ. "Now we have received not the spirit of the world, but the Spirit which is of God: that we might know the things that are freely given to us of God" (1 Corinthians 2:12). What hangs on all the Law and Prophets is love. What makes life tolerable for every being is the capacity to love, to care and show concern for one's fellowman. This love and concern for one's fellowman swells the heart and brings tears to one's eyes to witness relief efforts on behalf of a neighboring state (domestic) and the international community. In selfishness, every action becomes situational when it comes to truth, right, and wrong. It lies heavily on how one can benefit from the situation. Without God, we are empty and running on false hope and false happiness leading to darkness, a void within the existence of self. "Who by Him do believe in God, that raised Him up from the dead, and gave Him glory; that your faith and hope might be in God. Seeing you have purified your souls in obeying the truth through the Spirit to unfeigned love of the brethren, see that you love one another with a pure heart fervently: Being born again, not of corruptible seed, but of incorruptible, by the word of God, which lives and abides forever" (1 Peter 1:21–23).

Many have lost their way to reality and have taken their own lives, because of the heavy emptiness that lingers and hides deep inside. Without a true guide (light) to what is absolute in the universe and man's rightful relationship with God, the Creator of man, and the universe, man is unable to call upon the light or call upon the name of the Lord to disperse that darkness. There was darkness, there is darkness, and there will be darkness. But in God one can call on the light (Christ) when darkness approaches, and it will flee—a get-thee-behind-me-Satan moment. In the beginning, God stepped out and called upon the light, and it appeared, and darkness instantly separated itself; the two cannot coincide. Satan waits for an opportune time and whispers to take your life or the life of another as he lures you into his snare of captured souls.

How many incidents of school shootings can be traced back to a child (the shooter) who attended Sunday school regularly and the family who attended worship regularly? In the shooter's darkest and overwhelming moments, he did not know who to call on to disperse that darkness. Had the shooter established a relationship with the One beyond man to call on or to hold on to, who had the power to draw him or her back into the light (knowledge of God and his or her Savior, Jesus Christ)? How awful leaving this world believing what is taught in the public schools and universities:

that man evolved from a monkey; that God and religion are for only the weak minded and unintelligent; that our planet and universe came about by chance or because of some big bang; and that there is no consciousness after death—it's the end. One who is taught that he or she was created in the image of God and knows that his or her behavior should reflect that belief wouldn't commit such a horrific act on the creation or creatures of God. In these situations, the media and news stations sanitize their commentary by not mentioning the name of God to avoid offending the Antichrist and haters of God. In these situations, psychologists are called on for answers and solutions, for the healing of the minds, if you will, and for a way the public can wrap their minds around what has just happened. God isn't consulted, and Satan seeks his next opportune time to strike again.

It is Satan's lullaby and feel-good song to man that he isn't responsible for his own actions, especially in the following tune: "It is God who made me this way." The call still resounds from the mouth of Joshua. "Chose you this day whom you will serve." This statement silences the foolish talk of one having no power over his or her destination because it has already been predetermined. This silences the notion that genetics determines our behavior.

The Bible says that no temptation has come upon a person that he or she cannot overcome. Jesus was tempted in like manner and did not sin. But one sure thing is, if you tell yourself a lie long enough, yes, you will believe it. But this doesn't change the fact that a lie is a lie.

> Let no man say when he is tempted, I am tempted of God: for God cannot be tempted with evil, neither tempts He any man: But every man is tempted, when he is drawn away of his *own lust*, and enticed. (James 1:13–14, emphasis added)
> My brethren, count it all joy when you fall into divers temptations; knowing this that the trying of your faith works patience. But let patience have her perfect work, that you may be perfect and entire, wanting nothing. (James 1:2–4)

Truth is absolute. God's word is true. If you want to believe a lie, not what is written in the word of God, which does not change, God will allow you to believe that lie and then condemn you for believing it. Truth is a constant (not contingent on change), and a lie is a variable, which changes with who is in authority, popular opinions, majority rules, cultural beliefs, and even the changes of the times (centuries); for example, every wind and doctrines that come along. Examples include drinking the Kool-Aid of James Warren Jones (Jim Jones-Jonestown, Guyana) and any other flavored messages introduced from David Koresh, handling serpents in "will worship" to test one's faith, and speaking in tongues while dancing for the "Holy Ghost" until one foams at the mouth.

What a person believes to be true affects how he or she behaves. If you don't believe in God, certainly you will behave differently from an individual who does and certainly from one who believes, fears, and *obeys* God. In many third-world countries, in the name of God and religions, women and girls are second-class or less-than-second-class citizens. They are considered property to be sold and bartered. Grown women are beaten into submission in the streets by their husbands (not a love-thy-wife-as-thou-lovest-thyself faith). Many women are victims of arranged marriages and limited to little or no education, all in a systemic order of adhering to cultural rights or laws. The scriptures say what God has set free is free indeed. One has the freedom in Christ to remain unmarried and without sin. If one cannot contain self in a life without sin, he or she is told to marry to avoid fornication. Women are forced into marriages and devalued if not married: damned if you do and damned if you don't.

All knowledge is from God. Many black people in America were denied access to education; they were killed or beaten if they were found reading or writing. The black life was devalued and noted in documents as less than a man (three-fifths human), and the black man was denied voting privileges. Black people had no rights to choose and keep a wife or a husband or to nurture a family because children, husbands, and wives became property to be sold at will to other slave owners. This was the law, and many who believed or confessed to being Christians used their beliefs (*private interpretation of scripture*) to justify their behavior. Again, there was no concept of esteeming others higher than self in their oppressors' conduct. But God's word still warns, "Let God be true and every man a liar." There is ethnic cleansing done in the name of religion; again, no concept of love thy neighbor as thou lovest thyself. There is ethnic cleansing to create an idea of a superior race. In the above-mentioned situations, culture, laws, and belief played a role in man's behavior, but one can distinctly see that obedience to God played no role in how one esteemed himself and herself higher than others in these situations. In like manner, in this country's decision to mistreat black people, those who wrote and celebrated the enactment of laws to that effect did not represent biblical principles they purported. Chief justice John Roberts declared in his dissent that the decision to legalize gay marriage would be celebrated but would ignore the US Constitution.[13]

Truth is absolute, and God word is truth. If one's morals and ethics don't measure up to the truth of God's word, he or she falters because someone isn't using a true gauge, measuring stick, or correct manual. God observes man's attempt to call good evil and evil good. People who judge themselves by themselves are fools, and not wise. Is man more righteous than God? What is ethical and moral when it doesn't measure up to obedience to God's word? We only lie to ourselves and create a false sense of what we believe to be good. "Turn away my reproach which I fear: for your judgments are good" (Psalm 119:39). God has judged homosexuality to be an abomination in His sight and a sin that will keep man out of eternal life with Him. Man has determined that that lifestyle is good and acceptable and shouldn't be spoken against. Morals and ethics are God's way of schooling us on "Am I My Brother's Keeper?" And a resounding, absolute *yes* is the answer. "He has showed you, O man, what is good; and what does the Lord require of you, but to do justly, and to love mercy, and to walk humbly with your God?" (Micah 6:8).

A question to Christians: Would failing to warn the wicked of the wrath to come show that you are your brother's keeper? It's a big responsibility to be accountable for the souls of others. God says you are. If you fail to warn the wicked, his or her blood will be on your hands. That's something to think about when asked not to speak out or remain silent on the proliferation of the gay lifestyle here in America. The scriptures ask, "Is it better to obey God rather than man?"

Many are complacent in seeking out their soul's salvation because of the soft, pretty, nonthreatening clouds in the sky and the beautiful, warm sunshine. We should consider the scripture that says, "The Lord is not slack concerning His promise, as some men count slackness; but is longsuffering to us-ward, not willing that any should perish, but that all should come to repentance" (2 Peter 3:9). In other words, God loves man so much He is holding back, giving him plenty of time and opportunity to come to Him before it is everlastingly too late.

---

[13] Lydia Wheeler, "Chief Justice Decries Decision That Does Not 'Celebrate Constitution,'" *The Hill*, June 26, 2015, https://thehill.com/regulation/other/246256-chief-justice-decries-decision-that-does-not-celebrate-constitution.

📖 Book Corner Excerpt (A Critique)

Biblical Ethics & Homosexuality: Listening to Scripture, edited by Robert L. Brawley[14] and *Textual Orientation* by Choon-Leong Seow writes in chapter two of *Biblical Ethics & Homosexuality: Listening to Scripture*–Part 1, # 2, "The church has changed its mind on many issues as it confronts new situations and learns new truths."[15]

The church Christ built is based on scripture and cannot and will not change because the word of God will not change. The only "churches" that will and do change are denominational churches. And when they decide to obey God, they cannot and won't change with the times. There is nothing new under the sun; sin was sin then, and sin is sin now. Homosexuality was sin then, and homosexuality is sin now.

Seow writes, "There are many practices that the Bible actually permits—like polygamy."[16] The Bible calls everyone to repent (Acts 17:30). But from the beginning, it was not so. I know Mr. Seow and a vast number of others would like it that way, but God will no longer look the other way. He commands all to repent. Jesus has the plan of salvation and is "The Way." Let us get with the program (*God's plan of salvation*) and stop trying to comb the scriptures, looking for ways to justify our behavior.

Mr. Seow cites two incidents of human needs taking precedence over God's law:

1. David ate the showbread, which was lawful only for the priest to consume; and
2. Jesus stood up in the defense of His disciples, who plucked and consumed corn on the Sabbath, a practice against Jewish law.

In both instances, hunger was the issue. Food and water are the sustainers of life. You don't get to choose if you want to eat food and drink water; if you don't eat or drink, you die. Stop eating and drinking, and see what happens. Jesus is the Bread of Life (John 6:35). In His conversation with the woman at the well (Jacob's Well), He offered Himself as living

---

[14] Robert L. Brawley, ed., *Biblical Ethics & Homosexuality: Listening to Scripture* (Louisville, KY: Westminster John Knox Press, 1996).

[15] Choon-Leong Seow, "Textual Orientation," in *Biblical Ethics & Homosexuality: Listening to Scripture*, ed. Robert L. Brawley (Louisville, KY: Westminster John Knox Press, 1996), p.19

[16] Ibid., 19.

water, where one who drinks will never thirst (John 4:10-14). You get the opportunity to choose to be married or not and to have sex or not. And no one is going to die from celibacy—it's a choice and not a sin. Christ was very big on feeding the hungry or a crowd before He tried to teach them. Christ encourages and admonishes Christians to feed the hungry and give water to the thirsty, showing that when you do this to the least, you are doing it to Him. There is nowhere in scripture where Christ showed favoritism to homosexual and effeminate activity. In 1 Corinthians 6, scriptures show that it was when the effeminate changed his behavior: "And such were some of you, but you have been washed and sanctified" that favoritism was shown to the repentant heart, the new man and new creature in Christ. The angels in heaven rejoice over one sinner who repents. The act of aligning yourself with God (reconciling to the original status before the fall) makes the angels happy. They are so happy about having and welcoming you home in the end.

When God made man (male and female) and said it was "very good," there was no mention of any deviant activity ("oops" or "my bad") or something going wrong with the creation of man. As a matter of fact, as the world looked on at the incident of the alleged gay gene gone awry in Sodom and Gomorrah, God set the whole thing ablaze; enough said about God's feelings about men wanting to know or have sex with men. This wasn't a fire like the one set in Chicago or the one in Atlanta during the Civil War; God deliberately set this one. Chicago and Atlanta were rebuilt. Sodom and Gomorrah were not.

"Genesis does not, in fact, tell the full story of creation."[17] Really, Mr. Seow. Tell the rest of the story to us. Now, if you say you were there, let's move on. If you are wrestling with what is written, what will you do if God gives you more to handle? "These that were written were written for our learning" (Romans 15:4). Seow is interested in going beyond the written text (word). "And the way of wisdom [man's wisdom or interpretation], which gives credence to science and experience, is not at all unscriptural. It merely assumes a different textual orientation, one that ironically points us beyond the written texts."[18] God has made foolish the wisdom of this world. Let's stick with the inspired text.

Seow asks for a "different textual orientation" on our views of creation and the scriptural negativity on homosexual practice.[19] What he should be aware of is that he can't use a "penknife" on the scriptural text. Jehoiakim, king of Judah, had Jehudi read the roll (word of the Lord), which he cut up

---

[17] Ibid.
[18] Ibid., 31.
[19] Ibid., 26.

and burned, but received a double portion of scripture along with what he tried to change or burn up (Jeremiah 36:23-32). Mr. Seow continued to wrestle with scriptures, trying to school God. Mr. Seow writes, "At the same time, we must admit that procreation is not an essential element of our being human. People who are childless are no less human. Nor is heterosexual union an indispensable element of humanity."[20] Seow gives a litany of reasons (somewhat complaining) of why God-approved sexual activity shouldn't be held up as a measuring stick to condemn nonproductive homosexual sexual activity. Two members of the opposite sex have the tools for producing a whole child; it is God who allows the egg and sperm to meet up. Any couple who has tried to have a child for years and finally adopts and later ends up with a natural pregnancy can testify. The scripture reads "Your eyes did see my substance, yet being unperfect; and in Your book all my members were written, which in continuance were fashioned, when as yet there was none of them," (Psalm 139:16). No one gets into this world without God's say-so—not even for one day. The use of unauthorized tools by two people in opposition of God's plan is an abomination because God is all about being productive or bearing fruits. God didn't put Adam and Eve in the garden to do nothing. Ask the man with the one talent who hid or buried it. God is the one who makes the final decision after proper use of tools to give the increase. He came down to make man and started with Adam and Eve in *His* world. What's up with the homosexual putting a cramp in God's plan to replenish the earth? Not all seeds sown will produce, and not all humans will produce, but this fact doesn't make God's word a lie about seeds and reproduction or procreation. A seed of wheat or corn is an essential element of being corn or wheat, even if not every seed sown reproduces. When Onan in the Old Testament spilled his seed (unproductively) in act of defiance, his deed wasn't proper, and God was displeased. When gays spill their seed (unproductively) in an act of defiance, their act isn't proper, and God isn't pleased—you are not your own. Marriage (holy matrimony) isn't for everyone, and it is God who allows a person to make that decision, but he or she is required to stay faithful. But if the person can't contain (in celibacy), he or she should marry. Even in one's unmarried status, God expects one to bear the fruit of the Spirit in his or her relationship with Him. Stop procreating and see who will be around to challenge God or make any statements like Seow is trying to make.

Seow writes, "And the way of wisdom, which gives credence to science and experience, is not at all unscriptural. It merely assumes a different textual

---

[20] Ibid., 27.

orientation, one that ironically points us beyond the written text."[21] When one goes beyond what is written (which will save you in the last day), a good bit of wisdom would be to return to scripture, the Bible. There is nothing beyond or outside of God's word that is designed to save you. God warns that if an angel brings any other gospel (doctrine or message) than what the apostles, who were inspired by the Holy Ghost, (Comforter Jesus promised) preached, let him be a curse. Mr. Seow's wisest course would be to stick with the book. To go beyond what is written would leave one lost in space and experiencing many bad scientific (unscriptural) landings on dangerous planets (winds of doctrines). And perhaps never able to come back to earth or the Bible (one true doctrine) before the earth is folded and wrapped up like a garment, as prophesied in scripture. He or she would be lost forever.

The Bible

"And you shall know the truth and the truth shall make you free" (John 8:32). If it were not so, I would not have told you. There are many things beyond our comprehension, and no matter how intellectual we believe ourselves to be, there are some things about this universe that is just over our heads [pun intended]. "As you know not what is the way of the spirit, nor how the bones do grow in the womb of her that is with child: even so you know not the works of God who makes all" (Ecclesiastes 11:5). The scriptures establish facts and deliver a clear perspective of how man should view his place in this vast universe: "For My thoughts are not your thoughts, neither are your ways My ways, says the Lord. For as the heavens are higher than the earth, so are My ways higher than your ways, and My thoughts than your thoughts" (Isaiah 55:8–9).

We want to know. We just want to know, and certainly in what we know or think we know, we want it to be nothing but the truth. We'll do everything possible to research and justify or certify that knowledge about what we have come to believe is factual. The disciple of Christ who is often referred to as "doubting Thomas" just wanted to know the truth. He had walked with Christ and trusted that Jesus would be around for those things He had promised. But the situation existed that he watched Jesus die and be placed in a tomb. "This is the disciple which testifies of these things, and wrote these things: and we know that his testimony is true. And there are also many other things which Jesus did, the which, if they should be written every one,

---

[21] Ibid., 31.

I suppose that even the world itself could not contain the books that should be written—Amen" (John 21:24–25). God knows some stuff we don't know, and many wrestle with the stuff He allows us to know. The way we behave toward God and His word demonstrates that we simply can't handle the truth. We don't want to entertain the truth. "For whatsoever things were written aforetime were written for our learning, that we through patience and comfort of the scriptures might have hope" (Romans *15:4*).

Jesus wasn't thrown back by Thomas's disbelief. He loved Thomas (Didymus) as He loves all mankind. After all, that is why He went to the cross and the grave. He revealed Himself to Thomas and allowed him to examine His crucifixion scars. It was important to Jesus that Thomas keep the faith and believe, as it is to Him that all men do. "And Thomas answered and said to Him, My Lord and My God. Jesus said to him, Thomas, because you have seen Me, you have believed: blessed are they that have not seen, and yet have believed" (John 20:28–29).

Jesus conversed with God the Father and told Him, "While I was with them [His disciples] in the world, I kept them in Your name: those that You gave Me I have kept, and none of them is lost, but the son of perdition [Judas Iscariot]; that the scripture might be fulfilled" (John 17:12; also see Psalm 41:9). "And as they sat and did eat, Jesus said, Verily I say to you, One of you which eats with Me shall betray Me" (Mark 14:18; John 13:18–21). Jesus's prayer to God concerning the apostles, His disciples, whom He was leaving on earth and had commanded to preach the gospel to the world (Matthew 28:18–20), was this: "Neither pray I for these alone, but for them also which shall believe on Me through their word" (John 17:20). This is the essence of our faith that Jesus is who He says He is, the Son of God. And it is through Him that our salvation (alignment back with almighty God, the Father) has been worked out. Without this faith, it is impossible to please God. For all the doubting Thomases in the world, the message is the same: blessed are those who have not seen and yet believe.

It Is Written

There are a plethora of scriptures that show man that his knowledge is limited and that the Holy Bible is the *inspired* word of God (God breathed).

> Heaven and earth shall pass away, but My words shall not pass away. But of that day and hour *knows no man*, no,

not the angels of heavens, but My father only. (Matthew 24:35–36, emphasis added)

And many other signs truly did Jesus in the presence of his disciples, which are *not written in this book*: But these are written, that you might believe that Jesus is the Christ, the Son of God; and that believing you might have life through His name. (John 20:30–31, emphasis added)

And when he was disposed to pass into Achaia, the brethren wrote, exhorting the disciples to receive him: Who, when he was come, helped them much which had believed through grace: For he mightily convinced the Jews, and that publicly, showing by scriptures (Old Testament) that Jesus was the Christ (Acts 18:27–28).

God is faithful, loving, and true. Jesus is saying to man, "If this thing about you and Me and this place I have prepared for you with Me isn't true, I wouldn't bother telling you." No one likes being lied to, and yet religiously we are deceived and lied to every day, century upon century, about how we took up residence on this planet and our existence beyond the grave. God cannot lie and has no reason to deceive and toy with man's mind.

In Titus 1, the apostle Paul (a man like you and me) described himself as the servant of God and an apostle of Jesus Christ. Paul's faith in God and his knowledge of the truth about Christ, being one of the disciples who actually experienced first-century Christianity, and Paul's encounter (experience) on the road to Damascus while in the act of persecuting Christians before his conversion to Christianity were what brought about a "mind change:" a new man, once he heard and obeyed the truth. The way God delivers this message and news to the world is through peaching. Peaching is a command from God. Elsewhere in scripture, Paul conversed about the importance of preaching and his role in spreading the gospel. "For Christ sent me not to baptize, but to *preach* the gospel: not with wisdom of words, less the cross of Christ should be made of none effect. For the preaching of the cross is to them that perish foolishness; but to us which are saved, it is the power of God. For it is written, I will destroy the wisdom of the wise, and will bring to nothing the understanding of the prudent" (1 Corinthians 1:17–19, emphasis added).

The Lie at Ground Zero

Civilized nations accept nothing but the truth as the code of ethics in their social behavior, civil conduct, and legal affairs. A lie is simply destructive and often comes disguised as truth, like a newly constructed and seemingly flawless bridge, but the integrity of its foundation has been compromised, and it won't hold up to its promise of safety. Most often the blueprint or pattern wasn't followed. Satan has the ability to appear as an "angel of light," but what always thaws his deception is, "It is written." The scripture is man's blueprint and pattern to follow to achieve a perfectly built foundation of salvation.

A directive which comes straight from God's mouth: "Thou shalt not lie." We don't like being hurt by a lie, so we agree with that command readily; unfortunately, all too often when someone else is doing the lying. Of course, we most assuredly want him or her punished. The crime of perjury comes with a stiff penalty. The first sin entering the world puts a wedge between the relationship of God and man—was the Lie. The consequence is murder, bloodshed, death, pain, and suffering. Adam and Eve were forced out of paradise, the Garden of Eden.

"And the Lord God said, behold, the man is become as one of Us, to know good and evil: and now, less he put forth his hand, and take also of the tree of life, and eat, and live forever: Therefore the Lord God sent him forth from the Garden of Eden, to till the ground from where he was taken. So He drove out the man; and He placed at the east of the Garden of Eden Cherubims, and a flaming sword which turned every way, to keep the way of the tree of life" (Genesis 3:22–24).

God says, "You shall not raise a false report: put not your hand with the wicked to be an unrighteous witness. You shall not follow a multitude to do evil; neither shall you speak in a cause to decline after many to pervert judgment" (Exodus 23:1–2).

God cannot lie, and when He made a promise to Abraham because He could swear by no greater, He swore by Himself. "Wherein God, willing more abundantly to show to the heirs [man] of promise the immutability of His counsel, confirmed it by an oath: That by two immutable things, in which it was impossible for God to lie, we might have a strong consolation, who have fled for refuge to lay hold upon the hope set before us" (Hebrews 6:17–18).

The results of a lie have affected the life of man from ground zero to these present times. The LGBT community is telling a lie about God. God does not have anything to do with what they proclaim; their behavior is *not* His fault. The word of God goes out to man. "But though we, or an angel from heaven, preach any other gospel to you than that which we have preached to you, let him be accursed. As we said before, so say I now again, If any man preach any other gospel to you than that you have received, let him be a cursed" (Galatians 1:8–9). The apostle Paul wrote, "But I certify you, brethren that the gospel which was preached of me is not after man. For I neither received it of any, neither was I taught it, but by the revelation of Jesus Christ" (Galatians 1:11–12). There are well over three thousand distinct religious beliefs or faiths and practices in the USA alone, while the scriptures speak of one Lord, one faith, and one baptism. Many are still drinking the Kool-Aid (sugar water), sweet tasting, soft-to-the-ear sermons in "will worship." There are no gay Christians. "And such *were* some of you" (1 Corinthians 6:11, emphasis added). Some are killing in the name of religion and told they will have virgins in heaven. "For in the resurrection, they neither marry, nor are given in marriage, but are as the angels of God in heaven" (Matthew 22:30). A lie is designed to kill and put you straight in hell: separate you from God. "You are of your father the devil, and the lusts of your father you will do. He was a murderer from the beginning and abode not in the truth because there is no truth in him. When he speaks a lie, he speaks of his own: for he is a liar, and the father of it" (John 8:44).

Again, how important is it to have knowledge? Adam and Eve sought it. How important is it to have knowledge based on truth. Well they sort of missed the boat here and threw everything out of joint. They were deceived into committing a disobedient act that promised they wouldn't die (Genesis 3:3–4, 22–24). Who likes being deceived or lied to? God cannot lie, and Satan is the Father of Lies. Know the truth, and the truth will set you free. When you know the truth, you are at liberty to accept or reject it. Unlike not knowing the truth, you basically have nothing reliable to act on. You are literally trapped in a condition or state of stupid, a sitting duck, and an open minefield of a "make the best way through this thing called life" scenario.

What Exactly Is the Truth?

God that made the world and all things therein, seeing that He is Lord of heaven and earth, dwells not in temples made with hands, as though He needed anything, seeing He gives to all life, and breath, and all things; And has made of one blood all nations of men for to dwell on all the face of the earth, and has determined the times before appointed, and the bounds of their habitation; That they should seek the Lord, if haply they might feel after Him and find Him, though He be not far from every one of us: For in Him we live, and move, and have our being; as certain also of your own poets have said, For we are also His offspring. Forasmuch then as we are the offspring of God, we ought not to think that the Godhead is like to gold, or silver, or stone, graven by art and man's device. And the times of this ignorance God winked at; but now commands all men everywhere to repent: Because He has appointed a day in the which He will judge the world in righteousness by that Man whom He has ordained; whereof He has given assurance to all men, in that He has raised Him from the dead. (Acts 17:24–31)

Life is filled with truths; some hurt, and some put a smile on our faces. The trillion-dollar question is, What is the ultimate truth after all is said and done on this time-side of life? The only truth that matters is the gospel—the death, burial, and resurrection of Christ. It is a promise and plan to get man from earth to heaven. We can simply start with, "Let us hear the conclusion of the whole matter: Fear God and keep His commandments: for this is the whole duty of man" (Ecclesiastes 12:13). God created man in His own image. "For we are His workmanship, created in Christ Jesus to good works, which God has before ordained that we should walk in them" (Ephesians 2:10).

God is abundant (huge, large) in goodness and truth, and we are to be good—not our good but God's definition of *good*. As a matter of fact, no one can be good unless he or she is in Christ. "Walk in the light as I am in the light and we have fellowship one with the other." Out of all your goodness or righteousness, you are as a filthy rag in His sight (Isaiah 64:6). The only good one can ever possibly be is in Christ. Outside of Christ, there is no goodness in man. Don't be mistaken; we all think we are good, but our deeds end up being only charitable acts. They are helpful and needful acts of kindness on our part for the continuation of nonchaotic and somewhat pleasant dwellings. But for the act to be labeled "good," it has to come from God; and when done in the name of God, then it is good. The devil does kind and charitable things; can he do good things? This begs one to ask self, "Is there good in Satan?" Our goodness is an act of obedience, something Satan will not do. It is within Christ that our acts—not outside of Christ—are good. God created us for good works. Call no man good, for only God is good.

God Is Good

And Jesus said to him, Why call you me good? There is none good but one, that is God. (Mark 10:18)

When He shall come to be glorified in His saints, and to be admired in all them that believe (because our testimony among you was believed) in that day. Wherefore also we pray always for you, that our God would count you worthy of this calling, and fulfill all the good pleasure of *His goodness*, and that work of faith with power. (2 Thessalonians 1:10–11, emphasis added)

Or despise you the riches of *His goodness* and forbearance and longsuffering; not knowing that the goodness of God leads you to repentance. (Romans 2:4, emphasis added)

Behold therefore the goodness and severity of God: on them which fell, the severity of God ... but toward you, goodness, if you continue in *His goodness*. (Romans 11:22, emphasis added)

For You, Lord, are good, and ready to forgive; and plenteous in mercy to all them that call upon You. (Psalm 86:5)

Good and upright is the Lord; therefore will He teach sinners in the way. The meek will He guide in judgment: and the meek will He teach His way. (Psalm 25:8–9)

The Truth about Sin

We know some essential truths about God: He is good, He loves man, and He cannot lie. Let's take some time to learn a little about sin. Sin originated or was introduced into the world by Satan. Sin is death; this is sometimes instant and sometimes long and drawn-out suffering over centuries and generations. It literally separates man from his life source, God. Because of his disobedience, God allows man to experience (taste) the havoc of sin at the hands of the prince of this world, who is like a roaring lion, seeking whom he can devour. It is in God's nature to be forgiving and long-suffering. On this fact alone, God established a plan before the foundation of the world for the redemption of man. The first Adam (through disobedience) brought sin and death upon creation. The second Adam, Christ (through obedience of His death on the cross), brings eternal life to man. The world continues to witness the cruelty of sin through senseless beheadings, racial and civil unrest, violence in the name of religion, murders, sexual assaults, suicides, hopelessness, fear, ungodliness, lust and lewdness, lying and deception, wars, terrorist threats and attacks, pain, suffering, deaths of innocents, famines, droughts, pestilence, diseases, floods, earthquakes, torrential rains, and natural disasters.

Because of sin, the shedding of blood, suffering, and death entered the world. See Genesis 1:29–30; 2:8, 16–17; 3:17–19. "To Adam also and to his wife did the Lord God make coats of skins and clothed them" (Genesis 3:21). There is a TV program about survival called Naked and Afraid. I believe the characters or actors try to convey that this is how the first man lived—no cloths and no shelter. Scriptures say that when Adam and Eve discovered they were naked, they hid themselves (Genesis 3:7–10). Man, put some clothes on, please! In Genesis 3, some animals lost their lives: through their bloodshed and the stripping of their skins, clothing was made to protect Adam and Eve. God still cares and protects His creation, man. As you continue to follow man from this point on in suffering and death, the shedding of blood is at the forefront of his travel from Eden (Adam) to the cross (Christ). For the atonement of man's sin, God allowed animal sacrifices (bloodshed: pain, suffering, and death) for something the animal didn't do to be used as a temporary fix or atonement until the official sacrifice of the blood of Christ. Christ suffered, bled, and died for something He did not do. Man needs to understand that these blood sacrifices of innocent blood were all because God loved Him and gave him an opportunity to redeem himself, through obedience. The first time disobedience happened on earth was in the Garden of Eden. "For if we sin willfully after that we have received the *knowledge of the truth*, there remains no more sacrifices for sins" (Hebrews 10:26, emphasis added).

In these few pages, the reader has the truth. Now the reader has enough information about the Bible, the inspired word of God, to accept or reject it. Now there is no floundering around in the dark about the Bible or God. The person who believes and is baptized shall be saved. This isn't a lie, because God cannot lie. His promise to man is sworn by none other than Himself, because there is none greater than the almighty God Himself.

Connecting with God in Likeness

1. God is *angry* with the wicked every day;
2. Jesus *wept* at the death of Lazarus and *mourned* with his sisters, Mary and Martha;
3. The *wrath* of God is on the ungodly and the unrighteous;
4. It *repented* God that He had made man;
5. God *loves*, and God *forgives*;
6. God *laughs* at the wicked for He sees his day is coming (Psalm 37:13).
7. God *rested* on the seventh day; and
8. Jesus *broke bread* and *drank* the cup with His disciples.

The Holy Spirit makes intercession for us (expresses our concerns and thoughts that we cannot speak or express). In the spirit, we are connected with Him, and He is connected with us. Certainly, we know how to be angry, but scripture tells us to be angry and sin not. We love our spouses, children, family, and friends. We show compassion, kindness, and sympathy to others. Scripture tells us not to let the sun go down on our wrath but to be of a forgiving heart. Scripture calls us to repent of our sins. Man is told to work while it is day, for the night comes when no man can work. Work while you are young and healthy and before old age, when you aren't able to do for yourself. Jesus did a good work while He was on this earth.

Man displays attributes and characteristics of his Creator. God is eternal, and the spirit of man is eternal (God breathed). In the Garden of Eden, while the untarnished relationship existed, there was the tree of life and the tree of knowledge of good and evil. (Genesis 2:9) Man sinned, and a death sentence was upon man. "And the Lord God said, Behold the man is become as one of Us, to know good and evil: and now, less he put forth his hand, and take *also* of the TREE OF LIFE, and eat, and live forever; Therefore the Lord God sent him forth from the garden of Eden to till the ground from where he was taken" (Genesis 3:20–22, emphasis added). Christ had to experience death and shed blood for an atonement and price for sin. Only Christ (God the Son) qualified to conquer death, and it is only in Christ that man conquers death.

> Knowing that Christ being raised from the dead dies no more; death has no more dominion over Him. For in that He died, He died to sin once; but in that He lives, He lives to God. Likewise reckon you also yourselves to be dead indeed to sin, but alive to God through Jesus Christ our Lord. (Romans 6: 9–11)

But if the Spirit of Him that raised up Jesus from the dead dwell in you, He that raised up Christ from the dead shall also quicken your mortal bodies by His Spirit that dwells in you. (Romans 8:11)

Most importantly, we can discern good from evil, right from wrong. God allowed the children of Israel to have judges. God established laws, ordnances, and rules to govern the conduct of our lives. We cannot function as people without rules and laws from the smallest microcosm village or commune to the most advanced industrial society. Law and order come from God.

God didn't leave us alone here to wander in darkness and ignorance, creating our own rules and saving ourselves by our own rules. We don't have a heaven or hell to put ourselves in, but God does. If we were able, the cross or crucifixion wasn't necessary; man would have the power to save himself. It's not uncommon to hear someone say, "You go your way, and I will go mine (live on our own terms), and we both will be accepted in heaven by God. It doesn't matter as long as you believe." Jesus says He is the Way, the Truth, and the Life (John 14:6). The problem here is that no one bothers to check the blueprint, the Bible, for instructions to verify the foundational integrity of what he or she has built to enter eternal life. "According to the grace of God which is given to me, as a wise masterbuilder, I have laid the foundation, and another builds thereon. But let every man take heed how he builds thereupon. For other foundation can no man lay than that is laid, which is Jesus Christ" (1 Corinthians 3:10–11).

God has communicated with man through angels, prophets, apostles, and His written word: the Old Testament and the New Testament.

God, who at sundry times and in divers manners spoke in time past to the fathers by the prophets, has in these last days spoken to us by His Son, whom He has appointed heir of all things, by whom also He made the worlds; who being the brightness of His glory, and the express image of His person, and upholding all things by the word of His power, when He had by Himself purged our sins, sat down on the right hand of the Majesty on high; being made so much better than the angels, as He has by inheritance obtained a more excellent name than they. (Hebrews 1:1–4)

One Who Knows the Way

Some say they believe there is a God, but they don't believe in Christ.

Let not your heart be troubled, you believe in God, believe also in Me. In my Father's house are many mansions: if it were not so, I would not have told you. I go to prepare a place for you. And if I go and prepare a place for you, I will come again and receive you to Myself that where I am there you may be also. (John 14: 1–3)

If you had known Me, you should have known My Father also; and from hereafter you know Him, and have seen Him. (John 14:7)

What is most remarkable about Jesus, in comparison to all others who say they can save man, is that Jesus is the only One who declares that He knows the *way* from earth to heaven (John 14:6). No one else has made that claim. He was in heaven, came down to earth, and was received back into heaven. The account is in the book of Acts. Two angels informed the disciples that the same way they had seen Jesus ascend into heaven on a cloud was in like manner to His return for *saved or obedient* souls. All evident points to the fact that the so-called saviors (false messengers of God) are dead and buried and their graves are here with us today. And carvings (statures or idols) with eyes that cannot see, ears that cannot hear, and mouths that cannot speak are made by man's hands, and the unused parts are used for the fire or some other purchases for profit (Psalm 115:4–8). Christ was in heaven; He came to earth. He returned to heaven, and He is seated at the right hand of God. "And when He had spoken these things, while they beheld, He was taken up; and a cloud received Him out of their sight. And while they looked steadfastly toward heaven as He went up, behold, two men stood by in white apparel; which also said, You men of Galilee, why stand you gazing up into heaven? This same Jesus which is taken up from you into heaven, shall so come in like manner as you have seen Him go into heaven" (Acts 1:9–11).

God is an awesome God. What a relief that God only asked us to believe what He has presented to us in His written word. He who believes and is baptized shall be saved. Our tiny brains would blow a fuse trying to know all that God knows. This world couldn't contain the volume of books it would take to hold what can be written on what God knows. We can also believe that God delivered His word and what He wanted us to know, and Satan is busy trying to take His words out of the hearts of men.

Beloved, when I gave all diligence to write to you of the common salvation, it was needful for me to write to you, and exhort you that you should earnestly contend for the *faith which was once delivered to the saints.* For there are certain men crept in unawares, who were before of old ordained to this condemnation, ungodly men, turning the grace of our God into lasciviousness, and denying the only Lord God, and our Lord Jesus Christ. I will therefore put you in remembrance, though you once knew this, how that the Lord, having saved the people out of the land of Egypt, afterward destroyed them that believed not. And the angels which kept not their first estate, but left their own habitation, He has reserved in everlasting chains under darkness to the judgment of the great day. Even as *Sodom* and *Gomorrah*, and the cities about them in like manner, giving themselves over to fornication, and going after *strange flesh*, are set forth for an example, suffering the vengeance of eternal fire." (Jude 3–7, emphasis added)

This isn't going to be a rainbow or rainbow flag situation but fire.

There are many who question the authenticity of the Bible, the word of God, but unquestionably the sciences—archaeologist, paleontologist, geologist, historians, and so forth— show places, people, and times accurately depicted in Bible history; in other words, too many facts cannot be dismissed in the history of man's dwellings on earth over the centuries. In the days of the prophet Daniel, King Nebuchadnezzar is spoken of. "But there is a God in heaven that reveals secrets, and makes known to King Nebuchadnezzar what shall be in the latter days" (Daniel 2:28). The Bible gives an account of places like Babylon in the book of Daniel and Persia (Daniel 10:20), Greece, and Antiochus. Daniel spoke of the following places and the rise of tyranny in them: Egypt, Libya, and Ethiopia (Daniel 11). We see Jerusalem and Israel in Bible history. In reading the book of the prophet Ezekiel, we learn of the actions of kings and their time in Babylon. In 586 BC, Nebuchadnezzar destroyed Jerusalem and brought survivors to Babylonia. We find Solomon, third king of Israel (Jerusalem), around 973–933 BC. In the Bible, we read of the pharaohs of Egypt, including the Dead Sea (Scrolls); the Jordan River; Damascus; the Wall of Jerusalem (prophet Nehemiah), Nehemiah 12:37; Palestine; Mount Sinai; King of Cyrus, the Persian kings; Jeroboam I; Jeroboam II; the rise and fall of dynasties; and Assyria (2 King 17:4–7). The apostle Paul, who found himself imprisoned in Rome, composed letters or epistles from Rome. We find Paul at Corinth, Thessalonica (Acts 17:10), Macedonia, and Philippi with letters or epistles to the first-century church. There is much history of people and places we know today are in Bible history.

In the book of Acts, around AD 33, the church promised or foretold in prophecy came into existence in a spiritual way, unlike the tabernacle, built by hands in the Old Testament. The church became the saving vehicle for which Noah's ark was a prototype. The ark saved from water; the church saves from fire by way of water baptism. The church, a body of believers, is spiritual, and only Christ can add one to His church, the church of Christ, the kingdom of God, or the body of Christ through obedience to the gospel and water baptism. There are no Jews or Gentiles; all are one in Christ. No one can vote you into the body of Christ. Only your sins separate you from God. The first Christians added to the Lord's church went about, "praising God and having favor with all the people. And the Lord added to the church daily such as should be saved" (Acts 2:47). "Now when they heard this, they were pricked in their heart, and said to Peter and to the rest of the apostles, Men and brethren, what shall we do? Then Peter said to them, *Repent*, and be *Baptized* every one of you in the name of Jesus Christ for the remission of sins, and you shall receive the gift of the Holy Ghost. For the promise is to you, and to your children, and to all that are afar off, even as many as the Lord our God shall call [called by the gospel]. And with many other words did he testify and exhort, saying save yourselves from this untoward/perverse generation. Then they that gladly received his word were baptized: and the same day there were added to them about three thousand souls" (Acts 2:37–41, emphasis added). This is the beginning of the New Testament church, the church of Christ. This occurred on the day of Pentecost after Peter and other apostles' first sermon. These apostles were those the Holy Ghost empowered to preach to the crowd in tongues or languages they hadn't been schooled in or hadn't been born speaking (Acts 2:3). "And how hear we every man in our own tongue, wherein we were born?" (Acts 2:8).

The Bible is the inspired word of God: God breathed; holy men were moved by the Spirit and not by human wisdom to record the word of God. Jesus said, "Then said I, Lo, I come (in the volume of the book it is written of Me,) to do your will, O God" (Hebrews 10:7). The Godhead—Father, Son, and Holy Spirit did not leave man to figure out what to do or leave it to chance that man will figure it out on his own.

> However when He the Spirit of truth is come, He will guide
> you into all truth: for He shall not speak of Himself; but

whatsoever He shall hear, that shall He speak; and He will show you things to come. (John 16:13)

But the Comforter, which is the Holy Ghost, whom the Father will send in My named, He shall teach you all things, and bring all things to your remembrance, whatsoever I have said to you. (John 14:26)

You are asked to believe and given a personal invitation to come: "whosoever will, let him come." You have the sworn word of God Almighty, who cannot lie, that His word is true.

Paul wrote his epistles (letters) to the churches, and Peter (another writer of the inspired word) referred to Paul's writings as inspired (wisdom given to him) as well as other scriptures in the Bible in the following way: "As also in all his epistles, speaking in them of these things; in which are some things hard to be understood, which they that are unlearned and unstable twist, as they do also the *other scriptures*, to their own destruction. You therefore, beloved, seeing you know these things, before, beware less your also, being led away with the error of the wicked, fall from your own steadfastness. But grow in grace, and in the *knowledge* of our Lord and Savior Jesus Christ" (2 Peter 3:16–18, emphasis added).

Peter reminded followers of Christ of Paul's writings that the longsuffering of Christ (our Lord) is salvation. God has made preparation for your salvation, something you couldn't do. And from that perspective, the ball remains in your court to make the move toward salvation before the clock runs out and the game of life is called. Ever since the day Jesus died and resurrected (conquered death), he sat on the right hand of God and proclaimed His mission finished. The cross in obedience became the official sacrifice for sin and aligned man back with God. Since then, it has been man's move. That move would be to hear, believe, repent, confess, be baptized, and live faithfully until he or she departs this earth.

From Genesis to Revelation, the Bible reveals the beginning and ending, holding one concept: the creation, fall, and redemption of mankind. All books work in unison, concealing and revealing (Old Testament vs. New Testament) the mystery and the complete unveiling of the mystery of God's plan for salvation. There is neither Jew nor Greek; all are one in Christ Jesus. There is no more nation of Israel or chosen people but a spiritual Israel, people called by the Gospel. A spiritual Israel that does not serve God by the Law of Moses or temples made with hands, but serves God in Spirit and in Truth through His Son, Jesus Christ.

God masterminded the plan as noted in Scripture: "According as He has chosen us in Him before the foundation of the world, that we should be holy and without blame before Him in love: having predestinated us to the adoption of children by Jesus Christ to Himself, according to the good pleasure of His will, to the praise of the glory of His grace, wherein He has made us *accepted* in the beloved. In whom we have redemption through His blood, the forgiveness of sins, according to the riches of His grace; wherein He has abounded toward us in all wisdom and prudence; having made known to us the *mystery of His will*, according to His good pleasure which He has purposed in Himself" (Ephesian 1:4–9).

God has always been in control of how His word would reach man. He promised to send the Holy Ghost (Comforter) to bring to memory what Jesus had taught the disciples (apostles) when He was with them. These were men (vessels) God used to ensure that His inspired (God-breathed) word was recorded for instructions or directives to the church (body of believers and saved) and for those who would believe on Him through their word, the gospel. When sin entered the world through a lie and man's disobedience by adhering to that lie, it set in motion the plan to set things right again for all who chose to *believe* and *obey*. No liar will enter heaven; that will include those who lie on (against) God. God made me this way. "Blessed are they that do His commandments, that they may have a right to the Tree of Life, and may enter in through the gate into the city" (Revelation 22:14; see Genesis 3:22). Heaven is a prepared place for prepared people. "Wherefore the rather, brethren, give diligence to make your calling and election sure; for if you do these things, you shall never fall: for so an entrance shall be ministered to you abundantly into the everlasting kingdom of our Lord and Savior Jesus Christ" (2 Peter 1:10–11).

It behooves everyone to search the Scripture and to know what the will of the Lord is. Heaven has not been promised to good people, but obedient people. Notably, so, it was disobedience that separated, severed the relationship between God and man in the first place. "Will worshippers" won't find entrance through the gate; thus many will say, "Have I not done many wonderful works in God's name?" only to hear, "I never knew you, depart from me."

The Bible supports evidence of its claim to authenticity through historical documentation. We can verify people and places through archaeological findings that corroborate biblical events: kings, queens, princes, pharaohs, high priests, Roman governors, dynasties, emperors, and cities with accuracy. As the curiosity of man propels him, future excavations will discover even more biblical accounts to be accurate, thus leaving little doubts of the Bible's authenticity. Yet one is reminded of the conversation Jesus had with "doubting

Thomas" and the fact that God cannot lie. The Bible was written by over forty different men from various social and economic statuses: those learned and unlearned, tentmakers to physicians and scholars of the scrolls that span centuries yet kept the message on point. The message is in harmony, with no wavering over the centuries, and it attests to the fact that this was no human-designed task. God makes His will and word available so none will have an excuse not to believe and obey. "For God is not the author of confusion, but of peace, as in all churches [congregations] of the saints" (1 Corinthians 14:33). There were no writers doing a "one-up" on the other (claiming more knowledge and telling a different story of the same event). But you can see that the books corroborated historical events between writers and produced continuity from beginning to end or Genesis to Revelation. Our efforts to lend our own commentary (I think, I feel) to the Bible is debunked by "It is written." "Knowing this first, that no prophecy of the scripture is of any private interpretation" (2 Peter 1:20). In other words, GOD GOT THIS. Don't hurt yourself. "As also in all his epistles, speaking in them of these things; in which are some things hard to be understood, which they that are unlearned and unstable twist, as they do also the other scriptures, to their own destruction" (2 Peter 3:16).

The snake-handling worshippers seek to show their faith. The unlearned worshippers, not accepting blood transfusion, try to show their faith. Cult leaders who use sexual control over women and girls try to show their faith. Religious extremists, killing in the name of God, try to show their faith. Those who say they witnessed Jehovah and lived to tell they did try to show their faith. The Scripture says no man has seen God and lived (John 1:17; Exodus 33:20). There are those who say the earth won't burn up; they attempt to prophesy their faith. The Scripture says the earth will burn up (2 Peter 3:10), and the list goes on and on, with "will worshippers" twisting the scriptures. God has allowed man to gain the knowledge and ability to sustain life through the science of blood transfusions. Life of the flesh is in the blood; red blood cells carry oxygen to the brain and other parts of the body to sustain life. In Leviticus 17:11–14, Moses informed the children of Israel of this fact, which took science a while to discover.

God's Attitude about Sin

Have you ever wondered why God communicates with man through His Son, Jesus Christ? What is made clear throughout the writing of the Scripture is that man, now a sinner after that fateful day in Eden, stemming from his encounter with the serpent, who had allowed Satan to use him, couldn't make atonement for his own sins. He had placed himself in an imperfect state and needed another to dig him out. It is God's nature that He cannot stand the sight of sin. As a matter of fact, the presence of God is too good and righteous for man to behold. It would be detrimental for man to approach God's face in his sinful state. Moses (with God's assistance) was allowed to see only His backside.

> And He said, You cannot see My face; for there shall no man see Me, and live. (Exodus 33:20)
> No man has seen God at any time; the only begotten Son, which is in the bosom of the Father, He has declared Him. (John 1:18) See also John 3:13.

It took one who was perfect to approach God on man's behalf, a sinless one. God told man that Jesus was His Beloved Son and that He was pleased with Jesus and that mankind must hear Jesus. Can you fathom the degree to which sin is such a diseased and corrupt ailment in the flesh that when man tries to approach God without going through Jesus (mediator), he gets a "talk-to-the-hand; see Jesus" gesture from Him? Does man even understand and comprehend his predicament even yet? Yes, God is love, but don't forget the severity of God (Romans 11:22). The only way to approach God is through His Son, Jesus Christ—man's advocate with the Father (1 John 2:1). The following scriptures reveal a conversation between Jesus, His disciples, and one in particular, Philip: "If you had known Me, you should have known My Father also: and from hereafter you know Him, and have seen Him. Philip said to Him, *Lord, show us the Father*, and it sufficed us. Jesus said to him, Have I been so long time with you, and yet have you not known Me, Philip? He that has seen Me has seen the Father; and how say you then, Show us the Father. Believe you not that I am in the Father, and the Father in Me? The words that I speak to you I speak not of Myself; but the Father that dwells in Me; He does the works" (John 14:10, emphasis added).

Christ, the Messiah (promised redeemer), was prophesied from the Old Testament to the New Testament. "And he said to them, These are the words which I spoke to you, while I was yet with you that all things must be fulfilled, which were written in the law of Moses, and in the prophets, and in the psalms, concerning Me" (Luke 24:44). In the four Gospels or the first four books of the New Testament (Matthew, Mark, Luke, and John), you find the fulfillment of the promise in the birth of Christ, His death, and resurrection. Christ came of age and went about doing His Father's will. Christ taught the apostles (disciples) and commanded them to go into all the world and preach the gospel, baptizing in the name of the Father, Son, and Holy Ghost. Christ became obedient to the death of the cross, after which He pronounced, "It is finished." He took His seat in heaven at the right hand of God. A conversation Jesus had with God was about having "this cup" (His suffering the crucifixion and a cruel, agonizing, and shameful death; a scary moment of separation from God in death) not be so, but Jesus was obedient to the Father and said, "Not my will but thy will." Man needs to understand that God loved him enough to offer up His only begotten Son for his redemption. Can man ever comprehend the fact that sin is such a horrendous disease that it took deity to make amends on his behalf?

In the book of Acts, Christ sent back the Holy Spirit (day of Pentecost) and established the promised vehicle for saving souls, *The* Church. "Then comes the end, when He shall have delivered up the kingdom [church] to God, even the Father; when He shall have put down all rule and all authority and power. For He must reign, till He has put all enemies under His feet. The last enemy that shall be destroyed is death" (1 Corinthians 15:24–26).

Latter books of the New Testament reveal dialogue, with many congregations and epistles addressing conduct and behavior in the churches or congregations of the church of Christ. Similarly, Exodus, Leviticus, and Numbers communicated with the Hebrew nation about God's expectation of His chosen people. The church, the called by the gospel, is now His chosen people, with both Jews and Gentile, who are obedient to his will. And finally, the book of Revelation tells man what is to happen at the end of time when God comes to claim the people of His kingdom, the church. "The" church is distinct from "a" church or any denomination established after Pentecost. The church, in addition to the apostles and those who had believed and were baptized, (Peter addressed the crowd from every nation with the gospel) Christ added three thousand souls on the first day of coming into existence (Acts 2:41, 47). All obedient souls spend eternity in heaven with God, and all those disobedient spend eternity in the fires of hell with Satan. Note: churches in the New Testament refer to congregations of the church of Christ at various locations (cities), not different faiths and religions or religious practices and denominations of various faiths. "Salute one another with a holy kiss, the churches of Christ salute you" (Romans 16:16). Each of the following churches represents a local congregation (growing pains) in the community during the first century:

1. Ephesus (Revelation 2:1–7), the church that had forsaken its first love (2:4)
2. Smyrna (Revelation 2:8–11), the church that would suffer persecution (2:10)

3. Pergamum (Revelation 2:12–17), the church that needed to repent (2:16)
4. Thyatira (Revelation 2:18–29), the church that had a false prophetess (2:20)
5. Sardis (Revelation 3:1–6), the church that had fallen asleep (3:2)
6. Philadelphia (Revelation 3:7–13), the church that had endured patiently (3:10)
7. Laodicea (Revelation 3:14–22), the church that was lukewarm and lackadaisical (toward God) (3:16)

We are a generation all about knowledge and fact-checking. Discoveries by the medical society and other sciences—historians, biologists, and archeologists—reveal ancient cites, people, and religious purification ceremonies' restricted diets of clean and unclean animals. Parasites in pork (*Trichinella spiralis* and *Echinococcus granulois*) were discovered centuries and generations after God commanded Israel not to eat this cloven-footed, unclean animal (Leviticus 11:3). And circumcision on the eighth day in an infant's life is the safest because of the role vitamin K plays in the clotting or coagulation of blood (Genesis 17:12). These discoveries in the last one hundred to most recently fifty years have unearthed cultural practices that have had a significant impact on how we deal with certain health concerns in the twenty-first century.

Medical science discovered centuries after God initiated the procedure that the eighth day in a male's life, due to the level of prothrombin, which is a result of vitamin K (prevents hemorrhaging) produced in the liver, is the safest day to perform circumcision. God told Abraham to circumcise the male child on the eighth day.[22]

The rise and fall of kings and dynasties, which occurred in the lives of individual people and nations and lands, were foretold, including the coming of the birth of Christ, and when it came to fruition (Genesis 3:15; Galatians 4:4–5). Many of these ancient and biblical events surrounding the prophecy and life of Christ and the life and travels of His apostles and the activities of the first-century church corroborate historical accounts of people, cities, lands, and nations in the excavations and findings of the sciences. Certainly, it would take a concerted effort to disbelieve writings that can predict with great accuracy what will unfold centuries before the time of their occurrences. We have the book of Revelation,

---

[22] Thompson, Bert. "Rock-Solid Faith: How to Build It," pg. 238. Apologetics Press. Inc.
. This was a video

which predicts what will happen to the earth and man, the obedient and disobedient. What will happen is already sealed in a book. As Jesus has said, "If it were not so, I would not have told you." God tells man that nothing is left standing but His word, and the safest place to be standing is on the word of God.

Jesus in Prophecy (Acts 10:43)

OLD TESTAMENT	SCRIPTURE	NEW TESTAMENT	SCRIPTURE
Born of Woman	Genesis 3:15	Born of Woman	Galatians 4:4
Seed of Abraham, the Promise	Genesis 22:18	Seed of Abraham, the Promise	Luke 3:34
Tribe of Judah	Genesis 49:10	Tribe of Judah	Hebrews 7:14
Lineage of King David	2 Samuel 7:12	Lineage of King David	Luke 1:32
Born in Bethlehem	Micah 5:2	Born in Bethlehem	Matthew 2:1
Virgin Birth	Isaiah 7:14	Virgin Birth	Matthew 1:22
Bruise Satan's Head	Genesis 3:15	Bruise Satan Head	Hebrews 2:12–14; Galatians 4:4
Birth in Days of Roman Reign	Daniel 2:44; Genesis 49:10	Birth in Days of Roman Reign	Luke 2:1; Matthew 2:22
Born Both Human and Divine	Micah 5:2; Zechariah 13:7	Born Both Human and Divine	John 1:1, 14; 10:30; Philippians 2:6

Submit to God's Will	Psalm 40:8; Isaiah 53:11	Submit to God's Will	John 8:29; 2 Corinthians 5:21; 1 Peter 2:22
Rejected and Knew Grief	Isaiah 53:3	Rejected and Knew Grief	Matthew 8:17; Romans 4:25
Betrayed by a Friend for Forty Pieces of Silver	Psalm 41:9; Zechariah 11:12	Betrayed by a friend for forty pieces of silver	John 13:18; Matthew 26:15
His Hands and Feet Pierced	Psalm 22:16	His Hands and Feet Pierced	Matthew 27:39, 48
Numbered among Criminals	Isaiah 53:12	Numbered among Criminals	Matthew 27:38
Placed in a Borrowed Tomb	Isaiah 53:9	Placed in a Borrowed Tomb	Matthew 27:57
His Bones were not Broken	Psalm 34:20	His Bones were not Broken	John 19:33
His Flesh Would Not See Correction/ Be Raised from the Dead	Psalm 16:10	His Flesh Would Not See Correction/ Be Raised from the Dead	Acts 2:22
Ascend into Heaven	Psalm 110:1–3; 45:6	Ascend into Heaven	Acts 1:9–10

These prophecies spanned centuries yet unfolded with precisely calculated accuracy. God cannot lie and doesn't allow those that lie on Him to go unpunished.

"But the prophet, which shall presume to speak a word in My name, which I have not commanded him to speak, or that shall speak in the name of other gods, even that prophet shall die" (Deuteronomy 18:20).

From the Old Testament words of the prophets to the writings of the New Testament, God cannot lie, does not need to, and has and will always have man's best interest at heart. Let's be reminded of man's part: fear God and keep His commandments.

You Say You Don't Believe in God?

You get stopped dead in your tracks by the Creator with such foolishness. "The fool has said in his heart there is no God." "So what if some don't believe, will that make the word of God of no effect?" God won't poof in and out of existence based on you—that is, whether you believe He is. Satan is very happy about your alleged atheistic thoughts (unbelief); they make his job of stealing your soul so much easier. Satan is the first to introduce a lie (fathered a lie) in his conversation with Eve in the Garden of Eden, and he is honest enough to let man know his knowledge of the existence of God makes him tremble.

"For what if some did not believe? Shall their unbelief make the faith of God without effect? God forbid: yea, let God be true, but every man a liar" (Romans 3:3–4). The devil, if it were possible, would make it into heaven before any of you; that's something to think about. "He that believes and is baptized shall be saved: but he that believes not shall be damned" (Mark 16:16). Satan, though he believes, doesn't stand less than a minute chance of spending eternity with God. What does that say about your unbelief? You don't have a snowball's chance in hell, either by trying to get into heaven. Satan, the fallen angel, was with God and blew it. Now that you have your chance, he is working hard to make sure you blow it, too. "Then shall He say also to them on the left hand, depart from me, you cursed into everlasting fire, prepared for the devil and his angels" (Matthew 25:41). Satan knows he isn't going to enter heaven (because a home in heaven is based on obedience), and he knows he has a short time to win as many souls as he can take with him (steal from God). "Therefore rejoice you heavens, and you that dwell in them. Woe to the inhabitants of the earth and of the sea! For the devil is come down to you, having great wrath, because he knows that he has but a short time" (Revelation 12:12).

Since the time Satan (angelic creature/archangel) was kicked out of God's sight (heaven), he has taken vengeance on the souls of men. "Be sober, be vigilant; because your adversary the devil, as a roaring lion, walks about, seeking whom he may devour" (1 Peter 5:8). It was Jesus's mission when He left heaven to seek and save souls.

> For the Son of man is come to seek and to save that which was lost. (Luke 19:10)
> Verily I say to you, this generation shall not pass till all these things be fulfilled. Heaven and earth shall pass away, but My words shall not pass away. But of that day and hour knows no man, no, not the angels of heaven, but My Father only. (Matthew 25:34–36; Mark 13:32)

Jesus (the seed) was prophesied to spend a short time on earth, finishing what He needed to do to pay the debt man couldn't pay in the redemption of his sins. He has ascended back into heaven and says that where He is, we can be also.

> For He will finish the work, and cut it short in righteousness: because short works will the Lord make upon the earth. (Romans 9:28)
> And as Isaiah said before, Except the Lord of Sab'aoth had left us a seed (Christ), we had been as Sod'oma and been made like to Gomorrah. (Romans 10:29)

Searching the scriptures, we will come to know that because of Adam, we are all under sin. "Even the righteousness of God which is by faith of Jesus Christ to all and upon all them that believe: for there is no difference between the Jew/Greeks-Gentiles: For all have sinned, and come short of the glory of God; Being justified freely by His grace through the redemption that is in Christ Jesus: Whom God has set forth to be a propitiation through faith in His Blood, to declare His righteousness for the remission of sins that are past, through the forbearance of God" (Romans 3:22–25).

A sinner is one who has not submitted to the will of God. Good people are sinners. "For as in Adam all died, even so in Christ shall all be made alive" (1 Corinthians 15:22). "Where, as by one man sin entered into the world, and death by sin; and so death passed upon all men, for that all have sinned" (Romans 5:12). Let face it, folks, there is none righteous; no, not one (Romans 3:10). We are at a place in man's history on the planet earth where a force of evil has reappeared in this century, in this country, and in this nation that shows no fear toward God. They are haters of God. "There is no fear of God before their eyes" (Romans 3:18). Remember in Genesis 19 when the people of earlier-century BC hearts were so evil they wanted to molest the angels of God in Lot's house? This evil is back with a vengeance and with no fear of God and all that is righteous. Our hearts and minds are molested with lewd acts, openly perpetrated on this nation, this people, this society, and this country—USA.

It is very important that we know what is happening to us at this moment and space in time. The Father of Lies and deception is having a Field Day with America. We are people who realize very well that history does repeat itself. God is not pleased with those who commit sin, and He is not pleased with the ones who allow the sin (effeminate, unnatural affection) to permeate our lives, our nation. "Who knowing the judgment of God, that they which commit such are worthy of death, not only do the same but have pleasure in them that do them" (Romans 1:31).

There is no doubt that this book will bring a lot of debate and controversy, but isn't that just what Christ and His apostles and disciples brought to the established order—those who didn't believe in Christ as the Son of God, those who weren't willing to make a change, those who weren't willing to obey God, and those who didn't accept Christ as the messiah?

The Devils Believe in God

From "jump street," Satan is a step ahead of all mankind and then some. While we are wrestling with the issue of whether there is a God, Satan has put that issue behind him and he is working on our unbelief to his advantage. What it basically comes down to is this:

1. Do you believe in God?
2. Do you believe the Bible is His inspired word?
3. Ultimately, do you plan on being obedient to God (straight or gay)?

The problem with disobedience is that it was the one thing that got Satan (a fallen angel) kicked out of heaven in the first place. If you aren't planning on being obedient (your game plan), don't waste your time reading any further. Have fun with whatever you do—do what you do. Of course, it won't change the fact that God is God and that Judgment Day is coming.

> For God shall bring every work into judgment, with every secret thing, whether it be good or it be evil. (Ecclesiastes 12:14; Romans 2:16; 2 Corinthians 5:10)

So then every one of us shall give account of himself to
God. (Romans 14:12)
For what if some did not believe? Shall their unbelief
make the faith of God without effect? (Romans 3:3)

While it's essentially crucial for man's salvation that he trust the Holy
Bible as biblical authority, the inspired word of almighty God (Creator and
ruler of the universe), it is equally crucial to believe by faith that the Bible is
from God and not from man. God has given man the intellect to judge right
from wrong and has commanded him to search the Scripture daily, day and
night. The apostle Paul commended the people of Berea for being more noble
than those of Thessalonica because they were willing to search the scriptures
to see whether what Paul was saying (preaching) was true.

During my research, I discovered Apologetics Press. They employ a
team of scientists and auxiliary staff writers, who produce books, DVDs,
and other teaching and educational forms of media that provide proof of
the existence of the God of the Bible. What is interesting are the works
showing the inerrancy and divine inspiration of the Bible. As previously
stated, I was originally led to the website http://www.apologeticspress.org,
after listening to a DVD/video on *Rock Solid Faith: How to Build It* by Bert
Thompson. This is a thirteen-lesson video lecture series. A library copy of
the book was obtained for a more detailed chapter-by-chapter study of the
video sessions: Biblical faith, man in God's likeness, identifying the enemy,
origin and destiny of the soul, why family members stray from the faith, and
continuing to teach the gospel and contend for the faith (*paraphrased*). See
The Case for the Existence of God[23] and In *Defense of the Bible's Inspiration*.[24]

When it comes to how to conduct our lives before God and man,
scripture matters.

---

[23] Bert Thompson, *The Case for the Existence of God* (Montgomery, AL:
Apologetics Press, 2003), 123–181.
[24] Bert Thompson, *In Defense of the Bible's Inspiration* (Montgomery, AL:
Apologetics Press, 2003), 182–242.

Chapter 2
Freedom through Forgiveness

FREEDOM? FREEDOM? STOP! What freedom? Who do you really think you are? No, what do you really think you are? Let's not get things twisted. You are a servant—period! "Know you not that the Lord He is God: it is He that has made us, and not we ourselves; we are His people and the sheep of His pasture" (Psalm 100:3).

People walk around on this earth like characters in the movie *Poltergeist* (1982). They are dead, but they don't know it. Some believe we are here and don't know the who, what, why, when, or where we go from here facts of the matter. Some believe we evolved from some lower life form that came about from some cosmological bang or blast and that when we die, that's the end. Some believe man can be refurbished into other lower forms of life (animals or birds) to repeat an endless cycle of some state or terrestrial being.

We are God's handiwork. "For we are His workmanship, created in Christ Jesus to good works, which God has before ordained that we should walk in them" (Ephesians 2:10). Christ saves you from sin, and you become the servant of righteousness (Romans 6:16). Let not sin control you or yield to obey it, for what you obey, you are its servant. "Know you not, that to whom you yield yourselves servants to obey, his servants you are to whom you obey; whether of sin to death or of obedience to righteousness?" (Romans 6:16). Man is a servant and will always be a servant. A servant is man's status on earth. You are either a servant of Satan or a servant of Christ—period. There is no middle ground. To redeem man's soul from sin, Christ had to take on the role (form) of a servant, and scripture says Christ learned obedience through the things He suffered. We will have to be obedient, too. Now that you know you're just a servant and nothing else, keep reading to find out how you can work your way up to a freedman.

Freedom in Jesus Christ

Let's just establish one thing: your freedom is in Christ Jesus. You were created for His glory, you were created to serve, and you have only two choices: be a servant of righteousness or be a servant of sin. By sheer definition, 'not' of God means sin. Even the Most High, Jesus Christ, came down and took on the form of a servant to show man how to be a servant of God. Not only that, but He set man free from the hold of death. Okay, let's stop here. Did you have anything to do with your birth? Can you stop the day of your death? Okay, we are finished. We now understand who is in control. Let's continue on with how to obtain our freedom.

"Do you not know that to whom you present yourselves servants to obey, you are that one's slave whom you obey, whether of sin leading to death, or of obedience leading to righteousness—eternal life? But God be thanked that though you were slaves of sin, yet you obeyed from the heart that form of doctrine to which you were delivered. And having been freed from sin, you became the slaves of righteousness" (Roman 6:16–8).

Man's Religious Freedom

Make no mistake about it; God has always given man the freedom to choose right from wrong: eternal life or eternal damnation. People who try to force others to believe in God and live a God-fearing and Christian life don't understand the kingdom of God; it isn't by force and never will be or has been. This fact shines a light on the war-faring religious crusaders for God and the bloodthirsty religious terrorists. Jesus's invitation has always been "Whosoever will, come." Heaven is a prepared place for prepared people. On another note, far too many people believe *religion* is synonymous with *righteousness*. The Bible definition for a religious person is found in the book of James. "If any man among you seem to be religious, and bridles not his tongue, but deceives his own heart, this man's religion is vain" (James 1:26). The Bible defines *religion* this way: "Pure religion and undefiled before God and the Father is this, To visit the fatherless and widows in their afflictions, and to keep himself unspotted from the world" (James 1:27). As a matter of fact, Jesus's opponents were religious men: the Pharisees and Sadducees and scribes and rulers of the synagogue. To put religious acts or religion in perspective, it's a duty and responsibility to others in need.

The Bible talks about one Lord, one Faith, and one Baptism; yet when we look out over the universe, we see there are thousands of beliefs, faiths, and religious practices. If we aren't obedient to the one gospel the scripture speaks of, we are religiously wrong. In Acts 17:16–24, we read the account of the people of Athens. In this passage, the apostle Paul demonstrates that these people were too religious (superstitious) in their different religious beliefs. Here we see that it's not too farfetched of an idea or thought to realize or understand that people can be religiously wrong. Paul stops by to enlighten and educate the Athenians in his speech on Mars Hill on the one, true God. Many try to worship God and don't even know God. The simple solution is to be taught the one true gospel and obey it. Many look for a crutch or excuse while failing to search the scriptures: it's your "interpretation," not mine. Honest hearts will accept the word of God. "Knowing this first, that no prophecy of the scripture is of any *private* interpretation, for the prophecy came not in old time by the will of man; but holy men of God spoke as they were moved by the Holy Ghost" (2 Peter 1:20 –21, emphasis added).

God allows the rise and fall of everything. He sees the beginning and the end. Through His providence, He allows things to come about to test the hearts of men: homosexuality issues (again), judges, presidents or leaders, and the rise of violence and hatred in America. Even though He knows what is in people's hearts, God allows people to see themselves more closely and examine themselves to see whether they are walking with God. Those of you who profess to be righteous, search yourselves today in America. Here in these instances God allows you to see yourself and to make the necessary corrections into what you profess to be.

Hezekiah experienced success in his reign as king in Israel and prospered in all his works. At a time in his reign, Hezekiah became proud and failed an opportune time to glorify and acknowledge God to ambassadors from Babylon who were inquisitive about his success. The success God had allowed him to have. God left him to try him and *test* his heart (see 2 Chronicles 32-33). God has blessed America to be successful. America has become proud and boastful and has turned away from Him toward alternative lifestyles. Has God left America [rise of hatred, chaos, violence, and return *Sodom & Gomorrah*] to try us and test our hearts toward Him? What side of history will this century stand: with God or with Satan?

Honestly, if homosexuals, lesbians, heterosexuals, and any person(s) operating outside the *will of God* seem to be winning something, some position, some station or some status in this life, just stop and ask yourself,

"Are these victories in Christ Jesus?" What isn't God approved will come to naught, and people following their ways will perish (see Acts 5:38). The homosexual movement isn't going anywhere; it's fixed. Ask the residents of Sodom and Gomorrah. It was God who said that anything that isn't of righteousness will come to naught. God is and always will be in control. Take a look at Luke 17:27–29. "But the same day Lot went out of Sodom it rained fire and brimstone from heaven, and destroyed them all." People were eating, drinking, marrying, and being given in marriage until the day Noah entered the ark. The whole earth was destroyed; many were wiped off the face of the earth except Noah and his family, whom God saved. "But Noah found grace in the eyes of the Lord. These are the generations of Noah: Noah was a just man and perfect in 'his' generations, and Noah walked with God" (Genesis 6:8–9).

We love to give lip service to Mother Nature. Was the great flood an act of Mother Nature? After Adam and Eve sinned, was the cursing of the ground to bring forth thorns and thistles an act of Mother Nature? When Moses came down from the mountain and observed that the people were worshipping the golden calf, the earth opened up and swallowed many. Was that an act of Mother Nature? Rationalize as much as you please, but the scripture still says, "God judges the righteous, and God is angry with the wicked every day" (Psalm 7:11). God is saying to those who allow lewd, lascivious, and homosexual acts to permeate this generation and remain lukewarm and won't speak out against them that He will spew their prepend, so-called righteous selves out of His mouth; in other words, they make Him sick to His stomach (Revelation 3:16). Some things to consider are results of recent climate changes—mudslides, wildfires, volcano eruptions, and unprecedented ice storms for our times, are these events acts of Mother Nature, right? As in Daniel 5, King Belshazzar took and defiled what was God (belonged to God). We are tempting God by defiling the sanctity of marriage, the church, and children, His heritage. Is it possible because of our blasphemous ways we too can be staring at the same message: "MENE TEKEL U-PHARSIN"? (Daniel 5:25). For America, the handwriting is on the wall, if we fail to repent of our course.

Once again, it's not about homosexuality or the gay movement. If it's not gay, then it's bestiality, which is waiting in the wings, like the closet gays, for the right time to surface. Scripture says the imagination of man's heart is set in him to continue to do evil, so the situation is this; Will God find five or ten righteous and spare the city, the nation, the USA?

On Monday, February 24, 2014, there was a media storm over the fact that Uganda (Africa) had antigay laws. If one does believe the Bible, the word of God, it shouldn't be too mindboggling to accept some validity or to at least examine the rationalization and views of a country located in a place considered the cradle of civilization on the issue of homosexuality. They should have a lot to say to the rest of the world on this matter—that is, if we aren't too bright or smart to listen, since we (USA) are so advanced in knowledge and technological savvy. Africa isn't a country that has a pill for everything or multibillion dollars in drug research and drug manufactories to combat the spread of sexually transmitted diseases like AIDS. Many women have little say over their bodies in tribal marriages. And to think America isn't too far (just a few years) from addressing battered women syndrome issues. The rise of diseases from gay and bisexual activity would spread like wildfire from anal (toxic waste area of the body) to the (self-cleaning) vaginal sex part of the body. The people of Uganda have every right to protect their people from this Western homosexual movement.

Man's Sexual Freedom

An Internet article in *Reuters* (published July 2, 2015), "US Same-Sex Marriage Ruling Inspires Hope and Revulsion in Africa,"[25] said what other news media had reported about President Obama's response to the Supreme Court's favorable ruling on same-sex marriage; it came as a "thunderbolt" (swift change) that many in Africa, being socially conservative, didn't receive well or found hard to swallow or appreciate from a county that purports to believe in God and brandishes a motto throughout the international community: "In God We Trust."

The article recognizes that Africa is socially conservative and that South Africa is the only African country that permits gay or lesbian marriages. The scripture says, "A little leaven leavens the whole lump" (Galatians 5:9). The article stated, "In the streets, churches and corridors of power, from Uganda in the east to Zimbabwe in the south and Nigeria and Liberia in the west, the chorus of homophobic disapproval at the landmark U.S. decision rang out loud and clear."[26] It is appalling to read from this article's viewpoint that Africa's stand against homosexuality in their county could possibly affect

---

[25] MacDonald Dzirutwe, "Before Obama Trip, U.S. Gay Ruling Inspires Hope and Revulsion in Africa," *Reuters*, July 1, 2015, https://www.reuters.com/article/us-africa-gaymarriage/before-obama-trip-u-s-gay-ruling-inspires-hope-and-revulsion-in-africa-idUSKCN0PB4OY20150701.
[26] Ibid

Western donors' attitude in helping to support the fight against AIDS in Africa. Here's another statement from the article: Veteran Zimbabwe leader, Robert Mugabe, has called homosexuals worse than pigs and dogs. Simon Khaya-Moyo, a spokesman for his ruling ZANU-PF party, said same-sex marriage has no place in Africa. "It's taboo. We don't even talk about it here," he told *Reuters*. "Even animals know which is female and which is male ... Why should we not be able to know who is female, who is male? ... It is an insult to God."[27]

This ancient country can see the rise of Sodom and Gomorrah from a ways off, far across the oceans and seas into the West. This article reports that Medard Bitekyerezo, a Ugandan politician leading the push for tough antigay laws, sees the United States (West) descending back to the days of Sodom and Gomorrah, a place where the rulers (judges, presidents, or kings) are disoriented, and this behavior invokes only disgust from this ancient country. If they can't tell America anything about being more militarily supreme, more technologically savvy, they can tell America, historically speaking, how God destroys nations due to their depravity toward God's laws. Africa is in fear of what will become of America and how this result could possibly affect them. For now the politicians sentiments are, "But that's their [America's] business—they can't impose it [legalize homosexuality] on us [Africa]."[28]

Homophobia: The Rational Fear that "Gay Sex" Will Kill Homosexuals and Heterosexuals

Forgive me for putting this in the same sentence, but the issue of Black Life Matters doesn't compare to "Fecal or Anal Sex Matters." The media coverage of the N-word (Nigger) and the F-word (Fag): their coverage of gay rights activists trying to compare black people's civil rights with homosexuals' and lesbians' civil rights is overreaching because homosexuality lifestyle and lewd and sodomy activities go beyond one's imagination in comparing the two causes. When God stepped out on the face of darkness and said, "Let there be light," darkness fled. Like good and evil, the two causes (black people's civil rights and homosexuals' civil rights) are as far as the heavens are from the earth: corruptible versus incorruptible. It strains credulity to contend that the two are similarly situated with respect to black people's fundamental

---

[27] Ibid
[28] Ibid

struggles or cause was to be treated like human beings; human beings not living in a lifestyle, as a group of people, whom God labeled as abomination in His sight (Romans 1: 26-31; 1 Corinthians 6:9).

This behavior or lifestyle (selected orientation or self-identified) of intimate contact with feces puts one in contact with pathogens that help spread bacteria, diseases, and infections: hookworms, parasites, cryptosporidiosis, meningitis, E. coli, colitis, salmonella, and so forth. This is an extremely high-risk lifestyle that threatens the health of the general population. The ugly little secret is that many heterosexual males practice anal sex with their female partners; this is still a risky practice and presents a high risk to partners and the community at large, depending on individuals' promiscuity. Anal intercourse drives the HIV epidemic among gay and bisexual men. Possibly such activity by heterosexual males in sub-Saharan Africa may have helped spread the HIV epidemic in Africa and elsewhere in the world, where heterosexuals or bisexuals engaged in anal intercourse with female partners.

While the medical consensus is that smoking knocks from two to ten years off an individual's life expectancy, the *International Journal of Epidemiology* study found that homosexual conduct shortens the life span of gays by an astounding "8 to 20 years"—more than twice that of smoking.[29]

In light of irrefutable medical facts, although the gay population makes up a small fraction of America's population (1 to 2 percent), they account for an epidemic 64 percent of all syphilis cases. Because of their activity, US health regulations will not allow men who have sex with men to give blood (taxing the heterosexual population even more). Consider this fact: according to the Food and Drug Administration, MSM (men who have sex with men) "have HIV prevalence 60 times higher than the general population, 800 times higher than first-time blood donors, and 8,000 times higher than repeat blood donors." At present, these facts could have varied, but the risk factors are still of major concern to the general population.

Leave Them Alone—It Will Come to Naught

Any activity of man that is not God approved will come to naught (Acts 5:38). A lawyer and council, and a Pharisee name Gamaliel stood up and

---

[29] https://academic.oup.com/ije/article/26/3/657/742184; http://www.wnd. com/2008/04/61856/#iR0CuGqiqTu8hFDO.99 https://skeptics.stackexchange.com/questions/28211/do-homosexuals-have- a-shorter-life-expectancy-than-heterosexuals

instructed the people not to harm the apostles they had commanded not to preach the gospel of Christ because they feared their influence over the people, and because they can look back at other movements like Theudas (v.36) and Judas of Galilee (v.37) who in their days lead people to their death following their teaching and ideologies. He stated that if what Peter and the other apostles were teaching were not true, it will come to naught; so leave them alone. Case in point is the Exodus Institute's program that claimed to turn homosexuals straight.[30] Activities of anyone pretending to follow Christ will not produce Christians. All their plans, if not God approved, will fail. The last thing Christians should be alarmed about is evildoers, whose plans will come to naught. The ranting and raging over writing another bible that doesn't illuminate their abominable deeds and persecuting the Church for preaching the gospel when it comes to effeminate lifestyle will come to naught. After all, is man more righteous than God?

 BOOK CORNER (Excerpts)
reprinted by permission

Permission to use article entitled, *Medical Consequences of What Homosexuals Do*: **Homosexuals Die Young,**[31] by Dr. Paul Cameron, Psychologist and Chairman of Family Research Institute

Throughout history, the major civilizations and religions condemned homosexuality.[1] In the American colonies, homosexual acts were a capital offense. Thomas Jefferson said that homosexuality should "be punished, if a man, by castration, if a woman, by cutting through the cartilage of her nose a hole of one-half inch in diameter at least."[2] Until 1961 homosexual acts were illegal throughout America.

Gays claim that the "prevailing attitude toward homosexuals in the U.S. and many other countries is revulsion and hostility.... for acts and desires not harmful to anyone."[3] The American Psychological Association *and the*

---

[30] Christian Group Apologizes for Attempts to Turn Gays Straight," Associated Press, June 20, 2013. https://www.timesnews.net/News/2013/06/20/Christian-group-apologizes-for-attempts-to-turn-gays-straight.html 6:07 PM

[31] Paul Cameron. PhD in Psychology, Chairman of Family Research Institute. http://www.familyresearchinst.org/2009/02/medical-consequences-of-what-homosexuals-do/

American Public Health Association *assured the U.S. Supreme Court in 1986 that "no significant data show that engaging in... oral and anal sex, results in mental or physical dysfunction."*[4]

Is the historic stance against homosexuality merely one of prejudice? Is homosexual behavior really as harmless as gays and these health associations assert?

Homosexuals Die Young

Smokers and drug addicts don't live as long as non-smokers or non-addicts, so we consider smoking and narcotics abuse harmful. The typical lifespan of homosexuals suggests that their activities are more destructive than smoking and about as dangerous as drugs.

In a pioneering study[5], 6,737 obituaries from 18 U.S. homosexual journals during and after the height of the AIDS epidemic (13 years total) were compared to a large sample of obituaries from regular newspapers. The obituaries from the regular newspapers were similar to U.S. averages for longevity: the median age of death of married, never-divorced men was 75 and 80% of them died old (age 65 or older). For unmarried or divorced men, the median age of death was 57 and 32% of them died old. Married, never-divorced women averaged 79 at death; 85% died old. Unmarried and divorced women averaged age 71 and 60% of them died old.

The median age of death for homosexuals, however, was virtually the same nationwide — and, overall, about 2% survived to old age. If AIDS was the listed cause of death, the median age was 39. For the 829 gays who were listed as dying of something other than AIDS, the median age of death was 42 and 9% died old. The 163 lesbians had a median age of death of 44 and 20% died old.

Even when AIDS was apparently not involved, homosexuals frequently met an early demise. Three percent of gays died violently. They were 116 times more apt to be murdered (compared to national murder rates), much more apt to commit suicide, and had high traffic-accident death-rates. Heart attacks, cancer, and liver failure were exceptionally common. 18% of lesbians died of murder, suicide, or accidents — a rate 456 times higher than that of white females aged 25-44. Age distributions of samples of homosexuals in the scientific literature from 1858 to 1997 suggest a similarly shortened lifespan.

Follow-up studies of homosexual longevity have confirmed these general results. Comparison of gay obituaries who died of AIDS to official U.S. HIV/AIDS Surveillance data demonstrated very close agreement between the estimated median ages of death, as well as the 25th and 75th percentiles of the age-at-death distribution.[6] Another study looked at multiple lines of evidence — including more recent U.S. obituaries and patterns of homosexual partnerships in Scandinavia — again finding that homosexual behavior was associated with a shortening of life of probably two decades.[7]

What Homosexuals Do

Several major surveys on homosexual behavior are summarized in **Table 1.** Two things stand out 1) homosexuals behave similarly world-over, and 2) as Harvard Medical Professor, Dr. William Haseltine, noted in 1993,[8] the "changes in sexual behavior that have been reported to have occurred in some groups have proved, for the most part, to be transient. For example, bath houses and sex clubs in many cities have either reopened or were never closed."

Table 1. Homosexual Activities (in %)

behavior	US[9]	US[10]	US[11]	CAN[12]	US[13]	US[14]	ENG[15]	CAN[16]	AUS/ENG[17]
	1940s	1977	1984	1984	1983	1983	1985	1990	1991
	ever	ever	ever	ever	last yr	last mo	last mo	last 3mo	last 6mo
oral/penile	83	99	100	99	99	95	67	76	
anal/penile	68	91	93	98	95	69	100	62	
oral/anal	59	83	92	92	63		89	34	55/65
urine sex	10	23	29						
fisting/toys		22	41	47	34		63		
eating feces		4	8						
enemas		11	11						
torture sex	22	37	37						
public/orgy sex	61	76	88						
sex w/ minors	37	23	24						

Oral Sex: Homosexuals fellate almost all of their sexual contacts (and ingest semen from about half of these[18]). Semen contains many of the germs carried in the blood, so gays who practice oral sex incur medical risks akin to consuming raw human blood. Since the penis frequently has tiny lesions (and often will have been in unsanitary places such as a rectum), individuals so involved may become infected with hepatitis A or gonorrhea (and even HIV and hepatitis B). Since many contacts occur between strangers (70% of gays estimated that they had had sex only once with over half of their partners[19]), and gays average somewhere between 10^{20} and 110^{21} different partners/year, the potential for infection is considerable.

Rectal Sex: Surveys indicate that about 90% of gays have engaged in rectal intercourse, and about two-thirds do it regularly.[22] In a 6-month long study of daily sexual diaries,[23] gays averaged 110 sex partners and 68 rectal encounters a year.

Rectal sex is *dangerous*. During rectal intercourse, the rectum becomes a mixing bowl for

* saliva and its germs and/or an artificial lubricant,
* the recipient's own feces,
* whatever germs, infections or substances the penis has on it, and
* the seminal fluid of the inserter.

Sperm, which is immunocompromising[24], readily penetrate the rectal lining (which is only one cell thick), and tearing or bruising of the anal wall is very common during anal/penile sex. Because of this, these substances gain almost direct access to the blood stream. Unlike heterosexual intercourse — in which sperm cannot penetrate the multilayered vagina and no feces are present — rectal intercourse is probably the most sexually efficient way to spread hepatitis B, HIV, syphilis, and a host of other blood-borne diseases.

Tearing or ripping of the anal wall is especially likely during "fisting," where the hand and possibly arm is inserted into the rectum. It is also common when "toys" are employed (homosexual lingo for objects which are inserted into the rectum — bottles, carrots, even gerbils[25]). The risk of contamination and/or having to wear a colostomy bag from such "sport" is very real. Fisting was apparently so rare in Kinsey's time that he didn't think to ask about it. By 1977, a third of gays admitted to doing it.[26] The rectum was not designed to accommodate the fist, and those who do so can find themselves consigned to 'leakage' for life. Anal cancer is 24 times[27] and hepatitis C 10 times[28] more prevalent in gays.

Fecal Sex: About 80% of gays (see Table) admit to licking and/or inserting their tongues into the anus of partners and thus ingesting medically significant amounts of feces. Those who eat or wallow in it are probably at even greater risk. In the diary study,[23] 70% of the gays had engaged in this activity — half regularly over 6 months. Result? —the "annual incidence of hepatitis A in... homosexual men was 22 percent, whereas no heterosexual men acquired hepatitis A." In 1992, it was noted that the proportion of London gays engaging in oral/anal sex had not declined since 1984.[30]

While the body has defenses against fecal germs, exposure to the fecal discharge of dozens of strangers each year is extremely unhealthy. Ingestion of human waste is the major route of contracting hepatitis A and the enteric parasites collectively known as the Gay Bowel Syndrome. Consumption of feces has also been implicated in the transmission of typhoid fever,[31] herpes, and cancer.[32] About 10% of gays have eaten or played with [e.g., enemas, wallowing in feces].

In the late 1970s, the San Francisco Department of Public Health saw "75,000 patients per year, of whom 70 to 80 per cent are homosexual men.... An average of 10 per cent of all patients and asymptomatic contacts reported [to the Department]... because of positive fecal samples or cultures for amoeba, giardia, and shigella infections were employed as food handlers in public establishments; almost 5 per cent of those with hepatitis A were similarly employed."[33]

In 1976, a rare airborne scarlet fever broke out among gays and just missed sweeping through San Francisco.[34] A 1982 Swedish study "suggested that some transmission [of hepatitis A] from the homosexual group to the general population may have occurred."[35] The U.S. Centers for Disease Control reported that 29% of the hepatitis A cases in Denver, 66% in New York, 50% in San Francisco, 56% in Toronto, 42% in Montreal, and 26% in Melbourne in the first six months of 1991 were among gays.[36]

Urine Sex: About 10% of Kinsey's gays reported having engaged in "golden showers" [drinking or being splashed with urine]. In the largest survey of gays ever conducted,[37] 23% admitted to urine-sex. In a large random survey of gays,[38] 29% reported urine-sex. In a San Francisco study of 655 gays,[39] only 24% claimed to have been monogamous in the past year. Of these monogamous gays, 5% drank urine, 7% practiced "fisting," 33% ingested feces via anal/oral contact, 53% swallowed semen, and 59% received semen in their rectum during the previous month.

Other Gay Sex Practices

Sadomasochism: As Table 1 indicates, a large minority of gays engage in torture for sexual fun (15% of lesbians engaged in "piercing, cutting or whipping to the point of bleeding" with their lovers[40]).

Sex with Minors: 25% of white gays[41] admitted to sex with boys 16 or younger as adults. In a 10-state study,[42] 33% of the 181 male, and 22% of the 18 female teachers caught molesting students did so homosexually even though less than 3% of men and 2% of women are bisexual or homosexual.[43]

Depending on the study, the percent of gays reporting **sex in public restrooms** ranged from 14%[44] to 41%[45] to 66%.[46] The percent reporting sex in gay baths varies from 9%[47] to 60%[48] and 67%.[49] Furthermore, 45%,[50] 64%,[51] and 90%[52] said that they used **illegal drugs**.

Fear of AIDS may have reduced the volume of gay sex partners, but the numbers are prodigious by any standard. In Spain,[53] gays averaged 42 per year in 1989; in an eight year longitudinal study in Amsterdam, the figure was 25 per year in 1994.[54] Lesbians do not have as many partners, but neither is their sex life confined to other women. Of 498 San Francisco lesbians in a U.S. Centers for Disease Control study in 1993, 81% reported sex with men and 10% sex with gays in the last 3 years. Another 4% reported intravenous drug use.[55]

Medical Consequences of Homosexual Sex

Death and disease accompany promiscuous and unsanitary sexual activity. Between 70%[56] and 78%[57] of gays report having had a sexually transmitted disease. The proportion with intestinal parasites (worms, flukes, amoeba) has ranged from 25%[58] to 39%.[59] As of 2012, 55% of U.S. AIDS cases had occurred in gays and 30,000 U.S. gays were contracting HIV every year.[60]

The Seattle sexual diary study[61] found that, averaged on a yearly basis, gays:

• fellated 108 men and swallowed semen from 48;
• exchanged saliva with 96;
• experienced 68 penile penetrations of the anus; and
• ingested fecal material from 19.

No wonder 10% came down with hepatitis B and 7% contracted hepatitis A during the 6-month study.

The Gay Legacy

Homosexuals rode into the dawn of sexual freedom and returned with a plague that has destroyed many of them. Those who treat AIDS patients are at risk, not only from HIV infection, which as of 1996 involved about 200 health care workers,[62] but also from TB and new strains of other diseases.[63] Those who are housed with AIDS patients are also at risk.[64]

At least eight new sexually transmitted germs were identified between 1980 and 1997.[65] Dr. Max Essex, chair of the Harvard AIDS Institute, warned congress in 1992 that "AIDS has already led to other kinds of dangerous epidemics... If AIDS is not eliminated, other new lethal microbes will emerge, and neither safe sex nor drug free practices will prevent them."[66] At least eight, and perhaps as many as 30 patients[67] had been infected with HIV by health care workers as of 1992 including from dentists, nurses, and surgeons.[68]

The Biological Swapmeet

The typical sexual practices of homosexuals are a medical horror story — imagine exchanging saliva, feces, semen and/or blood with dozens of different men each year. Imagine drinking urine, ingesting feces and experiencing rectal trauma on a regular basis. Often these encounters occur while the participants are drunk, high, and/or in an orgy setting. Further, many of them occur in extremely unsanitary places (bathrooms, dirty peep shows), or, because homosexuals travel so frequently, in other parts of the world.

Every year, a quarter or more of homosexuals visit another country.[69] Fresh American germs get taken to Europe, Africa, and Asia. And fresh pathogens from these continents come here. Foreign homosexuals regularly visit the U.S. and participate in this biological swapmeet.

Unfortunately, the danger of these exchanges does not merely affect homosexuals. Travelers carried so many tropical diseases to New York City that it had to institute a tropical disease center, and gays carried HIV from New York City to the rest of the world.[70] Most of the 12,642 Americans who got AIDS from contaminated blood as of 1992 received it from homosexuals and most of the women in California who got AIDS through *heterosexual* activity got it from men who engaged in homosexuality.[71]

There is a pattern here that we ignore at our peril. Homosexual practices create a third-world level of sanitation and chronic disease unknown to most

Westerners. With the rise of new contagious diseases, homosexuality not only raises our medical costs, it increases the hazards of giving and getting medical care, receiving blood, and eating out.

Genuine Compassion

Society is legitimately concerned with health risks — they impact our taxes and everyone's chances of illness and injury. Because we care about them, smokers are discouraged from smoking by higher insurance premiums, taxes on cigarettes and bans against smoking in public. These social pressures cause many to quit. They likewise encourage non-smokers to *stay* non-smokers.

Homosexuals are sexually troubled people engaging in dangerous activities. Because we care about them and those tempted to join them, it is important that we neither encourage nor legitimize such a destructive lifestyle.

1. Karlen (1971) *Sexuality and Homosexuality* NY: Norton
2. Pines (1982) *Back to Basics* NY: Morrow, p211
3. Weinberg (1972) *Society and the Healthy Homosexual* NY:St. Martin's, preface
4. Amici curiae brief (1986) *Bowers vs. Hardwick*
5. Cameron, et al (1994) The longevity of homosexuals: before and after the AIDS epidemic. *Omega J of Death and Dying* 29(3):249-72
6. Cameron & Cameron (2005) Gay obituaries closely track officially reported deaths from AIDS. *Psychological Reports*, 96:693-97
7. Cameron, et al (1998) Does homosexual activity shorten life? *Psychological Reports*, 83:847-66
8. Haseltine (1993) AIDS prognosis. *Washington Times*, 2/13/93, C1
9. Gebhard & Johnson (1979) *The Kinsey Data* NY:Saunders
10. Jay & Young (1979) *The Gay Report* NY:Summit
11. Cameron, et al (1985) Sexual orientation and sexually transmitted disease. *Nebraska Medical J* 70:292-99; (1989) Effect of homosexuality upon public health and social order. *Psychological Rpts* 64:1167-79
12. Schecter, et al (1984) Changes in sexual behavior and fear of AIDS. *Lancet* 1:1293
13. Jaffee, et al (1983) National case-control study of Kaposi's sarcoma. *Annals Internal Medicine* 99:145-51
14. Quinn, et al (1983) The polymicrobial origin of intestinal infection in homosexual men. *New England J Medicine* 309:576-82

15. Beral, et al (1992) Risk of Kaposi's sarcoma and sexual practices associated with faecal contact in homosexual or bisexual men with AIDS. *Lancet* 339:632-35

16. Myers, et al (1991) *AIDS: Knowledge, Attitudes, Behaviours in Toronto* AIDS Committee of Toronto

17. Elford, et al (1992) Kaposi's sarcoma and insertive rimming. *Lancet* 339:938

18. Corey & Holmes (1980) Sexual transmission of Hepatitis A in homosexual men. *New England J Medicine* 302:435-38

19. Bell & Weinberg (1978) *Homosexualities* NY: Simon and Schuster

20. Hays, et al (1997) Actual versus perceived HIV status. *AIDS* 11:1495-1502

21. Corey & Holmes (1980) Sexual transmission of Hepatitis A in homosexual men. *New England J Medicine* 302:435-38

22. Hays, et al (1997) Actual versus perceived HIV status. *AIDS* 11:1495-1502

23. Corey & Holmes (1980) Sexual transmission of Hepatitis A in homosexual men. *New England J Medicine* 302:435-38

24. Manligit, et al (1984) Chronic immune stimulation by sperm alloantigens. *J American Medical Assoc* 251:237-38; Mulhall, et al (1990) Anti-sperm antibodies in homosexual men. *Genitourinary Medicine* 66:5-7; Ratnam KV (1994) Effect of sexual practices on T cell subsets. *Intl J of STDs and AIDS* 5:257-61

25. Adams (1986) The straight dope. In *The Reader* Chicago, 3/28/86 (Cecil Adams writes authoritatively on the counter-culture in alternative newspapers across the U.S. and Canada)

26. Jay & Young (1979) *The Gay Report* NY: Summit

27. Koblin, et al (1996) Increased incidence of cancer among homosexual men. *American J Epidemiology* 144:916-23

28. Ndimbi, et al (1996) Hepatitis C virus infection in a male homosexual cohort; risk factor analysis. *Genitourinary Medicine* 72:213-16

29. Corey & Holmes (1980) Sexual transmission of Hepatitis A in homosexual men. *New England J Medicine* 302:435-38

30. Elford, et al (1992) Kaposi's sarcoma and insertive rimming. *Lancet* 339:938

31. Dritz & Braff (1977) Sexually transmitted typhoid fever. *New England J Medicine* 296:1359-60

32. Beral, et al (1992) Risk of Kaposi's sarcoma and sexual practices associated with faecal contact in homosexual or bisexual men with AIDS. *Lancet* 339:632-35; Melbye & Biggar (1992) Interactions

between persons at risk for AIDS and the general population in Denmark. *American J Epidemiology* 135:593-602

33. Dritz (1980) Medical aspects of homosexuality. *New England J Medicine* 302:463-64

34. Dritz & Braff (1977) Sexually transmitted typhoid fever. *New England J Medicine* 296:1359-60

35. Christenson, et al (1982) An epidemic outbreak of hepatitis A among homosexual men in Stockholm. *American J Epidemiology* 116:599-607

36. Cameron, et al (1985) Sexual orientation and sexually transmitted disease. *Nebraska Medical J* 70:292-99; (1989) The effect of homosexuality upon public health and social order. *Psychological Rpts* 64:1167-79

37. Jay & Young (1979) *The Gay Report* NY:Summit

38. Cameron, et al (1985) Sexual orientation and sexually transmitted disease. *Nebraska Medical J* 70:292-99; (1989) The effect of homosexuality upon public health and social order. *Psychological Rpts* 64:1167-79

39. McKusick, et al (1985) AIDS and sexual behaviors reported by gay men in San Francisco. *American J of Public Health* 75:493-96

40. Lemp, et al (1995) HIV seroprevalence and risk behavior among lesbians. *American J Public Health* 85:1549-52

41. Bell & Weinberg (1978) *Homosexualities* NY:Simon & Schuster

42. Cameron & Cameron (1996) Do homosexual teachers pose a risk to pupils? *J of Psychology* 130:603-613

43. Laumann, et al (1994) *The Social Organization of Sexuality* U Chicago Press

44. Gebhard & Johnson (1979) *The Kinsey Data* NY:Saunders

45. Jay & Young (1979) *The Gay Report* NY:Summit

46. Cameron, et al (1985) Sexual orientation and sexually transmitted disease. *Nebraska Medical J* 70:292-99; (1989) The effect of homosexuality upon public health and social order. *Psychological Rpts* 64:1167-79

47. Rotheram-Borus, et al (1994) Sexual and substance abuse acts of gay and bisexual male adolescents. *J Sex Research* 31:47-57

48. Jay & Young (1979) *The Gay Report* NY:Summit

49. Cameron, et al (1985) Sexual orientation and sexually transmitted disease. *Nebraska Medical J* 70:292-99; (1989) The effect of homosexuality upon public health and social order. *Psychological Rpts* 64:1167-79

50. Rotheram-Borus, et al (1994) Sexual and substance abuse acts of gay and bisexual male adolescents. *J Sex Research* 31:47-57
51. Gebhard & Johnson (1979) *The Kinsey Data* NY:Saunders
52. Jafee, et al (1983) National case-control study of Kaposi's sarcoma. *Annals Internal Medicine* 99:145-51
53. Rodriguez-Pichardo, et al (1991) Sexually transmitted diseases in homosexual males in Seville, Spain. *Genitourin Medicine* 67:335-38
54. de Wit, et al (1997) Homosexual encounters. *Intl J STD and AIDS* 8:130-34
55. Lemp, et al (1995) HIV seroprevalence and risk behavior among lesbians. *American J Public Health* 85:1549-52
56. CDC (1997) *HIV/AIDS Surveillance Report* June
57. Cameron, et al (1985) Sexual orientation and sexually transmitted disease. *Nebraska Medical J* 70:292-99; Jay & Young (1979) *The Gay Report* NY:Summit
58. Jafee, et al (1983) National case-control study of Kaposi's sarcoma. *Annals Internal Medicine* 99:145-51
59. Quinn, et al (1983) The polymicrobial origin of intestinal infection in homosexual men. *New England J Medicine* 309:576-82
60. CDC (2012) *HIV Surveillance Report, 2012, vol. 24* November
61. Corey & Holmes (1980) Sexual transmission of hepatitis A in homosexual men. *New England J Medicine* 302:435-38
62. CDC (1996) *HIV/AIDS Surveillance Report* December
63. Dooley, et al (1992) Nosocomial transmission of tuberculosis in a hospital unit for HIV-infected patients. *J American Medical Assoc* 267:2632-35
64. Dooley, et al (1992) Nosocomial transmission of tuberculosis in a hospital unit for HIV-infected patients. *J American Medical Assoc* 267:2632-35
65. Wetzstein (1997) *Washington Times* April 12
66. Essex (1992) Testimony before House Health & Environment Subcommittee, February 24
67. Essex (1992) Testimony before House Health & Environment Subcommittee, February 24
68. Ciesielski, et al (1992) Transmission of human immunodeficiency virus in a dental practice. *Annals Internal Medicine* 116:798-80; *Houston Post* (1992) CDC Announcement, August 7
69. Biggar (1984) Low T-lymphocyte ratios in homosexual men. *J American Medical Assoc* 251:1441-46; *Wall St J* (1991) B1, 07-18-91;

Tveit (1994) Casual sexual experience abroad. *Genitourin Medicine* 70:12-14

70. Beral, et al (1992) Risk of Kaposi's sarcoma and sexual practices associated with faecal contact in homosexual or bisexual men with AIDS. *Lancet* 339:632-35; Melbye & Biggar (1992) Interactions between persons at risk for AIDS and the general population in Denmark. *American J Epidemiology* 135:593-602

71. Chu, et al (1992) AIDS in bisexual men in the U.S. *American J Public Health* 82:220-24

Call Fire Down from Heaven

Luke 9:54–56 says, "And when his disciples James and John saw this, they said, Lord, wilt thou that we command fire to come down from heaven, and consume them, even as Elias did?" Christians shouldn't go around cursing and condemning sinners to hell. A Christian's duty is to share the gospel in love, hoping to save someone's soul from eternal damnation. In Luke 9:56, Jesus told James and John, "For the Son of man is not come to destroy men's lives, but to save them." The scriptures instruct Christians to teach in love. No true Christian will condemn, harass, persecute, and gay bash, perhaps remembering that "such were some of you." Knowing what Jesus was or is about, you will understand the conversation He had with these two brothers (disciples) in Luke 9:55 when he rebuked them and said, "You know not what manner of spirit you are of." In other words, it's not about this world; it's about the one to come. Christians should have the spirit of saving themselves and others from the everlasting, fiery condemnation that is to come. Christians do not need to fight a battle that has already been won. Jesus has risen, and all power is in His hand. The only thing Christians have to do is obey God. Their responsibility to the homosexual and lesbian population is to share the gospel. It is up to them to receive it or reject it. That is as far as Christians are commanded to go: preach the word, be instant in season, out of season, reprove and rebuke—preach the word.

The Bible gives everyone his or her freedom to heed the call of the gospel. That is just as simple as it can get. "Whosoever will, let him come."

Freedom of Choice: Choose Whom You Will Serve

Joshua 24:2–16 says, "And if it seem evil to you to serve the Lord, choose you this day whom you will serve. And the people answered and said, God forbid that we should forsake the Lord, to serve other gods."

Again, heaven is a prepared place for a prepared people. In contrast hell is for the unprepared. It is for those who failed to make their election sure (2 Peter 1:10–11). The gospel calls everyone, but not all will hear or answer the call. There are some who will believe, but they won't go any farther than the Satan or devils, who believed, trembled, and didn't obey—James 2:19. Being a believer doesn't make one a Christian. "Be ye not hearers only, but doers" (James 1:22). Do not deceive yourself into thinking that you are a Christian because you believe in God; even the devils know God. It's the obedient soul who is saved and is added to the body of Christ, kingdom of God, and church of Christ.

God, an all-powerful being, has given you the freedom to make a choice as to whether to serve Him or not. *There's your freedom.* No creature of God should have a religious freedom issue. "Word up"—you are free. But as with anything else in this world, freedom comes with a price. Use your God-given, blood-bought freedom wisely.

God Does Not Compromise

In 2 Samuel 6:1–7 and 1 Chronicles 13:9–12, Uzzah (a Levite) had good intentions when he reached out to help keep the ark of the covenant of God sturdy while going over rough terrain. Unfortunately, this act cost him his life. Only individuals of the Kohathites (Levite tribe, specifically assigned) were instructed to handle the ark. They were instructed to shoulder the *Ark of the Covenant* on poles, but not touch the holy thing of God. Jews were knowledgeable of this fact as well as individuals today of the New Testament scriptures on the homosexual lifestyle, (Romans 1:26–32). Yet we tempt God with our personal, political, and popular views of worship. Worship is about following God's instructions on how He should be worshipped. When our thoughts and ways about worship aren't God approved, they will bring the same result: spiritual death or separation. God says to you that where He is you cannot come. There is a way that seems right unto a man, but the end is death (Proverbs 14:12).

There is nowhere in scripture where God compromised right for wrong. God expelled a fallen angel (Satan—*named after the fall*) out of heaven. We bargain with Satan when we compromise (offer up) our children or fruit of the womb—God's inheritance—to live in situations God condemns as abominable in His sight. Satan has deceived us into thinking that any home is better than no home, so we compromise and bargain with Satan for our children. Perhaps Uzzah felt that any help in keeping the Ark of the Covenant from falling was better than no help at all—only to realize this wasn't his call to make.

Coming Out

The Lord says, "Therefore *come out* from them and be separated, having nothing to do with evildoers and He will receive you" (2 Corinthians 6:17, emphasis added).

The very fact that you are called by the gospel to come out from among evildoers makes "coming out" in this sense a good thing. Unfortunately, the fashionable twenty-first century's "coming out" means leaving the closet of darkness to flaunt ones evil deeds and shake ones fists in the face of God. Considering that nothing is new under the sun, there is an argument to rewrite the Bible; one can cut out passages that reference effeminate: men with men and women with women. This is conduct (voiding out scripture) that was dealt with in the Old Testament in Jeremiah 36:23, which we will examine later.

Satan, liar and deceiver, continues to deceive the hearts of men to do the opposite of God's will. Just like the original sin, God said don't eat. Satan adds his two cents, changing the course of nature in the God-man relationship. God says, "Come out from sin and from evildoers." Satan would say to Come out of the closet, wave your rainbow flag, flaunt your sins, and establish your own unholy unions and community churches; for example, the Metropolitan Community Church, a gay "Christian" denomination founded in Los Angeles in 1968. There is nothing Christ-like in a homosexual lifestyle. But God is patient and loving and long-suffering, not willing that any should perish. The invitation remains the same: "Come out."

As the young people say, "Don't get this 'thang' twisted." God is the first to address the issue of "coming out" over two thousand years ago. He wants all to "come out," and He made it crystal clear how we are to come out. The Bible's "come out from among them" is entirely different from the satanic and abominable "coming out" of the closet. Back to square one: Satan lying to man. He started with Adam and Eve with "not." Now, it is "come out" of the closet and "not" from evildoers. Gays flaunt their lifestyle in God's sight with no shame, allowing Satan to alter the word of God as with Adam and Eve. Adam and Eve were honest enough to be ashamed of their disobedience. Pride comes before destruction (Proverbs 16:18). Adam's and Eve's downfall was the lust of the eye (the tree looked good), lust of the flesh (the tree tasted good), and the pride of life (they wanted to be like God), as it is with man today. Adam and Eve lusted after power to walk outside the commands of God and believed they could be as knowledgeable as God, (Genesis 3:5). They believed they could make wise decisions that needed to be made. They believed they could direct their steps in a garden, in a world where they had limited knowledge, and in things they weren't authorized to engage in or touch.

Satan's tactic has always been a little truth in his lie. It's very rare to fool someone with an all-out boldface lie. Satan never tells man the negative part or consequence of disobedience to God; like for instance, "This will be God's response to this action you are about to take." The thing was, Adam and Eve were already like God—good. God is good. In the book of Genesis, God said His creation of man was "very" good. After Eve disobeyed and persuaded her husband, Adam, to do so, they took upon themselves another characteristic or attribute: evil or sin. This was a death sentence on God's creation, man. This was Satan's goal to breach the relationship. Satan is going to hell, and he is doing everything he can to carry you there, too.

The scripture tells us that man is already free. Through His death on the cross, Jesus has set man free from death and eternal damnation. The homosexuals are demanding rights, and they have the ultimate right to eternal life through obedience to the gospel. The homosexuals want to blame God for being born gay. Adam and Eve did the blame game, too, and it got them nowhere. The LGBT community lusts for the federal benefits holy matrimony couples have (lust of the eye). The LGBT community lusts after the same sex (lust of the flesh). The LGBT community lusts for control of their lives given to them by God, shaking their fists in God's face; they are defiant to God's command and will for man (pride of life). Looking back over the course of man's existence on this planet, man hasn't left ground zero, the Garden of Eden. He accepts the lies of Satan and plays the blame game by engaging in the acts of the lust of the eye, the lust of the flesh, and the pride of life. We can clearly see that in the twenty-first century that nothing has changed.

📖 Book Corner (A Critique)

Kate Fagan, *The Reappearing Act: Coming Out as Gay on a College Basketball Team Led by Born-Again Christians*[32]

Fagan wrote that she spent much time around her college basketball teammates in Bible study while harboring and/or suppressing gay tendencies. But she concluded that she was satisfied with how she had determined to live her life, even in contradiction to scripture. It took 185 pages to say she would do what she wanted to do. She hardened her heart to her conscience of knowing she wasn't pleasing God and began to feel good about her choice to be gay.

What she gained from her lack of understanding scripture was enough information to hurt herself. "If the devil uses love to win souls, what makes him any different than God?"[33] Fagan expressed that her feelings (attractions to the same sex) weren't from the devil. Satan appears as an angel of light. Fagan answers her own question. The devil "uses" love. Scripture says God is love. Satan's strength and tactics are deception. The Bible talks of the pleasures of sin. Fagan feels her version of love in same-sex attraction feels good or pleasurable and can't be wrong or come from the devil. When it comes to right or wrong, who determines what is pleasing and acceptable to God? God, Satan, or man? In other words, Kate Fagan. If man determines what pleases God and how he is going to please God, whether God has a say-so in it or not, there could be some chaos. God is not the author of confusion. Because of her lack of scripture knowledge, Fagan concludes that she is open and accepting of everyone's faith and doesn't see right or wrong; nor does she even consider Christianity as the only right choice anymore [34]. Until Ms. Fagan accepts God's invitation for a true love relationship with Him and eternal love—which is her choice—Satan, whom she says uses love, is her choice.

---

[32] Kate Fagan, *The Reappearing Act: Coming Out as Gay on a College Basketball Team Led by Born-Again Christians,* (New York: Skyhorse Publishing 2014).

[33] Ibid., 116.

[34] Ibid., 185

You Did Not Build It

In Genesis 1:1, we read, "In the beginning, God created the heavens and the earth." Earth isn't yours; you don't get a say-so in its beginning or its ending. Hebrews 1:10–12 says, "And, you Lord, in the beginning have laid the foundation of the earth; and the heavens are the works of your hands: They shall perish; but You remain; and they all shall wax old as does a garment; And as a vesture shall You fold them up, and they shall be changed; but You are the same, and Your years shall not fail."

You didn't get a say-so in your birth (the day you were born) or your death (the day you leave this earth). If you don't believe this, try asking passengers from the *Titanic*, individuals in America's recent shooting massacres, or someone who is 150 years old today. What you do get is a say-so in where you spend eternity. No matter what you feel or believe, you don't get to stay here —you didn't build this. On the seventh day, God rested from His work, which He had made (Genesis 2:2).

It is by God's will that each and every human being enters and leaves this world. God made us for service to Him, and it is when we reach the age of accountability that our relationship changes from the innocent to the fallen stage or under the curse of Adam, the first man. "When I was a child, I spoke as a child, I understood as a child: but when I became a man, I put away childish things" (1 Corinthians 13:11).

When Adam and Eve ate of the tree of knowledge, God said they had become "as one of Us," knowing good from evil—(Genesis 3:22). When a child reaches an age of understanding or rationalizing the difference between good and bad, that child loses his or her innocence, protective veil, and spiritual embryotic sac. When Adam and Eve ate of the fruit, they lost their innocence. Their eyes were opened, and they understood and became individuals of accountability. They were naked before God. Once man reaches the age of accountability, he is forever naked before God, and no veil of innocence is an alibi. When one comes into the knowledge of the word of God (truth), there is no more claim of innocence or ignorance. "And the times of this ignorance God winked at; but now commands all men everywhere to repent: Because He has appointed a day, in the which He will judge the world in righteousness by that Man whom He has ordained; whereof He has given assurance to all men, in that He has raised Him from the dead" (Acts 17:30–31). Not only that, but God made sure that every soul (human being) is aware (inescapable or inexcusable) of the knowledge of His superior presence. And it is man's responsibility to seek or search the scriptures and learn of Him. "For this is the covenant that I will make with the house of Israel after those days, says the Lord: I will put My laws into their mind, and write them in their hearts: and I will be to them a God, and they shall be to Me a people: And they shall not teach every man his neighbor, and every man his brother, saying, Know the Lord: for all shall know Me, from the least to the greatest" (Hebrews 8:10–11; also see Jeremiah 31:33–43). We can go all atheism on God if we like (that's our freedom of choice); we know Him, and even the firmament declares His handiwork.

Because God loves man (male and female), His creation, He has put a plan of redemption in place: purchased our souls back through the blood of His Son, Jesus Christ.

For as in Adam all die, even so in Christ shall all be made alive. (1 Corinthians 15:22)

For all have sinned, and come short of the glory of God; being justified freely by His grace through the redemption that is in Christ Jesus. (Romans 3:23–24)

Do you not know that the unrighteous will not inherit the kingdom of God? Do not be deceived. Neither fornicators, nor idolaters, nor adulterers, nor homosexuals, nor sodomites, nor thieves, nor covetous, nor drunkards, nor revilers, nor extortioners, will inherit the kingdom of God. And such were some of you. But you were washed, but you were sanctified, but you were justified in the name of the Lord Jesus and by the Spirit of our God. (1 Corinthians 6:9–11)

Understand this: we all stand at a guilty distance from God. So when the church preaches on homosexuality and any other sins, it's not the creature, man (person's) position to go screaming that someone is infringing on his or her religious rights or freedom to live his or her lifestyle. If that were the case, every evildoer on "the list" could make the same claim. Perjury is on the books in states. Let the liars lobby for rights not be prosecuted for this sin—they are on "the list." Make no mistake about it, Mr. Obama ran for president in 2008 not a religious leader. It was within his job duty as president to protect any group's civil rights agenda, especially if it means helping him reach his political goal of election or reelection.

Again, don't get this "thang" twisted. Obama can go only as far as the grave with a gay person—after death, the judgment. Why would Obama have allowed a few abominable individuals hinder him from a greater good, serving as 44th president to a vast number of individuals who are God-fearing

Americans? His evolving could very well have been to the point of knowing he needed gay votes to help him get elected while battling a group of politicians who had vowed to do anything to keep him from being reelected. He evolved enough not to allow someone else's agenda to interfere with his agenda for a greater good. This reminds me of when certain characters in the Bible vowed not to eat or sleep until the apostle Paul was defeated. David, when he "was hungered," ate the showbread, which he wasn't supposed to do. Sometimes we have to be wiser than the tricks Satan hurls and take the hard, unpopular stand just to get things done.

Take a good look at Mr. Obama. He is married to an individual of the opposite sex, he fathered his children, and as far as anyone (news media and fact-checkers) knows, he is faithful—not an adulterer. If I were gay, I wouldn't allow Obama to sell me a ticket that doesn't look like his to the same fair. If salvation were based on his un-abominate lifestyle alone, Obama would get through the pearly gates, even though he conveniently agreed with the gays along the wayside as they traveled to the fair [heaven]. Obama agreed with them and with whatever issues they had about whatever, knowing at the end of the road or entry to the fair or pearly gates that they couldn't get in with the ticket they had. He was wise to agree with his adversary, who apparently could have used his response to hinder his personal goals to become president of the United States (see Matthew 5:25). There is no sin in ascribing to be president, but scripture proclaims that being effeminate is an abomination. Talking about the ole cliché (don't trust a politician). Obama, who professed to be a Christian, knows scripturally that gays aren't headed for eternal life with Christ. Mr. Obama de-evolves or reverts just enough not to get entangled with their agenda, which could possibly affect his agenda to be reelected as president of the United States. Note, he always said, "That's why I'm running for the president of the United States." I never heard him say, "That's why I running for your spiritual leader or campaigning to be your spiritual leader of the United States." Once again, don't get things twisted. If Obama decided to go into the ministry after his career as a politician and to be a Christian, he would have to continue his evolution or conversion back toward biblical truths. He would have to agree that a homosexual lifestyle is an abomination before God. Let's not filibuster through this. Obama's coattail isn't a safe place to hide when it comes to your salvation. For your political agenda—yeah! For your soul—nah! The house of God holds the controlling vote here.

Listen–Let's Get Straight Up

Biden wants to get the message out and believes everyone should be on this bandwagon that gay rights are straight-up human rights. God is far ahead of Mr. Biden here. Remember the scripture that says God has made man "upright"? (Ecclesiastes 7:29) "Straight up"! The government does and should protect the rights of every citizen, and that should include gay persons (citizens).

This very fact makes me understand why Obama and Biden feel compelled and obligated to take a stand for gays and the rights of any group of people with citizenship in this country. And everyone else should stand on the same principles of not being violent toward another human being and certainly not found casting stones at others' sins.

But in their zeal to do good, Obama and Biden tried to make a call the Creator of this universe hasn't authorized them to make. Remember Uzzah and the Ark of the Covenant in 2 Samuel 6 and 1 Chronicle 13? Uzzah tried to steady the ark, reached out to hold it, and was struck dead by the hands of God. All in Uzzah's presence saw him die for a seemingly good deed. But only individuals of the tribe of Levi (selected Levite member tribe) were allowed to handle the ark (with strict instructions) and not suffer death. Uzzah, in his zeal to do a good deed, died because his actions weren't authorized. Rulers of nations cause people to sin when their actions aren't aligned with the will of God. No one can stop people from living lives contrary to the will of God, their maker. Your choice of lifestyle is between you and God, your maker. God has given everyone that freedom: "Whosoever will, let him come." Judges are not authorized to legitimize a lifestyle—an abominable act before God. They force the nation to obey them instead of God.

The gay movement has hijacked and hitched a ride like a parasite on the civil rights movement of black people/African Americans in the USA and on the coattail of the first black president of the United States of America. Black people died, cried, prayed, carried their Bibles, and called on the name of God and Jesus Christ for deliverance from their ("hellrific") struggle and journey to freedom and basic human rights here in America. There are no recorded incidents in the gay movement where they called on the name of God or Jesus Christ, while carrying the Holy Bible, for freedom and equal rights. They have only demanded what they want while preying on the consciences of Americans, who wish to bury their history (America's history of brutality toward African American) and not repeat the ill treatment on any human being. Black people suffered because they were different from the majority of the country.

A gay individual has never been denied the right to vote because he or she is gay. A black person has never been able to hide his or her ethnicity (differences) in a closet or come with a choice to self-identifying or option to be a black person (African descent) or not. With political clout, gays positioned themselves to make demands on this country's moral fiber. They make demands while living in abomination and in unfruitful unions, for every federal benefit a union of male and female (a potential fruitful union) can bless God with and the United States and any thriving "civilized culture." They demand that the federal government recognize their abominable union (not *three-fifth of a union but a complete marriage*). They were determined to infiltrate the Boy Scouts and every religious, God-fearing (highly moral and principled) organization and business; even cake bakeries cannot escape their hatred toward God and righteousness. They even try to silence opposition by those who quote scripture, pointing out and bringing light to their deeds. The Boy Scouts pledge or oath says, "On my honor, I will do my best to do my duty to God and my country and to obey the Scout Law; to help other people at all times; to keep myself physically strong, mentally awake and morally straight." Homosexuals don't behave like a weak group suffering "civil rights" issues.

They were people waiting in the wings and ready to pounce on civilization once again like in the heydays of Sodom and Gomorrah. Their defeat or infiltration of the Boy Scouts of America is just as sweet to the gay population as their boast of having the first black president of America, Barak H. Obama, go down in history in support of homosexuality in America. The million-dollar question is, since the outcome will be the same as in the biblical account (God doesn't and didn't tolerate wickedness), how many people will go down with them this time? Will it be the whole United States of America? They took out the cities of the Plains: cities of Sodom and Gomorrah (Genesis 19:24–25). What archeologist will be unearthing the native plains of America in the distant centuries, attributing its destruction to the homosexual movement—a twenty-first-century Sodom and Gomorrah?

Straight up, God tells the gay person the same thing He told the first child born on the earth to Adam and Eve.

> "And the Lord said to Cain, Why are you angry? And why is your countenance fallen? If you do well, shall you not be accepted? And if you do not well, sin lies at the door" (Genesis 4:6–7).

No one on this planet is in a position to cast the first stone or stones at another person. Face the fact that all our sins are naked before the all-seeing eyes of God. Our challenge as a nation isn't to be weighing in the balance while the parasitic movement seemingly has its way with us (USA). This century is so intellectually stupid. People believe we are wiser and smarter than the Creator. Listen to how we measure up:

> "Woe to them that call evil good, and good evil; that put darkness for light and light for darkness; that put bitter for sweet, and sweet for bitter! Woe to them that are wise in their own eyes, and prudent in their own sight! Woe to them that are mighty to drink wine, and men of strength to mingle strong drink: which justify the wicked for reward, and take away the righteousness of the righteous from him!" (Isaiah 5:20–23).

When they meet opposition, why would gays be so surprised to discover their lifestyle is contrary to the religious beliefs and practices of America? "For this is thankworthy, if a man for conscience toward God endure grief, suffering wrongfully. For what glory is it, if, when you be buffeted for your fault, you shall take it patiently? But if, when you do well, and suffer for it, you take it patiently, this is acceptable with God" (1 Peter 2:20). Black people suffered wrongfully and took it patiently, waiting for God to deliver them. Gays are parading an abominable lifestyle and act as though the issue is with people who believe the Bible and not with them.

> "Let him eschew evil, and do good; let him seek peace, and ensure it. For the eyes of the Lord are over the righteous, and His ears are open to their prayers: but the face of the Lord is against them that do evil. And who is he that will harm you, if you be followers of that which is good? But and if you *suffer for righteousness' sake*, happy are you: and be not afraid of their terror, neither be troubled" (1 Peter 3:11–14, emphasis added).

Observationally speaking, the gay civil rights movement hasn't once mentioned any denied rights of a people or compared their movement to any other group other than African Americans, while deceitfully comparing their plight as a similar cause. They know not to position their lips in trying to associate any suffering or civil rights of a people with the Jews. History will show how immediately the Jews pounce on anything they feel diminishes their cause (remembrance of the Holocaust) and the history of suffering under the Germans and Nazis. And they will label it "anti-Semitic" with a quickness. There's nothing about anal sex that's kosher. A move in that direction to seek support from the Jews would have been met with a resounding "Hell to the No!"

The gay movement picked the least resistant target and trapped the first black (Hawaiian-born or Indonesia culture) president into overcompensating on their plight for "civil rights" because of the sins (inhumane treatment) of this country on African Americans. This was a very smart and strategic move on their part. "On May 9, 2012, Barack Obama became the first sitting U. S. president to publicly declare support for legalizing of same-sex marriage."[35]

They went in for the kill. Some black people stayed silent, and some joined in on the fray or disingenuous cause. If gays tried using gay "suffering" and gay "holocaust" in the same sentence to describe their civil rights agenda, they would have had to say it quietly and, if written, tear and chew up the paper it was written on. Many African Americans struggle with accepting the ugly facts of slavery, that they were enslaved and treated so inhumanly as a people. Many would like to forget, especially the younger generation, who are far removed from the realities of the past and its struggles. A thought to ponder: Homosexuality is a majority white male movement. Just visualize it being a majority black male movement. How many government-forced psych and research wards, Tuskegee-like disease testing government sponsored research laboratories, and "strange fruits" repopulated from southern states would one observe hanging from trees north and south (state-to-state)? Accusations of spreading HIV, acts against natural, un-Christian, abomination toward God, and harm to public health and society would set off a maelstrom of contention. There would be a relentless protest against and killings of this population for this behavior in American society—I digress.

It is reported that president Obama said his position on gay marriage evolved. Unfortunately for the Mr. Obama, he was damned if he did and damned if he didn't. Congress would surely have accused him of not supporting the law if he didn't support the federal and judicial rulings. His hard, personal work as a married family guy with aspirations for public office or public servant would be destroyed by the issue of an abominable self-identified sect of people.

The gay movement doesn't care about Obama, only about having its own way. Granted, he should have evolved enough not to let their agenda destroy him. For survival sake, because of hunger, King David ate the showbread

---

[35] "Obama Affirms Support for Same-Sex Marriage," ABC 25WPBF, May 9, 2012, http://en.wikipedia.org/wiki/Same-sex_marriage_in_the_United_States.

when it wasn't lawful. When all is said and done, all will have to give an account before God for the deeds done in their body. When Obama decides to follow Christ, surely he will have to re-evolve. He can repent. Will the homosexuals and lesbians repent?

The Jews won't forget their past or let anyone forgot and prey and profit from that past. Yes, the gay movement picked the right target. The gay movement picked the right place on this planet to launch their movement, the USA with its motto "In God We Trust." Once America loses its status and other nations' desire to look toward America for morals, Christianity, and hope for a better way of life in America fades, Satan has won what he set out to do—to kill and destroy. I heard a gospel minister say, "We are no longer a Christian nation but a nation with Christian in it." And we all thought this issue was about homosexuality. It's about the battle between good and evil. Satan wants what belongs to God—you!

"For we wrestle not against flesh and blood, but against principalities, against powers, against the rulers of the darkness of this world, against spiritual wickedness in high places" (Ephesians 6:12).

God's Glory and Man's Sanctification

Even everyone that is called by My name; for I have created him for My glory, I have formed him yea, I have made him. (Isaiah 43:7)

> According as He has chosen us in Him before the foundation of the world, that we should be holy and without blame before Him in love: Having predestinated us to the adoption of children by Jesus Christ to Himself, according to the good pleasure of His will. (Ephesians 1:4–7)

At some point, every knee will bow before God. Man was created for God and by God for His glory. The sooner homosexuals and all other sinners (for we all have sinned and come short of the glory of God) realize they are someone's servant (a slave and bondservant of God or a slave and bondservant to Satan), the sooner they will then begin to make wiser choices concerning where they will spend eternity. There is no middle ground. You don't even have the power to create a middle ground. You don't have the knowledge on how to go rogue or go over the wall of the pearly gate, mischievously stealing your way in. Again, there is no middle ground. I guess so much for freedom, other than the freedom one has in Christ Jesus. Because you are given the freedom of choice, you have the freedom to choose life or death. Freedom in Christ gives you that option. The fact is, you didn't have anything to do with being on this planet; you woke up and at some point between one year old and as late as five years old, you recognized you were a "you." And by the same breath, you have nothing to do with your dying. You will wake up on the other side of life, and you can't do a thing about that either, just like when you woke up here in this world and couldn't do anything about it.

What you can do (your only God-given freedom or rights) is decide whether you will spend eternity with God and His angels or with Satan and his angels. That's heavy stuff. But that's the card you have been dealt and the hand you must skillfully play. Cheer up, though; you have a manual, the Holy Bible, as well as tutors, preachers and Bible school teachers. You have a lifeline, the Holy Spirit to help you remember the moves or rules you have studied in scripture whenever you encounter tight spots in life. There is someone looking over your shoulders, whispering the correct play to make sure you make the right moves. Hear ye Him, Christ. Satan will try to deal you a bad hand. Angels are around, cheering you on as you play for the win for eternal salvation. Rest assured, God won't let a sincere and obedient player fail the game. He has got your back.

Slaves and Servants

"Know you not, that to whom you yield yourselves servants to obey, his servants you are to whom you obey; whether of sin to death, or of obedience to righteousness?" (Romans 6:16). When you get ready to talk about real freedom, you can thank God. "But God be thanked, that you were the servants of sin, but you have obeyed from the heart that form of doctrine [teaching] which was delivered you [the gospel] being made free from sin, you became the servants of righteousness" (Romans 6:17–18). Paul went on to say, "I speak after the manner of men because of the infirmity of your flesh: for as you have yielded your members servants to uncleanness and to iniquity unto iniquity; even so now yield your members servants to righteousness unto holiness" (Romans 6:19). "But now being made free from sin, and become servants to God, you have fruit to holiness, and the end everlasting life. For the wages of sin is death; but the gift of God is eternal life through Jesus Christ our Lord" (Romans 6:22–23).

We can't talk about freedom without talking about rights or civil rights: expressed freedom for equality. As we can see, once a foothold has been established comparing black people's struggles for rights in society to the gay people's struggles for rights in society, there is no stopping in an attempt to destroy the fabric of a God-fearing society. Black people marched with the Bible in their hands. Gays want to rewrite the Bible. It doesn't seem like they have the same message or agenda of black people or the plight of black people. Their present agenda is to get a foothold on the institution of marriage, another thing God created. Mimicking Black Lives Matter with "Equality Matters" is coat-tailing. It's feeding off the botched way equality was extended to black people/African Americans. It's feeding off the shame, fear, and guilt of the past, which still leaves a stench in America. The LGBT community brazenly bullies America into helping them push their agenda.

The Supreme Court in *Loving v. Virginia* defined marriage as a fundamental right because it is one of the basic civil rights of man—fundamental to our very existence and survival. The court ruled that anti-interracial laws were unconstitutional. The gays, playing on the guilt of this country's treatment of African Americans, want the courts to see them as a distinct group, which the population is discriminating against, just as were black people. Yet under no circumstances can they meet the scrutiny of a sect of people who are beneficial to the survival of the species, man, as in the case of biracial couples of the opposite sex who procreate in the perpetuation of our society. They don't fit in perfectly: feeling they should be viewed like normal, regular married couples; they try to persuade the courts and society, even in overwhelming evidence of their nonsubstantiality as a beneficial group to the survival of man's existence. They give nothing, feeding and preying off children in a facade of a solution in adoptive parenting to defy God. They strip federal benefits and bring this country to its knees, as the whole world, including the international community, watches to see how much we really trust in God. Once we have been proven a liar, it's hard to regain trust in what we say or purport.

Legalizing Same-Sex Marriage The Court's Distortion of the Constitution

Justice Thomas joins Chief Justice Roberts and Justice Scalia, dissenting.

In his dissent, Justice Clarence Thomas gave some clarity to "liberty" and "due process." He expressed that the argument is only a front to obtain substantive rights. The Constitution does guarantee "due process" before a person is deprived of life, liberty, or property. Thomas explained that this isn't the case in what is happening with the claims of the gay community toward rights to liberty and due process. They misunderstand and misinterpret the language of the Constitution, though successfully persuading the majority to their side on the issue.

Thomas said the Fourteenth Amendment uses the word *liberty* to refer to freedom from physical restraint, and the due process clause in the Fifth Amendment, used in the same sense, emphasizes protecting and safeguarding individuals' rights to life, liberty, and property. Thomas stressed that the original meaning of due process was deviated from in the majority's decision, since it referred to physical constraints. *Obergefell v. Hodges.* 576 U.S. ____, 135 S. Ct. 2584, 2631- 2634 (2015) (Thomas, J., dissenting).[36]

One can look back just slightly over one's shoulders to understand this physical constraint. The black man was physically constrained from keeping his family, his wife and children, together as a unit. He watched them be sold off on the auction block to other plantation owners. The black man was constrained from voting, reading, writing, owning property, or moving around and living where and how he desired while ordering his life. In short, the black man was physically constrained from life, liberty, and property. Thomas pointed out that gays and lesbians aren't physically restrained from participating in same-sex relationships. Black people and white people who wished to marry were physically restrained from marrying each other to the point of imprisonment. Jews and Germans were physically restrained from marrying each other. Before the ruling on June 26, 2015, those in the LGBT community had been able to cohabitate and raise their children without constraint or government interference. They are able to form civil unions or marriage ceremonies in states that recognize same-sex marriages.

Thomas wrote, "In the American legal tradition, liberty has long been understood as individual freedom from governmental action, not as a right to a particular governmental entitlement." *Obergefell v. Hodges.* 576 U.S. ____, 135 S. Ct. 2584, 2631- 2634 (2015) (Thomas, J., dissenting).[37]

Justice Thomas, with whom Justice Scalia joins, dissenting.

"The Court's decision today is at odds not only with the Constitution, but with the principles upon which our Nation was built. Since well before 1787, liberty has been understood as freedom from government action, not entitlement to government benefits. The Framers created our Constitution to preserve that understanding of liberty. Yet the majority invokes our Constitution in the name of a "liberty" that the Framers would not have recognized, to the detriment of the liberty they sought to protect. Along

---

[36] *Obergefell*, 135 S.Ct. at 2633
[37] *Id.* at 2631

the way, it rejects the idea--captured in our Declaration of Independence--that human dignity is innate and suggests instead that it comes from the Government. This distortion of our Constitution not only ignores the text, it inverts the relationship between the individual and the state in our Republic. I cannot agree with it."

"The majority's decision today will require States to issue marriage licenses to same-sex couples and to recognize same-sex marriages entered in other States largely based on a constitutional provision guaranteeing "due process" before a person is deprived of his "life, liberty, or property." I have elsewhere explained the dangerous fiction of treating the Due Process Clause as a front for substantive rights. *McDonald v. Chicago*, 561 U.S. 742, 811-812, 130 S. Ct. 3020, 177 L. Ed. 2d 894 (2010) (Thomas, J., concurring in part and concurring in judgment). It distorts the constitutional text, which guarantees only whatever "process" is "due" before a person is deprived of life, liberty, and property. U. S. Const., Amdt. 14, §1. Worse, it invites judges to do exactly what the majority has done here--"roa[m] at large in the constitutional field' guided only by their personal views" as to the "'fundamental rights'" protected by that document. *Planned Parenthood of Southeastern Pa. v. Casey*, 505 U.S. 833, 953, 965, 112 S. Ct. 2791, 120 L. Ed. 2d 674 (1992) (Rehnquist, C. J., concurring in judgment in part and dissenting in part) (quoting *Griswold* v. *Connecticut*, 381 U.S. 479, 502, 85 S. Ct. 1678, 14 L. Ed. 2d 510 (1965) (Harlan, J., concurring in judgment))."

"By straying from the text of the Constitution, substantive due process exalts judges at the expense of the People from whom they derive their authority. Petitioners argue that by enshrining the traditional definition of marriage in their State Constitutions through voter-approved amendments, the States have put the issue "beyond the reach of the normal democratic process." Brief for Petitioners in No. 14-562, p. 54. But the result petitioners seek is far less democratic. They ask nine judges on this Court to enshrine their definition of marriage in the Federal Constitution and thus put it beyond the reach of the normal democratic process for the entire Nation. That a "bare majority" of this Court, *ante*, at ___, 192 L. Ed. 2d, at 632, is able to grant this wish, wiping out with a stroke of the keyboard the results of the political process in over 30 States, based on a provision that guarantees only "due process" is but further evidence of the danger of substantive due process." *Obergefell v. Hodges*. 576 U.S. ____, 135 S. Ct. 2584, 2631- 2632 (2015) (Thomas, J., dissenting).[38]

---

[38] Id., S.Ct. at 2633

Power of the People

There is power in numbers. Naturally, this is believing and understanding one has power from his or her God-given rights to life, liberty, and property (legally or rightfully gained). These shouldn't be taken (or threaten to be taken) from him or her without due process in the legal sense. "Because that state of nature left men insecure in their persons and property, they entered civil society, trading a portion of their natural liberty for an increase in their security. Upon consenting to that order, men obtained civil liberty, or the freedom "to be under no other legislative power but that established by consent in the commonwealth; nor under the dominion of any will or restraint of any law, but what that legislative shall enact according to the trust put in it." [39]

It is the people who come together for the betterment of the whole in this society—strength of a civilized state or country. To do this, individual likes and dislikes are forfeited to a democratic process, yielding to majority rule. This is done through a political, legislative process. People vote on issues that affect their lives and elect officials to represent them in legislating laws for their state within the confines of the US Constitution. It is these laws the people establish through a legislative body. Under the guidelines of the US Constitution, the Supreme Court rules on established laws and doesn't create laws. Thomas wrote, "When the States act through their representative governments or by popular vote, the liberty of their residents is fully vindicated. This is no less true when some residents disagree with the result; indeed, it seems difficult to imagine any law on which all residents of a State would agree. What does matter is that the process established by those who created the society has been honored."[40] *Obergefell v. Hodges.* 576 U.S. _____, 135 S. Ct. 2584, 2637- 2638 (2015) (Thomas, J., dissenting).

Thomas said legislatures went to bat for the people on the matter of same-sex marriage. Thirty-five states put the issue to the people, and of the thirty-five, thirty-two opted to keep the understanding of traditional marriage as the definition of marriage, the union between a man and a woman. So the question is, What happened in the Supreme Court on June 26, 2015? Clearly the majority of "we the people, by the people, for the people" expressed what they believe marriage is.

Thomas wrote, "Aside from undermining the political processes that protect our liberty, the majority's decision threatens that religious liberty our

---

[39] https://en.wikipedia.org/wiki/Civil_liberties
[40] Obergefell v. Hodges, 135 S. Ct. 2584, 2637(2015)

Nation has long sought to protect." He wrote, "The First Amendment enshrined protection for the free exercise of religion in the US Constitution." He said that the federal government and the states reaffirmed their commitment to religious liberty by codifying protections for religious practice (Religious Freedom Restoration Act of 1993). Justice Thomas expressed his concerns that this decision will "have unavoidable and wide-ranging implications for religious liberty."[41] *Obergefell v. Hodges.* 576 U.S. ____, 135 S. Ct. 2584, 2636, 2638 (2015) (Thomas, J., dissenting).

Thomas pointed out that marriage isn't just a governmental institution; it is a spiritual institution.

Marriage is the oldest institution to man, given to him by God, where He placed the man and his wife and blessed the union with children.

Thomas wrote, "Had the majority allowed the definition of marriage to be left to the political process—as the Constitution requires—the People could have considered the religious liberty implications of deviating from the traditional definition as part of their deliberative process. Instead, the majority's decision short-circuits that process, with potentially ruinous consequences for religious liberty."[42] *Obergefell v. Hodges.* 576 U.S. ____, 135 S. Ct. 2584, 2631- 2639 (2015) (Thomas, J., dissenting).

Justice Thomas on Dignity

Thomas wrote, "[The] majority goes to great lengths to assert that its decision will advance the 'dignity' of same-sex couples."[43] *Obergefell v. Hodges.* 576 U.S. ____, 135 S. Ct. 2584, 2639 (2015) (Thomas, J., dissenting).

Dignity is addressed in several pages in this book. Justice Thomas clearly reflects my sentiment in his statement that government cannot give or take dignity from an individual. How one carries himself or herself, no matter what he or she faces in life, reflects the innate dignity the person possesses in his or her soul and spirit. Justice Thomas wrote, "Our Constitution—like the Declaration of Independence before it—was predicated on a simple truth: One's liberty, not to mention one's dignity, was something to be shielded from—but not provided by—the State.[44]" In other words, you have to already have dignity; it's how you carry yourself.

---

[41] Obergefell, 135 S. Ct. at 2638

[42] Id. at 2639

[43] *Id.*, 135 S. Ct. at 2639.

[44] *Id.* at 2640.

A large concern in Judge Thomas's dissent is that "By straying from the text of the Constitution, substantive due process exalts judges at the expense of the People from whom they derive their authority."[45] *Obergefell v. Hodges.* 576 U.S. ____, 135 S. Ct. 2584, 2631, 2639-40 (2015) (Thomas, J., dissenting).

The framers of the Declaration of Independence acknowledged that every person or human being is created equal and is "endowed by their Creator with certain unalienable Rights." Justice Thomas said this statement shows the framers "referred to a vision of mankind in which all humans are created in the image of God and therefore of inherent worth. That vision is the foundation upon which this Nation was built."[46] *Obergefell v. Hodges.* 576 U.S. ____, 135 S. Ct. 2584, 2631- 2639 (2015) (Thomas, J., dissenting).

What Do the LGBTQ (Self-Identified) People Really Want?

Justice Thomas wrote, "Petitioners do not ask this Court to order the States to stop restricting their ability to enter same-sex marriage, to engage in intimate behavior, to make vows to their partners in public ceremonies, to engage in religious wedding ceremonies, to hold themselves out as married, or to raise children. The States have imposed no such restrictions. Nor have the States prevented petitioners from approximating a number of incidents of marriage through private legal means, such as wills, trusts, and powers of attorney. Instead, the States have refused to grant them governmental entitlements."[47] *Obergefell v. Hodges.* 576 U.S. at____, 135 S. Ct. 2584, 2635 (2015) (Thomas, J., dissenting).

This is their argument for liberty, which Justice Thomas explained had nothing to do with the understanding of "liberty" in the US Constitution. What they want is what traditional married (holy matrimony) couples have; they think that if they win this fight, this will legitimize the unnatural behavior and give them some form of dignity to their state of existence. Once again, they miss the mark; God has given every man dignity. He has made man upright—the ability to do right and make wise choices. "Lo, this only have I found, that God has made man upright; but they have sought out many inventions" (Ecclesiastes 7:29). Dignity is the manner in which one carries himself or herself; it is one's lifestyle

---

[45] *Obergefell v. Hodges*, 135 S. Ct. 2584, 2640 (2015)
[46] *Id.* at 2631
[47] *Obergefell*, 135 S. Ct. 2584 at 2635

that destroys his or her dignity. Man has sought out all kinds of ways (inventions) to bring himself below the status to which God has called him to walk. Justice Samuel Alito wrote:

> In short, the "right to marry" cases stand for the important but limited proposition that particular restrictions on access to marriage *as traditionally defined* violate due process. These precedents say nothing at all about a right to make a State change its definition of marriage, which is the right petitioners actually seek here. See *Windsor*, 570 U.S., at ___ , 133 S. Ct. 2675, 186 L. Ed. 2d at 852 (Alito, J., dissenting)[48]

Some states are looking out for themselves through self-preservation in taxes, sales of marriage licenses, and voters from "newly" self-identified group/sect of people. Gays aren't able to give back to government. They aren't an investment to the continuation of society or civilization, but they boldly demand compensation from government for their unproductive and unfruitful unions. They want to be rewarded in the same manner as an institution of millennial status with a proven history of sustainability and benefits to life on this planet. They haven't provided any history of sustainability, and they have global ties to the deathly AIDS epidemic, resurfacing from a shameful closeted life thousands of years after Sodom and Gomorrah debacle, which is remembered only for the death it brought to the plains of those cities. Who is going down now? Is it the cities of the plains of the United States of America? When they run their course this time around in history, will the USA go down in history like Sodom and Gomorrah, uninhabitable and never to rise again? Just like Satan persuaded Eve, "You will not surely die," he is telling America, "You are too big to fail or go to a state of ruins like Sodom and Gomorrah." Could this twenty-first century gay movement (*God turns protection away from America*) be our closet sleepers; our Trojan horse; our home-grown terrorist; our inside-job of a takedown of life as we know it in America; and orchestrated by Satan who is seeking whom he can devour? The issue isn't about the gays anyway; it's about good versus evil. The battle has already been won. God is just testing the ones who purport to follow Him. Who will stand in the gap? Who will seek the old past and stand therein? Who will speak out against evil and proclaim His word?

---

[48] *Id.* at 2619

Inalienable Rights

In the most bizarre and disrespectful way, the right to be treated like the human being God created (God breathed life into man on the sixth day of creation) is being compared to an act and lifestyle God calls an abomination. What is equally puzzling is that the comparison is almost being accepted. Some black people are silent about the comparison, and some support it.

Gays wouldn't even dare try to remotely suggest they have been mistreated or have struggled for rights as a people like the Jews in Hitler's Germany. But they sound their trumpets, wave their flags, and protest on some comparison to black people's mistreatment or struggles for rights as a people in Jim Crow's early America. They know an anti-Semitic protest and backlash would follow any attempt at a platform that compared discrimination of the two groups and rights of a sect of people who deserve equal protection and recognition, too. They picked an easy, less-resistant target—African Americans. Remember the indignity black people suffered just to be treated like humans (inalienable rights) while not breaking any laws of God? Homosexuals who haven't suffered in this manner as a group of people fight for the rights to live in an undignified and unnatural manner—something God didn't create or authorize.

The Holocaust is the Nazi's persecution and genocide of Jews. African Americans suffered forced labor and were murdered in a systemic and a systematic state-sponsored devastation on a people: Tuskegee Syphilis Tests—an unethical experiment in human trials study. Jews' property was taken from them, and they were forced to live in ghettos, as were African Americans in the USA. The word *Holocaust*, the Greek word *holokauston*, means "sacrifice by fire." Many black people suffered burnings and hangings. As they prospered, despite Jim Crow, black-owned businesses were burned. Black owners were forced off or stripped of their property, citizenship, and voting rights, jobs, and dignity as humans; even places of worship were burned. Jewish businesses were burned, and Jews suffered the pillaging and burning of synagogues through "Kristallnacht" ("Night of Broken Glass"). In the Holocaust Jews suffered medical experiments, so did black men, as mentioned earlier, at the Tuskegee Institute when they were given dangerous drugs to treat syphilis. Black people were prohibited from marrying white people, and Jews were prohibited from marrying Germans. Many black slaves suffered branding like cattle. Nazis ordered Jews to wear the yellow Star of David on their clothing so they could be easily recognized and targeted. Need I go on about discrimination, civil rights of a people, and God-given, inalienable rights of people? People who weren't living abominable lifestyles in God's sight yet were targeted by hate? "If you be reproached for the name of Christ, happy are you; for the Spirit of glory and of God rests upon you: on their part He is evil spoken of, but on your part He is glorified" (1 Peter 4:14).

Yes, the Nazi even persecuted gays. If you are a people who don't serve and love God and keep His word, choosing to "defile [yourselves] with mankind," know that it's much better to suffer persecution for doing right than for doing wrong. Your reward is in heaven. "Knowing this, that the law is not made for a righteous man, but for the lawless and disobedient, for the ungodly and for sinners, for unholy and profane, for murderers of fathers and murderers of mothers, for manslayers, for whoremongers, for them that defile themselves with mankind, for menstealers, for liars, for perjured persons, and if there be any other thing that is contrary to sound doctrine; according to the glorious gospel of the blessed God, which was committed to my trust" (1 Timothy 1:9–11).

What the Nazi did to Jews and what the white people did to black people, being their murderers and/or men stealers, didn't make them right; nevertheless, be as it may, the homosexual agenda doesn't compare to denied rights and suffrage of a people to gain some foothold to a legitimate argument for civil rights as self-identified people to practice sodomy. African Americans and Jews, despite their ("hellrific") pasts, marry and procreate; they live productive lifestyles in the sight of God. The gay or homosexual lifestyle gives nothing back in the way of the survival and continuation of a people, a nation. But those in the movement want it all, blessings of marriage, husband and wife holy unions (dignity).

Obergefell v. Hodges Opinion of the Court State Legislation and Judicial Decisions Legalizing Same-Sex Marriage

In Judge Thomas's dissenting statements, he made a strong point that was clearly overlooked by society: freedom *to* versus freedom *from*. Black people (in forced slavery) fought for "freedom from" ("hellrific") discriminating restraints on their natural, God-given liberty and pursuit of happiness. Homosexuals fight for "freedom to" engaged in the liberty of unnatural pursuits. Even before the June 2015 ruling, gays were at liberty to engage in same-sex relationships, cohabitate, and raise their children or adopt children without being harassed. Their fight is to have the "freedom to" have federal benefits extended to them in their unnatural unions.

Thomas wrote, "Petitioners cannot claim, under the most plausible definition of 'liberty,' that they have been imprisoned or physically restrained by the States for participating in same-sex relationships."[49] *Obergefell v. Hodges.* 576 U.S. ____, 135 S. Ct. 2584, 2635 (2015) (Thomas, J., dissenting). They have been at liberty to marry in states that recognize same-sex marriages. They are able to travel the country and make their homes where they like. They have no governmental restrictions to go about their daily lives, unlike black people (early history in this country), whom they use to justify their cause for their civil rights movement. Justice Thomas wrote, "Instead, the States have refused to grant them governmental entitlements. Petitioners claim that as a matter of 'liberty,' they are entitled to access privileges and benefits that exist solely because of the government. They want, for example, to receive the state's imprimatur on their marriages—on state-issued marriage licenses, death certificates, or other official forms. And they want to receive various monetary benefits, including reduced inheritance taxes upon the death of a spouse, compensation if a spouse dies as a result of a work-related injury, loss of consortium damages in tort suits. But receiving governmental recognition and benefits has nothing to do with any understanding of 'liberty' the Framers [of the Constitution] would have recognized." Judge Thomas farther wrote, "To the extent that the Framers would have recognized a natural right to marriage that fell within the broader definition of liberty, it would not have included a right to governmental recognition and benefits ... Petitioners misunderstand the institution of marriage when they say that it would 'mean little' absent government recognition"[50] *Obergefell v. Hodges.* 576 U.S. ____, 135 S. Ct. 2584, 2635- 2636 (2015) (Thomas, J., dissenting).

Thomas wrote, "In a concession to petitioners' misconception of liberty, the majority characterizes petitioners' suit as a quest to 'find ... liberty by marrying someone of the same sex and having their marriages deemed lawful on the same terms and conditions as marriages between persons of the opposite sex.' But liberty isn't lost, nor can it be found in the way petitioners seek. As a philosophical matter, liberty is freedom only *from governmental* actions, not an entitlement *to governmental* benefits..."

Obergefell v. Hodges. 576 U.S. ____, 135 S. Ct. 2584, 2637 (2015) (Thomas, J., dissenting).

---

[49] *Obergefell,* 135 S.Ct.at 2635
[50] 135 S.Ct. at 2636

(P. 13 Cite as: 576 U.S. _____ (2015) Thomas, J., dissenting).[51]

Man has found how to create hybrids in the seedless watermelon and the mule. They are sterile—not an original design in nature. By God's design, all plants and animals are able to produce after their own kind. God didn't create sterile people and then command them to be fruitful and replenish the earth. God finds the deliberate act of homosexuality against nature an abomination.

The parasitic nature of this movement has tried to create and influence public policy and gain acceptance on the plight of the black man's struggles in these United States of America. God created man in His own image; from the first man and his wife, Eve, all nations through procreation populated the earth (fruitful and multiply). God tells man to be holy as He is holy; an abominable lifestyle (homosexuality) doesn't fit the character of God in his definition of "holy." And the bed is undefiled in marriage; it is designed for a man and his wife.

It is a natural right of man to be treated like a human being. This is a right from God, who made man—and made him upright. In contrast, one's access to legal rights are granted by the society and prevailing thoughts of the culture; for example, the black man's rights to be treated with dignity is from God, yet the prevailing attitude of slave owners (kidnappers of men) didn't honor God. Legal rights granted by the culture in this country (USA) allowed permission to treat the black man (slave) poorly ("hellrific"). The gay movement uses civil rights interchangeably with legal rights and statutory rights for cultural and political victory. They demand that Congress, the legislature, Supreme Courts, and states' rules and ordinances grant them legal rights or civil rights to express their freedom in practicing homosexuality in a county founded on religious principles and values; but this is a lifestyle God has condemned as abominable in His sight.

Gays have always had their civil rights. They haven't been treated less than human though their sexual activities aren't the norm in society. There are no signs for gay waiting rooms, gay water fountains, and gay entrance to establishments only through the back door. They aren't denied voting rights or the right to move into certain neighborhoods.

No one in the history of this country has had to fight for civil rights in mainstream America (excluding Native Indians, who rejected mainstream America) other than the black man and women, who demonstrated that they shouldn't be deemed as property. They own property and are granted

---

[51] *Id.* at 2637

Clarence Thomas, "Free to vs. free from," p. 13, cite as: 576 U.S.__(2015).

the same privileges as the white male in voting and wages for equal labor or equal pay and representation on a political front in this country.

Abominable acts aren't what Martin Luther King Jr. and freedom marchers fought, died, and marched for with their Bibles in hands. The civil rights movement participants—black people, white people, and Jews—fought and died to raise the God-fearing conscience of America on the black man's inalienable rights to be treated like a human being and granted equal privileges and access to liberties and the pursuit of happiness enjoyed by the white population and all American citizens.

We live in a democracy and in a country where the rights of everyone are granted; even homegrown terrorists are read their Miranda rights. What is distinct about homosexuals is the lewd act of sodomy. There is no trace of a gene factor in comparison to heredity and simple Mendelian genetics.

Going back to "the list," if each sinner on "the list" fought as hard as do the homosexuals for their rights to be recognized as a group because they also have one, two, or all of either genes (fornicator, adultery, thief, liar, and so forth), then they shouldn't be morally responsible for their behavior either. And they should be accepted in a society built on morals and Christian values despite their actions. Why does this society still punish and send people from "the list" to jail? The liars (perjury) and the thief (burglary, robbery, and larceny) go to jail. The courts award the non cheating party in a divorce more property or settlement. In North Carolina, an innocent spouse can sue a third party who has broken up the marriage.

The Pleasure of Sin

Heterosexuals (those who aren't of the homosexual persuasion) can make the assumption or come to the conclusion that one who engages in such acts finds them pleasurable; therefore, the Bible warns of the pleasures of sin.

> And have no fellowship with the unfruitful works of darkness, but rather reprove them. For it is a shame even to speak of those things which are done of them in secret. (Ephesians 5:11–12)

One can conclude only that it must be a very strong pleasure that can lure one to an area designated for the expulsion of waste, which is unbeneficial and potentially toxic to the human body, to seek pleasure. Well over twenty years ago, there were rumors alleging practices of gerbil shooting: inserting live gerbils up the rectum for sexual stimulation. There must be an overwhelming pleasure that causes one to insert a live eel or rodent into the rectum to obtain some level of pleasurable sensation; this means using the body (God created) in a manner for which it wasn't designed. This is an example of how Satan takes you places you didn't plan to go and causes you to stay longer than you wanted or planned to stay. Once a physician has to remove a deceased rodent out of your rectum or a surgeon has to remove an eel, which has busted through your body cavity, to save your life, during those critical moments one has to be thinking, *How did I get here? I've gone too far.* When you give your mind over to Satan, he is in control. You are his servant. When you give your mind over to God, God is in control, and you are His servant. You have fellowship with Him by having the mind of Christ. God loves man and will not hurt him. Satan wants to destroy man just to get back at God.

While Satan (the Father of Lies) holds you captive, he deceives you into thinking you are calling the shots, when in actuality he is at the wheel and driving you further and further away from God (your Creator). He is taking you to distant places, where he hopes you become lost and disoriented there so you can't find your way out or back. Satan comes to steal, kill, and destroy. Satan's desire is for death to overtake you before you realize what is happening to you. Jesus says that if you die in your sins, where He [Jesus] is, you cannot come (John 8:21). Man must understand that the wages of sin is death, not eternal life. If he dies in his sins, he will belong to Satan forever, not God. Satan knows he is going to the lake of fire. He knows that it hurts God when he steals one of His creatures (man or woman) from Him. You are just a little pawn Satan uses to get back at God. Satan is very happy when someone flaunts and parades his or her gay lifestyle because he knows he has that person and has God angry. "God is angry with the wicked every day."

Freedom

When we think about freedom, all kinds of scenarios pop into our heads—mostly free will. Then there are constitutional liberties and civil rights. We even think of political freedom, freedom of speech and of the press, and the freedom of assembly and personal wealth in economic freedom. The list goes on in man's philosophy of what his idea is of expressed free will.

The freedom and rights people of America enjoy were fought for and claimed in their victories over oppressors. When the ideas of rights are examined, everyone has his or her idea of what is right; being persuaded by how what is desired will affect him or her personally. So rights can be for the greater good or for who is calling the shots. Let's look at the right to life, for example; is it the expectant mother's freedom to do what she will with her own body or is it the unborn child's freedom or rights to life? Or even more so, is it the rights of political and judicial outsiders to force or intervene and make the decision concerning her (the mother's) body and that of the unborn child? There are rights to equal treatment of the law for minorities and women. There are natural rights from God, called "moral rights" or "inalienable rights." African Americans fought for these basic rights. The parasitic actions of gays don't measure up to the civil rights Martin Luther

King Jr. and civil rights marchers, leaders, and activists fought and died for. In the shameful history of the United States, there were legal rights in societal laws, statutes, and customs in opposition to God's law of love for one's fellowman when it came to the right to vote (be counted), citizenship, and rights as human beings.

Let's stop here for a moment and reflect on the fact that the whole duty of man is to fear God and keep His commandments (Ecclesiastes 12:13).The first commandment is to love the Lord your God with all your heart, soul, and mind; and the second is like unto it—love your neighbor as yourself. Healing starts when the oppressor seeks and asks for forgiveness (makes amends) and when the oppressed forgives. This step can happen only when God's commands are accepted as the common denominator of the two parties or groups.

We can research the etymology of the word *right*. We can read the history of the word *right*. We can study the philosophy of the word *right*. But the fact remains that if our definition doesn't reflect God's definition of right, we are still tripping over and stumbling over ourselves to our own demise. It isn't in man to direct his steps (Jeremiah 10:23). Civil and political rights protect our freedom from government repression, unwarranted infringement, and an organization's discrimination. Individuals have the right to freedom of speech or expression, freedom of press, freedom to assemble, freedom of religion and self-defense, and freedom to petition and vote—to name a few. These are human rights based on citizenship and fairness.

In the 17th century, English common law judge Sir Edward Coke revived the idea of rights based on citizenship by arguing that Englishmen had historically enjoyed such rights. The English Bill of Rights was adopted in 1689. The Virginia Declaration of Rights, by George Mason and James Madison, was adopted in 1776. The Virginia declaration is the direct ancestor and model for the US Bill of Rights (1789) ... In the 1860s, Americans adapted this usage to newly freed black people. Congress enacted civil rights acts in 1866, 1871, 1875, 1957, 1960, 1954, and 1991 ... T.H. Marshall notes that civil rights were among the first to be recognized and codified, followed later by political rights and still later by social rights ... Civil Rights movements began as early as 1848 in the USA with such documents as the Declaration of Sentiment. Consciously modeled after the Declaration of Independence, the Declaration of

Rights and Sentiments became the founding document of the American women's movement, and it was adopted at the Seneca Falls Convention, July 19 and 20, 1848.[52]

We can look into individual rights versus group rights (rights in politics, civil rights, and those warranting equal protection under the law), granted, they all have their place in society and foster and propel our use of the moral compass to make justice, rights, and fairness work for the greater good of society. But remember, real freedom and liberty have already been won for you, and you only need to accept it. Live as a freeman—free from sin, death, and the york of bondage. Live and walk in your liberty in Christ (Galatians 5:1).

Escape to Freedom

If we felt we were held against our will, the only thing we could think about is an avenue of escape. When we hear of individuals who have been held against their wills for decades, we often say, "If that had been me, I would have escaped."

The vast majority of us are unaware that we are held captive; therefore, we aren't even looking for an avenue of escape. Everyone since the fall of Adam and Eve has been held captive and is in need of an escape. "Wherefore, as by one man sin entered into the world, and death by sin; and so death passed upon all men, for that all have sinned" (Romans 5:12). We have become so acclimated to sin in our lives and in society that the shackles of darkness and the captivity of Satan are deceptive and unrecognizable; we know not what to look for. John talks about knowing the truth and says the truth will set you free. If you commit sin, you are the servant of sin. Jesus came to set you free from sin. In the book of Romans, Paul explained that whomever you obey is whom you serve, whether it is sin to death or of obedience to righteousness (John 8:30–36; Roman 6:16–17). When you allow Jesus to rule your life, you become His servant, and that is unto righteousness and eternal life.

When we reach the age of accountability, knowing right from wrong, we are able to personally and individually make preparations for our souls' eternal home. Remember when God and Jesus had the conversation about

---

[52] Wikipedia, s.v. "Civil and Political Rights," accessed April 30, 2013, http://en.wikipedia.org/wiki/Civil_and_political_rights. (last edited 2 December 2019, at 06:31)

Adam and Eve. "They have become as one of Us knowing good from evil." When we can rationalize and choose between the right way and the wrong way, as spelled out in the will of God (His holy word; the Bible), we are accountable human being in the sight of God. When we choose wrong over right, we have sinned (Romans 3:10–12). Whosoever knows to do good and does it not, that is sin. Your choice to sin holds you "captive" and brings you death, both physically and spiritually. And this is why you need to know you are *not* free, even with your earthly civil liberties and ability to practice your religious freedom contrary to the will of God. Self-will religions make you disobedient to God. There are a lot of tangible freedoms and rights we cry out for and use on our worldly lust and pride of life that is temporal, while we are silently and blindly being led in shackles to the guillotine of hell as servants of sin and Satan.

God has provided us a way to escape this deceptive kidnapper of souls. Jesus tells us He is the way, the truth, and the life; no man comes to the Father but by Him (John 14:6). Are we listening to Jesus? He is giving us a way out. Are we too busy fighting to have our way at all costs? We are fighting the wrong battle. Gays are trying to win a fight that is over. The battle has already been won, when Jesus said, "Grave, where is your stain, and death, where is your victory?"

Save yourselves from this untoward generation. Trying to coattail on African Americans' real struggles for civil rights or freedoms, which were their inalienable rights, is insulting when homosexuals' civil rights agenda is fighting to redefine the institution of marriage that God created. This is the relationship between male and female that God created; and also wanting to steal children (through adoption). God's gift to the union and His inheritance (Psalm 127:3) are their *real* and only platform for civil rights and freedom. Free yourself from the shackles of sin and obey God. When God sets you (heterosexual and homosexual) free, you are free indeed. God doesn't discriminate.

As heaven and its hosts are witnesses, God has set before you this day life and death, blessing and cursing: therefore you have the opportunity and freedom to choose life. Honestly, how much more freedom can one ask for than for life's blessings from God and a life eternally with God, the master of the universe? See Deuteronomy 30:19–20. Your *freedom* is in Christ Jesus, and you have the right to enteral life in Christ Jesus through your obedience to the gospel.

Now, these are your rights and freedom none discriminatorily granted to you by God.

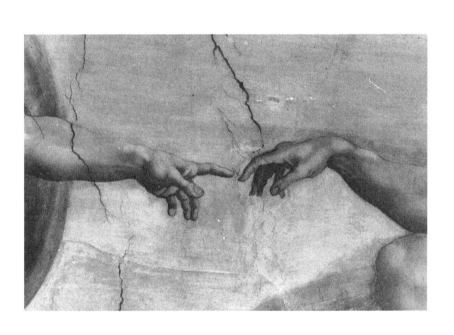

Chapter 3
Only One Relationship Is Everlasting

THERE WILL BE many relationships we form while on earth, be it parent, teacher, boss, sibling, friend, or spouse—even enemy. Our main focus should be the one relationship that extends beyond the physical grave: your spouse, significant other, or whoever cannot go beyond the grave with you.

When your soul and eternal salvation are at stake, it's not the time to go all Al Green. The musical artist song, "If Loving You Is Wrong, I Don't Want To Be Right.[53]" To be right and acceptable in the sight of God ("which is your reasonable service," Romans 12:1–2), there are some relationships we will have to give up or end. It isn't extreme, unreasonable, or insensitive to be asked to give up a worldly and temporal pleasure in exchange for eternal pleasures in heaven. The scriptures declare that if your eye offends you, you should pluck it out and be ready to enter heaven blind (lame) than to have the whole body enter hell. "And if thy right eye offends thee, pluck it out, and cast it from thee: for it is profitable for thee that one of thy members should perish and not that thy whole body should be cast into hell" (Matthew 5:29; 18:9; Mark 9:47). These scriptures teach us that denying licentious passions and mortifying our members (of the body) in self-denial are worth it because these decisions will lead to eternal life. Eternal life is traded for this temporal stay on earth—only to face eternity in hell and a life without God. This is

---

[53] Stax Records "If Loving You Is Wrong, I Don't Want To Be Right," songwriters Homer Banks, Carl Hampton, and Raymond Jackson (1960s)

a life without a proper relationship, which was from the beginning in the creation before Adam sinned.

It's time to modify our minds and thought patterns to achieve the only worthwhile goals: a home in heaven and a restored relationship with God, the Father, through Jesus Christ, His Son. This is the relationship we had with God before Adam sinned. This relationship is restored when we meet Christ in obedience through the watery grave of baptism, rising to walk in newness of life. "If you then be risen with Christ, seek those things which are above, where Christ sits on the right hand of God" (v. 1). This occurs when you take your mind off the pursuit of worldly relationships, unauthorized by the holy scripture, and place yourself in a position to "set your affections on things above; not on things on the earth" (v. 2). This is a call for action on man's part. "Mortify therefore your members which are upon the earth; fornication, uncleanness, inordinate affection [unnatural desire of homosexuality and bestiality], evil concupiscence, and covetousness, which is idolatry; For which things' sake the wrath of God comes on the children of disobedience" (vv. 5–6). When you do make a change, you can also say, "In the which you also walked some time, when you lived in them" (v. 7). See Colossians 3:1–8.

God-Man Relationship

"While He yet talked to the people, behold, His mother and His brethren stood outside, desiring to speak with Him. Then one said to Him, Behold, your mother and your brethren stand outside desiring to speak with you. But He answered and said to him that told Him, Who is My mother? And who are My brethren? And He stretched forth His hand toward his disciples, and said, Behold My mother and My brethren! *For whosoever shall do the will of My Father which is in heaven, the same is My brother, and sister, and mother*" (Matthew 12:46–50; Mark 3:35, emphasis added).

What is man that God is mindful of him? "And God saw everything that He had made, and, behold, it was very good. God said of each of his creation: sun, moon, stars, fowls of the air, fish of the sea, cattle, trees, (etc.) that it was good. And God said, Let Us make man in Our image, after Our likeness ... So God created man in His own image, in the image of God created He him; male and female created He them," (Genesis 1:27). It's not until God created man that one reads, "God saw everything that He had made and behold it was *very* good" (Genesis 1:31, emphasis added). Now that heaven and earth were built and the entire host, its inhabitants, were in place, the evening and the morning were the sixth day; it was on the seventh day when God ended His work or rested. He built it. See Genesis 2:2. Now, what's our complaint?

God spoke His creation into existence, but when it came to man, He applied a hands-on approach. "And the Lord God formed man of the dust of the ground, and breathed into his nostrils the breath of life [some of Him]; and man became a living soul" (Genesis 2:7).

Man was so important to God that He provided a home for him. "And the Lord God planted a garden eastward in Eden; and there He put the man whom He had formed" (Genesis 2:8). He provided food for him to eat. "And out of the ground made the Lord God to grow every tree that is pleasant to the sight, and good for food" (Genesis 2:9). God even supplied man with wealth: gold, bdellium, and onyx stone (Genesis 2:11–12). And God didn't stop there. He gave man a J-O-B. "And God took the man and put him into the Garden of Eden to dress it and to keep it" (Genesis 2:15). Again, I ask, What is our complaint?

Unbeknownst to man at creation, God had plans for man to be with Him in heaven, leaving his earth-bound, terrestrial dwelling place and transforming into a celestial dwelling place. "Going away to prepare a place for you that where I'm am you will be also." Man ultimately will receive a robe and crown. We will talk about that part later. Let's work on our relationship, which comes with benefits that were even before the foundation of the world.

Marrying and Giving In Marriage

When was it that homosexuals and heterosexuals weren't equal? All have sinned and come short of the glory of God, and all have to do the same thing to be restored to the grace of God. All have the same enemies: Satan, death, and hell. All have the same friends: Christ, everlasting life, and home in heaven. Any form of being unequal comes about by one's own volition when he or she chooses to live beneath the station in life to which he or she is called—called to do good works.

President Obama's reaction to the justices' ruling on same-sex marriage was this: "And then sometimes, there are days like this when that slow, steady effort is rewarded with justice that arrives like a thunderbolt."[54] The article

---

[54] Greg Hernandez, "Obama's Reaction to Supreme Court' Ruling on Gay Marriage," https://www.gaystarnews.com/article/obama-us-supreme-courts-gay-marriage-ruling-real-change-possible260615/

and video are found under the Associated Press by Jim Kuhnhenn and Lisa Lerer[55] and *The Hill* by Ben Kamisar [56]

"America needed this kind of thunderbolt raining down on them from the hands of the Supreme Court judges just as much as Sodom and Gomorrah felt they needed fire raining down on them from the hands of God. Not!

Evolving Publicly

In his 2006 book, *The Audacity of Hope*, Obama said that his own faith was a reason to oppose same-sex marriage, though he also wondered whether "in years hence I may be seen as someone who was on the wrong side of history."[57] The Bible makes it clear in examples that some people ended up on the wrong side of history, and the former president can safely take his cue. Any time one is in opposition to God, he or she is on the wrong side of history. Pharaoh opposed God and His servant, Moses, a messenger or preacher for God's word. He and his army drowned in the Red Sea. Pharaoh ended up on the wrong side of history. Dathan instigated a rebellion against Moses, a man of God, in leading others to make a god, a golden calf, to worship. The people who followed him chose not to obey God; they were swallowed up by the ground and stood on the wrong side of history. See Exodus 32:26; Numbers 16:32. "And as it was in the days of Noah, so shall it be also in the days of the Son of Man. They did eat, they drank, they married wives, they were given in marriage, until the day that Noah entered into the ark, and the flood came, and destroyed them all. Likewise also as it was in the days of Lot; they did eat, they drank, they bought, they sold, they planted, and they built. But the same day that Lot went out of Sodom it rained fire and brimstone from heaven, and destroyed them all" (Luke 17:26–29). Certainly, one can see that the homosexuals (effeminates) and those who tolerated their behavior

---

[55] Jim Kuhnhenn and Lisa Lerer, https://www.ksl.com/article/35257808/for-obama-and-clinton-twisty-paths-to-yes-on-gay-marriage (modified Dec. 22, 2019); https://oklahoman.com/article/feed/856956/for-obama-and-clinton-twisty-paths-to-yes-on-gay-marriage

[56] Ben Kamisar, "Scalia: Gay Marriage Decision Shows Court Is America's 'Ruler,'" *The Hill*, June 26, 2015, https://thehill.com/blogs/blog-briefing-room/news/246249-scalia-gay-marriage-decision-shows-americas-ruler-is-supreme

[57] Barack Obama, *The Audacity of Hope: Thoughts on Reclaiming the American Dream. Crown Publisher: New York* (2006)

were on the wrong side of history then and still are. People who don't obey God, homosexuals and heterosexuals alike as in the days of Lot (Sodom and Gomorrah) and Noah (flood), ended up on the wrong side of history; they were lost forever. Things will be the same when the Lord (Christ) returns. Will you be on the wrong side of history, disobedient to the will of God? See Matthew 24:36–39.

National Gay Human Rights Group

Fred Sainz of the Human Rights Campaign, National Gay Rights Group, said Obama now stands as one of the great champions of gay rights.[58] It would be nothing better, almost beyond or at least on the same footing as the actions of the Supreme Court, for the LGBT community to equate the first black president as a champion of gay rights, somehow superseding and sweeter than their victory in the Supreme Court on Friday, June 26, 2015. Hence, it would be connecting African America with something so disturbingly non-Christian and abominable in the sight of God. Once again, Satan is like a roaring lion, seeking whom he can destroy. The assassin (who is intentionally nameless in this book) in the church massacre on June 17, 2015, in Charleston, South Carolina, was bent on bringing evil and pain. He brought an end to this display of the evil symbol of hatred in that state, other states, retailers, and manufacturers of that confederate flag. In like manner, the decision of the Supreme Court to usurp authority over the people of these United States ("we the people, for the people, by the people") will bring some changes to an unelected group, whose job is to legislate the law and not create it. God will hear the cries of His people—He always does.

Ironically, there were Africans who came to America who were royalty. Their tribal enemies sold them to the slave trade bound for America, and of that bloodline one made it to the capitol of America and became America's royalty—leader of the free world. It was a sight to behold; nations around the world celebrated with the USA when Obama was elected president of the USA. In the distant future, many won't care to talk about his extraordinary leadership or great political victories or accomplishments, but they will remember that while in office he was an advocate of gay rights and anal sex—a lifestyle God calls abominable in His sight. Fred Sainz is happy to make such

---

[58] https://www.lgbtqnation.com/2015/06/for-obama-and-clinton-its-been-a-long-journey-to-yes-on-marriage-equality/ Original article by Jim Kuhnhenn and Lisa Lerer, Associate Press June 27, 2015.

a proclamation (statement) and to mar Obama's presidency. Obama is the first and only president to go down in history credited with advancing the cause of homosexuality in a Christian nation. It's a much sweeter victory (for one who shakes his fist in the face of God) than the actual ruling from the Supreme Courts for gays in America. This isn't something Martin Luther King or Nelson Mandela would have wanted to face the almighty God with on their record on this side of history.

Supreme Court's Justice Chastens Judges

Justice Antonin Scalia chastened the Supreme Court's justices over the landmark decision legalizing same-sex marriage. Scalia argued in his opinion that the court was increasingly creating policy rather than serving as a neutral arbiter. Scalia wrote, "Today's decree says that my Ruler, and the Ruler of 320 million Americans coast-to-coast, is a majority of the nine lawyers on the Supreme Court … This practice of constitutional revision by an unelected committee of nine, always accompanied (as it is today) by extravagant praise of liberty, robs the People of the most important liberty they asserted in the Declaration of Independence and won in the Revolution of 1776: the freedom to govern themselves."[59] (Scalia, Antonin.Dissenting opinion. *James Obergefell v. Richard Hodges*. 576 U.S. ____, 135 S. Ct. 2584, 192 L. Ed. 2d 609 (2015). Dissenting judges expressed that the actions of this court were a threat to American democracy. He and other dissenters noted that the issue should have been left to the states and not to the Supreme Court. "The actions of the courts invalidate the marriage laws of more than half the States and ordered the transformation of a social institution that has formed the basis of human society for millennia."[60] (Roberts, John. Dissenting opinion. *James Obergefell v. Richard Hodges*. 576 U.S. ____, 135 S. Ct. 2584, 192 L. Ed. 2d 609 (2015). Justice Roberts accused Justice Kennedy and the four other justices who ruled in favor of same-sex marriage of engaging in policymaking free of a constructional foundation. Celebrate the decision if you favor it, he said in the concluding lines of the dissent (p. 68). "But do not celebrate the Constitution. It had nothing to do with it." Chief Justice John Roberts wrote in his dissenting statement, "Celebrate the achievement of a desired goal. Celebrate the opportunity for a new expression of commitment to a partner, Celebrate the availability of new benefits, but do not celebrate

---

[59] Obergefell v. Hodges, 576 U.S. ___, 135 S. Ct. 2584, 2627 (2015).

[60] *Id.*, at 2612

the Constitution. It had nothing to do with it."[61] (Roberts, John. Dissenting opinion. *James Obergefell v. Richard Hodges.* 576 U.S. ____, 135 S. Ct. 2584, 192 L. Ed. 2d 609 (2015) www.supremecourt.gov/opinions/bounvolues.aspx. The dissenting judges on the court which were made up of Harvard and Yale graduates, who mostly grew up on the coast; none were evangelical Christians or Protestants, religions that make up a significant sum of the population in America. Yet a decision to allow same-sex marriage to become law by a group of nine justices that doesn't represent the populous or cross section in its opinion on this issue violates something more fundamental than "no taxation without representation." The fact is that American opinion wasn't properly represented in the social transformation that will affect our lives in this country. Yes, for now, the decision seems like a victory, but the question that still lingers is, Was it constitutional? The next question is, How long do you think God will put up with it? Historians, check to see how long Sodom and Gomorrah existed before God let go of them.

Religious Affiliation of the Signers of the Declaration of Independence[61]		
Religious Affiliation	# of Signers	% of Signers
Episcopalian or Anglican	32	57.1%
Congregationalist	13	23.2%
Presbyterian	12	21.4%
Quaker	2	3.6%
Unitarian or Universalist	2	3.6%
Catholic	1	1.8%
Total	56	100%

As showed in the table above, mostly to a great degree, the signers were Protestant in their religious beliefs. Over 90 percent of these men were married and fathered children. They recognized God as the higher source of power and rule. They were inspired by the word of God, which was echoed in

---

[61] *Id.,* at 2626
Id. at Wheeler, "Chief Justice Decries Decision."
[62] B. J. Lossing, *Signers of the Declaration of Independence* (New York: George F. Cooledge & Brother, 1848), reprinted in Benson J. Lossing, *Lives of the Signers of the Declaration of Independence* (Aledo, TX: WallBuilder Press,1995), 7–12, http://www.adherents.com/gov/Founding_Fathers_Religion.html. Last modified 7 December 2005.

the wording of the document that would govern a people and nation under God (in whom we trust), understanding that this new nation exists because of the providence of God.

Judges Don't Cause My People to Sin

Supreme Court justices Roberts, Alito, Scalia, and Thomas may be the four Justices who go on record as the USA's saving grace—the right side of history. Chief Justice Roberts in his dissent said that "Unfortunately, people of faith can take no comfort in the treatment they receive from the majority today."[63] *Obergefell v. Hodges*. 576 U.S. at ____, 135 S. Ct. 2584, 2626 (2015) (Roberts, J., dissenting). In their dissent, they took the blood of the people off their hands, but will it be enough to stay the hands of God? Surely the number isn't five or ten that God promised Abraham He would consider sparing the city. What is to become of America, who has chosen to go down (return to) this dark path? Consider what Justices Alito, Scalia and Thomas said about the concept of liberty in the Constitution: "Today's decision casts that truth aside. In its haste to reach a desired result, the majority misapplies a clause focus on 'due process' to afford substantive rights, disregards the most plausible understanding of the 'liberty' protected by that clause, and distorts the principles on which this Nation was founded. Its decision will have inestimable consequences for our Constitution and our society."[64] *Obergefell v. Hodges*. 576 U.S. at ____, 135 S. Ct. 2584, 2626 (2015) (Alito, J., dissenting).

DISSENT BY: Roberts; Scalia; Thomas; Alito[65]

Chief Justice Roberts, with whom Justice Scalia and Justice Thomas join, dissenting.
Petitioners make strong arguments rooted in social policy and considerations of fairness. They contend that same-sex couples should be allowed to affirm their love and commitment through marriage, just like opposite-sex couples. That position has undeniable appeal; over the past six years, voters and legislators in eleven States and

---

[63] *Obergefell* 135 S. Ct. at 2626.
[64] *Obergefell* 135 S. Ct. at 2640.
[65] *Obergefell v. Hodges*, 135 S. Ct. 2584, 2611 (2015).

the District of Columbia have revised their laws to allow marriage between two people of the same sex.

But this Court is not a legislature. Whether same-sex marriage is a good idea should be of no concern to us. Under the Constitution, judges have power to say what the law is, not what it should be. The people who ratified the Constitution authorized courts to exercise "neither force nor will but merely judgment." The Federalist No. 78, p. 465 (C. Rossiter ed. 1961) (A. Hamilton) (capitalization altered).

Although the policy arguments for extending marriage to same-sex couples may be compelling, the legal arguments for requiring such an extension are not. The fundamental right to marry does not include a right to make a State change its definition of marriage. And a State's decision to maintain the meaning of marriage that has persisted in every culture throughout human history can hardly be called irrational. In short, our Constitution does not enact any one theory of marriage. The people of a State are free to expand marriage to include same-sex couples, or to retain the historic definition.

Today, however, the Court takes the extraordinary step of ordering every State to license and recognize same-sex marriage. Many people will rejoice at this decision, and I begrudge none their celebration. But for those who believe in a government of laws, not of men, the majority's approach is deeply disheartening. Supporters of same-sex marriage have achieved considerable success persuading their fellow citizens--through the democratic process--to adopt their view. That ends today. Five lawyers have closed the debate and enacted their own vision of marriage as a matter of constitutional law. Stealing this issue from the people will for many cast a cloud over same-sex marriage, making a dramatic social change that much more difficult to accept.

The majority's decision is an act of will, not legal judgment. The right it announces has no basis in the Constitution or this Court's precedent. The majority expressly disclaims judicial "caution" and omits even a pretense of humility, openly relying on its desire to remake society according to its own "new insight" into the "nature of injustice." *Ante*, at ___, ___, 192 L. Ed. 2d, at 624, 631.

As a result, the Court invalidates the marriage laws of more than half the States and orders the transformation of a social institution that has formed the basis of human society for millennia, for the Kalahari Bushmen and the Han Chinese, the Carthaginians and the Aztecs. Just who do we think we are?

The gays picked their targets and masterfully reeled in their prey. So they believe. Mr. Obama as well as anyone else who speaks of his or her faith (presumably the Christian faith) is tested by the Almighty. Homosexuality and bestiality stand clearly on the minds of those that hate God and hate what is right in the sight of God; the heart of man is set in him to do evil continually. It's God who tests the ones who profess Him; those who profess to believe are the ones whom God tests. It's not enough to "believe" in God; Satan does, too. We are challenged to "obey" God. If you believe Him, why not obey Him?

It's astonishing how the LGBT community latched on to the landmark cases related to the black man's civil rights movement and to the first black president of the United States to advance their cause. Obama wasn't fully oriented in the Jim Crow culture, born and reared in the Indonesia culture; and understandably, his scars may not run as deep. No African American born person, that I can recall ever, raised his or her voice at any time within the two and a half years I followed the nightly news, Internet articles, and talk shows concerning gay marriage and the DOMA-*Defense of Marriage Act*; even though, the homosexuals tried to use their same-sex marriage case, citing *Loving v. Virginia*, which struck down racial restrictions on marriage, to compare discrimination of black people with those of gays and lesbians when it came to marriage rights for same-sex couples.

Talk show host Piers Morgan and other networks show hosts offensively and inaccurately made comparisons to the gay and black struggles or plights here in America (N-word and F-word). The events in Ferguson, Missouri; Charleston, South Carolina; and Boston will show, their plights aren't, have never been, and will never be the same. God hasn't called an ethnicity (black man) an abomination. As noted in chapter two, if the LGBT community had cracked one side of their mouths to compare their plight with Jews and even the way the Germans or Nazis treated homosexuals in connection to any form of discrimination and tried to associate that with Jews' discrimination or the Holocaust, a backlash would have resounded from earth to the heavens. African Americans never opened their mouths in protest to such insults in the media's comparisons of their suffering (civil right struggles) when discussing the N-word and F-word and, how the LGBT community used them and their landmark cases on discrimination and systemic injustices to advance the gay agenda.

Justice Samuel Alito, in his dissent, saw the majority opinion as a threat to religious views of this country or greater society. "It will be used to vilify Americans who are unwilling to assent to the new orthodoxy," Justice Alito wrote. "In the course of its opinion, the majority compares traditional marriage laws to laws that denied equal treatment for African-Americans and women. The implications of this analogy will be exploited by those who are determined to stamp out every vestige of dissent."[66] *Obergefell v. Hodges.* 576 U.S., at ____, 135 S. Ct. 2584, 2642 (2015) (Alito, J., dissenting).

In his dissent, Justice Scalia took a similar view, saying that the majority's assertiveness represented a "threat to American democracy."[67] *James Obergefell v. Richard Hodges.* 576 U.S. ____, 135 S. Ct. 2584, 2626 (2015) (Scalia, J., dissenting).

Trying to justify that interracial marriage discrimination is the same as homosexual (same-sex) marriage discrimination is disingenuous. Interracial marriage produces offspring (fruit of the womb), isn't an abomination, and isn't in violation of the laws of nature. Judge Roberts compared the same-sex marriage case to *Loving v. Virginia*, which struck down racial restrictions on marriage. The two, he said, are different because the decision didn't aim to change the core definition of marriage—union between a male and female. "Removing the racial barriers to marriage therefore did not change what a marriage was any more than integrating schools changed what a school was."[68] *James Obergefell v. Richard Hodges.* 576 U.S. at ____, 135 S. Ct. 2584, 2619 (2015) (Thomas, J., dissenting).

The LGBT community is moving like kudzu across the plains of America, destroying and snuffing out the light of whatever is holy, righteous, and good in God's sight. Their goal is to change marriage (the bedrock of society), an institution God built. There in the home God placed the father (male), mother (female), and the fruit of the womb (children) His inheritance in the union. The home and family are so precious to God that He compares them to His church, the saving institute He places man in, in preparation to be presented to God. The church (she) is the bride of Christ (He) and produces children (Christians). This process to align man back to God as in the beginning before Adam sinned is found in the instructions of the Holy

---

[66] Id., 135 S. Ct. at 2642
[67] Obergefell, 135 S. Ct. at 2626
[68] Obergefell, 135 S. Ct. at 2619

Bible. The gays are attacking the church, Christians, and seek to rewrite or reinterpret scriptures to advance their cause. It is Satan (a fallen angel) who got kicked out of heaven and is doing this (good vs. evil), and the gays are his pawns—being deceived into believing they are in control and winning some kind of victories over the church and this country's Christian values. Satan is trying to claim as many souls as he can because even he knows the game is already won (outcome set); all that isn't of God will come to naught.

The thing is, all God doesn't approve will come to naught. There are no real victories outside of "in Christ" anyways. But who will the gay rights movement bring down with them? Is it the tolerant? Who in Sodom and Gomorrah just tolerated the homosexuals and didn't speak out because of fear of what others my think or feel about them not being on the right side of history? What did they think or feel when fire and brimstone came down from heaven? Were they not caught up in the fire and brimstones? They went down, too. The Bible says only Lot's family made it out, so some people (tolerant souls) went down. When one stands up for righteousness, he or she is bound to create an enemy or two in this life.

Dignity

There is no dignity in anal sex, in the area where feces and harmful bacteria leave the body. Intellectualize it, legislate it, proposition it, get upset about it, bully retail shop owners over it, scream discrimination and bigots because of it, and do whatever else you don't like about it; dogs don't even have anal sex. To make that statement isn't mean; it's just not so. Lower animals don't have anal sex. They don't. They have little puppies, kittens, or whatever their mommies and daddies are. They aren't as intelligent as man, but they still aren't confused about following the laws of nature. But to be fair, they don't have the intellect to make a choice, and that is why man is answerable to God and they are not. God stamps "abomination" across your forehead, and there it will stay. Only Jesus can take it off, not the courts.

Homosexuals feel that bans on gay marriages demean their dignity. Those who were "in the closet" having anal sex believe someone can demean them. And when they finish complaining about how mean you are, they ask to adopt your children. God puts the "holy" in matrimony. God adds the children to this union. It is God who gives dignity; it cannot be legislated. "Lo children are a heritage of the Lord: and the fruit of the womb is His reward. As arrows are in the hand of a mighty man; so are children of thy youth. Happy is the man that has his quiver full of them: they shall not be ashamed, but they shall speak with the enemies in the gate" (Psalm 127:3–5). God gives the marriage union its dignity and children its nobility. Jesus suffered the greatest indignity, the cruel death on the cross (crucifixion), and arose victorious on the other side of death. Jesus suffered indignity for our sins, redeeming us from the curse of the Jewish Law. "Cursed is every one that hangs on a tree" (Galatians 3:13).

Gays have successfully convinced the Supreme Court that they love the idea of marriage and want to be part of the marriage institution—not without federal benefits, of course. The court legislates an age-old institution and attempts to write gay marriage into it without the blessing of the Creator of *said* institution. Well, enough said. Wrap your minds around that and see where you might be standing when it's time for God to call and you to answer. To the lesbian—come, where is your husband? To the homosexual—come, where is your wife?

Go, Call Your Husband

Don't let the gays be found like the woman at Jacob's Well. Jesus asked about her husband (significant other, life partner). "Jesus said to her, go, call your husband, and come here. The woman answered and said, I have no husband. Jesus said to her, You have well said, I have no husband: For you have had five husbands; and he whom you now have is not your husband: in that said you truly" (John 4:16–18).

Gays believe they have won some victory. Jesus will ask, "Go call your husband." Two men can't come to Jesus and say, "The other man who is with me is my husband." Likewise, two women can't come and certainly call the other woman a husband or wife. God is not the author of confusion. Gays will get the same judgment (from God this time). "The one you are with isn't yours." It wasn't from the beginning and never will be that way.

Love

To love someone, you have to know that individual and seek to please and have a desire to please him or her. To truly love someone, you have to show that individual that you love not in words only but in actions and deeds. God loved us first. "For God so loved the world that he gave his *only* begotten Son" (John 3:16, emphasis added). Our love is manifested only in our obedience.

Jesus learned obedience through the things He suffered. He loved the Father, and the Father loved Him.

When we talk about or think of relationships, the first thing that comes to mind is usually the word *love*. I read an old article *written several years ago*, where author Jeff Chu, along with the cover of his book, was featured.[69] Dan Savage reviewed the article titled "Does Jesus Really Love Me?" Savage's comments focused on Mr. Chu's expressed feelings that churches don't offer gays [*gay Christians*] the solace of a place of worship. If I have ever heard of an oxymoron (gay Christian) concept, this would be this statement. I don't even believe Mr. Chu knows what he is saying. What Christ is he talking about? The word *Christian* means a disciple of Christ, a follower of Christ and Christlike. "The disciples of Christ were first called Christians at Antioch—(Acts 11:26).

Let me interpret. In his gay Christian experience, he would be saying the gay, emulating-Christ experience; the gay obedience-to-the-Father (God) experience, who is the same God, who said it is an abomination for mankind to lie with mankind as he would lie with womankind. Based on the definition of *Christian*, what gay Christian experience is he alluding to?

Mr. Chu says his faith in God is secure and that no one has the authority to tell him whom he loves. I'm not sure whether the "He" is God or Mr. Chu himself. The book of Hebrews among Bible scholars is referred to as the "book of faith" or the "hallmark of faith." It covers the faithful acts of the patriarchs Abel, Enoch, Noah, Abraham, Jacob, Joseph, Moses, and an individual named Rahab. Their faith produced obedience, which moved them to action. Faith without works is dead. "But without faith it is impossible to please Him; for he that comes to God must believe that He is, and that He is a rewarder of them that diligently seek Him" (Hebrews 11:1–40).

It seems Mr. Chu knows very little about Jesus, whom he says he loves. It is Jesus who gives Christians the authority to preach the word, reprove, and rebuke. Yes, Mr. Chu, there are individuals (Christians) who have the authority from God to tell you "what thus saith the Lord."

> I charge thee therefore before God, and the Lord Jesus Christ, who shall judge the quick and the dead at His appearing and His kingdom; Preach the word; be instant in season, out of season; reprove, rebuke, exhort with all

---

[69] Jeff Chu, *"Does Jesus Really Love Me? A Gay Christian's Pilgrimage in Search of God in America"* Dan Savage, https://www.nytimes.com/2013/04/14/books/review/does-jesus-reallylove-me-by-jeff-chu.html

longsuffering and doctrine. For the time will come when they will not endure sound doctrine; but after their own lusts shall they heap to themselves teachers, having itching ears; And they shall turn away their ears from the truth, and shall be turned unto fables. But watch thou in all things, endure afflictions, do the work of an evangelist (preacher), make full proof of thy ministry. (2 Timothy 4:1–5)

Today, in twenty-first century America, we are dealing with the biggest fable that has ever been told. It is something else to be told about the Three Little Pigs and the Big Bad Wolf, Goldilocks and the Three Bears, and Henny Penny or Chicken Little, but turning to fables of "I'm gay because God made me this way"—no other fables lied on God. Really, did God make you and condemn you for being effeminate? I have heard that if you tell a lie long enough, you will start to believe it. Is America starting to believe it? But it doesn't change the fact that it's a lie. The most frightful thing about this lie is lying 'on' God. When you decide to act in an abominable way and blame God for it, God gives you up, allows you to pursue your vile ways, lets you believe what you are saying, and allows what you engage in to destroy you (Romans 1:24–32).

Many confuse belief in God as synonymous with Christianity. The devils believed and trembled; that's more than I can say for a lot of people, who are haters of God. The devil believed and didn't obey God. If he did, he wouldn't be the devil. Having faith and/or believing in God without obedience doesn't produce a Christian. Mr. Chu needs to examine the scripture and then ask himself whether he is really secure in his faith. If it's without works, obedience to the will of God, his faith is vain and worthless—dead. Mr. Chu described himself as a conflicted believer. Satan is a believer and isn't conflicted—he knows the deal. And his mission is to confuse and deceive man and cause conflict with the word of God.

The scripture says God is angry with the wicked every day. God will tell Mr. Chu, whom He really loves, the truth about salvation and the church, the bride of Christ. Is Mr. Chu willing to listen to God? Consider the "rich young ruler." He came running up to Jesus with kind salutations. He had heard about living forever and wanted to know how to inherit eternal life. Jesus engaged him in conversation about sins that would keep one out of heaven: adultery, murder, theft, lying, covetousness, and dishonoring parents. He told Jesus he had kept these commandments from his youth. Jesus looked on him and *loved* him. Mr. Chu and everyone should know that Jesus loves man, and it pleases Him when man lives right. The "rich young ruler's" sin and our sins are that we don't want to make a sacrifice and give up the one sin that keeps us at a guilty distance from the proper relationship we should have with our Lord: our total obedience and surrender to His will. To love God, there are some relationships we will have to give up: be it effeminate, adultery, and fornicating partners, to name a few.

Mr. Chu should understand that there are no fornicator Christians, liar Christians, thief Christians, murder Christians, or effeminate Christians because all won't enter the kingdom of God. You will meet Christians who will tell you that before they became a Christian, they participated in such acts. Stop fighting with man-made denominations or churches, obey the gospel, be added to the body of Christ through baptism, walk faithfully until death, and receive a crown of righteousness, which God has prepared for all who obey Him. Christ adds one to His church, the one He died for, and no one can separate you but your sins, which you personally and continually commit or live in.

Mr. Chu asks, "Does Jesus Really Love Me?" He should answer the question "Does he really love Jesus?" Jesus says that if you love Him, you will keep His commandments. How much does Jesus have to do for Mr. Chu to demonstrate that he loves him? Does Mr. Chu really know Jesus? Does he know what Jesus has already done for him—that Jesus died for him so he could live with Jesus forever in heaven?

To Whom Little Is Forgiven, the Same Love the Little

"As it is written, there is none righteous; no, not one" (Romans 3:10). In Luke 7, Simon, a Pharisee (religious person), asked Jesus to come to his house and dine with him. Many others who believed themselves to be righteous attended the dinner and behaved as if they were on the same level of righteousness as Christ; after all, that's how and why He received the invitation to dine in Simon's house with them. While Jesus sat at meat with Simon and his other guests, who believed themselves to be "righteous" folks, a woman the scriptures noted to be a sinner came and stood at His feet behind Him, weeping, washing His feet with her tears, and wiping them with the hairs of her head. She kissed His feet and anointed them with ointment. This was a woman, obviously engaged in some public lifestyle, and everyone around knew she was a sinner. Jesus knew she was a sinner, the people knew she was a sinner, and most importantly, the woman knew she was a sinner. Are we as honest as this woman, today?

When she found out Jesus was in Simon's house, she bought her expensive alabaster box of ointment because she wanted to do something nice for Him. It was customary to wash the feet of travelers and guests who had to travel on unpaved and dusty roads in sandals. It was a kind gesture, like offering a glass of cold water, cola, or tea to a guest visiting one's home on a hot summer day.

Everyone at the dinner questioned Jesus's righteousness and felt He should have nothing to do with the woman—a sinner, especially anyone of that sinful nature. What Jesus had to say was an eye-opener for Simon, the Pharisee (preacher, teacher, religious and moral individual). Jesus posed a question, a type of scenario to Simon. "There was a certain creditor which had two debtors: the one owed five hundred pence, and the other fifty. And when they had nothing to pay, he frankly forgave them both. Tell me, therefore, which of them will love him most?" See Luke 8:41–42. Simon told Jesus he supposed the one who owed the greater debt would love the most. Jesus told Simon he made a wise observation or judgment. Jesus then turned to the woman and said to Simon that from the time He had entered Simon's house, Simon hadn't offered Him water for His feet, but the women had washed His feet with her tears, wiped His feet with her hair, and anointed His feet with ointment. Jesus told Simon that Simon hadn't greeted Him with a kiss, but the woman, since He entered Simon's house, hadn't stopped kissing His feet.

Here is a lesson for everyone. Jesus told Simon that this woman's sins, which were many, were forgiven, for she loved much. But to whom little was forgiven, the same loved little. Jesus told the woman that her sins were forgiven. This woman saw herself as a sinner who needed Jesus, while Simon failed to acknowledge his sins, and she was able to walk away with her sins forgiven. Many times we aren't ready to surrender all our sins to Jesus; there are just a few we want to acknowledge. If we trusted God to forgive all our sins, we can give Him all our love.

The question is still on the table for Mr. Chu to answer. Does he really love Jesus? If so, how much does he love Jesus? How much of his sins is he willing to give to Jesus? If he wants to give up a few of his sins, then obviously he has only a little love for Jesus. If he plans to give Jesus *all* of his sins, including what the scripture refers to as an abominable lifestyle (effeminate or men having sex with men), then it is obvious he really loves Jesus a lot. "To whom little is forgiven, the same loveth little." Jesus wants to forgive us of all our sins (Luke 7:47). The gospel requires that we repent of all our sexual immorality, which would include homosexuality, lesbianism, fornication, adultery, bestiality (zoophiles), and child molestation (pedophilia), and submit in obedience to the word of God—Son of God.

Yes, Jesus Loves Me

And how do I know this? Well, because the Bible tells me so. Man is the crown of His creation; created in His image and likeness, man became a living soul (Genesis 2:7). God gave man dominion over His creation: fish of the sea, fowls of the air, and other living creatures (Genesis 1:28; 2:15–20). Although man was created to live forever, it was sin that separated and destroyed the relationship, creating a physical and spiritual death. God loved man so much that He made a plan that would redeem man and place him back in a proper relationship with Him. This will come about through Faith + Obedience = Salvation. The wages of sin is death. When we sin, we become guilty of death (Romans 6:23). Even all the way back in the Garden of Eden, man was given hope (Genesis 3:15; Galatians 3:16). God's plan was to send His Son to set men free from the death sentence and eternal separation from Him (John 3:16; 2 Corinthians 5:21). God entrusted man with this relationship, and man failed miserably in his part, but God was willing to forgive him and set him on a course of mending this relationship. We will talk later about what God offers, His plan, and what requirements man will have to meet to qualify for redemption and pardon.

God's Word Will Last Forever

Many times when we don't like what the Holy Bible has to say and what the messenger of the Word has to say, we want to cut it out of the Holy Bible or rewrite the Holy Bible. How absurd—gays demanding their own bible, one that leaves off passages condemning effeminate and abominable acts. Once again there is nothing new under the sun. Jeremiah 36:23 says, "And it came to pass, that when Jehudi had read three or four leaves, he cut it with the penknife, and cast it into the fire that was on the hearth, until all the roll was consumed in the fire that was on the hearth." Just like Jehudi, we try to destroy the word of God. In Jeremiah 36:28, God not only had the scroll rewritten word per word based on what was written in the original roll or book that Jehoiakim king of Judah had burned in the fire, but in verse 32, He instructed that more would be added.

The Withered Fig Tree

Examining Mark 11:12–14 and Matthew 21:18–22, one can find many lessons drawn from the cursed fig tree, including being unfruitful. This tree had leaves and from all practicality should have had fruit somewhere on it because the budding fruit appears on the fig tree before the leaves come out, and the leaves get larger and cover the fruit. There was no fruit to be found, even though it had enticed Jesus from afar to approach with anticipation and expectation of some figs to eat. Parading around as married couples in same-sex unions won't produce fruits—accursed union with no chance of ever producing fruit—ever.

Parable of the Talents

"But he that had received one went and dug in the earth, and hid his lord's money" (Matthew 25:18). This man was called wicked and slothful, and he was cast out (Matthew 25:26, 30).

God made His creatures: man, beasts, fowls of the air, fish of the sea, crawling insects, and trees to produce after their own kind. "And God blessed them, and God *said* to them, Be fruitful and multiply, and *replenish* the earth" (Genesis 1:28, emphasis added). After the flood, God blessed Noah and his sons, and He said to them, "Be fruitful, and multiply, and replenish the earth" (Genesis 9:1). God commands all His creation to bring forth after their kind (Genesis 1:11, 21, 24).

The Spiritual Family of God

In the church, which is Christ's bride or wife, saved souls are added through baptism, producing children or Christians of the kingdom. God is our Father, and Christ is our Brother. This is an institution or union that works to produce saved soul. The obedient is born again spiritually and becomes a child of God. This is a union that produces Christians. This is a relationship that produces a family of God. Everything about the God-man relationship is about being fruitful and giving Him our best. A deviant lifestyle of same-sex relationships produces nothing and is an abomination before God. The scriptures clearly show God's contempt toward unfruitfulness. Bear much fruit (John 15:5–8), and faith without works is dead (James 2:26; Galatians 5:22–23).

Branded A Teen Sex Offender

If you had access to the Internet or TV, most Americans in the western hemisphere, not to mention some other countries, had followed tweets or heard about the incident of a teenager (eighteen years old) in Florida who was charged with a felony for sexual acts (lascivious and lewd battery) on a fourteen-year-old.

A state law, effective July 1, 2009, lists teens as young as fourteen on the same website as adults who are convicted pedophiles and sexual predators. Florida legislation complies with the Adam Walsh Child Protection and Safety Act, qualifying for millions in federal funds.

Even though the eighteen-year-old contends that the activity was consensual, the law (in the state where the act was committed, Florida) is emphatic that a person under the age of sixteen isn't legally able to give consent to sex. The article said that if you are fifteen years old, you better have some ideas of right and wrong. Most prosecutors don't have a problem prosecuting teens that age who rape or commit some lewd act on a ten-year-old.

If convicted, the eighteen-year-old could face a prison term of fifteen years. This fact set off a maelstrom of controversy. It reminds me of the question "Why do the heathen rage?" CNN legal analyst Sunny Hostin (currently, *The View* talk show panelist) took some tongue-lashing for just reporting the fact that the offender (eighteen years old) had admitted to the relationship with the underage teen and that the act was a felony. "Am I therefore become your enemy, because I tell you the truth" (Galatians 4:16). If that isn't shameful enough, the tongue lashers went after the mother for trying to protect her daughter by exposing the offender after alleging she had asked the offender to stay away from her daughter, when a neighbor brought the incident to her attention.

God has commanded us to love and protect our children. This is her duty as a mother and wife.

> And so train the young women to love their husbands and children. (Titus 2:4)
>
> Behold, children are a heritage from the Lord, the fruit of the womb a reward, like arrows in the hand of a warrior are the children of one's youth. Blessed is the man who fills his quiver with them! He shall not be put to shame when he speaks with his enemies in the gate. (Psalm 127:3–5)

Let the mother of the underage teen not be afraid to protect her child and stand strong against the tongue-lashing, accusing her of gay bashing. Many will speak evil of people trying to do right and in this instance merchandise this into a media maelstrom of controversy. "And many shall follow their pernicious ways; by reason of whom the way of truth shall be evil spoken of and through covetousness shall they with feigned words make merchandise of you; whose judgment now of a long time lingers not, and their damnation slumbers not. For if God spared not the angels that sinned, but cast them down to hell, and delivered them into chains of darkness to be reserved to judgment; and spared not the old world, but saved Noah the eight person, a preacher of righteousness, bringing in the flood upon the world of the ungodly" (2 Peter 2:2–5). The parents of the underage teen have a God-given right to bring up their child in a lifestyle that's not an abomination or one that is not lewd or lascivious in the sight of God. "Train up a child in the way he should go; even when he is old he will not depart from it" (Proverbs 22:6).

The article cited the eighteen-year-old offender's defense lawyer, who blamed the social structure, environment, and state that created the environment of how we educate children. The lawyer tried to blame the state, environment, and facilities for allowing pre-K, kindergarten, elementary schools, junior highs, and high schools where oftentimes different age-groups can possibly be housed and schooled in the same facility. The offender's lawyers want to blame school programs where contact through communications and activities can be blamed but not the actions of the eighteen-year-old, who is of the age of accountability. Can you think of another situation? Remember, Adam told God that his sin was the fault of the woman He had given him. Adam wanted to blame God for putting Eve in the same place (Garden of Eden) and giving her to him for a wife. Remember, state laws (authority of God), environment (contact or communication), and facility (garden). Please know that Adam knew the rules: don't eat of the tree. Adam broke God's commandment. We are all responsible for our actions, whether we are educated or not about the law. Laws put in place to protect are still binding, no matter whether we are ignorant of them or not. Adam couldn't have claimed ignorance, so he blamed God. The lawyer for the eighteen-year-old who molested the fourteen-year-old couldn't have claimed ignorance, so he blamed society, the state, and the teen's social environment.

Speaking of pride before destruction, when the offender was offered some type of leniency—a plea deal, even an acknowledgement that she knew and understood that she had broken the law (beforehand knowledge or not), she rejected it. Man, a fallen creature, has been extended leniency and forgiveness for sin, but his pride won't let him accept the fact that he is a sinner and needs the blood of Christ (mediator) on the cross and his obedience (acceptance of the plea deal) to save him, to stay out of prison (hell). The article stated that the eighteen-year-old sex offender was offered an "extremely" lenient plea that would have afforded her the opportunity to avoid a felony, incarceration, or stigma of being a sex offender; yet knowing she had committed the felony, whether it was known to her at the time when she engaged in the act, decided to press the gay (lesbian) agenda. She had allowed her heart to become arrogant and hardened with pride. Her attitude was that of the larger gay community, which has set itself up against the Lord of heaven and the institution He built. He offered marriage and the gift He gave to this institution, children. Again, pride comes before destruction.

The article so eloquently stated that high school relationships may be fleeting, but being convicted of a sex offense on a child is a felony conviction and is forever on one's record.

The American Civil Liberties Union came to the teen's defense and rallied for signatures in support, in light of the scripture that reads, "Broad is the way that leads to destruction, and many there be which go in thereat" (Matthew 7:13). Does it really matter what organization is behind you and how many signatures you get? Once you leave this side of life, the American Civil Liberties Union cannot say a word on your behalf. But Jesus can. Make sure your actions won't cause Him to deny you on your journey to the other side of this life. "But whosoever shall deny Me before men, him will I also deny before My Father which is in heaven" (Matthew 10:33). If being in a big number guarantees what is right, the minority that's trying to deny temptations to do wrong can just stop and join the larger group. But scripturally speaking, that is quite the contrary. "Because strait [no pun intended for being effeminate] is the gate, and narrow is the way, which leads to life, and few there be that find it" (Matthews 7:14).

Back to Al Green, who wrote, "If loving you is wrong, I don't wanna to be right." C'mon—really? Even if your actions mean eternal damnation? Going to jail? Staying out of hell?

We all need to examine our relationships, whether we are gay, straight, or teens who are disobedient to parents. All relationships are fleeting; death robs us of them. "For in the resurrection, they neither marry, nor are given in marriage, but are as the angels of God in heaven" (Matthew 22:30).

Being a sinner or offender of the cross is a blasphemous conviction forever on your record. God has made it possible for us to take the plea deal: being born again through baptism, like a whole new creature coming into a forgiven or pardoned relationship. This is a nonfleeting relationship that can and will, through our continuous walking in the light of the cross of Christ until He returns, last forever.

Let us fight, march, campaign, vote, and lobby for the relationship that is God approved. All unscriptural relationships will come to naught.

Biblical Relationships Referenced in Scripture

* God the Father, God the Son, and God the Holy Ghost *(Matthew 28:19, Luke 3:22)*
* Jesus Christ, the Son of God *(John 3:16, Matthew 17:5)*
* Christians, children of God *(Acts 2:47, Acts 11:26)*
* The church, the bride of Christ *(Ephesians 5:23-33; Acts 2:37–47)*
* The church, the kingdom of God *(Colossians 1:24, Matthew 16: 18–28)*
* Brother and sisters in Christ in the kingdom, in the church (Christians) *(2 Timothy 1:9-10, Matthew 12: 50, Luke 8:19-21, Hebrews 13:1)*
* The bed undefiled in marriage: male and female unions blessed by God through holy matrimony *(Mark 10:9, Hebrews 13:4)*
* Children, obey your parents in the Lord *(Ephesians 6:1–3: Colossians 3:20)*
* Wives, submit to your own husband *(Ephesians 5:22, 24–25, Colossians 3:18)*
* Young women and young men, love your children and be sober minded *(Titus 2:4, 6)*
* Fathers, provoke not your child to wrath *(Ephesians 6:4, Colossians 3:21)*
* Husbands, love your wife as Christ loves the church and gave Himself for it *(Ephesians 5:25; Colossians 3:19)*
* Elders and overseers of the flock (a congregation of the church or body of Christ) *(1 Peter 5:1-40)*
* Evangelists, preachers, teachers, and members (admonish one another in the gospel) *(2 Timothy 4:5; Romans 15:14; Colossians 3:16)*
* Love the Lord, your God, with all your heart and your neighbor as yourself (God and man). *(Matthew 22:35-40; Mark 12:31)*
* Obey those who have the rule over you through laws and ordinances. *(Hebrews 13:17-19)*
* Rulers cause not the people to sin and turn from God *(1 kings 22:52–53, Isaiah 9:16)*
* The church is responsible for widows in deeds *(1Timothy 5, James 1:27)*
* Honor those women who labor with you in the Lord *(Romans 16:1–6, 12)*
* Respect elderly women as mothers *(1Timothy 5:2: Titus 2:3–4)*
* Respect younger women as sisters *(1 Timothy 5:2)*
* Older women should teach younger women *(Titus 2:3–5)*

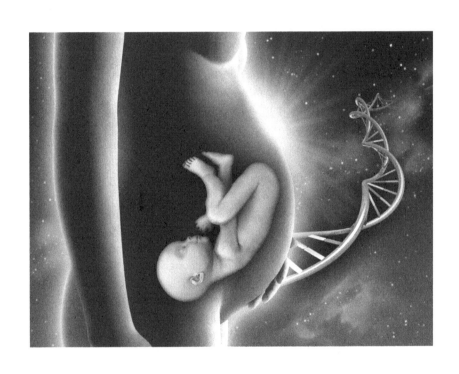

Chapter 4
I Was Born Gay, I Was Born Again

THERE HAVE BEEN many discussions and explanations about why some people believe they were born gay or born with "gay genes." Chromosome research in the Human Genome Project offers an explanation.[70] Scientists and geneticists try to wrap their minds around an age-old issue, homosexuality, which has existed since the biblical days of the patriarch Abraham and his nephew, Lot. Almighty God has already addressed the issue of homosexuality, sexual relations between members of the same gender.

Many scientists in institutions of biotechnology around the globe have spent countless hours and millions of dollars studying and analyzing the human X and Y chromosomes; using the sequences from the Human Genome Project, they couldn't find anything that identified a "gay gene." The conclusion drawn is from unreplicated claims. In an article at LifeSiteNews.com, Dean A. Byrd wrote that Dr. Francis S. Collins, one of the world's leading scientists who works on the cutting edge of DNA research, concluded that "there is an inescapable component of heritability to many human behavioral traits." However, he added, "for virtually none of them, is heredity ever close to predictive." Dr. Collins would agree, environment can influence gene expression, and free will determines the response to whatever predispositions might be present." From his research, Dr. Collins,

---

[70] Wikipedia, s.v. "Human Genome Project" https://en.wikipedia.org/wiki/Human_Genome_Project

concluded, "Sexual orientation is genetically influenced but not hardwired by DNA, and that whatever genes are involved represent predispositions not predeterminations." Dr. Collins noted that environment, particularly childhood experiences, as well as the role of free will and choice affect us all in profound ways.[71]

This gene in mankind, which scientists are trying to identify as a "gay gene," is the same sin-sick-causing gene found in all individuals' behaviors on "the list" in the book of 1Corinthians. The liar, the thief, the adulterer, the fornicator, and the effeminate (men having sex with men) and lesbian (women having sex with women) behaviors have already been identified thousands of years ago as this terrible disease called "sin." Save your research dollars and time in the research labs.

> And God saw that the wickedness of man was great in the earth, and that every imagination of the thoughts of his heart was only evil continually. (Genesis 6:5)
>
> All we like sheep have gone astray; we have turned everyone to his own way; and the Lord has laid on Him the iniquity of us all. (Isaiah 53:6)

The Living Dead: Dead Men Walking

Consider the disease, *Sin*, and its symptoms. Satan, the carrier, has the ability to infect in an insidious and contagious manner. When sin was found in Adam, all mankind failed under sin. The disease attaches itself to the unsuspecting man, mostly at his weakest and most vulnerable moments, either through lack of knowledge of the will of God for his (protection gear— whole armor of God) or his own lust and evil desires (carelessness or free will and choice). Man's immune system is low or depleted of spiritual food (the word of God, the Bread of Life), Christ. The horror of the disease is that it has the ability to replicate cells and make cells look like the original, but the basic genetic code of the false cell is very destructive. Satan, the carrier, appears as an angel of light. He deceives the host, man, and blinds him to what is actually happening to his body and soul. The carnal scientists and geneticists aren't educated or skilled enough to identify this gene that has

---

[71] National Association for Research and Therapy of Homosexuality—May 24, 2014 .Dean A. Byrd, "Homosexuality Is Not Hardwired," LifeSite News, March 20, 2007.

gone awry (wild or free radical). They are simply using the wrong textbooks. Only an individual who holds a spiritual MD (the Master's Doctrine) and has a spiritually trained eye can recognize the DNA of this viral contagious strain is able to discern the disease-causing, viral, and contagious gene strain (Hebrews 5:14; 1 Kings 3:9). This degree of knowledge is gained under the tutelage (studies) of the inspired textbooks of the Master, who first (isolated) identified the viral strain and named the disease, *Sin*. God made man upright, and that strain couldn't hide from the sight of God or the trained eye, which works under the microscope of the Holy Ghost. It divides asunder both spirit and flesh, even cutting to the morrow of the bones. This is a technique not found in man-made dissecting labs, Petrie dish, or surgical instruments.

Satan's (the parasite, feeding on God's children) tactics are to take over and do as much damage as possible before the host knows what is happening to him or her. The horror of the disease (*sin*) wreaks its zombie-like, living-dead effect on the creatures, man. He becomes a Satan-controlled, decaying servant who reeks an odorous stench in the sight and nostrils of God, fit only for the fires of hell. Man walks around in this euphoric sensation as if he is actually in control of his own life and destiny, which is the deathly and deceptive effect of the sin's enzymes that ooze into his and her (mankind) system—soul. He or she is made to feel proud of his or her ways and actions without a clue about the underlying consequences that will befall him or her once the disease, *sin*, has full control. People are unaware of what happens if death overtakes them without the cure Christ offers? When sin takes over, it turns people into creatures of unrighteousness, lacking faith (knowledge) of God. Most people are horrified at the thought of running into a zombie, but the gene slowly turns men into creatures controlled by Satan and into a living-dead state, ugly and vile and fit for punishment and pain in a place without God–forever. Satan only wants to injure and hurt others who want to do right in the sight of God.

Sin is contagious and hurts a lot more people than its hosts—the people who are infected by the strain of the gene or virus. When Adam sinned, he hurt God. "And it repented the Lord that He has made man on the earth, and it grieved Him at His heart" (Genesis 6:6). The earth or ground was cursed; animals were sacrificed for clothes after man was driven from the Garden of Eden. And animals became sacrificial blood offerings for sin. The relationship that man (the creature) had with God was breached. Because of sin, this breach demanded a sacrifice, a perfect or sinless sacrifice; it required the blood of God's Son, Jesus Christ. One can say a blood transfusion for the cure. When people sin, they hurt members of their family, society, and nation. No man is an island (words of a poet). What you do and say can have devastating effects on others in society and country. Thou shalt not kill, steal, or lie. Yes, espionage falls into *stealing* secret information and *lying* or concealing the act.

You want to get a mental picture of how bad sin is? It is something that deceitfully looks good, smells good, and tastes good to man. Sin is the cause of Jesus's death on the cross. Digest that. Really wrap your mind around the fact that it took someone (deity) to come down from heaven and submit to the cruel death on the cross, all because of this disease, identified as *Sin*. Jesus had to fight this kryptonite of an enemy and win, telling God the Father, "Not my will, but your will be done." If you could see through the sweet-smelling, beautiful, and cunning disguises, look at them face on, you'll see they are the most unimaginably and horrifyingly dark and evil things one could ever witness. The thought puts me in mind of the 1983 (TV Miniseries), *The V Aliens*, written by Kenneth Johnson. The film was about reptile-like monsters disguised to look like humans but came from another planet to take over earth. Yes, we see the symptoms and results of brushes with sin (daily) in our society, but are we able to see sin or the prince of darkness head-on? The reality is, probably not. If so, would one live to tell about it? When it finishes with man (outside of Christ), it kills and steals the soul. It has a tendency to disguise itself—it's deceptive. It makes people feel like they are in control when in reality one can be only a servant of Satan or a servant of Christ. There is no middle ground. Think about it: very few people, if any, would readily agree to follow Satan if he walked up to them and identified himself as Satan. His origin was heaven before he rebelled against God and convinced some angels to follow him.

Moses couldn't, because of man's terrestrial state, look upon God (the most righteous), but he was allowed to see God's backside (Exodus 33:22–23; also see John 1:18 and 1 John 4:12). We see the results of sin, but in our terrestrial state can we look at Satan face-to-face in his undisguised form? When Satan does approach man, he appears as an angel of light (through acceptably convincing messages) in his persuading and enticing man to sin against God. We find ourselves engaging in sin a lot of times before we realize what is happening; that's Satan's deceptive trait. Satan makes sin look attractive and enticing, but this isn't the true face of *Sin*. If Satan did show his true face, you would be horrified and immediately run away from him. He disguises sin to taste good, feel good, look good, and even appear righteous. The word of God identifies his tactics as the pleasures of sin. That is why knowing (feasting on) the word of God is very important to the spiritual immune system; it's a buffer to help us see what's happening before we become involved in the sinful act (become infected). The word of God is our antioxidants, that buffer against those free radicals of sin. Remember when Satan tried to tempt Christ. Christ's response was, "It is written." What powerful medicine or antitoxin we can use to ward off sin: "It is written." This is spiritual food for the immune system of the soul.

The Cure for Sin

One of the greatest blessings of heaven is that sin won't be there (Revelation 21:3–4). God, knowing that people would sin, prepared a cure for them. Without Jesus, there can be no healing. The healing process comes when people can see sin as God does. They have to understand the horror sin causes to the body and soul, and the hurt it causes God. People need to accept the cure God has provided and prescribed: the shed blood of Jesus Christ, obtained through baptism.

Amputations to Save the Body

It may be a hard pill to swallow when we discover we have to lose to gain. But when the end results are lifesaving and/or beneficial, we know it's for the best. Think about the scripture that says, "If my eye offends, I would pluck it out and enter heaven lame than go to hell with two eyes." There is yet another warning from scripture. "Let not sin therefore reign in your mortal body, that you should obey it in the lusts thereof. Neither yield you your members as instruments of unrighteousness to sin; but yield yourselves to God" (Romans 6:12–13). God will tell you that He created you for "good" works. "For we are His workmanship, created in Christ Jesus to good works, which God has before ordained that we should walk in them" (Ephesians 2:10).

Don't blame God for being gay. Adam told God he had sinned because of the woman God gave him. Eve blamed the serpent. "It beguiled me." Now, where am I going with this? From the scriptural account, we see that Adam was cursed, Eve was cursed, the serpent was cursed, and their sins caused the earth, the ground, to be cursed. Because of their actions, not even the ground could escape damnation. This truth makes one wonder whether this country's attitude toward God is the reason for the climate changes we want to blame on Mother Nature or global warming. Between the flood in Noah's days and the burning or fire and brimstone of Sodom's and Gomorrah's days, don't the gays know we have already been shaken up? Let find our liberty in

Christ Jesus and assurance for eternal life. God has a history of destroying evil nations.

Today many are still trying to pull an Eve on God by going all Flip Wilson, who said, "The devil made me do it." And gays have the audacity to pull one of Adam's old moves by blaming God and saying, "God made me this way." Adam told God, "The woman *you gave me* caused me to sin" (emphasis added). Hello, folks, blaming it on the serpent and on God didn't work with God when Adam and Eve tried it. The problem still remains the lust of the eye, the lust of the flesh, and the pride of life. Let us lay aside the sins that so easily beset us and move on to righteousness and perfection in Christ.

More Than You Are Able to Bear

Do you feel that God isn't fair with you? He has made you a thief, a liar, a fornicator, an effeminate, and so forth and now expects you to behave differently. What? And against your natural desires to live as such? Let's talk about this issue a little bit. The scripture says Christ was tempted in like manner but didn't sin. Christ was about His Father's will, and He expressed that when He had to go to the cross and be the official sacrifice for the sins of the world. Christ learned obedience through the things He suffered, even unto death on the cross. If Christ obeyed God, where does man fit on the totem pole or hierarchy? When we learn the truth about God and our predestined relationship with Him, it's about time we also come to be about our Father's will. And please stop *lying on* God. C'mon, please! It's about time that we become obedience to the gospel; learn obedience, take up our cross, and follow Him—daily.

Stop trying to find excuses to sin and at worst blame God for it. The most distasteful excuse I have ever heard was the one that rolled off the actor's, Terrence Howard, lips in the character of Quentin whom he played in the 1999 movie *Best Man*. "If God wanted us to have one woman, He would not have all this p'sy out there." [72]What a lack of knowledge and what a bad blame game on God. Let him seek the answers to the following question. Why would God say let every man have his own wife and let every woman have her own husband? "Let a man leave his father and mother and cleave to his wife, and the two shall be one flesh." Howard's character in *Best Man* is totally ignorant of God's plan for man. God said it's an abomination for man to lie with mankind as with womankind, and He said to let every man

---

[72] *Best Man*, directed by Malcolm D. Lee (1999) 40 Acres and A Mule FlimWorks.

and woman have his or her own spouse. Like Mr. Howard's movie character, who engages in fornication and adulterous acts, in real life, gays are saying that despite what God has commanded, God made them this way. "Born this way" is another bad game of blaming God. Please, let America not hear from the gays in their blame game, saying, "If God didn't want us to have anal sex, He wouldn't have all these anuses or rectums out there." Thank God the ear canals and nostrils haven't been violated; it's too late for the mouths. I can't help but recall the infant a male in Africa raped because he felt a virgin would cure him of the disease of AIDS in his body; no doubt he had AIDS because of his sin of fornication or adultery. The young prince of England cradled this tiny, pain-ridden, torn body in his arms in a photo as the world looked on in horror at the effects of sin. Many are too blind to recognize this behavior as sin.

God isn't going to require any more of a gay person, in line of obedience, than He would of Jesus (who learned obedience through the things He suffered), than of Satan and his angels (whom He kicked out of heaven for disobedience), than of Adam and Eve (whom He kicked out of the Garden of Eden for disobedience), and than of the heterosexual, who is living in sin. God says to all, "Where I am you cannot come." God's requirement for a gay person and straight person is that you "present your bodies a living sacrifice, holy and acceptable to God; not be conformed to this world, but transformed by the renewing of your mind, that you also are able to prove in Scriptures what is good and acceptable and perfect; that is the will of the Lord for you" (Romans 12:1–2). *Now, know this that obedience to God makes all equal in the sight of God, not bills of rights, laws, propositions, or amendments.*

The New Birth

Whether you are gay or straight, every person born of the flesh (corruptible) has to be born again, born of the spirit (incorruptible). "That which is born of the flesh is flesh and that which is born of the spirit is eternal." It's time to examine the scripture for what it really means and how one is truly born again. It doesn't matter how you found yourself in your corruptible state, born a liar, fornicator, thief, straight or even gay; you must be born again. Honestly, it's not about the blame game—why you are the way you find yourself outside of Christ. You need to find your way out of that sinful state. "Seek and you shall find; knock and it shall be opened; asked and it shall be given." Christ has made the opportunity available for you to find a new lease on life (incorruptible and eternal). "And such were some of you" (1 Corinthians 6:9–11).

For those seeking a home in heaven, Jesus declares there is only "one" way in; you must be born again. You believe you were born gay; Christ has a solution to your dilemma. You have the opportunity to be born again. Everyone has an opportunity to be born again. No one is without an excuse for walking contrary to the will of God.

There are two essential elements involved in this new birth: water and Spirit (John 3:5–7). Every Christian is saved the same way. Everyone is born into the family of God the same way. One must *hear* the gospel (Romans 10:17), *believe* (John 8:24), *repent* (Luke 13:3), *confess* (Romans 10:10), and be *baptized* (Acts 2:38). There is no deviation from God's plan for how one is born into the family or added to the body of Christ. We don't get to do our own thing when it comes to salvation. Ask Aaron's two sons who decided to worship God as they willed.

Aaron's two sons (Nadab and Abihu), who offered up strange fire to God, were consumed by fire (Leviticus 10:1–3). Many religious denominations are offering up strange worship—"will-worship" to God. He didn't authorize, and they will be met at the gates of heaven with "Depart from Me, I never knew you."

New Testament Conversions

All who have reached the age of accountability and have the mental capability to choose right from wrong must be converted to be saved. That would be saved from eternal damnation in the fires of hell. And what exactly is conversion? Many have a misconception of biblical conversion—from weird to miraculous, to supernatural happenings, and to an unexplainable experience. Conversion brings about a change, a repented heart; thus, the scripture alludes to the old man and the new man. It pictures taking off the old and putting on the new. The purpose of conversion is to turn a sinner into a saint, a Christian. The only way one can successfully be converted is to search the scripture and understand and observe examples of conversions. "Verily I say to you, Except you be converted, and become as little children, you shall not enter into the kingdom of heaven" (Matthew 18:3). These are moral and spiritual changes to one's attitude and way of life. These are changes one must make personally as he or she is taught and persuaded by the word of God, the gospel. "It is written in the prophets, And they shall be all *taught* of God. Every man therefore that has heard, and has learned of the Father, comes to me" (John 6: 45, emphasis added). To do this, we must become teachable, humble, and obedient like innocent children. This is a change from being a slave to sin (bad deeds; self-will) and becoming a slave to righteousness (good deeds; obedient). An arrogant, self-willed, high-minded individual no doubt believes the gospel serves only weak people who need something to believe in and isn't for him or her. He or she is too haughty in spirit to be childlike and teachable.

What happens to a repented heart is the result of one's seeking forgiveness of past sins and acting on that by his or her obedience through baptism. The act on the part of the sinner brings about his or her pardon. "Let the wicked forsake his way, and the unrighteous man his thoughts: and let him return to the Lord, and He will have mercy upon him; and to our God, for He will abundantly pardon" (Isaiah 55:7).

Man has a part to play in his salvation. He doesn't stubble into heaven and doesn't know how he got there. Mankind has to accept the invitation from God, which requires obedience (action) on his or her part. Side note, the pope can't do this. "Why does this man thus speak blasphemies? Who can forgive sins but God only" (Mark 2:7). Here Jesus established that He forgives sins.

In this chapter, you will learn that no saved person "got religion." Religion is a work and duty. "Pure religion and undefiled before God and the Father is this, to visit the fatherless and widows in their afflictions, and to keep himself unspotted from the world" (James 1:27). But each and every one who *heard* (teaching of the truth, John 6:44) the gospel (death, burial, and resurrection) of Christ and the redemption it plays in man's eternal salvation (reestablished relationship with God, the Father) *believed* (faith), *repented* of sins, *confessed* that Jesus is the Christ, and was willing to be *baptized* for the remission of sin; thus, he or she becomes a Christian, a follower of Christ. This is the doctrine of the New Testament church. "For I am not ashamed of the gospel of Christ: for it is the power of God to salvation to everyone that believes; to the Jew first, and also to the Greek" (Romans 1:16).

While you examine the number of conversions recorded in the book of Acts and the New Testament books, note the *pattern* of how one obtained salvation (added to the body: kingdom or church) was enacted or accomplished through the obedient believers' actions in scriptures referenced in the book of Acts on the following pages. Let's start with the first three-thousand-plus souls added to the church on the day of Pentecost in AD 33, the beginning of the New Testament church, as the prophet Joel prophesied. These accounts of one being saved included Saul, who later changed his name to Paul; the eunuch; the Philippian jailer; Lydia and her household; and others.

The apostle Paul (who was Saul of Tarsus before his conversion) persecuted the church. He had a change of heart, a new mind-set about the church (faith). His actions and way of life changed. He no longer hauled Christians off to prison after he was convinced of the truth and repented of his actions. Paul was baptized and became a Christian. Let's read more about other conversions in the New Testament church. To become fully converted, all will follow the pattern of Paul.

1. A change of mind or heart through faith in the gospel. "For with the heart man believes to righteousness; and with the mouth confession is made to salvation" (Romans 10:10).
2. A change of actions or repentance of old ways. "I tell you Nay but except you repent, you shall all likewise perish" (Luke 13:3).
3. A change of relationship or Baptism will establish one from servant of Satan to servant of God. "For as many of you as have been baptized into Christ have put on Christ" (Galatians 3:27).

"Then Peter said to them, Repent, and be baptized every one of you in the name of Jesus Christ for the remission of sins and you shall receive the gift of the Holy Ghost. For the promise is to you, and to your children, and to all that are afar off, even as many as the Lord your God shall call. And with many other words did he testify and exhort saying save yourselves from this untoward generation" (Acts 2:38–40).

In the conversion process, baptism consummates the relationship or marriage. The "I do—I believe" is professed to the one you have submitted your life to or become betrothed to before witnesses (confess before men). The converted soul (unmarried to married or sinner to Christian) becomes part of Christ's body, His bride, the church, or family. The two become one: Christian or one in Christ. "He that believeth and is baptized shall be saved" (Mark 16:16). If you stay faithful (unadulterated by false teachings, unauthorized worship practices—"will worshippers") this is an everlasting relationship; death doesn't separate. This relationship is about pleasing God by shunning, rejecting, or despising other suitors and love interests that will pull you away from God. You are the one for Him, His betrothed, the apple of His eye—a Christian.

Honest hearts can confidently trust the pattern of conversion and plan of salvation for lost souls found in the book of Acts.

Acts 2:1–47

The apostle Peter preached the first sermon of the New Testament church, the church of Christ. "Now when they heard this [the gospel: death, burial, and resurrection] they were pricked in their heart, and said to Peter and to the rest of the apostles, Men and brethren, what shall we do [to be saved] … Then Peter said to them, Repent, and be baptized every one of you in the name of Jesus Christ for the remission of sins, and ye shall receive the gift of the Holy Ghost" (Acts 2:37–38). The Lord added to the church daily such as should be saved. This wasn't a mourning-bench situation, candidate-for-baptism situation, or voted-on membership situation. "Then they that gladly received his word were baptized; and the same day there were added to them about three thousand souls" (Acts 2:41).

Acts 8:5–13

When the people of Samaria heard Philip preach the gospel to them, they believed, and both men and women were baptized (v. 12). "But when they believed Philip preaching the things concerning the kingdom of God, and the name of Jesus Christ, they were baptized both men and women. Then Simon himself believed also: and when he was baptized, he continued with Philip and wondered beholding the miracles and signs which were done" (Acts 8:12–13).

Acts 8:26–39

As Philip finished preaching in Samaria (village in Jerusalem), he traveled to Gaza (desert land) and saw a man, a eunuch of great authority under Candace queen of the Ethiopians, riding back from worship, reading from the scriptures concerning Isaiah the prophet. Philip explained the gospel/New Testament, and the eunuch believed and asked to be baptized (v. 36). On the surface, this man was religious, read the scriptures, and attended worship, but he needed someone to bring him into the light of the gospel. Know the truth, and the truth will set you free. Philip preached (taught) him about Christ. He heard the gospel (the death, burial, and resurrection of Jesus as the Savior of man), believed the gospel, confessed his faith in Christ, and asked Philip to baptize him. He became a Christian. This pattern (married to Christ or in the church or body through baptism) of salvation has continued throughout the history of the New Testament church.

Acts 9:1–18

Saul of Tarsus, who is later recognized in scripture as the apostle Paul, was initially persecuting the church, hauling Christians off to jail who professed Christ. He was on a very personal mission, persecuting Christ and His disciples until the day he met Jesus on the road to Damascus. He was stricken blind by the very light of the presence of God, the Son. After the encounter, following instructions, he was led to the house of Judas. There Ananias, a disciple, received instructions from the Spirit of God to seek Saul in the house of Judas. God had chosen Saul as the vessel to bear His name before the Gentiles, kings, and the children of Israel (v:15). Saul was to be shown great things by God and was to suffer for Jesus's name sake. Although Ananias was reluctant due to fear of Saul's history with the church, he obeyed the Lord. Ananias went into Judas's home, laid his hands on Saul, and addressed him as Brother Saul. Saul immediately received his sight. Ananias explained Jesus more perfectly to Saul. He arose and was baptized (v. 18).

Acts 10

Cornelius was described as a devout man and one who feared God. He held the office of a centurion in an Italian band in Caesarea. He and his household or family were religious people, charitable to the poor, and Cornelius prayed to God constantly. Cornelius was seeking God, and he found Him through a vision. "Your prayers and your alms are come up for a memorial before God" (Acts 10:4). This encounter with an angel or messenger of God led him to the apostle Peter (vv. 5–6). In Acts 10, we find Peter being a bit reluctant in sharing the gospel with anyone outside the Jewish ethnicity (v. 28). Peter had received a vision (v. 20) about clean and unclean things, and in that vision, Peter understood that the word of God had come to all nations, both Jews and Gentiles.

> What God has cleansed, that call not you common. (v. 15)
> Then Peter opened his mouth, and said, of a truth I perceive that God is not respecter of persons: But in every nation he that fears Him, and works righteousness, is accepted with Him. (vv. 34–35)

Cornelius was the first of the Gentiles to become baptized and become a Christian.

> Can any man forbid water, that these should not be baptized, which have received the Holy Ghost as well as we? ... And he commanded them to baptized in the name of the Lord. Then prayed they him to tarry certain days. (Acts 10:47–48)

And the apostles and brethren that were in Judaea heard that the Gentiles had also received the word of God. (Acts 11:1)

Peter had to defend his actions with other Jews for baptizing and receiving Cornelius (the first Gentile to be converted) as a brother in Christ. "Forasmuch then as God gave them the like gift as he did to us, who believe on the Lord Jesus Christ; what was I, that I could withstand God? When they heard these things, they held their peace, and glorified God, saying, then has God also to the Gentiles granted repentance to life" (Acts 11:17–18).

Acts 16

We read of Paul preaching the gospel in various regions of the country and in Philippi, the chief city Macedonia. On the Sabbath, Paul held a prayer service and taught the gospel. He met Lydia, a businesswomen (a seller of purple) from the city of Thyatira, who had come out to worship. She heard and understood Paul's message of the gospel and was baptized. Lydia and her family or household believed and were converted; they became Christians (Acts 16:14–15).

Acts 16

Paul continued to conduct prayer services and taught the gospel in the region of the country of Philippi. A damsel (young woman) possessed with a spirit of divination (maybe some fortune-telling talents) made a lot of money for the person she was enslaved or indentured to, attended one of these prayer meetings, and started following Paul and brethren with him, saying, "These men are the servants of the Most High God, which show to us the way of salvation" (Acts 16:18). She did that for many days, and Paul became annoyed and commanded the spirit that she possessed or possessed her to come out. And it came out immediately (Acts 16:18). This put an end to the money-making scheme of her owner. He brought charges against Paul and the other gospel preachers (vv. 19–21).

Paul and Silas ended up in prison from these charges. There Paul and Silas had an opportunity to preach the gospel to the jailer or keeper of the prison, who believed the gospel and was baptized. "And brought them out, and said, sirs, what must I do to be saved? And they said, Believe on the Lord Jesus Christ, and you shall be saved, and your house. And they spoke to him the word of the Lord, and to all that were in his house. And he took them the same hour of the night, and was baptized, he and all his, immediately" (Acts 16:30–33).

Acts 18

While in Corinth, Paul continued to reason in the synagogue every Sabbath and persuaded the Jews and the Greeks. He testified to the Jews that Jesus was Christ. Many Jews took issue with the message, so Paul started speaking exclusively to the Gentiles. "And Crispus, the chief ruler of the synagogue, believed on the Lord with all his house; and many of the Corinthians hearing believed, and were baptized" (v.8). Paul stayed in Corinth a year and six months after a vision from God to stay and continue to preach the gospel there despite the attitude of some of the Jews, who were trying to cause him grief. "Then spoke the Lord to Paul in the night by a vision, Be not afraid, but speak, and hold not your peace: For I am with you, and no man shall set on you to hurt you: for I have much people in this city" (Acts 18:9–10).

Acts 19

The apostle Paul found disciples who knew only the baptism of John, the Baptist. "He said to them, Have you received the Holy Ghost, since you believed? And they said to him, We have not so much as heard whether there be any Holy Ghost. And he said to them, to what then were you baptized? And they said to John's baptism. Then said Paul, John verily baptized with the baptism of repentance, saying to the people, that they should believe on Him which should come after him, that is, on Christ Jesus. When they heard this, they were baptized in the name of the Lord Jesus" (Acts 19:2–4).

Acts 22:16

The apostle Paul gave an account of his conversion, recounting the incident that had happened to him on the road to Damascus. He showed baptism was essential for his conversion to Christianity.

📖 Book Corner Excerpt (A Critique)

BORN GAY: The Psychobiology of Sex Orientation by Glenn Wilson and Qazi Rahman

One of several books viewed for content that supports the gay lifestyle and is found to be a message in opposition to the gospel of Christ and the New

Testament church is *Born Gay* by authors G. Wilson and Q. Raham.[73] It is my goal in writing this book to compare the two views.

Reasons offered in support of being gay pretty much take one back to ground zero, the blame game found in the Garden of Eden with Adam and Eve. It's the smothering mothers, missing fathers, some heterosexual encounter in childhood or early teens, and genetics, or God's fault, to cite a few. God was in control when He first gave instructions to man on how to live and please Him then, and He is still in control is today. Adam and Eve were disobedient then, and man is still disobedient today; nothing really has changed. To Adam and Eve, God said not to eat fruit from a certain tree in the Garden of Eden. In the New Testament and Old Testament scriptures, Man is instructed *not* to have intercourse (sex) with another man or a woman with another woman— (Leviticus 18:22, Romans 1: 27). God is still giving instructions on how to live, and after generations upon generations and centuries upon centuries, man is still a disobedient creature. He wants to intellectualize himself into whatever he wants to do, yet scriptures tell mankind there is a way that seems right unto a man, but the end thereof is death.

Being gay is no longer characterized by the field of psychiatry as a mental illness or disease, and it is now accepted and protected by law in this society, but guess what? All who claim to speak with authority on this matter are new kids on the block compared to God Almighty. God is the Creator, and they have *no lot in this matter.* They are a little shy of a couple of centuries too late to chime in and are certainly eternally too late to offer an opinion; this hypothesis is based on their limited understanding. God holds all knowledge. Job would ask them (researchers and scientists), "Where were you when God created the universe?" The gays are claiming God created them. Yet God created everything (every seed) to produce after its own kind. Somebody is lying here. It's still the responsibility of those who are Christians to share the gospel, so all will hear (will be taught) and have an opportunity to obey.

Maybe the bigger issue is this: Did God make a mistake, leave off this little tidbit of information about mistakenly creating gay people, and worst of all, condemn them for being gay—stamping an abomination seal across their foreheads? The gays have come out of the closet and no longer want to protect God from this little mistake or secret in creation. God said everything He had made and done in creation was *good.* God said He can't lie. He created Adam and Eve, and they produced after their kind. The gays can't produce after their own kind; no two men can produce a child by having sex together,

---

[73] Glenn Wilson and Qazi Raham, *Born Gay: The Psychobiology of Sex Orientation.* London, England: Peter Owen Publishers 2008

and no two women can produce a child by having sex together. You don't have to be a scientist to figure out who is lying. From the sons of Noah, all nations came about; that would include the black man. There are no closeted black men hiding their blackness or being forced to choose between being a black man or not. God has never referred to a nation or ethnicity of people as an abomination outside the sinful acts or lifestyle of a people or nation.

If you are experiencing any type of orientation that isn't of God or through the word of God, that leaves you void of grasping or taking hold of your full potential as a child of God in your defined roll (created for good works in Christ Jesus) in this relationship with your Creator, it's time to reexamine the source of this orientation. Is it of God? It isn't in man to direct his steps; in other words, you are just not as smart as God. Let the word of God direct your path.

In the book *Born Gay: The Psychobiology of Sex Orientation* by Glenn Wilson and Qazi Rahman, the concept of psychobiology is introduced (p. 10).[74] We can use psychobiology, overlapping of science research in disciplines such as genetics, psychology, biology, and so forth, into just what we want to believe and think, but the bottom line is that the whole duty of man is to fear God and keep His commandments. No LGBTQ or heterosexual individuals, or anyone else can rewrite the scriptures to justify their cause. Jehudi cut out and burn the scripture (scroll) per the king's request, but the king received a double portion of the word (Jeremiah 36:23). God said His word will not change—that would mean from culture to culture, generation to generation, and century to century. And surely there is no private interpretation of scripture—(2 Peter 1:20). God is not the author of confusion— (1 Corinthians 14:33). Understand that God has His plan of salvation and instructions for man on how to obtain eternal life down to a science, too. He is so serious about it that He warns that if an angel brings another message or gospel, let him be accursed. When it comes to who is really the "Master of Science," God says no one knows how the bones form in the womb—(Ecclesiastes 11:5). Let's not think we can "out-science" God. His psychic ability is as high as heaven is above the earth, and His understanding of biology leaves Him as the only one capable of creating a human being with all the neuroscience and endocrinology. No one who thinks he or she is smarter than his or her Creator needs to try explaining it to Him. The authors of *Born Gay* feel science is our best tool for seeking truth. "Although work on the origins of sexuality has been sensitive from the outset, the accumulation of evidence from independent laboratories across the world has shown that the biological

---

[74] Ibid., 10.

differences between gay and straight people cannot be ignored. Science is our best tool for seeking truth about nature even if the facts it provides are sometimes counterintuitive or discomforting."[75] The scriptures say God's word is truth. Stop researching fallible man; study God's word, and you will know the truth. It's not until we decide to obey God that we will stop trying to defy God and prove Him wrong.

A story is told of some students to whom their professor had given recognition as his top and brightest students. The students plotted against the professor in an effort to find fault and prove he could be wrong or make mistakes. They decided to take a bird and conceal it behind a curtain. They asked the professor to guess whether the bird was dead or alive. If he said it was dead, they would let the bird fly out from behind the curtain. If he said the bird was alive, they would squeeze the life out of the bird and present the dead bird to the professor. When they posed this situation to the professor, his response was, "Whatever thy willeth. The bird is whatever you want it to be." This response stunned the students, who for a moment felt they were smarter than their teacher.

The Bible is whatever you want it to be to you. Yet many are combing the scripture to find God at fault. Is Jesus dead or alive to you? Can Jesus be seen living in you? Is the Bible real or not real to you? It's whatever you want. Jesus's invitation remains the same: "Whosoever willeth, let him come. And he that believeth and is baptized, shall be save."

The authors boldly state their belief in the preface of the book, and they set out to support it in their writing of the book. "Modern scientific research indicates that sexual orientation is largely determined by the time of birth, partly by genetics, but more specifically by hormonal activity in the womb arising from various sources."

Ask yourself what the physic "going-on" was in the brains of Adam and Eve when they decided to disobey God. More than likely it's the same physic in our brains we have today when we decide to disobey God. One thing, just straight off the bat, is that they were listening to Satan, and so are we when our lives are contrary to God's will. He got their hormones (endocrinology) enticed to want to be like God—that is pride. Surely their nerves were in overdrive when they realized they were naked and nervously hid in fear of being discovered that they had disobeyed. Surely their brains were in overdrive while working up an excuse (neuroscience). The scriptures tell man that Satan is like a roaring lion, seeking whom he shall devour. Satan understands that his time is limited, and it would be wise for man to

---

[75] Ibid., 10.

understand that his time is limited, too. Man speaks of God's unconditional love but doesn't understand that the offer of salvation is *conditional*: If you believe and are baptized, you will be saved—(Mark 16:16). If you die in your sins, where I am you cannot come – (John 8:21).

God's hands are tied. He cannot lie. Satan is the Father of Lies; he introduced the first lie. Could Eve have had a hormonal problem that caused her to disobey God? Maybe being created from Adam's ribs somehow created a genetic alteration or defect. Could Eve have blamed various sources, including the serpent, for her disobedience? Certainly, if some science (scientists) could have been employed in the Garden of Eden, some justification could have been presented in her case. But results would be the same with Adam as with the gays today—blaming God, who gave him Eve. Gays blame God for having gay genes and suggest possibly something went wrong in the womb: some androgen receptor and 5a- reductase situations and so on.

Wilson and Rahman believe they have presented a sufficient amount of scientific research and data in their book to support or show "that sexual orientation is something we are born with and is not 'acquired' from our social environment."[76]

This is science and an argument (based on scripture) that cannot be won. Be honest and stop deceiving yourselves. Admit you are sinners and don't want to do right. Justifying a sin won't change your status as a sinner. Hope for grace and mercy that you have the opportunity to have a change of heart toward God before it's eternally too late—that's all.

The authors point out instances when LGBT individuals have been demonized and forced to hide their abominable desires and attraction to the same sex. Scripture says that if you suffer for what you do wrong, you can't compare to one who suffers and has done nothing wrong (forced slavery in the United States). In Walkerton, Indiana (in the news, April 2015), the LGBT community directed threats of bodily harm toward a shop owner who (because of religious conviction) decided not to cater a gay wedding. There were no reports of black people threatening to burn down Woolworth because of discrimination at its lunch counters. They took the ill treatment and trusted in God to bring about peace. It is very obvious that the LGBT community is disingenuous and bullies with a nefarious agenda, all the while riding on the civil rights struggles of black people in America. Ironically, African Americans at present (twenty-first century) are still suffering or experiencing racial injustice; they have challenged age-old voting rights laws and discrimination in a society that welcomes, condones, and legalizes

---

[76] Ibid., 145.

effeminate activities or lifestyle the scripture condemns. The scripture doesn't condemn a man for being black, whether he is Jew, Gentile, male, or female.

The farther I read into the pages of *Born Gay*, the more Wilson and Rahman came up with excuses based on scientific studies to support homosexuality, even blaming it on maternal stress, developmental instability, and birth order, to cite a few. In their conclusion,[77] the authors supported the belief or research that man's nearest relative is the bonobo. That could very well be the problem and not any other scientific reasons offered in their book. Certainly if you believe you are related to monkeys and apes, you could pretty much justify any reason for acting in a subhuman way through anal sex. God has made man upright—know that.

Wilson and Rahman praised gay contributions to society. Gays couldn't have made any form of contributions to society ("science, music, art, literature, politic and philanthropy") without heterosexual parents (through nonabominable acts) because they wouldn't have existed or been born. The accomplishments and acclamations go to the heterosexuals. And give God the glory for His marvelous creation. Be fruitful and multiply and replenish the earth.

New Creature in Jesus Christ: Born Again

Make no mistake about it; all men are born the same way, with the sperm or seed, the egg or fertile soil, blood, water, and spirit. Make no mistake about it; all men are saved the same way: the blood of Jesus, water baptism, and the gift of the Holy Spirit. The gospel is the seed of the word, and your spiritual heart (mind) is the fertile ground of incubation for the growth and development into a disciple from babe to maturity in Christ. There is no "You go your way" and "I go my way," and we both get to heaven because we believe in the same God. There is only one God, and there is only one plan of salvation, and we all have to be saved or reborn the same way. God is so serious about this that He said if an angel comes with another gospel of how to be saved, let him be accursed (Galatians 1:8). There is no special gay gospel, and there are no gay Christians. The scripture asks, "How can two walk together unless they agree?" We all have to obey God, and He doesn't have one person saved one way and another person saved another way. God isn't the author of confusion. If it makes no difference what one believes,

---

[77] Ibid., 150.

then it would be unfair to condemn a man if he believes a lie. You need to believe this: God has given us the truth. His word is truth, and we will be held accountable for our sins. We are responsible for searching the scriptures to learn and know what thus says the Lord. "That they should seek the Lord, if haply they might find Him" (Acts 17:27; Romans 1:18–32).

As we examined a few conversions in the New Testament, we saw that all followed the same pattern: *hear* the gospel and learn how Jesus died for sins; *repent* of sins; *believe* the gospel (the death, burial, and resurrection of Christ); *confess* faith in Jesus as the Christ, the Son of God; and be *baptized* to have their sins washed away. It didn't matter whether they were religious people; they stood in need of salvation, the plan God offers man. Even though the disciples of John thought themselves to be saved (Christians), as many moral or religiously "good" person(s) today think. But it isn't until one is taught the gospel: hears, believes the gospel, confesses faith in Christ, and is baptized (final stage of conversion: sinner to saint) that he or she becomes a Christian. He is one that is pleasing to God. In other words, he or she is not a "will worshipper": people who make up their minds to vainly worship God the way they want and expect to be saved.

> For as many of you as have been baptized into Christ have put on Christ. (Galatians 3:27)
>
> Know ye not, that so many of us as were baptized into Jesus Christ, were baptized into his death? Therefore we are buried with Him by baptism into death: that like as Christ was raised up from the dead by the glory of the Father, even so we also should walk in newness of life. For if we have been planted together in the likeness of His death, we shall be also in the likeness of His resurrection. Knowing this that our old man is crucified with Him, that the body of sin might be destroyed, that hereafter we should not serve sin. For he that is dead is freed from sin. Now if we be dead with Christ, we believe that we shall also live with Him. (Romans 6:3–8)
>
> For by one Spirit are we all baptized into one body, whether we be Jews or Gentiles, whether we be bond or free: and have been all made to drink into one Spirit. (1 Corinthians 12:13)

From the first three-thousand-plus souls on the day of Pentecost, who were added to the church, the body of Christ (Acts 2:38, 41), to the Ethiopian eunuch, who was baptized (became a Christian) and went on his way, rejoicing (Acts 8:38), and on to any sincere soul today who must recognize that he or she is a sinner, the first step is to allow the gospel of Christ to save you through your obedience to His word. You may have been born one way, but you have every opportunity to be born again.

BAPTISMS

Baptism for the Remission of Sins

Jesus is baptized to fulfill all righteousness. In Acts 2:37–38, Peter said, "Repent and let every one of you be baptized in the name of Jesus Christ for the remission of sins, and you shall receive the gift of the Holy Spirit." *Remission* means to "take away or forgive." Remember that Adam brought death and that Christ brought life. Now that you know this much, you still will not profit in blaming anyone— not even Adam, Eve, or God for your state of sin; just take the free card out, man! Take it! Salvation is free. The blood of Jesus Christ purchased your freedom.

The Bible teaches us that God is able to remember our sins no more (Hebrews 8:12). He casts our sins into the depths of the sea (Micah 7:18). God will do this for you when you repent and are baptized (Mark 16:16). The purpose and goal of baptism are the forgiveness of sins. This places you back in a perfect relationship with God as if you never sinned and as if Adam and Eve never sinned in the Garden of Eden. They never severed the man-God relationship and brought separation (spiritual and physical) or death to mankind.

In Luke 13:3, Jesus told the Jews they had to repent and be baptized. This was about washing away sins (Acts 2:38; 22:16). It's a biblical fact that all men have sinned; they have been separated from God and are lost (Romans 3:23; 6:23). Isaiah said, "Your sins have separated you from your God and your iniquities have hidden His face from you" (Isaiah 59:1–2). The scriptures tell us God is too holy to look upon sin (Habakkuk 1:13). How often do you hear individuals boast that God loves them? They don't want you trying to tell them anything or correct them on anything. The reality is that God can't stand them. He doesn't even want to look at them. Christ steps in to be our advocate. Christ will make right for us again the relationship that once existed in Genesis 3. Christ will deliver the church or kingdom (saved souls) over to God. Now you can approach God and only then.

Let's examine what being baptized into Christ means. In this chapter, we will weigh in on what the Holy Bible says about scriptural conversions and remission of sins through baptism in Christ. Since mourners' bench, outward signs and inward grace, religious opinions that one is saved before baptism, and other catechism aren't found in the New Testament scriptures, they will not be addressed.

Baptisms Found in the Bible

"There is *one* body, and *one* Spirit, even as you are called in *one* hope of your calling; *one* Lord, *one* faith, *one baptism*, *one* God and Father of all, who is above all, and through all, and in you all" (Ephesians 4:4–6, emphasis added).

There are five to six different baptisms mentioned in the Bible; some scholars claim as many as seven, listing the baptism of Jesus as separate from John's baptism. In this chapter, the one baptism needed today for men to enter heaven will be examined. It's important to understand the different baptisms that occurred in the Bible and which one puts man (people) in a right relationship with God. "Know you not, that so many of us as were baptized into Jesus Christ were baptized into His death? Therefore we are buried with Him by baptism into death: that like as Christ was raised up from the dead by the glory of the Father, even so we also should walk in newness of life. For if we have been planted together in the likeness of His death, we shall in the likeness of His resurrection: Knowing this, that our old man is crucified with Him, that the body of sin might be destroyed, that hereafter we should not serve sin" (Romans 6:3–6).

The Baptism of Cloud (1 Corinthians 10:14)

"Moreover, brethren, I would not that you should be ignorant how that all our fathers were under, and passed through the sea; and were all baptized to Moses in the cloud and in the sea; and did all eat the same spiritual meat; and did all drink the same spiritual drink: for they drank of that spiritual Rock that followed them: and that Rock was Christ."

It was through the water and by the cloud that God delivered the children of Israel. Looking closely at these verses, we see that when Moses and the people of Israel left Egypt, Jesus (who was with God in the beginning) was there with them. Note: "that Rock that followed was Christ." They were saved by water as they went through the sea. Their enemy and oppressor, Pharaoh and his army, tried to follow. But they found themselves separated from the people of Israel by the sea. And when they tried to pursue Israel, they were downed in the sea.

This should also be a lesson for getting wet and being baptized. Moses and the people followed God's instructions and were baptized. Pharaoh's army went into the same water and got wet, and they died. God instructed Moses to lead the people of Israel through the sea, which was their salvation. Pharaoh didn't receive instructions from God to enter the sea; therefore, his action was unauthorized. Pharaoh and his army went into the same water and weren't baptized (saved), but they got wet and were ultimately destroyed (drowned).

Unfortunately, this is the fate of will-worshippers. These are those who create their own way of worship and doctrines unauthorized by God, who warns angels not to bring any other gospel. Let them be a curse—destroyed. This makes one rethink the first church in Acts 2:38 and the three-thousand-plus different and distinct religious practices today. According to the *World Christian Encyclopedia* (Oxford University Press, 2nd Edition, 2001), "There are 33,000 distinct denominations in 238 countries all professing to be Christians."[78] Of the fast-food, have-it-your-own-way or church-of-your-choice mentality, even angels were warned to tread lightly and stay clear.

The Baptism of John (Matthew 3:1–17)

John's message was repent for the kingdom of heaven is at hand (Matthew 3:2). The prophet Isaiah spoke of John the Baptist (*baptizer*) making and preparing the way for Jesus (Isaiah 40:3). John said to the people who came to be baptized of him, "I indeed baptize you with water to repentance: but He that comes after me is mightier than I, whose shoes I am not worthy to bear: He shall baptize you with the Holy Ghost, and with fire" (Matthew 3:11). When Jesus came to John to be baptized of him, John was hesitant, telling Jesus he needed Jesus to baptize him. Jesus was on a mission to do His Father's will and therefore instructed John to do this. "And Jesus answering said to him, allow it to be so now: for it becomes us to fulfill all righteousness." Then John (His cousin), the baptizer, baptized Jesus. When Jesus came up out of the water, the heavens opened to Him, and John saw the Spirit of God descending

---

[78] Oxford University Press, 2nd Edition, 2001

like a dove on Jesus. And he heard a voice from heaven, saying, "This is My beloved Son, in whom I am well pleased" (Matthew 3:13–17).

John's message was to repent for the kingdom of heaven was at hand (Matthew 3:2). Now that the kingdom is come, Jesus's church (the body of Christ or His bride; see Colossians 1:13–28; 1 Thessalonians 2:12, 14; Revelation 1:9), the baptism of John is no longer necessary. It served its purpose. In Acts 19, Apollo, who knew only the baptism of John, the baptizer, was preaching in the synagogue. When Aquila and Priscilla heard him preach, they explained "the way" of God more accurately or perfectly; they said that Christ had died and purchased His church with His own blood. Also in Acts 19, Paul found other disciples who knew only John's baptism. Paul told them that John's baptism was for repentance, telling the people they must believe on Christ Jesus. So when Paul explained "the way" more accurately to those disciples, they were baptized in the name of the Lord Jesus. It was about twelve that this happen to, and afterward, they went into the synagogue, preaching, disputing, and persuading the things concerning the kingdom of God.

The Baptism of the Holy Spirit (Matthew 3:11; Acts 1:5)

We understand the scriptures reference the Holy Spirit or Holy Ghost as the Comforter. Jesus (Godhead) discussed with His disciples that the Father (Godhead) would send them the Comforter, the Holy Ghost (Godhead), who would bring to their remembrance whatsoever things He had taught them and said to them while He was with them on earth (John 14:26). The Comforter, the Spirit of truth coming forth or proceeding from God, will testify of Jesus. The disciples will bear witness because they have been with Jesus from the beginning of His ministry (John 15:26–27). The Spirit of truth guiding the disciples into all truth was the conversation Jesus had with His disciples before His crucifixion (John 16:13–16). *This baptism delivered the power to perform miracles and was given to the apostles and whomever the apostles laid hands on to receive the baptism of the Holy Ghost.* This measure of or baptism of the Holy Spirit isn't to be confused with the gift of the Holy Ghost, which all Christians are promised upon baptism.

The Baptism of Fire (Matthew 3:11; Acts 1:5)

He shall baptize you with the Holy Ghost and with fire (Matthew 3:11). He will burn up the chaff with unquenchable fire (Matthew 3:12). "And death and hell were cast into the lake of fire." John wrote,

> And I saw a great white throne, and Him that sat on it, from whose face the earth and the heaven fled away; and there was found no place for them. And I saw the dead, small and great, stand before God; and the books were opened: and another book was opened, which is the book of life: and the dead were judged out of those things which were written in the books according to their works. And the sea gave up the dead which were in it; and death and hell delivered up the dead which were in them: and they were judged every man according to their works. And death and hell were cast into the lake of fire. This is the second death. And whosoever was not found written in the book of life was cast into the lake of fire. (Revelation 20:11–15)

Paul wrote, "Seeing it is a righteous thing with God to recompense tribulation to them that trouble you: And to you who are troubled rest with us, when the Lord Jesus shall be revealed from heaven with His mighty angels, In flaming fire taking vengeance on them that know not God, and that obey not the gospel of our Lord Jesus Christ" (2 Thessalonians 1:6–8).

Peters wrote, "Seeing then that all these things shall be dissolved, what manner of persons ought you to be in all holy conversation [conduct and lifestyle, way of living] and godliness, Looking for and hasting to the coming of the day of God, where in the heavens being on fire shall be dissolved, and the elements shall melt with fervent heat" (2 Peter 3:11–12).

The Baptism of Water (Mark 10:38–40)

The baptism of suffering or death on the cross puts one in heaven. Two brothers (sons of Zebedee), James and John, asked Jesus whether they could sit one on His left hand and the other on His right hand in glory. Jesus replied and told them they didn't really know what they were asking, and it wasn't for Him to say. He asked them whether they would stand strong in the faith and drink of the cup He would drink of and be baptized like He was (water), and they said to Jesus that they would or could. Jesus affirmed that they would break bread (body of Christ) and drink of the cup (blood shed on the cross) with Him.

The disciples broke bread and drank the fruit of the vine in communion with Jesus in the Last Supper. New Testament Christians break or eat unleavened bread and drink the cup or fruit of the vine in memorial of Christ's blood, which He shed on the cross, with His body pierced or broken. This memorial of Christ's death, burial, and resurrection is upon the first day of each week (Sunday) as the apostles practiced and instructed in the New Testament. New Testament Christians are doing what the two brothers did; they are communing with Christ. The apostles told Christians that "as often as you do this, you do it in His memory" (1 Corinthians 11:23–25).

What Does It Mean to Be Baptized?
A Look at Romans 6

"Know ye not, that so many of us as were baptized into Jesus Christ were baptized into his death? Therefore we are buried with Him by baptism into His death: that like as Christ was raised up from the dead by the glory of the Father, even so, we also should walk in newness of life" (Romans 6:3–4). Baptism puts us in a relationship. We are no longer outsiders. We are married (church, bride, body of Christ) and part of a family (children of God).

What does someone who is gay need to know about baptism?

> For if we have been planted together in the likeness of His death [baptism], we shall be also in the likeness of His resurrection: Knowing this, that our *old man* is crucified with Him, that the body of sin might be destroyed, that *hereafter* we should not serve sin. For he that is dead is freed from sin. Now if we be dead with Christ, we believe that we shall also live with Him. Knowing that Christ being raised from the dead dies no more; death has no more dominion over Him. For in that He died, He died to sin once; but in that He lives, He lives to God. Likewise reckon you also yourselves to be dead indeed to sin, but alive to God through Jesus Christ our Lord. Let not sin therefore reign in your mortal body, that you should obey

it in the *lusts* thereof. Neither yield you your members as instruments of unrighteousness to sin: but yield yourselves to God, as those that are alive from the dead, and your members as instruments of righteousness to God. For sin shall not have dominion or control over you: for you are not under the law, but under grace. What then? Shall we sin because we are not under the law, but under grace? God forbid. Know you not, that to whom you yield yourselves servant to obey; whether of sin to death or of obedience to righteousness? But God be thanked, that you *were* the servants of sin, but you have obeyed from the heart that form of doctrine which was delivered you. Being then made free from sin, you became the servants of righteousness." (emphasis added)

Paul said that *before* you acted in a carnal and fleshly manner, going after and yielding your body, becoming a servant to uncleanness and to iniquity; but *after* accepting Christ (through obedience) you *now* yield your body to be a servant of God in doing holy (not abominable) acts.

"For when you were the servants of sin, you were free from righteousness. What fruit had you then in those things whereof you are now ashamed? For the end of those things is death. But now being made free from sin, and become servants to God you have your fruit to holiness, and the end everlasting life. For the wages of sin is death, but the *gift of God* is eternal life through Jesus Christ our Lord" (emphasis added).

Our baptism in water is in a similitude manner to Jesus: "For I delivered to you first of all that which I also received, how that Christ died for our sins according to the Scriptures; and that He was buried, and that He rose again the third day according to the Scriptures" (1 Corinthians 15:3–4). Remember the brothers James and John and what Jesus told them; He said they would drink the cup, drink His blood. Christians commemorate the death, burial, and resurrection of Jesus each Lord's Day (Sunday) when they drink the cup, the fruit of the vine (blood), and eat the unleavened bread, the body of Christ. To do this, one becomes part of the body; added to His kingdom or church through water baptism, that would be going down into the liquid grave of baptism and rising from the water to walk in newness of life.

It was only Jesus's blood, not animal sacrifices, that was a perfect sacrifice for the sins of man in redeeming him and putting him back into a right relationship with God, the Father.

Wherefore when He comes into the world, He says, Sacrifice and offering You would not, but a body have you prepared Me: In burnt offerings and sacrifices for sin You have no pleasure. Then said I, Lo, I come (in the volume of the book it is written of Me) to do Your will, O God. (Hebrews 10:5–7)

For He has made Him to be sin for us, who knew no sin; that we might be made the righteousness of God in Him. (2 Corinthians 5:21)

At this point, the reader must know as much as the two sons of Zebedee, James and John. Yes, you can be baptized with the baptism Jesus was baptized with (water) and drink of the cup and eat the bread every first day of the week in remembrance of His death, burial, and resurrection—unleavened bread (body) and fruit of the vine (blood).

The Baptism of the Father, Son, and Holy Ghost (Matthew 28:19–20)

The Great Commission Baptism puts one into Christ. "Go you therefore and teach all nations, baptizing them in the name of the Father, and of the Son, and of the Holy Ghost. Teaching them to observe all things whatsoever I have commanded you (the apostles): and, lo, I am with you always, even to the end of the world. Amen" (Matthew 28:20). *The baptism of the Father, Son, and Holy Ghost is the one that will last unto the end of the world.* This is the *one* Lord, *one* faith, *one* baptism, and *one* God and Father of all, who is above all and through all and in you all (Ephesians 4:5–6).

Peters told the Jews in Acts 2 that they had crucified Jesus. God had made Him both Lord and Christ. "Then Peter said to them, *repent*, and be *baptized* every one of you in the name of Jesus Christ for the remission of sins and you shall receive the gift of the Holy Ghost" (Acts 2:38, emphasis added). Water baptism in the name of the Jesus saves man.

Which sometimes were disobedient when once the longsuffering of God waited in the days of Noah, while the ark was a preparing, wherein few, that is, eight souls were saved by water. WATER, the like figure whereto even baptism does also now save us (not the putting away of the filth of the flesh, but the answer of a good conscience toward God,) by the resurrection of Jesus Christ. (1 Peter 3:2–21)

For as many of you as have been baptized into Christ have put on Christ. There is neither Jew nor Greek, there is neither bond nor free, there is neither male nor female: for you are all one in Christ Jesus. (Galatians 3:27–28)

In summary, for one to scripturally be in Christ, he or he must obey the following:

1. Hear the word of the gospel (Romans 10:17).
2. Believe Jesus died for our sins, was buried, and rose the third day (John 8:24).
3. Repent of past sins (Luke 13:3).
4. Confess that Jesus is the Son of God (Romans 10:10).
5. Be baptized for the remission of sins (Acts 2:38).

Whether you are gay or straight, look back at "the list." It is futile and vain to continue to make excuses, whatever they might be about your failure to obey God. If the righteous will barely make it in, what about the sinners and the ungodly? Once again, take the free gift, man! Here is the free pass or ticket out of hell. Obey. Christ did even unto the death of the cross.

FAITH

FAITH: Without Faith It Is Impossible to Please God

Now that we understand that baptism puts us into Christ, how do we even get to the point of baptism? Our spiritual lives start with faith and end with faith. "But without faith, it is impossible to please Him for he that comes to God must believe that He is, and that He is a rewarder of them that diligently seek Him" (Hebrews 11:6). Revelation 2:10 lets us know about the reward of being faithful unto death, which is the crown of life. We all want to be winners, and we can be through faith. It has been penned in the lyrics: faith is the victory that overcomes the world.

Faith and Belief

Faith and belief are often used interchangeably, and we cannot have faith if we don't believe. The major difference is that someone can believe but not have faith. Remember, Satan believed and trembled. Faith is something that is evidence of some action. "What does it profit, my brethren, though a man say he has faith, and have not works—can faith save him? ... Even so faith, if it has not works, is dead, being alone. Yea, a man may say, You have faith, and I have works: show me your faith without your works, and I will show you my faith by my works. You believe that there is one God; you done well: the devils also believe, and tremble" (James 2:14, 17–19).

Some prefer to look at faith as an unknown, invisible, and mysterious factor, while faith is an obedient response to evidence. Faith comes by hearing (first) and hearing (the gospel) and then believing the gospel (Romans 10:17). The apostles preached the word of faith. Christ brought an end to the Law of Moses and animal sacrifices, and He made redemption or pardon of sins through His blood on the cross to everyone who believes, both Jews and Gentiles. So what is our faith? *The faith that Christ died for our sins and rose again to die no more, conquering death that held all mankind hostage.* "But the righteousness which is of faith speaks on this wise, Say not in your heart, Who shall ascend into heaven? [that's to bring Christ down from above] or, who shall descend into the deep? [that's to bring up Christ again from the dead]" (Romans 10:6–7). After hearing and believing what was preached by the apostles, which is the gospel—the death, burial, and resurrection—our obedience is evidence of our faith. The scripture says, "That if you shall confess with your mouth the Lord Jesus and shall believe in your heart that God has raised Him from the dead, you shall be saved. For with the heart man believes to righteousness, and with the mouth confession is made to salvation. For the Scripture says, Whosoever believes on Him shall not be ashamed" (Romans 10:9–11).

Here is salvation as simple and plain as day. Yet the scripture says many have a zeal to do what's in their own minds and own will, and they sadly have gone about in their ignorance of God's righteousness—His plan of salvation to establish their own righteousness. They have established their own churches, religions, and faiths; and they won't submit themselves to the righteousness of God. That is why the *one* Lord, *one* faith, *one* baptism, and *one* Lord and Father of all we find in scripture become over thirty-five-hundred-plus-and-growing different faiths and religious practices in "will" and "vain" worship of God (Romans 10:1–3).

The scripture asks, How shall we escape the wrath to come and hellfire if we reject God's plan of salvation, which is so simple? Jesus came down personally and delivered it to His hand-picked disciples (twelve apostles), and the disciples (apostles) confirmed what He had taught them while He was on earth with them. God the Father acknowledges Jesus (His beloved Son) and sent the Holy Ghost to bear witness to the apostles with signs, wonders, and miracles, confirming the word (Hebrews 2:3–4). "And many other signs truly did Jesus in the presence of his disciples, which are not written in this book; But these are written, *that you might believe that Jesus is the Christ, the Son of God; and that believing you might have hope*" (Romans 15:4, *emphasis added*).

The other disciples told Thomas they had seen Jesus. Thomas (Didymus) asked for evidence, and he wasn't denied his request. On several occasions after His resurrection, Jesus appeared to His disciples, and this time Thomas was with them. Jesus was aware of Thomas's expressed concerns. "Except I shall see in His hands the print of the nails, and put my finger into the print of the nails, and thrust my hand into His side, I will not believe" (John 20:25). When Jesus entered the room where Thomas and the other disciples were gathered, He approached Thomas and said, "Reach here your finger and behold My hands and reach here your hand and thrust it into My side and be not faithless, but believing" (John 20:27). Thomas told Jesus that he believed. Jesus's response was, "Thomas, because you have seen Me, you have believe: blessed are they that have not seen, and yet have believe" (John 20:29).

Righteousness through Faith

The book of Hebrews is regarded as the "Hall of Faith" or "Chapter of Faith" because of the many biblical characters recorded there, including Abel, Enoch, Noah, Abraham, Sarah, Jacob, Joseph, Moses, Rahab (the harlot), and many others who demonstrated faith and faithfulness through their action and response to the word of God. "Now faith is the substance of things hoped for, the *evidence* of things not seen. For by it the elders obtained a good report" (Hebrews 11:1–2, emphasis added). In Romans 4:3, we read that Abraham believed God, and his faith was counted or imputed to him for righteousness. "Even as Abraham believed God, and it was accounted to him for righteousness" (Galatian 3:6).

God is righteous and faithful.

God is *faithful*, by whom you were called to the fellowship of His Son Jesus Christ our Lord. (1 Corinthians 1:9, emphasis added)

There has no temptation taken you but such as is common to man: but God is *faithful*, who will not suffer you to be tempted above that you are able, but will with the temptation also make a way to escape that you may be able to bear it. (1 Corinthians 10:13, emphasis added)

But the Lord is *faithful*, who shall stablish you, and keep you from evil. (2 Thessalonians 3:3, emphasis added)

Let us hold fast the profession of our faith without wavering (for He is *faithful* that promised). (Hebrews 10:23, emphasis added)

If we confess our sins, He is *faithful* and just to forgive us our sins, and to cleanse us from all unrighteousness. (1 John 1:9)

In short, these scriptures support the fact that God has your back and will follow through on His promises with action. He has done it all to receive you, and it is now your move. Show your faith in His promises to you by being obedient to His will—by actions or works.

📖 Book Corner Excerpt (Interview)

"Former Homosexual Says 'No one is born gay,'" CBN, July 21, 2003.[79] The full excerpt of the interview is not included.

Stephen Bennett is a former homosexual who lived the "gay" lifestyle for eleven years. Today he is married with children. He professes to be a born-again Christian and has a ministry targeted at lesbians and homosexuals, whom he says want to be set free from homosexuality. The following quoted paragraph is from an interview with Lee Webb, the *700 Club* interviewer, in 2003.

I said to them specifically, "I am living proof that there's no basis whatsoever for any kind of legislation equating

---

[79] Stephen Bennett, CBN, "Former Homosexual Says 'No One Is Born Gay,'" July 21, 2003, http://www.sbministries.org/. http://www.greaterhope.org/stephen-bennett/

homosexuality with heterosexuality." For the fact that I was gay. I lived the gay lifestyle until I was 28 years old, probably for about 11 years. Well, with over 100 men sexually, many of whom are dead today from AIDS. I've buried countless boyfriends in the ground because of AIDS.

I was in love with another man who was going to be my partner for life, until a Christian woman showed up at my door one day with a Bible and said that I could be set free from my homosexuality. That was back in 1990 and my life has never been the same again.

I reached out to Mr. Bennett for comments on his 2003 interview on CBN with Lee Webb, and he expressed concerns about the title of this book, *I Was Born Gay, I Was Born Again*. I agreed with Mr. Bennett's understanding of scripture that "no one is born gay," but is concerned about the merchandising of the gospel.

The gospel saves, not programs. That was a weakness and flaw with the leader of Exodus International. Exodus International fronted itself as a Christian ministry that had no authority scripturally, yet it tried to supersede the authority of the Bible for personal glory, profit, and recognition. Only Jesus saves, and only His way of salvation and His word convert the heart of man; that would exclude man-made institutions and programs that cannot save souls. God's word won't fold to man's demands or apologize to man.

For more information on Stephen Bennett and Stephen Bennett Ministries, please visit his website at http://www.sbministries.org/.

Commanded to Walk by Faith

Faith is the key to the Christian life. "For we walk by faith, not by sight" (2 Corinthians 5:7). We look not on the things seen but to the things unseen, for what we see now is temporal (2 Corinthians 4:18).

> For we know that our earthly house of this tabernacle were dissolved, we have a building of God, an house not made with hands, eternal in the heavens. (2 Corinthians 5:1)
>
> The heavens declare the glory of God and the firmament shows His handy work. (Psalm 19:1)
>
> Be still and know that I am God. I will be exalted among the heathen. I will be exalted in the earth. (Psalm 46:10)

Let us be individuals who will believe to the saving of our souls (Hebrews 10:39). Once we have obeyed, let's not just get wet and die. But after we are baptized, we have an obedient and working faith that produces fruit in saving ourselves and bringing other lost souls to Christ.

This is a simple, uncomplicated message. Don't act like Naaman when he wanted to be cleansed of leprosy. The prophet Elisha sent him to dip seven times in the Jordan River. He was angry and upset because he held some mega-church mentality and wanted grandeur. He wanted Elisha to come and showboat by waving his hands over him and calling on the Lord. He even questioned the choice of river waters. He wanted more prestigious rivers (Abana and Pharpar Rivers of Damascus were better than all the waters of Israel) to perform his salvation from his leprosy. "And his servants came near, and spoke to him and said, My father, if the prophet had bid you do some *great thing*, would you not have done it? How much rather then, when he says to you, Wash, and be Clean?" (2 Kings 5:13, emphasis added). It wasn't until Naaman obeyed and dipped seven times in the Jordan River that he was cleaned (saved) from that disease (2 Kings 5:14).

Man has come up with so many elaborate ways to be saved when the way is as simple as hear, believe, repent, confess, and be baptized; then live faithfully (work in the kingdom church) until death.

If you believe you were born gay, well, all hope isn't lost. The solution to pleasing God and saving your soul is to be born again. It isn't an elaborate ritual. Jesus has done all the work, which involved His death on the cross, His resurrection from the dead, and His ascension to heaven. And through your obedience, He has promised you that you may be where He is, with a mansion in heaven prepared for you. Your choices are the temporal pleasures, short-lived victories life has to offer, or the eternal home in heaven. It's your move! It has always been your choice to move back to or toward God. What is man that God is mindful of him? Think that over. God wants you back, and He sent Jesus to make that possible. Satan wants you, too. He wants to get back at God for condemning him to hell by seeking to destroy you and your chance for eternal life with God. Your personal victories on this time side of life aren't important in the greater scheme of things. They are at the most short lived; you are leaving here one day. The battle is between good (God) and evil (Satan). Now, what side you chose to stand on is the only victory that will matter, and the question to you is, Will it be in Christ Jesus?

Chapter 5
Ye Are Gods–Judges and Magistrates

God stands in the congregation of the mighty; He judges among the gods. How long will you judge unjustly, and accept the persons of the wicked? ... They know not, neither will they understand; they walk on in darkness; all the foundations of the earth are out of course. I have said, You are gods; and all of you are children of the most High. But you shall die like men, and fall like one of the princes. Arise, O God, judge the earth: for You shall inherit all nations." (Psalm 82:1–2; 5–8)

Jesus answered them, Is it not written in your law, I said, You are gods? If He called them gods, to whom the word of God came, and the scripture cannot be broken; Say you of Him, whom the Father has sanctified, and sent into the world, You blaspheme; because I said, I am the Son of God? (John 10:34–36)

HERE IS EVIDENCE that God is always in control. He always *knows what is going on*. He remains the Supreme Judge. He uses judges to execute His wrath on those who do evil and praises on those who do good, whether or not the judges know and understand how God uses them as vessels and ministers for His purpose. Judges save the souls of men by judging righteously and leading men and nations in the right paths (to Christ); that is the providence God provides. The rulings of Supreme Court judges provide America and all humanity with an opportunity to keep a good and righteous position of protection by God's divine providence. The court's ruling on gay marriage should have reflected America's motto or mantra: "In God We Trust."

Every person should be in subjection to the governing authority. For there is no authority except from God, and *those that exist are established by God.* Therefore whoever resists authority has opposed the ordinance of God, and they who have opposed it will receive condemnation on themselves. Rulers aren't a cause of fear for good behavior but for evil. Do you want to have no fear of authority? Do what is good, and you will have praise from the same, for the authority is a minister of God to you for good. But if you do what is evil, be afraid, for authority doesn't bear the sword for nothing; it is a minister of God and an avenger that brings wrath on the one who practices evil (Romans 13:1–4).

What Do The Judges of This Nation Have to Say?

Roberts, C.J., Dissenting

Kenney, J., delivered the opinion of the Court, in which Ginsburg, Breyer, Sotomayor, and Kagan, JJ., joined. Roberts, C.J., filed a dissenting opinion, in which Scalia and Thomas, J., joined .Thomas, J., filed a dissenting opinion, in which Scalia, J., joined. Alito, J., filed a dissenting opinion, in which Scalia and Thomas, JJ., joined. State Legislation and Judicial Decisions—Legalizing Same-Sex Marriage "Petitioners make strong arguments rooted in social policy and considerations of fairness. They contend that same-sex couples should be allowed to affirm their love and commitment through marriage, just like opposite-sex couples. That position has undeniable appeal; over the past six years, voters and legislators in eleven States and the District of Columbia have revised their laws to allow marriage between two people of the same sex."

Roberts, Scalia and Thomas contend that this Court is not a legislature. "Whether same-sex marriage is a good idea should be of no concern to us. Under the Constitution, judges have power to say what the law is, not what it should be. The people who ratified the Constitution authorized courts to exercise "neither force nor will but merely judgment." The Federalist No. 78, p. 465 (C. Rossiter ed. 1961) (A. Hamilton) (capitalization altered).

"Although the policy arguments for extending marriage to same-sex couples may be compelling, the legal arguments for requiring such an extension are not. The fundamental right to marry does not include a right to make a State change its definition of marriage. And a State's decision to maintain the meaning of marriage that has persisted in every culture throughout human history can hardly be called irrational. In short, our Constitution does not enact any other theory of marriage. The people of a State are free to expand marriage to include same-sex couples, or to retain the historic definition."

"Today, however, the Court takes the extraordinary step of ordering every State to license and recognize same-sex marriage. Many people will rejoice at this decision, and I begrudge none their celebration. But for those who believe in a government of laws, not of men, the majority's approach is deeply disheartening. Supporters of same-sex marriage have achieved considerable success persuading their fellow citizens—through the democratic process—to adopt their view. That ends today. Five lawyers have closed the debate and enacted their own vision of marriage as a matter of constitutional law. Stealing this issue from the people will for many cast a cloud over same-sex marriage, making a dramatic social change that much more difficult to accept."[80] [S.Ct. Reporter Pagination at 2611-2612 (Roberts, John. Dissenting opinion. *James Obergefell v. Richard Hodges*. 576 U.S. ____, 135 S. Ct. 2584, 192 L. Ed. 2d 609 (2015) www. supremecourt.gov/opinions/boundvolumes.aspx]

After this ruling, many Americans were left feeling like *"no one knows what is going on."* The 2016 presidential candidate, Donald Trump, was able to capitalize on the June 2015 ruling and on the winds of the tide of the times in American's dissatisfaction with the powerful elite, people in office they had trusted who had let them down. Yes, his base didn't care whether

---

[80] Obergefell v. Hodges. 576 U.S. ____, S.Ct. 2584 at 2611-2612 (2015)

he stood in the middle of the streets and shot somebody; they certainly felt like doing the same. It now seems like so many children are standing in the middle of schools, shooting somebody, whether their classmates or school officials. His base didn't care whether he was a potty mouth; they wanted to swear at the judges and political representatives they had voted into office, who allowed this ruling to happen in a Christian nation.

This ruling opened the portal and allowed the evil spirits of chaos and hatred to resurface and increase, severing God's divine providential protection. Once again, hear this. God, the Supreme Judge, is always in control and knows what is going on. He allows things to happen to let us see ourselves for who we are. See Judges 9:8-16. He allows the undesirable to rule over a disobedient nation and to bring about a change (uncomfortably), allowing America to repent (change course) and humble itself to the will of God, the highest rule of authority. The question is, Will we repent before we are ultimately destroyed? "MENE, MENE, TEKEL, UPHARSIN."

Is Being Gay the Problem?

America has become an abominable nation and flaunts its sins in the sight of God. It appears that being effeminate wasn't the only offense on "the list." It also appears that some who had been gay were no longer effeminate, "for such were some of you." The problem seems to have been disobedience, and the solution was obedience.

Politics wasn't a topic of discussion; neither was political correctness or even tolerance for abominable acts. There were no issues of gay bashing or any sinner bashing; only they had sin in their lives. Being effeminate was one of the sin issues, and they obeyed God and took that sin out of their lives.

On Thursday, November 7, 2013, the *New York Times* reported, "Breaking News Alert: Senate approves Ban on Antigay Bias in Workplace."[81] What was strikingly interesting about this article, compared to the struggles black

---

[81] "Senate Approves Ban on Antigay Bias in Workplace," *New York Times*, November 7, 2013.
https://blog.seattlepi.com/seattlepolitics/2013/11/07/u-s-senate-votes-to-ban-anti-gay-workplace-bias/
https://www.truthdig.com/articles/senate-approves-ban-on-anti-gay-bias-at-work/
https://www.wsj.com/articles/senate-passes-gayrights-bill-banning-discrimination-1383853128 (Nov. 7, 2013)

people faced in the three-fifths or less than a man treatment in this country (while peacefully marching for their God-given, inalienable rights not to be discriminated against), was that civil rights for the African-American man didn't get this level of political and bipartisan support for his (more than a social) issue of being treated poorly and unequally because he was of a different race or ethnicity. I guess this is like one not of the human race.

Noah had three sons, and of these three, the earth was repopulated. And God didn't biblically describe the black man as abominable. Yet here we see where one is defiant in his response to the Creator's command that man shouldn't lie with mankind as with womankind; it is an abomination, and the other has Bible in hand, tears, and prayers to God. Now, don't miss this: It was reported that it was the first time in the Senate's history that there was a bipartisan vote, 64 to 32, in support of including gay, lesbian, bisexual, and transgender into USA nondiscrimination law; this banned discrimination in the workplace. It makes one wonder what history will report was the ratio in the Senate's voting bipartisan in support of banning discrimination in the workplace for black Americans. The one can get a job and complain about discrimination on the job for being gay, live and buy where he or she wants, and has never experienced discrimination in access to public facilities. The other one can't even get the job because of discrimination due to the color of his or her skin.

"A Judge in Texas Struck Down the Ban on Same-Sex Marriage" is the headline in an article Manny Fernandez wrote for the *New York Times* on February 27, 2014.[82] This judge believed the ban violated the US Constitution, which has been amended to accommodate the gay lifestyle here in America. God's word doesn't change or accommodate situational ethics. The Texas Constitution, passed in 1997 and 2003, defines marriage as a union between a man and a woman. This judge felt this definition discriminated against gay marriages and demeaned their dignity in their marriage unions. In other words, one's religious views—Judaic Christian views—aren't a legitimate reason to condemn same-sex unions. In Judge Orlando L. Garcia's opinion, God doesn't rule here. The government alone will decide what is right, just, and legitimate. There is no room, in other words, in our U.S. Constitution for what the Bible

https://www.expressnews.com/news/us-world/us/article/Senate-approves-ban-on-anti-gay-bias-in-workplace-4965928.php

[82] Manny Fernandez, "A Judge in Texas Struck Down the Ban on Same-Sex Marriage," *New York Times*, February 27, 2014. https://www.nytimes.com/2014/02/27/us/texas-judge-strikes-down-state-ban-on-same-sex-marriage.html

has to say about being effeminate or about men having sex with men. This is a brutish and blasphemous statement against the will of God for man. It has been said from Judge Garcia's mouth to God's ears. We will all give account for every word spoken out of our mouths. "But I say to you, that every idle word that men shall speak, they shall give account thereof in the Day of Judgment (Matthew 12:36). We all heard or read what the judge said. Let us examine scripture.

> O Lord, I know that the way of man is not in himself: it is not in man that walks to direct his steps. (Jeremiah 10:23)
> For my thoughts are not your thoughts, neither are your ways My ways, says the Lord. For as the heavens are higher than the earth, so are My thoughts than your thoughts. (Isaiah 55:8–9)

Job asked, "Shall mortal man be more just than God? Shall a man be more pure than his maker?" (Job 4:17).

Amendment Ten gives citizens of the state the freedom to vote on the laws and elect representatives who will protect their votes on these laws and issues of concern while serving their elected terms in office. Even though many people in these United States voiced their opinions against gay marriages, the courts have usurped their rights. In the news in April 2015, senators (politicians) were challenging religious freedom to practice one's religious belief when it came to homosexuality and the Christian businessperson. Christian business owners are forced to participate in gay activities (catering gay weddings) against their beliefs in the Bible. This is the opinion of Governor Rick Perry. We see that, based on the original Constitution, it is unconstitutional to take away the rights of the people of the United States of America to vote on their state's laws and not to have that right usurped by the courts.

Suffer Little Children to Come unto Me

In this same article from The New York Times, February 27, 2014, Manny Fernandez wrote about a situational ethics view among gay and lesbian couples who expressed that biblical principles and the rights of others to exercise and express their religious rights (Christian belief) caused them much anguish in perpetuating discrimination against this lifestyle in financial, legal, and emotional ways. The gay couples were distraught because they were challenged when it came to them being considered parents in the traditional way, as mothers and fathers. The gay or lesbian couples feel that discrimination against this lifestyle demeans their definition of family and belittles the parent-child relationship; they are denied equal protection in government benefits in this "family-tax-eligible status" they seek. The movement is trying to claim on their finances and taxes what belongs to God. "Lo, children are an heritage of the Lord: and the fruit of the womb is His reward" (Psalm 127:3). In Matthew 19:14 and Luke 18:16, Jesus expressed His love and concern for children. No one should stand in the way of children knowing and accepting Jesus Christ. "Permit little children and forbid them not, to come to Me: for of such is the kingdom of heaven." The Bible shows God's displeasure and punishment to those who taint (morally contaminate) what is acceptable and righteousness in the innocent minds of children. Children's innocence should not be offended by what is contrary to the will of God. Children shouldn't be placed in adoption situations or environments where the homosexual lifestyle is taught to them (Matthew 5:19; 18:6; Mark 9:42). God is angry with the wicked every day. The advocates for gay rights believe God is love. Yes, God is love, but He is also a consuming fire. We can recall in Genesis what He did with some of that fire in Sodom and Gomorrah.

If one were to say that these children have the opportunity to make up their own minds about their sexuality or even that Christian principles won't be withheld, the Bible speaks of a house divided against itself will not stand. No one in a gay relationship is going to teach his or her children what the Bible says in 1 Corinthians 6 and Romans 1:21–32; it is an abomination for man to lie with mankind as with womankind or for women to be in sexual relationships with other women. Matthew 12:25 and Mark 3:24–26 teach that a house divided against itself will not stand.

It never ceases to amaze me when people (mankind) think they are more righteous or smarter than God. Take a look at the table below. It is so hypocritical and discriminatory to punish everyone on this list except homosexuals, but we should jail and prosecute everyone else. These sins will keep everyone who commits them out of heaven. God called all these acts "sin," and He went on to say that the effeminate (unnatural affection) or homosexual was an abomination in His sight. But special preparation and laws are being formed to protect only those who are effeminate. Someone needs to see the handwriting on the wall before it's too late.

Sin	Bible	Crime	Punishment
Fornicator	Scriptures condemn behavior	Prostitution or underage sex acts; pedophilia	Jail
Adulterer	Scriptures condemn behavior	On books in some states; example: North Carolina	Divorce court or fines and fees
Effeminate Homosexuality (gay or lesbian)	Scriptures condemn behavior	Lewd acts and sodomy	protected by law Amended US Constitution
Bestiality	Scriptures condemn behavior	Sex with animals; zoophilia felony	Jailed
Thieves	Scriptures condemn behavior	Robbers, burglars, muggers, pansy schemes, cheating on tax returns	Jailed
Drunkards	Scriptures condemn behavior	Drunk drivers, disorderly conduct	Jailed
Extortioners	Scriptures condemn behavior	Unlawful gain by unacceptable means	Jailed
Men stealers	Scriptures condemn behavior	Kidnappers/ traffickers	Jailed
Liars	Scriptures condemn behavior	Perjury	Jailed
Revilers	Scriptures condemn behavior	Non peaceful assembly	Jailed

Is it fair to jail and prosecute all other sinners but not those committing homosexual acts? After all, it is God who said they were all sinning or sinners. Why discriminate against the liars, kidnappers, and thieves? Amend something so they can be free to disrupt and change the course of this nation? Absurd. And so is the gay lifestyle permeating this nation. Get ready for the arguments for bestiality, now that the gays have opened the floodgates. Felony charges of animal cruelty were brought against a man having sex with the family's pet Chihuahua.[83]

---

[83] "Felony Charges for Sex with Family Pet Chihuahua," CBS, February 6, 2015, https://www.nydailynews.com/news/national/florida-man-tomas-bautista-busted-sexually-assaulting-chihuahua-police-article-1.137623 ; https://www.dailymail.co.uk/news/article-2943193/Man-sex-CHIHUAHUA-jailed-wife-spots-abusing-family-pet.html

If you don't stand up against sin, you will fall (be persuaded) by every wind and doctrine that come along. Satan takes you places where you didn't mean to go and keeps you there longer than you planned to stay. America, save yourselves; get back on course.

Homosexuality from Biblical Times to Ancient Rome to Twenty-First-Century America

Again, the question to be answered, "Is homosexuality the real problem?" There are many who try to write scholarly about the subject, indulging in mounds of research and relying on PhD philosophy and understandings for acceptance of this lifestyle contrary to scripture. The most threatening concerns are the people who stand by and allow sinful acts to cause a nation to be cursed. Look at the history of man; this isn't the first time the issue of homosexuality has plagued a nation. Remember Sodom and Gomorrah. Remember—Adam, Eve, and the serpent weren't the only ones cursed, but their actions led to the ground being cursed, too (Genesis 3:17–18). When a people or nation isn't governed by righteousness, the nation suffers in derision. The ground you stand on wants to spew you out! Observe the climate changes we haven't seen in fifty to one-hundred-plus years, fires, earthquakes, hurricanes, floods, mass shootings and killings of children (for such is the kingdom of God), vicious acts on women (the crown of creation, glory of man, and vessel through which the Savior came to earth to save mankind), growing racial tension, high crimes, and terrorist threats.

The Bible talks about man being "gods" and man's ability to govern, rule, and judge a nation of people. "Behold the man is become as one of Us, to know *good* and *evil*" (Genesis 3:22, emphasis added). We know right from wrong, and there are people elected and placed in positions of authority (by the will of God) in a civilization to maintain peace, lawfully judge, and punish the unlawful in that particular society.

Homosexuality has been around since biblical times; so is the real problem with effeminate and lewd acts, or is it with the society (nation) that allows it to flourish? Take a look at the Roman Empire; where is it now? We know the biblical account of Sodom and Gomorrah. Where are these cities now? The scriptures tell us there is nothing new under the sun. Recent events are evidence as hundred-year-old climatic weather devastations make their circuits back to landmarks that were once destroyed. Tropical Storm Sandy and others make their circuit, revisiting places once devastated by the waters from the seas and oceans. Still, earth's inhabitants' salvation is once again dependent on God's promises to save man—if he is obedient to the will of God. The promise of the rainbow, that He won't destroy the earth and mankind by water, is a reminder of that covenant. Man's inventions have come a long way since the flood, Noah, and the ark. There won't be any need for submarines—water won't be the issue. There won't be any need for spaceships; the moon will turn to blood, the sun will fail to shine, and the earth will burn up. Don't try to look for any fire retardants on that day! Just like Noah's days, you won't see the event coming; it will be too late for preparations.

Satan is bent on destroying man, and his most successful tactics are deception and lies. The scripture says he is the Father of Lies. And God cannot lie. Gays have convinced this nation that God is lying when He says a man shall leave father and mother and cleave to his wife and that they two shall become one. Gays want America to believe marriage should be between two people (same sex) who are attracted to each other and committed to one another in a "loving" relationship. Gays would like to convince or persuade the heterosexual population to believe it is God's fault they are the way they are; in other words, "God made me this way." If God made a person gay, wouldn't He know about it too? Ground zero: Adam and Eve already played the lying and blame game, and they didn't win. Sidebar: according to the book of Genesis, the ground and the serpent were cursed. Instead of America being blessed, will it receive a curse too?

The gays didn't build the institution of marriage, but they want to destroy it, to change it to fit their agenda. God said, "Be fruitful and multiply and replenish the earth" and that children are His inheritance. To further their agenda, gays have convinced this society (nation) to sacrifice or offer up their children to their abominable agenda. They fight for and demand the right to adopt, seeking legal avenues that allow the system to give over God's inheritance, children, to them in adoption; because any home (gay on gay or lesbian on lesbian) is better for the child (God's inheritance) than no home at all. These are more of Satan's all-so-innocent lies and deceptions. We give away God's inheritance and place them in an abominable environment—not the home God built (instituted for the husband and wife); and we have the audacity to ask God to bless us, to bless America. What hypocrites we are when we get angry with Jeremiah Wright who said, "God damn America." It was over ten years ago, March 2008, since Mr. Wright made the statement. President Trump can be heard on many occasions saying: 'our country's going to hell,' before and after he was elected president, and no one is offended by it. No one has challenged Mr. Trump on his statement. What are the differences between the two statements, which have the same outcomes: God damn America versus America is going to hell?

We are dealing with Satan, the Father of Lies and deception, who wants only to kill, steal, and destroy man. The gays want to take what God has given to the marriage and have convinced society that we, the American people, are unfair. They can't give; they just want to take. They can't perpetuate a continuation of life; they just want to seize what you have as rights of the giver or perpetrator of continued civilization. What parasites! It won't be long before married employees will be informed by their employers that two men sleeping together and not adding anything to perpetuate civilization—not one pain in childbirth—can afford the same benefits as a married employee who can produce the next generation of senators, congressmen, presidents, governors, doctors, lawyers, judges, actors, athletes, laborers, or workforce. God's way maintains a future functioning civilization. My mistake, that has already happened.

There are religious leaders who haven't suffered on the cross but have elevated themselves to high priests. Jesus has earned the position of High Priest. Jesus came to the fig tree, and it was fruitless, and He cursed it. Remember the one-talent, two-talent, and five-talent servants in the Bible. Their master took the one-talent servant's talent and gave it to the five-talent servant. God created animals, trees, and all of nature to produce after its own kind. God didn't produce a fruitless anything; even the sun and moon take part in keeping the earth in a position of production or reproduction in bringing in the change of seasons and photosynthesis of plants for food. If it isn't of God, then it is of Satan. God didn't create man to have fruitless sex with another man or a woman to have fruitless sex with another woman.

How far as a nation will we allow this to go? Just like the handwriting on the wall in the biblical prophecy, we can be assured that Satan will never stop seeking whom he can destroy. We will have to change our ways and ask God for forgiveness. Once gays have a stronghold on this nation's family, the institution of marriage and home, and the adoption of children ("Blessed is the man that has his quiver full of them"), this nation will be dealing with bestiality (zoophilia) on the same agenda and political level as the gay issue. People will soon be fighting for rights to marry animals and be afforded the same tax breaks as the rest of society. Scary? Some finance guru into animals will tell you it's all about the money, taxes, and finance. Well, the same lewd acts of homosexuality and bestiality are in the same chapter in the Bible. Satan always takes you where you didn't plan to go and always keeps you longer than you plan to stay. The call still stands: resist the devil, and he will flee from you. As a nation of people, we need to resist the pressure to conform to what God calls abominable or an abomination. We need not tempt God with our sinful ways. The scriptures once mentioned that it repented God that he had made man. Are we trying to make it back to that circuit in history, in that nothing is new under the sun? What can we do as a nation to make it right with God so we can rightfully and confidently say, "God, bless America"?

For Ye Are Gods

They have become like Us, discerning good and evil. Our appointed judicial officials have been given the authority and power to make the ultimate decisions of what will judge and govern our nation and civilization. This is an awesome amount of power, one the Almighty (El Elyon) will hold accountable for the nation.

The high arch of authority from the Supreme Court to the local police officers exercising a lawful duty to rule over the citizen in society for the betterment of the people in righteousness toward God exalts any civilization.

> Submit yourselves to every ordinance of man for the Lord's sake: whether it is to the king, as supreme; or to governors and to them that are sent by him for the punishment of evildoers, and for the praise of them that do well. For so is the will of God, that with well doing you may put to silence the ignorance of foolish men. As free, and not using your liberty for a cloak of maliciousness, but as the servants of God. Honor all men, love the brotherhood. Fear God. Honor the king. Servants, be subject to your masters with all fear; not only to the good and gentle, but also to the froward (1 Peter 2:13-18).
>
> Obey them that have the rule over you, and submit yourselves: for they watch for your souls, as they that must give account, that they may do it with joy, and not with grief: for that is unprofitable for you. (Hebrews 13:17)

We are so quick to say, "God, bless America." I remember when the nation was in an uproar after hearing Jeremiah Wright say, "God damn America." Let's not be so quick to get upset or throw stones until we examine our lives here in the USA; could there possibly be some truth to his statement?

What can we do as a nation of people to ensure that God continues to bless America? If our lives are abominable and odorous as a nation of people toward God, can we continue to expect God to bless America? Are we headed toward Mr. Wright's prediction or prophecy of damnation on America?

God Does Judge Nations

> Behold, this was the iniquity of your sister Sodom; pride, fullness of bread, and abundance of idleness was in her and in her daughters, neither did she strengthen the hand of the poor and needy. And they were haughty, and committed abomination before Me: therefore I took them away as I saw good. (Ezekiel 16:49–50)
>
> Thou shalt not lie with mankind, as with womankind: it is an abomination. (Leviticus 18:22)
>
> Even as Sodom and Gomorrah, and the cities about them in like manner, giving themselves over to fornication, and going after strange flesh, are set forth for an example, suffering the vengeance of eternal fire. Likewise, also these filthy dreamers defile the flesh, despise dominion, and speak evil of dignities. (Jude 1:7–8)
>
> The outcry of Sodom and Gomorrah is indeed great; and there is exceedingly grave. (Genesis 18:20)

Let us look back at Mr. Wright's statement in reference to scripture quoted above. God lets us know that the abominable lifestyle of the people defiles the land and brings the judgment of God. We also know from scripture that God holds accountable those judges He puts in place to govern the people. Just like when Adam and Eve sinned, the earth was cursed; when judges fail to execute judgment that is righteous before God, the nation suffers the consequence. Know that!

> He that justifies the wicked, and he that condemns the just, even they both are abomination to the Lord. (Proverbs 17:15)
>
> Whoso rewards evil for good, evil shall not depart from his house. (Proverbs 17:13)

Let not the Supreme Court cause evil not to depart from America in calling evil (homosexual marriage) good.

It should be no surprise when there is talk of al-Qaeda, ISIS, and terrorists plotting against America. Don't be so quick to get upset with Mr. Wright; his cry could be no less than the cry Jonah had when God had something against Nineveh (Jonah 1:1–2). The wicked shall be turned into hell as well as the nations that forget God.

> Put them in fear, O Lord: that the nations may know themselves to be but men—Selah. (Psalm 9:17, 20)
>
> Whatsoever the Lord please, that did He in heaven, and in earth, in the seas, and all deep places ... Who slew some great nations, and slew mighty kings; Sihon king of the Amorites, and Og king of Bashan, and all the kingdoms of Canaan. (Psalm 135: 6, 10–11)
>
> "Then it will be seventy years are completed I will punish the king of Babylon and that nation," declared the Lord, for their iniquity. (Jeremiah 25:12)

As for Me and My House

On Thursday, March 14, 2013, on CNN, GOP Senator Rob Portman announced his support of same-sex marriage, saying he'd had a change of heart after his son revealed to him that he was gay. He now supports gay marriage and the ideology that gay unions should afford the same benefits provided to couples who can produce offspring to populate the planet and continue civilization, based on a commandment from God to "be fruitful and multiply and replenish the earth." In their disobedience and flaunting of their abominable acts, they demand every opportunity afforded to biblically marriage couples and give nothing in return. Anyone with a brain in his or her head and logical deduction can understand that if an island or planet had just two females (or only two males), liberally speaking, within a hundred years of no fruit (offspring/ replenishing), civilization would not commence in those places. The USA was founded on Christian principles. If gays had had their way at the USA's beginning, right now we wouldn't be discussing the present issue in this two hundred and forty-plus-years -old country; there wouldn't be many around to debate this issue. And certainly there would be no offspring of the two scenarios cited above. Gays and lesbians would die at the hands of their own volition, without artificial means or help from this society, which offers up God's inheritance to them. They demand our children for a facade of a family just to fit an agenda, and they shake their fists in God's face while we help them do so. The LGBTQ community wants America to believe they have a sustainable cause. This is Satan leading men to their doom (the fires of hell) all over again, like the fallen angels who followed him. You can't go against God and expect a good outcome. God will not be mocked (Galatians 6:7).

Fortunately for homosexuals, the gene they claim to have inherited is reversible, unlike one born with diabetes or Down syndrome genes. No medical exam is needed, just a change of heart toward God and His commands. Resist the devil, and he will flee from you.

We cry and mourn over God's heritage (temporarily put in our care) when children are taken from us in mass shootings, but we don't shed a tear when gay adoptions take place as they use God's heritage to front their agenda-driven goals in an abominable lifestyle. They attack and try to redefine an institution God created and sanctioned.

> And Adam said, "This is now bone of my bones, and flesh of my flesh: she shall be called Woman, because she was taken of Man." (Genesis 2:23)
> Therefore shall a man leave his father and his mother, and shall cling to his "wife: and they shall be one flesh." (Genesis 2:24)

Gays didn't create marriage, and they don't have any God-given authority to mess with it; they should leave it alone. And God-fearing citizens shouldn't be forced to shut up, but they should speak out to their elected officials.

What I found so riveting was that this man, Rob Portman, decided not to be a father and leader of his household. He decided to allow his son to dictate the morals of his household, representing his family to the nation. To be the father and head of his household doesn't mean he doesn't love his children when and if he doesn't condone their behavior or choices in life; the situation should be quite the contrary. Remember the scriptures that say, "Spare the rod, spoil the child" and "God chastens whom He loves." One can love and be a disciplinarian. Portman went as far as to say he had consulted with a mortal man, Dick Cheney, for advice—not the holy word of God, but Mr. Cheney— another politician with his own personal frailties like his. He used the wrong measuring gauge here. Again, is man more righteous than God? The first thing that popped into my mind when I saw the interview by news reporter Dana Bash was that if she had interviewed Joshua, his response would have been, "As for me and my house, we will serve the Lord." He wouldn't have compromised because of an unfaithful son or daughter, whom he loved, because God comes first. Remember our currency: "In God We Trust."

It is the righteous lives and prayers of righteous men and women that are keeping America from the wrath of God and the brink of war. Let's not bring America to its knees like Sodom and Gomorrah. Will God find twenty or ten righteous persons, who would cause Him to spare this country –America? Don't be deceived. Looking out over the history of man and civilization, we see that many kingdoms, dynasties, and nations have fallen, sometimes to less mighty adversaries. "Remember, except the Lord keep the city, the watchman watches in vain." If God doesn't keep the city or nation, our military might is useless against any sized enemy.

Consider Abraham's conversation with God in Genesis 18:25. "Far be it from You to do such a thing, to slay the righteous with the wicked, so that the righteous and the wicked are treated alike. Far be it from You! Shall not the Judge of all the earth deal justly?" In Genesis 32, Abraham said, "Oh may the Lord not be angry, and I shall speak only this once; suppose ten are found there?" And He said, "I will not destroy it on account of the ten."

Many have read this account of God destroying Sodom and Gomorrah because not one righteous person was found outside of Lot's family. In America let us pray that God can find at least ten righteous persons. It is being said that many Americans are coming to accept the homosexual lifestyle. Well, the count is on. Will God find ten righteous and spare the nation? In reading 2 Chronicles 33:2, we note that Manasseh did evil in the sight of the Lord according to the abominations of the nations, whom the Lord dispossessed before the sons of Israel. The Supreme Court in its decision should note 2 Chronicles 33:9. See Isaiah 9:16; Isaiah 10:1–7. Thus Manasseh misled Judah and the inhabitants of Jerusalem to do more evil than the nations whom the Lord destroyed before the sons of Israel. One of many ways God deals with sinful nations is to cause them to cease to exist or reduce them in glory and power. Let this not be the fate of the USA over the issue of sins of abomination: the alternative lifestyles of homosexuality and the LGBTQ community.

The concern that citizens of this nation should have is, Will God use unrighteous or non-Christian nations (China, Korea, Russia, Syria, terrorist cells, and so forth) to judge the USA and/or destroy America? History is full of examples of how not-so-mighty things have crumbled big and mightier things; let that not be so of the USA.

No One Knows What Is Going On

The scriptures say there is nothing new under the sun. The conclusion to be drawn here is that man has a short memory or selected memory.

Put your ears to the wind, listen to the crowd of protestors, and observe the times. The cry is the same as in ancient times. Crucify the righteous one, who has a proven track records of decency ("Lock Him up"), and let us have Barabbas, a murderer and known offender of what is decent. Deplorable people are found in every culture and century throughout the history of man. The deplorable, religious sects (of biblical days) deemed themselves more righteous than God (self-righteous or will worshippers) and wanted to destroy Christ. They were mud slingers who tried to bring in false witnesses to discredit Christ.

These individuals feed on fear and hate. They accept and encourage vile behavior, knowing that the scriptures condemn those who do wrong and are supporters of those who do wrong; they are one in the same. They are an abomination to God, because they refuse to do right; even when they have the opportunity to change, they will not.

Trump supporters will vote for him no matter what he says or does, because he is divisive and supports a hate message, the evil they love.

To be fair to Trump, he doesn't fully understand what is going on—past or currently. He was running neck and neck in the polls with politicians who were overly qualified and well out of his league, but he is seemingly defeating them at their own game or on their turf.

When America lies and says, "In God We Trust" while making laws that are against scripture, things that "cause the people [nation] to sin," God takes His protection away and allows things to happen that will bring America to its knees. To sin against God this way opens up the portal and allows this evil spirit to enter the hearts of the people. This spirit brings the chaos and hatred America is witnessing at this present time. "Righteousness exalts a nation: but sin is a reproach to any people" (Proverbs 14:34).

God uses evil to serve His purpose. King Ahab (king of Israel) heard the flattery of four hundred of his prophets instructing him to show his power and go to battle, but not Micaiah, the prophet of God, who told him it was not a good decision. "Now therefore behold, the LORD has put a lying spirit in the mouth of these your prophets and the LORD has spoken evil against you" (2 Chronicles 18:22). To serve His purpose, see a few other scriptures where God allowed evil spirits to visit man: Job 1:12; Judges 9:23; 1 Samuel 16:23.

Trump is only a vessel God uses as an eye-opener to encourage America to repent before He allows Satan to bring America to its knees. While Trump has his fingers on the nuclear codes and the White House (due to the Electoral College), it can be an "It is finished" moment for the USA as we know it at any juncture in the near future. T-Rex (terrorists) just might want to test that electric fence (boasted military might).

Trump communicates on a very low unpresidential level. He ran against overqualified presidential candidates in education and experience. The polls showed him winning in many states. Trump's famous line is, "No one knows what is going on." What is going on is that God wants Americans who say, "In God We Trust" to repent and not make laws that cause a nation to sin. Everyone has the right to live the way he or she chooses and is answerable to God individually for his or her life choices, but a nation or country shouldn't make legal any act or behavior that is against the God in whom they purport to trust. Let's repent and close that portal (evil spirits that have entered this country) before things get worse or irreversible for the USA.

There Is Nothing about Trump's Resilience

Trump is even dumbfounded that he is able to maintain high numbers in the polls after all his transgressions against many groups of people of this nation. His supporters (including some of the religious conservatives or evangelical sects, who believe themselves to be more righteous than God and are will-worshippers) aren't interested in Trump's transgressions. They want a Barabbas (murderer –hater without cause or vile individual they can manipulate through misuse of scripture) over Hillary Clinton (a good and not vile and nasty mouth or guile; mud-sling, name calling) found in her mouth individual— see 1Peter 2:22); nothing is new under the sun. It makes one wonder how many evangelical male voters preferred a Trump over a female leader for the United States of America. It's nothing new or strange that God uses small things or less qualified things to bring down or destroy large and stronger or mightier things. Trump is in the White House because God allowed Satan to touch America, and Trump is the vessel He used. To show His power, God allowed Satan to touch Job, but not destroy (Job—Job 2:6). Many voters felt they had to choose evil (*supporters of gay marriage candidates*) over their religious belief in order to vote for their state's representatives in the Democratic Party, and many didn't vote or decided to vote for the Republican Party candidates. Will this happen again? Will Trump get his second term? Will America still be standing? Will God allow Satan to bring America down? Will Jeremiah Wright's prophesy come true; "God dam America?" God allowed Satan to touch Job's body with sores and boils but stayed his hands from ultimately destroying Job. God allowed Trump to take over an established party and *touch it with vileness*, so we can see how frail we are. In Trump's words, "Nothing like you have seen before." Now repent before God allows Satan to bring America to its knees or, worse, experience the same demise as Sodom and Gomorrah—uninhabitable.

America needs to change its course, repent, and pray that God doesn't use Trump as a vessel to totally destroy America. "Except the Lord keeps the city, the watchman watches in vain." We have no military might against a large nation or a small one. It is God who allows things to be.

Trump is just a vessel God uses for His set purpose. Mr. Trump doesn't even know what is going on. His behavior is vile and vulgar, but he is still viable in the number of votes in the polls. What is going on? There is nothing new under the sun. Give us Barabbas and crucify Christ. Lock her up! See Matthew 27.

Clinton is a female, and Trump doesn't think Clinton has the stamina to be president because she is female. He should check out Israel's first female judge, Deborah, in the book of Judges; see her roar. See Judges 4–5.

In 2016, presidential candidate Hilary Clinton, who was highly qualified and pretty much overqualified, succumbed to a less qualified candidate in the run for U.S. president. Supporting an agenda that isn't God approved assisted with the ushering in of the opening of the portal to evil spirits or wormhole to what followed in this country: chaos and disarray. God is always in control and allows the undesirables to bring us to our knees until we repent and follow Him. Consider the biblical account of the Bramble Bush—Judges 9:14. A great number of Americans wanted Trump to come rule over them, despite many tell-tell signs of that of a bramble bush's character.

America, look in Daniel 5. Belshazzar, son of Nebuchadnezzar, who lifted himself up against the Lord of heaven in his sinful acts, saw the writing on the wall; he was going down. Nebuchadnezzar was brought to understanding through suffering, humbled his heart, and understood that the Most High God ruled in the kingdom of men. "MENE, MENE, TEKEL, UPHARSIN." Our days are numbered, too. Will we repent of our course? As a people, a nation, will our handling of the gay or homosexual movement of the twenty-first century leave us weighed in the balances and found wanting? What country or little terrorist regime or cell is waiting in the wings to take our mighty nation down? Let us see the writing on the wall and ask for the righteous to pray that God will continue to protect the USA.

Will the judges watch and keep our souls by allowing biblical principles to rule the lives of the citizen of this great nation, on which it was built?

Who Told You That You Were Naked?

In defining and identifying morals and immorality in today's modern-day society, as it relates to being homosexual or effeminate, do we need to return to scripture? The answer is yes. In Genesis, God asked Adam and his wife, "Who told you that you were naked?"(Genesis 3:11–13). Of course they started the blame game: the woman you gave me; [the gene you gave me]. Today, going to scripture in Romans chapter 1, who tells homosexuals, they are immoral with vile affections? Isn't God still in the equation? We want to debate what is moral and immoral. Well, here's a news flash; this is God's world. He built this. He made the rules, which supersede any and all other rules. His word doesn't change with the current issues of the century. His word will last forever. You have an opportunity to obey—if you want to. The choice has always been yours. Choose you this day whom you will serve: Christ or Satan. Debate over. The homosexuals complain about equality. God doesn't discriminate. We all have sinned and come short of the glory of God, and we all have to repent, gay and straight alike. We all have to obey God, gay and straight alike. We all have the freedom to come out from darkness (sinful deeds) and walk in the "light"—Christ Jesus.

In his dissent in *Windsor v. the United States*, Supreme Court Justice Alito said it was expected that the court endorsed a consent-based view of marriage and rejected the traditional view. The act of legalizing gay marriage, in his opinion, puts the Supreme Court in a powerful position to decide on an issue historians, social scientists, philosophers, and theologians, whom he expressed, were more qualified to address.

Everyone wants to take credit: historians, social scientists, philosophers, and theologians. But they didn't come up with that out of the blue; it was God, the Creator of mankind. It was God's idea of marriage and what it meant to be married, with a husband, wife, and children. We recognize this as tradition, because it has been with man since the beginning of time, as recorded in the book of Genesis. When the Constitution was written, marriage was about traditional marriage in a Christian-oriented belief.

Alito also wrote that the issue of same-sex marriage was so new to the country; there was no knowing the broader implications of allowing such an institution, citing the "ancient and universal human institution" of family. "At present, no one—including social scientists, philosophers, and historians—can predict with any certainty what the long-tern ramifications of widespread acceptance of same-sex marriage will be. And judges are certainly not equipped to make such an assessment."[84] 570 U.S., at ____, 133 S. Ct. 2675,186 L.ED.2d808 at 852 (dissenting opinion) (footnote omitted)

The scriptures say that there is nothing new under the sun. Here are four words for the judges: "Remember Sodom and Gomorrah?" There is nothing left to do now. The deliberation on the ramification is moot; it has already been set in place. If Alito and other judges' dissents are to show that they won't stand for what ancient biblical history calls an abomination, then clearly the nation's blood won't be on those judges' hands; they didn't fail to warn this nation of the consequence of allowing gays or the homosexual lifestyle to alter the ancient and universal human institution of family. But is that what happened in the Supreme Court's ruling to make the gay issue of marriage versus traditional or biblical marriage a federal issue that governs all states? The Supreme Court holds God-fearing individuals hostage by forcing them to live in places they believe to be in abomination toward God without an avenue to flee to states that honor Him. These are states that believe in moral values in a Christian nation built on Christian principles that are "purported" by the founding fathers of our Constitution. Many Christians and God-fearing individuals cannot now choose a state where it would have the authority to decide what is marriage, based on the citizen of the state; therefore, this leaves defiant ones open and not hidden because of the Supreme Court ruling, which umbrellas all states. Many wolves can walk in sheep's clothing under this ruling. Satan in his deception was at work.

📖 Book Corner Excerpt (Majority Opinion-US Supreme Courts)

Majority Opinion of the US Supreme Courts—June 26, 2015 (excerpt from https://en.wikipedia.org/wiki/Obergefell_v._Hodges)[85] *Obergefell v. Hodges*, 576 U.S. at ____, 135 S.Ct. 2584 at 2593- 2608, (2015).

> Chief Justice Roberts and Justices Scalia, Thomas, and Alito each wrote a separate dissenting opinion. The Chief Justice read part of his dissenting opinion from the bench, his first

---

[84] *Obergefell v. Hodges.* 576 U.S. ____, 135 S. Ct. 2584, 2642 (2015).
[85] Obergefell v. Hodges, 576 U.S. at ____, 135 S.Ct. 2584 at 2593 -2608(2015) Wikipedia, s.v. "Obergefell v. Hodges," last modified May 13, 2019, https://en.wikipedia.org/wiki/Obergefell_v._Hodges.

time doing so since joining the Court in 2005. Majority opinion: Justice Anthony Kennedy authored the Court's opinion declaring same-sex couples have the right to marry.

Justice Anthony Kennedy authored the majority opinion and was joined by Justices Ruth Bader Ginsburg, Stephen Breyer, Sonia Sotomayor, and Elena Kagan. The majority held that state same-sex marriage bans are a violation of the Fourteenth Amendment's Due Process and Equal Protection Clauses.

"The Constitution promises liberty to all within its reach," the Court declared, "a liberty that includes certain specific rights that allow persons, within a lawful realm, to define and express their identity." Citing *Griswold v. Connecticut*, the Court affirmed that the fundamental rights found in the Fourteenth Amendment's Due Process Clause "extend to certain personal choices central to individual dignity and autonomy, including intimate choices that define personal identity and beliefs", but the "identification and protection" of these fundamental rights "has not been reduced to any formula." As the Supreme Court has found in cases such as *Loving v. Virginia*, *Zablocki v. Redhail*, and *Turner v. Safley*, this extension includes a fundamental right to marry.

The Court rejected respondent states' framing of the issue as whether there were a "right to same-sex marriage", insisting its precedents "inquired about the right to marry in its comprehensive sense, asking if there was a sufficient justification for excluding the relevant class from the right." Indeed, the majority averred, "If rights were defined by who exercised them in the past, then received practices could serve as their own continued justification and new groups could not invoke rights once denied." Citing its prior decisions in *Loving v. Virginia* and *Lawrence v. Texas*, the Court framed the issue accordingly in *Obergefell*.

The Court listed four distinct reasons why the fundamental right to marry applies to same-sex couples, citing *United States v. Windsor* in support throughout its discussion. First, "the right to personal choice regarding marriage is inherent in the concept of individual autonomy." Second, "the right to marry is fundamental because it supports a two-person union unlike any other in its importance to the committed individuals", a principle applying equally to same-sex couples. Third, the fundamental right to marry "safeguards children and families and thus draws meaning from related rights of childrearing, procreation, and education"; as same-sex couples have children and families, they are deserving of this safeguard—though the right to marry in the United States has never been conditioned on procreation. Fourth, and lastly, "marriage is a keystone of our social order", and "[t]here is no difference between same- and opposite-sex couples with respect to this principle"; consequently, preventing same-sex couples from marrying puts them at odds with society, denies them countless benefits of marriage, and introduces instability into their relationships for no justifiable reason.

The Court noted the relationship between the liberty of the Due Process Clause and the equality of the Equal Protection Clause and determined that same-sex marriage bans violated the latter. Concluding that the liberty and equality of same-sex couples was significantly burdened, the Court struck down same-sex marriage bans for violating both clauses, holding that same-sex couples may exercise the fundamental right to marry in all fifty states.

Due to the "substantial and continuing harm" and the "instability and uncertainty" caused by state marriage laws differing with regard to same-sex couples, and because respondent states had conceded that a ruling requiring them to marry same-sex couples would undermine their refusal to hold valid same-sex marriages performed in other states, the Court also held that states must recognize same-sex marriages legally performed in other states.

Addressing respondent states' argument, the Court emphasized that, while the democratic process may be an appropriate means for deciding issues such as same-sex marriage, no individual has to rely solely on the democratic process to exercise a fundamental right. "An individual can invoke a right to constitutional protection when he or she is harmed, even if the broader public disagrees and even if the legislature refuses to act", for "fundamental rights may not be submitted to a vote; they depend on the outcome of no elections." Furthermore, to rule against same-sex couples in this case, letting the democratic process play out as "a cautious approach to recognizing and protecting fundamental rights" would harm same-sex couples in the interim.

Additionally, the Court rejected the notion that allowing same-sex couples to marry harms the institution of marriage, leading to fewer opposite-sex marriages through a severing of the link between procreation and marriage, calling the notion "counterintuitive" and "unrealistic". Instead, the Court stated that married same-sex couples "would pose no risk of harm to themselves or third parties". The majority also stressed that the First Amendment protects those who disagree with same-sex marriage.

In closing, Justice Kennedy wrote for the Court: No union is more profound than marriage, for it embodies the highest ideals of love, fidelity, devotion, sacrifice, and family. In forming a marital union, two people become something greater than once they were. As some of the petitioners in these cases demonstrate, marriage embodies a love that may endure even past death. It would misunderstand these men and women to say they disrespect the idea of marriage. Their plea is that they do respect it, respect it so deeply that they seek to find its fulfillment for themselves. Their hope is not to be condemned to live in loneliness, excluded from one of civilization's oldest institutions. They ask for equal dignity in the eyes of the law. The Constitution grants them that right."[86]

Yes, this defiance toward God's holy union will follow you beyond the grave—past the first death. Are you willing to stand in judgment found in a union that God didn't grant? Yes, marriage is civilization's oldest institution. God knows that, because He created it. Remember the first couple or union, Adam and Eve? God took a rib from Adam and created Eve. God returned part of Adam back to him (presented to Adam his wife), and through their

---

[86] *Obergefell*, 135 S. Ct. 2584 at 2593 -2608
https://en.wikipedia.org/wiki/Obergefell_v._Hodges.

union, God made the two one again—greater than they were apart. That is the power of God. This union was for His glorification.

Man is created to glorify God. God expects something from this union—an inheritance (children, the fruit of the womb). A man-made court cannot duplicate that power of uniting two people, making one in a union. It was God who decided what man needed and what He wanted man to have, so He gave man a wife. When man steps outside that order, he makes himself unproductive in preforming undignified acts. God created everything to produce after its kind, thus this act of disobedience become an abomination to His will for man. Only God can grant dignity to this type of union, and only God is able to deem that the bed is undefiled in holy matrimony. The twenty-two male chromosomes and the twenty-two female chromosomes union can deliver up to God a *whole person* in everyone born. Adam and Eve were able to reproduce after their kind after the operation of God on the first man, Adam. Listen, the Supreme Court doesn't need to help God out here. Remember Uzzah (Perez-Uzzah) trying to keep the ark from falling (2 Samuel 6:7, 1Chronicles 13:9–14). Don't think God is unfair in His judgment.

Dissenting Opinions

In his dissent, Chief Justice John Roberts argued that same-sex marriage bans didn't violate the Constitution.

> Chief Justice John Roberts wrote a dissenting opinion, which was joined by Justices Scalia and Thomas. Roberts accepted substantive due process, by which fundamental rights are protected through the Due Process Clause, but warned it has been misused over time to expand perceived fundamental rights, particularly in *Dred Scott v. Sandford* and *Lochner v. New York*. Roberts stated that no prior decision had changed the core component of marriage, that it be between one man and one woman; consequently, same-sex marriage bans did not violate the Due Process Clause. Roberts also rejected the notion that same-sex marriage bans violated a right to privacy, because they involved no government intrusion or subsequent punishment. Addressing the Equal Protection Clause, Roberts stated that same-sex marriage bans did not violate the clause

because they were rationally related to a governmental interest: preserving the traditional definition of marriage.

More generally, Roberts stated that marriage, which he proposed had always had a "universal definition" as "the union of a man and a woman", arose to ensure successful childrearing. Roberts criticized the majority opinion for relying on moral convictions rather than a constitutional basis, and for expanding fundamental rights without caution or regard for history. He also suggested the majority opinion could be used to expand marriage to include legalized polygamy. Roberts chided the majority for overriding the democratic process and for using the judiciary in a way that was not originally intended. According to Roberts, supporters of same-sex marriage cannot win "true acceptance" for their side because the debate has now been closed.[87] Roberts also suggested the majority's opinion will ultimately lead to consequences for religious liberty, and he found the Court's language unfairly attacks opponents of same-sex marriage.

Justice Antonin Scalia wrote a dissenting opinion, which was joined by Justice Thomas. Scalia stated that the Court's decision effectively robs the people of "the freedom to govern themselves", noting that a rigorous debate on same-sex marriage had been taking place and that, by deciding the issue nationwide, the democratic process had been unduly halted. [88]Addressing the claimed Fourteenth Amendment violation, Scalia asserted that, because a same-sex marriage ban would not have been considered unconstitutional at the time of the Fourteenth Amendment's adoption, such bans are not unconstitutional today. He claimed there was "no basis" for the Court's decision striking down legislation that the Fourteenth Amendment does not expressly forbid, and directly attacked the majority opinion for "lacking even a thin veneer of law".[89] Lastly, Scalia faulted the actual writing in the opinion for "diminish[ing] this Court's reputation for

---

[87] *Obergefell v. Hodges*, 576 U.S. at___, at 135 S. Ct. 2584, 2625 (2015) https://en.wikipedia.org/wiki/Obergefell_v._Hodges.

[88] *Id.* at ___,135 S. Ct. 2584, 2627

[89] *Id.* at 2628

clear thinking and sober analysis" and for "descend[ing] from the disciplined legal reasoning of John Marshall and Joseph Story to the mystical aphorisms of the fortune cookie."[90]

Justice Clarence Thomas wrote a dissenting opinion, which was joined by Justice Scalia. Thomas rejected the principle of substantive due process, which he claimed "invites judges to do exactly what the majority has done here—roa[m] at large in the constitutional field guided only by their personal views as to the fundamental rights protected by that document"; in doing so, the judiciary strays from the Constitution's text, subverts the democratic process, and "exalts judges at the expense of the People from whom they derive their authority." [91]Thomas argued that the only liberty that falls under Due Process Clause protection is freedom from "physical restraint." Furthermore, Thomas insisted that "liberty has long been understood as individual freedom *from* governmental action, not as a right *to* a particular governmental entitlement" such as a marriage license. According to Thomas, the majority's holding also undermines the political process and threatens religious liberty. Lastly, Thomas took issue with the majority's view that marriage advances the dignity of same-sex couples. In his view, government is not capable of bestowing dignity; rather, dignity is a natural right that is innate within every person, a right that cannot be taken away even through slavery and internment camps.[92]

Justice Samuel Alito wrote a dissenting opinion, which was joined by Justices Scalia and Thomas. Invoking *Washington v. Glucksberg*, in which the Court stated the Due Process Clause protects only rights and liberties that are "deeply rooted in this Nation's history and tradition", Alito claimed any "right" to same-sex marriage would not meet this definition; he chided the justices in the majority for going against judicial precedent and long-held tradition. Alito defended the rationale of the states, accepting the

---

[90] *Id.* at 2630. https://en.wikipedia.org/wiki/Obergefell_v._Hodges

[91] *Id.* at ___,135 S. Ct. 2584, 2631

[92] Id., at 2639

premise that same-sex marriage bans serve to promote procreation and the optimal childrearing environment. Alito expressed concern that the majority's opinion would be used to attack the beliefs of those who disagree with same-sex marriage, who "will risk being labeled as bigots and treated as such by governments, employers, and schools", leading to "bitter and lasting wounds". Expressing concern for judicial abuse, Alito concluded, "Most Americans—understandably—will cheer or lament today's decision because of their views on the issue of same-sex marriage. But all Americans, whatever their thinking on that issue, should worry about what the majority's claim of power portends." [93]

Satan, a Liar and Deceiver from the Beginning

The issue isn't really about gays and the gay or lesbian movement. Satan is busy about finding something or someone to get at God through His creation. The real issue, unbeknownst to man, is the spiritual warfare between Satan and God, good and evil. Those who profess to be gay and believe they are running the show and gaining victories are just pawns in the hands of Satan. What can they win? We are all leaving here one day—what then? Are we (homosexual and heterosexual) going to meet God as an obedient servant or not? What rights and freedoms does anyone really need beyond the freedom in Christ and rights to eternal life? Satan goes about, seeking whom he may destroy, deceiving and lying and separating man from God, his Creator. When you choose evil over good, Satan wins; he can claim you as his own. God has given us the power to resist Satan, and when we make the wrong choice, Satan wins. Again, it's not about the sin of homosexuality and gay marriage. It's about whether you, man, will make the right choice when given the opportunity.

Homosexuality isn't the only sinful act on "the list." The heart of man continues to do evil (Genesis 6:5, Jeremiah 17:9). Take a good look at the man in the mirror—and don't think it isn't a possibility that the Supreme Court judges will have to, in some distant future, rule on the civil rights of people as a separate sect or group petitioning for the rights to practice bestiality: getting their animals social security numbers and tax benefits,

---

[93] Obergefell, 135 S.Ct. at 2643

health care policies, and so forth. The gays have opened the floodgates into the next chapter—bestiality. If a man can have anal sex with another man, then certainly he can have sex with an animal. It's in the Bible. Think it isn't so? Read the book of Leviticus. The same issue will be about the money, tax benefits (inheritance tax) and so on to get on the ticket of someone or some group's political agenda.

"If in this life only we have hope in Christ, we are of all men most miserable" (1 Corinthians 15:19). If the gay community feels they have made the right choice and that there is nothing beyond the grave, then let them have a ball on this time side of life. Let them flaunt their lifestyle in the face of God, march in their parades, and wave their rainbow flags. This is their only time to do so, no matter how short lived; eat, drink, and be merry.

God has given man everything he needs. God created the woman for the man. God made the area of the body where His inheritance enters the world in a clean, healthy, safe, and self-cleaning place for the man and woman's relationship and procreation. The deceitfulness of Satan lures man to an area of the body where waste is expelled and where seeking pleasure takes place in non-life-giving properties. This is a place where toxins, germs, bacteria, and potentially disease-causing feces leave the body. It was the improper disposal of human waste, which rats ingested, that caused the spread of the bubonic plague. It was the anal sexual activities of the homosexual or bisexual community that helped spread the AIDS virus to the general population. Nothing good for man comes from the area where waste is discarded, even though we try to "intellectualize" ourselves out of the possibility that this is true. How far will we let Satan take us away from God and His plan for our lives? Man doesn't need a road map or master drawings to demonstrate what part of the body God designed for use. But when we reject God, we are destined to follow the wrong trail.

It was in May 2018, a week before submitting my manuscript to the publisher's editorial service and three years after writing the above paragraph, that I discovered that "Poop Pill"[94] research is done to help people with clostridium difficile-- *JAMA*, 2017; 318 (20): 1985 DOI: 10.1001/ jama.2017.17077. The feces from a healthy person (donor's stool) is put in the intestine of the infected person to help restore a healthy balance of bacteria in the gut of the person with clostridium difficile.

---

[94] "Poop Pill," *ScienceDaily*, https://www.sciencedaily.com/releases/2017/12/ 171201091026.htm.
ScienceDaily. www.sciencedaily.com/releases/2017/12/171201091026.htm (accessed January 3, 2020)

Jesus Saves

An article in Associate Press, June 20, 2013 headlines read, "Christian group apologizes for attempts to turn gays straight."[95] The first thing that came to my mind when I read this article was Acts 19:15. "And the evil spirit answered and said, 'Jesus I know, and Paul I know, but who are you?'"

> Then certain of the vagabond Jews exorcist, took upon them to call over them which had evil spirits the name of the Lord Jesus, saying, "We adjure you by Jesus whom Paul preacheth." (v. 13)
>
> And there were seven sons of one Sceva, a Jew, and chief of the priest, which did so. (v. 14)
>
> And the man in whom the evil spirit was leaped on them, and overcame them, and prevailed against them, so that they fled out of that house naked and wounded. (v. 16)

The leader of Exodus International, a commercial Christian ministry, assumed he had authority scripturally, and attempted to supersede the authority of the Bible for personal glory, profit, and recognition. Only Jesus saves, and only His way of salvation and His word can convert the hearts of men—that would exclude man-made institutions with specialized programs to **cure** sin but cannot save souls without the *unadulterated* message of the gospel.

The devil watches and waits for his opportunity to leap on you when you don't know Jesus or His apostles who wrote and left Jesus's word in scripture to study and obey. Alan Chambers, whose ministry worked to help people repress same-sex attraction, apologized to the gay community for inflicting "years of undue suffering" and plans to close the organization. Gay rights activists welcomed Chambers's apology while reiterating their belief that Exodus had caused great damage[96].

---

[95] "Christian Group Apologizes for Attempts to Turn Gays Straight," Associated Press, June 20, 2013. https://www.timesnews.net/News/2013/06/20/Christian-group-apologizes-for-attempts-to-turn-gays-straight.html 6:07 PM

[96] https://en.wikipedia.org/wiki/Alan_Chambers_(activist). Former President of Exodus International

God has promised even greater harm. He is a consuming unapologetic fire (Hebrews 12:29, Deuteronomy 4:24; 9:3)

Not understanding God—the true God, Ruler, and Creator of the universe—the creature (man), after experiencing what he believes is a victory in his pursuit, states, "Now we need them to take the next step to leadership and persuade all other religious-based institutions that they got it wrong." In other words, we feel we are making some progress here in destroying what God has built; help us to get other religious-based institutions that speak out against homosexuality out of our way.

Lord, if I Find Ten Righteous?

The question again, to America and to the Supreme Court, "Is homosexuality the problem?" Judas asked Jesus, "Is it me?" That's the question all who turn a blind eye to homosexuality in this nation should ask themselves. The scripture says you may as well be committing the same act. Take a closer look at scripture. God said He would spare the city if He found a number of righteous men, regardless of the fact that homosexuals had attempted to take over and even press on Lot's home, demanding to send the angels out so they may "know" (have sex) with them. So the question is still on the table here. Sin isn't going away. But are homosexuals the problem here, right now, in America? Is it not with the people who allow their behavior to permeate our society, causing God to turn His protection away from this land, this people, this country, this nation—America? I heard a minster say America is no longer a Christian nation, only a nation with Christians in it. My question is, Will God find ten?

> Why do the heathen rage, and the people imagine a vain thing? The kings of the earth set themselves, and the rulers take counsel together against the Lord, and against His Anointed, saying Let us break their bands asunder, and cast away their cords from us. He that sits in the heavens shall laugh: the Lord shall have them in derision. Then shall He speak to them in His anger, and vex them in His sore displeasure. (Psalm 2:1–5)
>
> Be wise now therefore O ye kings: be instructed, you judges of the earth. Serve the Lord with fear, and rejoice

with trembling. Kiss the Son, less He be angry, and you perish from the way, when His wrath is kindled but a little. Blessed are all they that put their trust in Him. (Psalm 2:10–12)

In God We Trust.
God, bless America.

Chapter 6
Jesus Did Not Come to Condemn

JESUS DIDN'T COME to find righteous people (Mark 2:17). Do you not know that Jesus is on your side? He came to win you back from Satan, redeem you, and save you. His purpose on earth was to offer mankind a clean slate by becoming the official sacrifice for our sins. He was on earth a short period of time, cleaning up Adam's disobedience, which caused all to fall under sin; Satan's trap is physical and spiritual death.

Whether you want to consider it or not, you are a sinner. There is no neutral ground in this spiritual warfare. You are a winner (righteous or sheep) or a loser (sinner or goat). If this fact is hidden, it's hidden from the ones who are lost. Save yourself from this untoward generation. Jesus sacrificed His life for you and offered salvation. Of course, while it's free, it is also conditional (*if* you walk in the light, *if* you believe, *if* you follow me). Since we don't know the way, following Jesus who has come from glory and returned to glory would be a sure bet on finding our way to heaven, where Jesus now sits on His throne at the right hand of God.

Not only is man's salvation conditional; it is time sensitive. If you die in your sins there, you cannot come. No one knows the hour of the day; be ready when He comes.

Invitation for Coming Out

Coming out is the *original* invitation from God. Yes, please come out! Come out and be sanctified, setting yourselves apart from the world of evildoers. And one important thing about coming out is that God isn't looking for the qualified (there aren't any), but He does qualify the called in the gospel, meaning, upon your obedience to the gospel. He is calling on all of mankind to come out; come out of the darkness of evil deeds and bad conversation (lifestyle) and into the glorious light of righteousness in Christ Jesus. Jesus declares that He is coming. He is coming back to claim His own. Your "coming out" should be in such a fashion that you will be able to behold His "coming out," out of the clouds from heaven. If this isn't the case, you will be running and calling on the rocks to fall on you and hide you from the wrath to come, because you have failed to heed His invitation.

No Purchase Necessary

"Free this or free that. Please respond by …" "No purchase necessary. Just fill in your name and address and phone number, and mail to the address on the card." "You can get this item or these funds at no cost to you. Complete the contact information and return with your signature to the sender by a particular date."

We all have seen this type of advertisement described in the above paragraph in some fashion or form and in one way or another. We respond to this type offer of material wealth far more readily than to the invitation for eternal life Christ offers. In both instances, we are getting something free. But we have to believe it to respond and give of ourselves and our time to complete the requirement(s). We understand that we need to do something to get something, and following the instructions in a timely manner is what determines whether we qualify to receive the *free* offer.

"The List": Such Were Some of You

Being effeminate is called out not just as a sin, but it is abominable in the sight of God. Now is this to say that being effeminate (homosexuality; males having sex with males) is worse than the other sins on "the list"? I will leave that up to the debaters of this world. I have always heard that a hit dog will holler and tell the truth and shame the devil. Are not those who say that when the church speaks out on the sins on "the list" in 1 Corinthians 6:9–11 that they are gay bashing? Where are the cries from the fornicators, adulterers, and thieves? I would say that the gay community's response would be very much like a hit dog—they holler. Read Revelation 22:15. It begs one to ask oneself, "Why do the heathens rage?" They got called out for their abominable deeds. The apostle Paul said they were classified as abominable. They didn't ask, but Paul certainly told them about themselves. He wasn't trying to be politically correct but helped them identify and correct what was lacking; to take hold on to the opportunity for eternal life. As far as "the list" goes, there is no room for gay bashing or being dogmatic. But we do understand that a convicted felon is one who commits a felony. Now, if you commit one felony or one hundred, you are still classified as a felon. Many on "the list" must understand the scripture when it says that if you commit one sin, you are guilty of all—no sin or sinner will enter heaven. What is interesting is that of all the sin or sinners on "the list," the effeminates are the most vocal. They blame God for who they are and what they do, void of all responsibility for their life choices. They ignore scripture, which says, "Choose you this day whom you will serve." No thieves, liars, fornicators, or adulterers step out to be recognized as a special group, bullying, organizing, and demanding rights to be accepted as part of God's holy institutions: church and marriage. No one serving in the church wants members to know they are big-ole liars, drunkards, thieves, fornicators, and adulterers. An adulterer knows he or she needs to make changes in his or her life, if the marriage is going to work. But homosexuals don't want to be accountable for their sins. They want to be accepted as they are in these holy places, with the scriptural union of marriage and the scriptural church, Christ's bride. Christ (He) and His bride, the church (she), produce children (Christians). His offspring or children of the kingdom are born into the family of God the same way—by hearing, believing, confessing, repenting, and being baptized. To be in the family of God, His children (Christians) have a responsibility to work to create disciples of all men, adding to the body of Christ. There is no part of God's creation that God doesn't command to be productive. To be viewed as unproductive, one needs only to recall Jesus's reaction to the fig tree. Why does God deem being effeminate an abomination and not the other sins or sinners on "the list"? Let the debaters of this world debate it. Let those who want eternal life obey it.

No other sinners on "the list" blame God for their sinful deeds and/or lifestyle they have chosen to live or a gene that causes them to behave in such a manner (lying, stealing, fornicating or committing adultery, and so forth).

What is a fact is that all sins separate man from God. Another fact is that man was created by God, and that fact makes him precious and valuable to God—more valuable than earth itself or the things on the earth. Man is a part of God, who breathes a part of Himself into the creature, man. "Lo, this only have I found, that God has made man upright; but they have sought out many inventions" (Ecclesiastes 7:29). In other words, man continues to come up with ways to defy God and His authority in his life. Without Jesus Christ nothing that exists would exist; that includes man.

In Psalms (8:4–6) David asked, "What is man, that thou are mindful of him?" Hebrews 2:6–8 echoes David's thought. But in a certain place, David, the psalmist, said, "What is man that thou are mindful of him? Thou has put all things in subjection under his feet." In Genesis 1: 26–28 God said, "Let Us make man in Our image, after Our likeness: and let them have dominion over all the earth, and over every creeping thing that creepeth upon the earth. So God created man in His own image, in the image of God created He him; *male* and *female* created He them. And God blessed them, and God said unto them, Be *fruitful*, and *multiply*, and *replenish* the earth and subdue it: and have dominion over the fish of the sea, and over the fowl of the air, and over every living thing that moveth upon the earth" (emphasis added).

A point referenced throughout the chapters in this book, mankind is still up to the same old blame game as his parents, Adam and Eve, which started in the Garden of Eden. As scripture lets us know, nothing is new under the sun. It's the twenty-first century, and here we go again. "God made me this way," says the effeminate. Remember Adam. "The woman you gave me." Eve said, "The serpent beguiled me." Can we recognize the lust of the eyes, the lust of the flesh, and the pride of life scenario in the Garden of Eden? Man couldn't resist what he was told not to partake of or do. Even today man is trying to be equal with God. Gay marriage is equal with holy matrimony—really? Pride got Satan kicked out of heaven (Isaiah 14:12–15).

"But every man is tempted when he is drawn away of his own lust and enticed. Then when lust has conceived, it brings forth sin. Sin, when it is finished, brings forth death" (James 1:14–15). "For all that is in the world, the lust of the flesh, and the lust of the eyes, and the pride of life, is not of the Father, but is of the world. And the world passes away, and the lust thereof; but he that does the will of God abides forever" (1 John 2:16–17).

"Little children, it is the last time: and as you have heard that antichrist shall come, even now are there many antichrists; whereby we know that it is the last times. They went out from us, but they were not of us; for if they had been of us, they would no doubt have continued with us; but they went out, that they might be made manifest that they were not all of us … And now, little children, abide in Him; that, when He shall appear, we may have confidence, and not be ashamed before Him at His coming. If you know that He is righteous, you know that every one that does righteousness is born of Him" (1 John 2:18–19... 28–29).

If Your Eye Offends, Pluck It Out

At the time of their ignorance, God winked at, but now commands all to repent. God does not make exceptions for sin.

> And if thine eye offend thee pluck it out: it is better for thee to enter into the kingdom of God with one eye, than having two eyes, to be cast into hell fire. (Mark 9:47)
> And if thy right eye offend thee, pluck it out, and cast it from thee: for it is profitable for thee that one of thy members should perish, and not that thy whole body should be cast into hell fire. (Matthew 5:29; 18:19)

Whatever it is in your life that is causing you to stumble or keep you out of heaven, you need to find some way to separate yourself from it. "There hath no temptation taken you but such as is common to man, but God is faithful, who will not suffer you to be tempted above that ye are able; but will with the temptation also make a way to escape, that ye may be able to bear it" (1 Corinthians 10:13).

What Are Eunuchs?

"For there are some eunuchs, which were so born from their mother's womb; and there are some eunuchs, which were made eunuchs of men; and there be eunuchs, which have made themselves eunuchs for the kingdom of heaven's sake. He that is able to receive it, let him receive it" (Matthew 19:12). As the text shows, some have even become celibate for the kingdom of God's sake. The apostle Paul (who wished that all were as he, unmarried; 1 Corinthians 7:7–9) didn't have to care for a wife and was busy spreading the gospel from place to place. If he had had a wife, he would have had family obligations, and if he hadn't been willing to submit to those, he would have been classified as worse than an infidel. To have a wife, Paul understood that the wedding vows made him obligated to a responsibility he was commanded to keep. But in Christ he was free to be unmarried, and he chose that status for the kingdom's (church) sake in devoting himself to the spreading of the gospel.

In examining the article "What Are Eunuchs?" by Tony Warren,[97] we see that the biblical distinction was clearly drawn between what the Bible defines as a eunuch, looking at Acts 8:27 and Esther 2:3, 14, and effeminate. The Bible has no condemnation for one who was a eunuch (celibate or castrated male) but clearly condemns those classified as effeminate. If the gay gene is causing one to stumble (which is just being discovered thousands to perhaps millions of years by man after the creation of man, and Scripture explicitly condemns mankind for lying with mankind as with womankind), we honestly need to examine the word of God. "Let every man be a liar, but God be true" (Romans 3:4). We should believe God rather than man. We should also know that as far as what researchers have to say about a gay gene, there are as many opinions as there are noses; everyone has one. God took care of the opinions of men in the Transfiguration. "This is my beloved Son, hear ye Him."

Concerning the Married and Unmarried

> Nevertheless he that stands steadfast in his heart, having no necessity, but has power over his own will, and has so decreed in his heart that he will keep his virgin, does well. So then he that gives her in marriage does well; but he that gives her not in marriage does better. (1 Corinthians 7:37–38)
>
> But if they cannot contain, let them marry; for it is better to marry than to burn. (1 Corinthians 7:9)
>
> Marriage is honorable in all and the bed undefiled: but whoremongers and adulterers God will judge. (Hebrews 13:4)

To be unmarried isn't a sin. To commit adultery and fornication are sins. God has never forbidden scriptural marriage.

Even though many look at the tradition of the priesthood in the denominational teaching of the Catholic Church, God never command it; nor was it practiced in the priesthood of God's people.

---

[97] Tony Warren, "What Are Eunuchs?" accessed June 5, 2013, http://www.mountain-retreat.org/faq/what_are_eunuchs.shtml.

And Aaron took him Elisheba, daughter of Amminadab, sister of Naashon, to wife; and she bare him Nadab, and Abihu, Eleazar, and Ithamar. (Exodus 6:23)

And Eleazar Aaron's son took him one of the daughters of Putiel to wife; and she bare him Phinehas: these are the heads of the fathers of the Levites according to their families. (Exodus 6:25)

I'm not sure why the man-made priests don't marry. But in this denominational religion, it has become a hotbed for molestation of altar boys (homosexuality or pedophilia). The new pope, Pope Francis, doesn't want to talk about homosexuality, while homosexuality runs rampantly in the USA, as it did in Sodom and Gomorrah. He wants to move to other subject matters; well, that's not the view of Christians, followers and disciples of Christ. That decision can be made only if you are the *head of your own church*, so I guess that is why the pope can make that decision. "For the husband is the head of the wife, even as *Christ is the head of the church*; and He is the Savior of the body, therefore as the church is subject to Christ, so let the wives be to their husbands in everything. Husbands love your wives even as Christ also loved the church, and gave Himself for it; That He might sanctify and cleanse it with the washing of water by the word" (Ephesians 5:23–26). Jesus is the High Priest, and He makes decisions concerning His church. "And being made perfect, He became the author of eternal salvation to all them that obey Him; Called of God an high priest after the order of Melchisedec" (Hebrews 5:9–10). "*Preach* the word: be instant in season, out of season: reprove, rebuke, exhort with all longsuffering and doctrine. For the time will come when they will not endure sound doctrine; but after their own lusts shall they heap to themselves teachers, having itching ears; and they shall turn away their ears from the truth, and shall be turned to fables" (2 Timothy 4:2–4, emphasis added). Christ and Christians or disciples of Christ will tell Pope Frances it is still in season to preach against the effeminate. The church saves souls. It does not change with the times and cuddle up with the world and evildoers. Be *productive*, not abominable or unfruitful in His kingdom; help save a soul from the fires of hell. Tell the truth; God's word is truth. He has said that His word will not go out void. Just tell the truth; preach the word. Honest souls will hear and obey.

Stop Lying on God

I suspect that if gays stop lying on God, the gay gene will dissipate—flee from the gay person's body. The scientists and researchers would stop looking to find one, too. "Submit yourselves, therefore to God. Resist the devil, and he will flee from you" (James 4:7). There will be no bullying God to let them through the pearly gates. And those who worship (creating their own churches—Metropolitan Community Church, for example) vainly under false teaching will experience weeping and gnashing of teeth. If gays think there is a possibility that they could argue their case, guess how long that conversation with God will last? It won't even get up to the count of nearly a twinkling of an eye.

Those who are Christians when Jesus returns on a cloud will be caught up and changed within a twinkling of an eye. Nothing follows what deals God will make with gays, for God made man, and male and female made He them. There will only be a separation of the sheep and goats. Sheep are those who hear Jesus's, the Shepherd of the soul, voice welcoming them home. Goats are the ones trying to get into heaven by arguing their case with God, which they can't do within a twinkling of an eye's time. This is time they won't have anyway; it will be over then. Those who are within the age of accountability have had plenty of time on this time side of life (on earth) to choose to deny self and follow Christ. Those who have decided or chosen to follow Christ will enjoy heaven; as one lyric says, "Heaven is cool inside." Those who follow the devil, as the sexual lyric goes, will experience "dropping it like it's hot," taking on a whole new meaning.

There will be no supreme courts, no presidents, no polls, no political parties or lobbyists, no freedoms or rights, no nothing or anything—just Satan welcoming you home as his slave and servant of sin or evil deeds. Any freedoms and rights you achieved on earth will not pass over to the other side as slaves and servants of Satan. And it's too late to consider the freedom in Christ as His servants and slaves of righteousness. Don't be fooled or deceived. You have been purchased with the blood of Jesus, and your freedom is in Christ. Take Jesus up on the offer or lose out forever.

Created for Good Works

We are all supposed to be with God. "For we are His workmanship, created in Christ Jesus to good works, which God has before ordained that we should walk in them" (Ephesians 2:10).

Think about it. The LGBTQ community is fighting for gay rights and to be recognized in a Christian nation as a dignified sect or group of people. Even if they get those rights in the USA and other places on God's green planet, what happens when he or she [gay person] dies outside of the will of God for his or her life? Think about it; would a person (mankind) rather miss out on life everlasting in heaven just for a meager seventy, eighty, and (if at best) one hundred fleeting years on the earth, and then have to spend eternity in the fires of hell? Again, think about it. For those who commit these sins won't enter the kingdom of God. Well, that's what honest souls are reading out of the BIBLE (Basic Instructions Before Leaving Earth).

Due to their success at bullying mainstream America into accepting their parasitic and abominable lifestyle, gays are planning to silence God and cut His word out of the Bible. Will they create their own Bible, have a Holy Bible burning, or ban the gospel from being preached? "How beautiful are the feet of those who carry the gospel" (Isaiah 52:7; Romans 10:15). That's what I'm reading out of the good book, the Bible.

"Then said Jesus to his disciples, If any man will come after Me, let him deny himself, and take up his cross, and follow Me. For whosoever will save his life shall lose it: and whosoever will lose his life for My sake shall find it. For what is a man profited, if he shall gain the whole world, and lose his own soul? Or what shall a man give in exchange for his soul? For the Son of man shall come in the glory of His Father with His angels; and then He shall reward every man according to his works" (Matthew 16:24–27).

What God Purposed for Man

God has saved and called us with a holy calling, not according to our works but according to His own purpose and grace, which was given us in Christ Jesus before the world began (2 Timothy 1:9). Jesus suffered, bled, and died (official sacrifice) for the sins of man, placing man back into a proper relationship with God, the Father. Jesus's resurrection from the dead abolished death, making life and immortality a reality through the gospel (His death, burial, and resurrection).

Adam brought death to man. Jesus, the only acceptable sacrifice, brought life eternal to man. When we accept Christ and the gift of salvation through obedience of the gospel, and live faithfully until He calls us to glory, we will have a home eternal with God.

Go and Sin No More

Get started on the right path. So you have lived your life as a homosexual, lesbian, transvestite, adulterer, fornicator, drunkard, liar, kidnapper or stealer of men, thief, and so forth. Wherever you find yourself, harden not your heart toward the truth, God's word; repent, obey the gospel, and go and sin no more.

Should We Call Down Fire from Heaven?

Jesus said no. Jesus came but for one purpose: to redeemed man's soul. You (individually) are the only one who can mess that up by rejecting Him. Still, His invitation stands: "Whosoever will; let him come." You cannot join Christ's church. Christ adds you to His body, not man. You are added upon your obedience to the gospel. No one can keep you out of Christ's church, only you and your deeds or lifestyle. There are many denominations—man-made religious institutions—that can vote on your membership or vote against your membership. Even in this, gays—not knowing scripture and the differences between man-made religions and the church in the Bible—are disingenuous in their attempt to force religious organizations to accept the gay lifestyle in worship assemblies. Unscriptural as some places of worship are, their gay agenda is the only thing they really want, not God. God will never keep honest and obedient hearts out of worship to Him; only you and your sins can separate you from the love of God and true worship. Christ didn't come to condemn. The words He spoke, the apostles taught, gospel preachers preach, and Christians or disciples teach (which you—only you—can fail to obey) will condemn you in the end. You can't save yourself, so God sent Jesus to save you, not condemn you.

Cast the First Stone

Gay, murderer, thief, liar, fornicator, adulterer, kidnapper—and the list goes on. We all have to do the same thing: *repent*. It's time to be honest with ourselves. "All have sinned and come short of the glory of God." If you find yourself on "the list," I can make a pretty good guess or calculation that that list has been around long before you or I (present-day people) came on the scene on planet earth. There is no time to cast stones, no time to blame God or some nonexistent gene. If that were the case, the people of Sodom and Gomorrah would have already made a case. And even if they had back then, they and you would still be back at ground zero: "The woman you gave me" and "The serpent beguiled me."

Apostle Peter's Lesson: Learn about Unclean Persons (Sinners)

In Acts 10, Peter experienced a vision while waiting on food to be prepared to eat. The vision came to him of all manner of four-footed beasts of the earth: wild animals, fowls, and creeping things. These were things Peter considered unclean and not worth touching and consuming. The thing with this vision Peter had was that he heard a voice. A voice asked him to get up and eat or partake of the feast spread out before him. For Peter, *in all his righteousness*, that wasn't going to be the case—*ain't happening.* "And the voice spoke to him again the second time, 'What God has cleansed, that call not you common.' This was done thrice: and the vessel was received up again into heaven" (Acts 10:15–16). As you begin to read Acts 10, you meet Cornelius, a man who prayed, sought God, and had an honest desire to be saved. You see this was Peter's first encounter with Cornelius after his vision of unclean food. And the lesson is yours: "Then Peter opened his mouth, and said of a truth I perceive that God is no respecter of Persons. But in every nation he that fears Him, and works righteousness, is accepted with Him" (vv. 34–35). This should be the attitude of every straight and gay person—to be a Cornelius, seeking salvation through obedience to the gospel. This should be the attitude of every Christian: not to condemn but to willingly (like Peter) share the gospel with all seeking salvation and the knowledge of the truth.

Jesus already did the suffering and dying for our sins. Because we all have sinned and come short of the glory of God, no one is in a position to cast stones or behead a person for being gay or an adulterer. God is patient and long-suffering, not willing that any should perish. When we hear about zealous and religious groups judging and condemning their own fellowman (male or female) to death, obviously they have their own personal agenda. It is almighty God (the righteous Judge) who judges man, and it is God who values all souls and demonstrated this when He allowed His only begotten Son, Christ, to die and redeem man's soul.

Ninety-Nine Just and One Lost

It is *you* God loves. It's you. *Come out* and be ye separated. The angels in heaven rejoice over one soul who repents, and who is saved from the deceitful snares of Satan. Don't be found [*a hard-hearted person*] where saints are instructed to cast not their pearls before swine [*lifestyle refuse to hear or accept the gospel*] or knock the dust from off their shoes—[*give up talking to you and move on to someone who wants to hear the gospel*]. The gospel is time sensitive. Your successful obedience to it is based on before the return of Christ or before your departure from this world, but no one knows when it will happen.

To God Be the Glory

Because of His pardon, we can see that God is gracious and isn't interested in sending anyone to hell. Jesus's sole purpose was to come and redeem man, not send him to hell. It is a sad, sad day when we do all we can to send ourselves to hell. We have a way out, and we are the only ones who can make that choice. "Whosoever will let him come."

Don't Lie with a Male as with a Woman (Leviticus 18:22)

In 1 Corinthians 6:1–11, the apostle Paul listed the sin of homosexuality (being effeminate) in the same group with others who wouldn't enter heaven. What was distinct in the classification of the identified sins in "the list" was that the homosexuals were not only committing sin, but their acts were deemed an abomination in the sight of God. Looking into the scriptures, we can go back to the third book of the Bible, Leviticus. The book paints a vivid picture of God's attitude about homosexuality, His instructions for moral living, and His judgment against those who violate His commandments and ordinances.

"If a man also lies with mankind, as he lies with a woman, both of them have committed an abomination: they shall surely be put to death; their blood shall be upon them" (Leviticus 20:13). Here in the same chapter of Leviticus, bestiality is addressed. "And if a man lies with a beast, he shall surely be put to death: and you shall slay the beast. And if a woman approach to any beast, and lie down thereto, you shall kill the woman, and the beast: they shall surely be put to death; their blood shall be upon them" (Leviticus 20:16).

Now, move over to the New Testament again to examine how homosexuality was dealt with after Christ gave instructions on how to get to heaven. In Romans 1, Paul enlightened the reader that because of homosexuality, God gave them (Gentiles) up to their vile ways.

> Wherefore God also gave them up to uncleanness through the lusts of their own hearts, to dishonor their own bodies between themselves. Who changed the truth of God into a lie, and worshiped and served the creature more than the creator, who is blessed forever. Amen. For this cause God gave them up to vile affections: for even their women did change the natural use into that which is against nature. And likewise also the men, leaving the natural use of the woman, burned in their lust one toward another; men with men working that which is unseemly, and receiving in themselves that recompense of their error which was meet. And even as they did not like to retain God in their knowledge, God gave them over to a reprobate mind, to do those things which are not convenient; Being filled with all unrighteousness, fornication, wickedness, covetousness, maliciousness; full of envy, murder, debate, deceit, malignity; whisperers. Backbiters, haters of God, despiteful, proud, boasters, inventors of evil things, disobedient to parent, Without understanding, covenant-breakers, *without natural affection*, implacable, unmerciful: Who knowing the judgment of God, that they that which commit such things are worthy of death, not only do the same, but have pleasure in them that do them. (Romans 1:24–32, emphasis added)

Christ Died for You (Romans 5:8)

In the same book, in Romans 8, we learn about hope in Christ—something that wasn't there in the Old Testament, the Law of Moses. Those who committed an offense died on the spot; there was no grace, no mercy. *Those found committing homosexuality and bestiality were stoned on the spot.*

For when we were yet without strength, in due time Christ died for the ungodly. For scarcely for a righteous man will one die: yet perhaps for a good man some would even dare to die. But God commends His love toward us, in that, while we were yet sinners, Christ died for us. Much more then, being now justified by His blood, we shall be saved from wrath through Him. For if, when we were enemies, we were reconciled to God by the death of His Son, much more, being reconciled, we shall be saved by His life. And not only so, but we also joy in God through our Lord Jesus Christ, by whom we have now received the atonement. Wherefore, as by one man sin entered into the world, and death by sin and so death passed upon all men, for that all have sinned. (Romans 5:6–12)

It cannot be emphasized more than what we found in the previous verses—that Christ didn't come to condemn. He came to clean up Adam's act and put man back into a proper relationship with God. That was something because of man's sinful nature he couldn't do. The blood of animals couldn't do. Only the blood of a sinless one could do. Christ who knew no sin became sin (human) and the official sacrifice for the sins of the world. (2 Corinthians 5:21)

The Gift of Preaching

The Word of God, the Gospel (Good News)

And how shall they preach, except they be sent? As is written, How beautiful are the feet of them that preach the gospel of peace, and bring glad tidings of good things? (Romans 10:15)

For the preaching of the cross is to them that perish foolishness; but to us which are saved it is the power of God. For it is written, I will destroy the wisdom of the wise, and will bring to nothing the understanding of the prudent. Where is the wise? Where is the scribe? Where is the disputer of this world? Has not God made foolish the wisdom of this world? For after that in the wisdom of God, it pleased God by the foolishness of preaching to save them that believe. (1 Corinthians 1:18–21)

Base things of the world, and things which are despised, has God chosen, yea and things which are not, to bring to naught things that are: that no flesh should glory in His presence. But of Him are you in Christ Jesus, who of God is made to us wisdom, and righteousness, and sanctification, and redemption: That, according as it is written, he that glories, let him glory in the Lord. (1 Corinthians 1:28–31)

Take hold of God's word and live. Its whole purpose is to prepare you for a life with Christ. The BIBLE (Basic Instructions Before Leaving Earth) was left. If God was interested only in condemning you to hell, Jesus wouldn't have died and left instructions on how to save yourselves from this untoward generation.

But if our gospel be hid, it is hid to them that are lost: in whom the god of this world has blinded the minds of them which believe not, less the light of the glorious gospel of Christ, who is the image of God, should shine to them. For we preach not ourselves, but Christ Jesus the Lord; and ourselves your servants for Jesus sake. For God, who commanded the light to shine out of darkness, has shined in our hearts, to give the light of the knowledge of the glory of God in the face of Jesus Christ. But we have this treasure in earthen vessels, that the excellency of the power may be of God, and not of us. (2 Corinthians 4:3–7)

We Shall All Stand before the Judgment of God

Make no mistake about it; don't get this "thang" twisted. It has nothing to do with whether you believe in God. "For we shall all stand before the judgment seat of Christ" (Romans 14:10). The sea will give up its dead (including cremation or being eaten by wild animals). Yes, all will stand before the judgment seat of God. No excuse; you can't claim you were never told. Here it is in black and white. The scriptures ask, "Are you angry because I tell you the truth?"

That is the nature of man; many who are not interested in the truth find themselves offended.

"And then shall many be offended, and shall betray one another, and shall hate one another.

And many false prophets shall rise and shall deceive
many. And because iniquity shall abound, the love of many
shall wax cold. But he that shall endure to the end, the
same shall be saved. And this gospel of the kingdom shall
be preached in all the world for a witness to all nations; and
then the end come" (Matthew 24: 10–14).

Who Can Separate You from the Love of God?

Again, Jesus is not in the condemning business—take advantage of that! But
know that every word He has spoken will condemn you in the end. Your life
and opportunity to do something about your state of being are time sensitive;
it's here and now. A true Christian isn't in the business of condemning and
gay bashing. His command is only to share the gospel so others might have
the opportunity to hear the gospel and become a Christian (a child of God),
too. His responsibility and duty are to share the gospel. By sharing the truth
of God's word, no one is deprived of the only rights and freedom God has
given him or her. "Whosoever will, let him come." But for those who know
the truth and fail to warn the wicked, the wicked person's blood will be on
their heads. "Nevertheless, if you warn the wicked of his way to turn from it;
if he does not turn from his ways, he shall die in his iniquity; but you have
delivered your soul" (Ezekiel 33:9).

GRACE

The Grace of God: His True Attribute

"GRACE IS FAVOR or kindness shown without regard to the worth or merit
of the one who receives it or in spite of what the person deserves"[98] (Nelson
Bible Dictionary).

When we talk about faith and salvation, we must understand they are not
possible without grace. We all need grace. And most often in our society, we
demand and seek mercy and pardon for our indiscretions. We like making
off like bandits with the loot from the lotto and super-discounted prices, a

---

[98] Defined as Unmerited Favor of God. Nelson Bible Dictionary published
by Thomas Nelson: HarperCollins Christina Publishing, Inc. Nashville, TN

bang for our bucks. It's, for the most part, our nature. Let's be honest: a lot of us want something for nothing or very little effort on our part. Well, we have won heaven's lotto. Just take the ticket, pick it up at the altar, the cross, and follow Christ to a home in heaven. A prize of a mansion and eternal life awaits. We've got God's heartstrings; we were loved even when we were sinners and unworthy. God loved us first. We are winners. We are getting this gift without our blood being shed and being crucified. Jesus has already purchased the winning ticket for us with His blood.

Let's take a look at grace: *free* stuff, a gift. Salvation is free to all. It starts with a pardon for personal wrongs against God. Since *all* are guilty of sin, *all* deserve hell; it just that simple. Be all surprised if you wish. Talk to Adam and Eve about that, but no need—it's a done deed. Through one man, Adam, sin and death entered the world. Now, on the other hand, it's a done deal when it comes to your pardon and salvation from sin. Talk to Jesus about that; through Christ there is forgiveness of sin and life everlasting. We are saved by grace; something received without merit.

> Wherein in time past you walked according to the course of this world, according to the prince of the power of the air, the spirit that now works in the children of disobedience: Among who also we all had our conversation in times past in the lusts of our flesh, fulfilling the desires of the flesh and of the mind; and were by nature the children of wrath, even as others. But God, who is rich in *mercy*, for His great love wherewith he loved us, Even when we were dead in sins, has quickened us together with Christ, (by *grace* you are saved;) and has raised us up together, and made us sit together in heavenly places in Christ Jesus: That in the ages to come He might show the exceeding riches of His *grace* in His kindness toward us through Christ Jesus. For by grace are you saved through faith; and that not of yourselves; it is the gift of God: Not of works, less any man should boast. (Ephesians 2:4–9, emphasis added)

Now, before some of us lazy individuals (God did it all, folks) get too happy about no work and something for nothing, there is something one *must* do to be saved; this isn't a couch potato faith. Remember the free advertisement to complete and return in the mail? Talking about bringing a horse to water, but you can't make him drink. Keep reading, and you will see the significance of water baptism. It is up to you to submit to water baptism.

Grace allows us the *means* and opportunity to approach God; by grace we are saved through faith. No amount of work on our part is good enough to merit salvation. "Who has saved us, and called us with an holy calling, not according to our works, but according to His own *purpose* and grace, which was given us in Christ Jesus before the world began" (2 Timothy 1:9, emphasis added).

We will never get to the point in our mortal existence that we are so good and righteous that God owes us for our good deeds. There is no such thing as being so good, right, and spotless (on our own) that God should save us. "As it is written, There is none righteous, not one: There is none that understands, there is none that seeks after God. They are all gone out of the way, they are together become unprofitable, there is none that does good, no, not one ... For all have sinned, and come short of the glory of God" (Romans 3:10–12, 23).

Many have rejected the plan of salvation God offers. Many have refused to accept the "grace offer" He has extended. Many have gone all Sinatra on God, saying, "I did it my way." When a person rejects what God has to offer, he doesn't move out of the guilty position of sin, that one finds himself or herself in at the age of accountability. This is, unfortunately, a disobedient state, deserving the punishment of a sin-guilty individual. "For the wages of sin is death; but the gift of God is eternal life through Jesus Christ our Lord" (Romans 6:23).

How Does One Get This Grace?

Grace is what we get from God through Christ Jesus. We can't do anything about our undone condition without Him.

> But we see Jesus, who was made a little lower than the angels for the suffering of death, crowned with glory and honor; that He by the grace of God should taste death for every man. (Hebrews 2:9)
> For you know the grace of our Lord Jesus Christ, that, though He was rich, yet for your sakes, He became poor, that you through His poverty might be rich. (2 Corinthians 8:9)
> In whom we have redemption through His blood the forgiveness of sins, according to the riches of His grace. (Ephesians 1:7)

Works of Obedience vs. Works of Merit (Earned)

Ultimately, grace is received by one's obedience to the gospel, the preaching of Christ's death, burial, and resurrection. "Though He were a Son yet learned He obedience by the things which He suffered. And being made perfect, He became the author of eternal salvation to all them that obey Him" (Hebrews 5:8–9). A young minister once stated, "It is sad that God has done so much and yet so few have come to receive the free gift of grace!"

Grace is extended and offered to all men (people), but many because of unbelief and lack of faith won't receive it. Out of all the preaching and teaching the cross and what the death, burial, and resurrection mean to man and his salvation, the Bible informs us that "all will not be saved." "Enter you in at the strait gate: for wide is the gate, and broad is the way that leads to destruction, and many there be which go in thereat. Because strait is the gate, and narrow is the way, which leads to life, and few there be that find it ... Not everyone that says to Me, Lord, Lord, shall enter into the kingdom of heaven, but he that does the will of My Father which is in heaven" (Matthew 7:13–14, 21).

Law of Liberty vs. the Law of Sin and Death

Under the Law of Moses, there was no grace. You sinned, and you died. One found guilty was stoned to death and often punished in a timely manner. Under the "law of Christ," the "law of liberty," one is given the opportunity to confess, repent, seek forgiveness, and make the necessary changes in his or her life. As you can see, even with grace, mankind is still under a law, the law of Christ. "To them that are without law [Law of Moses], as without law, (being not without law to God, but under the law to Christ,) that I might gain them that are without law" (1 Corinthians 9:21). The apostle Paul was interested in reaching people at whatever station in life they found themselves; then he could educate and bring them to Christ under the law of liberty.

> But whosoever looks into the perfect law of liberty, and continues therein, he being not a forgetful hearer, but a *doer* of the work, this man shall be blessed in his deed. (James 1:25, emphasis added)

For the law of the Spirit of life in Christ Jesus has made
me free from the law of sin and death. (Romans 8:2)

Grace is something we should seek, and when we receive it, we should work to hold on to it. It's a ticket to the free gift, salvation. We don't want to misplace or lose it. It's free, but it shouldn't be dealt with nonchalantly. Faith without work is dead. By works a man is justified and not by faith alone (James 2:24). Many lotto winners have lost their winning tickets and a financial opportunity for a better life. The loss to them is forever and results in millions of unclaimed dollars going into the state funds and revenue budget. Consider the biblical warnings of falling from grace:

1. "Wherefore let him that thinks he stands take heed less he fall" (1 Corinthians 10:12).
2. "Let us labor, therefore, to enter into that rest, less any man fall after the same example of unbelief" (Hebrews 4:11).
3. "For if after they have escaped the pollutions of the world through the knowledge of the Lord and Savior Jesus Christ, they are again entangled therein, and overcome, the latter end is worse with them than the beginning" (2 Peter 2:20).
4. "Christ is become of no effect to you, whosoever of you are justified by the law; you are fallen from grace. For we through the Spirit wait for the hope of righteousness by faith" (Galatians 5:4–5).

Clearing up all misconceptions, let me say that grace isn't universal without any effort on man's part to obtain it and hold on to it, because it is something, if not careful, that can be lost, as indicated in the scriptures in the above list.

The Lord Talking with Moses

"And the Lord descended in the cloud, and stood with him there, and proclaimed the name of the Lord. And the Lord passed by before him, and proclaimed, The Lord, the Lord God, merciful and gracious, longsuffering, and abundant in goodness and truth" (Exodus (34:5–6). What an awesome God, who sent His Son, Jesus, to save man, extending grace and not condemning. Will we condemn ourselves by not obeying His word?

Heaven and Hell: Real Places

As far as scriptural references, hell is just as real as heaven. If an honest heart person believes in one, certainly he or she can't justify the nonexistence of the other. They hold in their possession claims of an eternal home for the soul. One is as equally inexpressible or indescribably pleasant as the other is inexpressible or indescribably tormentous. What person believes in the day (light) but doesn't believe in the night (darkness)? Certainly, both exist. People get to experience both day and night on this side of the cross. Remember Jesus's conversation with doubting Thomas? "Blessed is the one who believes without seeing [faith]." The fact is, you will one day leave this walk of life, and there is a sure bet that you will face the reality of heaven or hell as you pass over into the spiritual realm of your eternal existence. Because you possess the spirit God breathed into man, you are an eternal being; like God, your life-giving source, you can never cease to exist. Man (people) will experience an eternal home somewhere: hell or heaven. The gospel plea to man is to choose wisely; Joshua did. The fool has said in his heart that there is no God.

In chapter four, we had a conversation about faith. Without faith it is impossible to please God. We proclaim that God loves everybody, and scripturally this is so. God so love the world that He sent His Son, Jesus Christ, to die and shed His blood of atonement for the sins of man. The scriptures also tell man that God will cast the wicked into hell, all sinners into the lake of fire. We chose to ignore or not accept that fact; we should have faith in our own judgment. We exhibit very little faith when we demonstrate that we believe some of what God says but not all of what God says .

Hello out there. Hello out there, world. God is patient and long-suffering; He is not willing that any should perish. *God has no desire to send anyone to hell.* Remember that God sent His only begotten Son, Jesus Christ, to die to purchase man's (people's) souls back from eternal damnation in the fires of hell, from a spiritual death and separation. You are His investment. He may not show up in your lifetime, but that doesn't make Him slack concerning His promise. Take Him up on His offer before you run out of time on this side of the cross; that's New Testament salvation.

Sin Is Sin Is Sin

In Luke 9:54, the disciples James and John asked Jesus whether they should call down fire from heaven to consume individuals who didn't see eye to eye with them. Jesus's response was a no. In other words, "You know not what manner of spirit you are of; For the Son of man is not come to destroy men's lives, but to save them" (Luke 9:55–56).

In a news article by NBC News June 2014, vice president Joe Biden is quoted as saying that "prejudice is prejudice."[99] This statement was in defense of violence against gays in different cultures around the globe. While attending an international forum for gay rights, Biden iterated that he and President Barack Obama were advocates for the rights of gays, bisexuals, lesbians, and transgender lifestyles. Biden went as far as to say that he didn't care about different cultures' views; the rights of individuals in abominable lifestyles trump those views. I would interpret this to mean cultures that have a history older than the United States, dating back to biblical days, too.

If we back this up a little, maybe about a couple of hundred thousand years, maybe back around the time of the culture when the book of Leviticus was written, this statement would sound very blasphemous. Malachi 3:6 and Matthew 24:35 inform man that throughout cultures, times, centuries and to the end of this world and eternality, God changes not. He cannot lie, so this means His word doesn't change from the ancient cultures to the present times in the history of this universe.

While Biden exclaims that prejudice is prejudice, Jesus exclaims that sin is sin. Many have exalted themselves above the knowledge of God, even trying to be godlike in power and proclamations. It is the Christian duty today, as it was with our spiritual brother, the apostle Paul, to inform the erring souls with meekness and gentleness of Christ. "For the weapons of our warfare are not carnal, but mighty through God to the pulling down of strong hold; Casting down imaginations, and every high thing that exalts itself against the knowledge of God, and bringing into captivity every thought to the obedience of Christ" (2 Corinthians 10:4–5).

Biden's interpretation of the treatment of gays in our society or civilization as "the civil right issue of our day" is putrefying and it is insulting to equate

---

[99] Https://www.nbcnews.com/news/prejudice-prejudice-biden-says-gay-rights-trump-culture-n140121
2014 NBCNews.com, The Associated Press, First published June 24, 2014.
"Prejudice Is Prejudice: Biden Says Gay Rights Trump Culture

with the suffrage and black holocaust: USA-sponsored genocide or systemic persecution and murder of black people in America, leaning ones thoughts toward a mental flashback in the minds of those who can take a very short walk back in history to Jim Crow laws, police dogs, water hoses, separate public water fountains, hospital waiting rooms, public transportation, and bodies hanging from trees as a norm for the landscape. Even today in America, take a quick look over your shoulders at profiling, redlining, unequal wages, and home and business loans. These were acts perpetrated against a group of people who weren't in abomination to the will of God. It's sickening to attempt a comparison between black people's rights to be recognized as human beings and gays' rights to live unnatural and unseemly ways in the sight of God and man.

The civil rights movement of African Americans brought this country to its *knees in prayer* to God for the betterment of the whole. The civil rights movement for homosexuality will bring this county to its knees in the destruction of people living in disobedience to God. The two movements don't compare in any shape, form, or fashion.

I admired George W. Bush's stand on biblical principles while in the office of president. He didn't cower to demands from gays to change the definition of marriage or entertain judges who would lead the hearts of people away from God. Because of the providence of God, America exists and enjoys its status on the globe and must remain a nation that trusts in God. Bush later expressed support of FMA-*Federal Marriage Amendment*-because of the pressure of the courts. It was the courts that questioned whether Obama would abide by their rulings and go along with the gay or LGBT agenda or on any other rulings.

Bush Administration's Stance

In 2003 the White House declined to take a stand on the amendment (FMA/ *Federal Marriage Amendment*), although press secretary Ari Fleischer relayed that President George W. Bush believed marriage was between a man and a woman. In his State of the Union address on January 20, 2004, President Bush alluded to the recent court decision in Massachusetts that ordered the state to recognize same-sex marriages beginning in May. "Activist judges ... have begun redefining marriage by court order, without regard for the will of the people and their elected representatives ... If judges insist on forcing their arbitrary will upon the people, the only alternative left to the people would be the constitutional process." [100]On February 24, after the same Massachusetts court reiterated that it was insisting on marriage and that civil unions were insufficient, Bush expressed support for this amendment for the first time. In August, Vice President Cheney neither endorsed nor condemned the FMA, arguing that same-sex marriage was for the states to decide. Cheney stated his support for same-sex marriage on a state-by-state basis. On the other hand, of the eleven states in which amendments defining marriage were on the ballot, all passed handily. Bush won in nine, including Ohio. Interpretation of some exit polling suggests that the amendments may have brought out one million additional voters, most of whom came out for the first time to cast their ballots for Bush. Notably, a vast majority of these states hadn't voted for a Democrat in many years. The two states that Bush didn't win, Michigan and Oregon, still passed amendments limiting official recognition of marriage to one man, one woman unions. In the 2000 presidential election, there was some speculation that many evangelicals didn't go to the polls and vote because of the October surprise of George W. Bush's drunk-driving arrest record. In a dozen swing states that decided the presidential election, moral values tied with the economy and jobs as the top issue in the campaign, according to Associated Press exit polls.

In our zeal not to discriminate, we have taken up a fight we weren't called to fight or authorized to fight. Even some members of the Supreme Court expressed these sentiments. Read Judge Alito's dissenting remarks. Yes, it is always right not to discriminate or perpetrate violence against another human being. Jesus is an advocate for not being violent to people who may not do things your way or to your likening. He told His disciples, James and John, they couldn't act that way. Jesus has set men free. When Jesus sets you free, you are free indeed. There is no tolerance for a bloodthirsty "Crusaders for Christ" religious mentality that kills people because they don't convert to Christianity or want to live a life in some other faith or not worship God at all. The almighty God has always given man a choice. But the overly righteous are warned and understand that God won't condone or disregard writing sinful acts into law and forcing people to turn their thoughts and hearts away from God.

In the words of Biden, "There is a price to pay." Better yet, God won't be mocked. This article says Obama was asking that gay rights be made a

---

[100] https://en.wikipedia.org/wiki/Federal_Marriage_Amendment#Bush_administration's_stance
Wikipedia, s.v. "Federal Marriage Amendment," last modified May 28, 2019, http://en.wikipedia.org/wiki/Federal_Marriage_Amendment

priority and declared his support of gay marriages. When a nation becomes so emboldened that it stands up in opposition to God's laws, it invokes the handwriting on the wall.

> And have no fellowship with the unfruitful works of darkness, but rather reprove them. For it is a shame even to speak of those things which are done of them in secret. (Ephesians 5:11–12)
>
> God has put a rainbow in the sky. There is hope. If only in this world you have hope, of all men you are most miserable. "I do set my bow in the cloud, and it shall be for a token of a covenant between Me and the earth" (Genesis 9:13).

LET
GOD
BE
TRUE
but every man a liar
Romans 3:4

Chapter 7
Debaters of This World

"BUT YOU, O Lord, shall laugh at them; you shall have all the nations in derision" (Psalm 59:8).

Piers Morgan (*Piers Morgan Live* on CNN) expressed sentiments that the Bible needs to be amended so it supports same–sex marriage; he was so hilariously ignorant. I can imagine the residents of heaven laughing at him—what a silly man. Mr. Morgan bellowed out of his mouth his contempt for the authority of God's word, suggesting it had no more authority in the lives of people than a fallible, man-made instrument like the U.S. Constitution. And like the Constitution, it can be changed or amended by the people and with the times; after all, it's for the people, by the people, and of the people. The Bible is the word of God and doesn't change with the times. Psalm 59:12 points out the sin of the mouth, the words of their lips; let them be taken in their pride and for the cursing and lying they speak. The apostle Paul penned,

> Where is the wise? Where is the scribe? Where is the disputer of this world? Has not God made foolish the wisdom of this world? For after that in the wisdom of God the world by wisdom knew not God, it pleased God by the foolishness of preaching to save them that believe. For the Jews require a sign, and the Greeks seek after wisdom; But we preach Christ crucified, unto the Jews a stumbling block, and unto the Greeks foolishness; But unto them which are called, both Jews and Greeks, Christ the power of God, and the wisdom of God. (1 Corinthians 1:20–24)

Mr. Morgan made one of the most foolish remarks I have ever heard; he wanted God to obey the will of man instead of man obeying the will of God. When I first heard this, I laughed. But it's really sad when God laughs at our foolishness (Psalm 2:4). Paul went on to say, "For after that in the wisdom of God, it pleased God by the foolishness of preaching to save them that believe … Because the foolishness of God is wiser than men; and the weakness of God is stronger than men" (1 Corinthians 1:21, 25).

Mr. Morgan will understand, as will every man, that "the preaching of the cross is to them that perish foolishness; but to Christians, which are saved, it is the power of God." Scripture says God will destroy the wisdom of the wise, and will bring to nothing the understanding of the prudent (1 Corinthians 1:18–19).

> Because the foolishness of God is wiser than men; and the weakness of God is stronger than men. For ye see your calling, brethren, how that not many wise men after the flesh, not many mighty, not many noble, are called: But God hath chosen the foolish things of the world to confound the wise, and God hath chosen the weak things of the world to confound the things which are mighty; And base things of the world, and things which are despised, hath God chosen, yea, and things which are not, to bring to naught things that are: that no flesh should glory in his presence. But of him are ye in Christ Jesus, who of God is made unto wisdom, and righteousness, and sanctification, and redemption: That, according as it is written, He that glorieth, let him glory in the Lord. (1 Corinthians 1:25–31)

God's word will go forth and it will not return to him void, but will accomplish that which it was designed to do. The preaching of the gospel will bring honest and obedient hearts to God. (Isaiah 55:11)

> Let the wicked forsake his way, and the unrighteous man his thoughts: and let him return to the Lord; and He will have mercy upon him; and to our God, for He will abundantly pardon. For My thoughts are not your thoughts, neither are your ways My ways, says the Lord. For as the heavens are higher than the earth; so are My ways higher than your ways, and My thoughts than your thoughts. (Isaiah 55:7–9)

On Friday, March 15, 2013, talk show, Piers Morgan had his audience entertain the thought that his guest was calling homosexual behavior wrong, and the second guest stated that the solution to the problem in America was that we needed more marriages. The solution for Uzzah to keep the ark from falling was to reach out and try to balance it. The hand of God struck him dead, because only the priests from a specific Levite tribe could handle the ark. "There is a way that seems right unto a man, but the end thereof is death" (Proverbs 14:12;16:25). The ark was God's thing, and unauthorized activity was punished. Marriage is God's thing, and unauthorized activity will be punished.

Debating the N-Word and F-Word

On November 19, 2013, *Piers Morgan Live*, CNN's nightly nine o'clock at night news hour, aired a debate I found absolutely disturbing. There on the panel sat three men: a CNN anchorperson, a writer or columnist for the *New York Times*, and an editor of a section of the *Huffington Post*. They were discussing the n-word and f-word as if to equate the black people's struggles in America with gay and lesbian struggles in America. What was more appalling was that the African-American community didn't speak out against such a comparison. As mentioned before and in previous chapters, if gays had even tried to part their lips and compare their discrimination and suffering to that of the Jews (Holocaust) in any way remotely, there would have been an immediate backlash or anti-Semitic outcry from that community. But oddly there was nothing from the black community while the gay civil rights movement hitches itself to the civil rights movement of African Americans to gain ground in their agenda to change a nation—but not for the better. This change would lead only down a dark and disturbing path that even a Supreme Court judge cited; we don't know the outcome. The rise of present-day events in the news concerning racial discrimination should send a clear message that the two have nothing in common as they relate to civil rights of a people. Unfortunately, the portal was opened when the Supreme Court decided to accept a lifestyle God deemed abominable. We will see more sexual crimes against animals surface; this nation will return to more overt racial divides, crimes against women and children, devastating weather and climate changes, and threats of terrorism local and internationally. We have removed our only protection: "In God We Trust." We are proud and trust in our own presumed wisdom, knowledge, and military might.

What Is Marriage? Man and Woman: A Defense by Ryan T. Anderson

Same-Sex Marriage in the Supreme Court: The issue to debate is whether the Supreme Court will redefine marriage for this nation or allow each of its fifty states's citizens to determine by their vote what will be legalized for that particular state.

At the time of this research, forty-one states forbid same-sex marriages, defining marriage as between a man and a woman. Nine states allowed same-sex marriage. There were one hundred and twenty thousand same-sex couples who have married; this can't really be done unless it is a man-made institution. It's something tampered with, and once you do that, because God doesn't dwell in evil, you don't know what you have, even though man is calling it a marriage. For one thing, it is virtually impossible scripturally anyway. Here's an example of man tampering with what God has put in place: the mule is sterile, and the seedless watermelon is sterile. They are incapable of reproducing without some intervention. Male with male and female with female cannot produce an offspring and often solicit the assistance of surrogate births or sperm donate in the case of lesbians. Put either man with man or woman with woman on an island, and nothing will happen as far as a continuation of their seed: man, plant, or animal. The seedless watermelon and the mule are hybrids, not something God designed. The thing is, if marriage was something man put together (for example, the U.S. Constitution), then it could be amended to fit the times and whims of the people. No matter what understandings courts or people have of marriage, it is a God-created institution between a man and a woman. Tampering with God's blueprint will automatically disannul it. There will never be a gay marriage in the sight of God. "Lo, this only have I found, that God has made man upright; but they have sought out many inventions" (Ecclesiastes 7:29). "And God saw that the wickedness of man was great in the earth, and that every imagination of the thoughts of his heart was only evil continually" (Genesis 6:5).The bed is undefiled only in holy matrimony. Jesus told the woman at the well that she had had five husbands, and the one she presently lived with wasn't hers. Gays can say they have a spouse in their unholy union; Jesus will say that the person they call a spouse or live with isn't theirs. The bed is undefiled in marriage, and God doesn't sanction men lying with men as they would lie with women.

God said a man shall leave father and mother and cleave to his wife, and they then shall be one. And be for real; if you don't want your union to be blessed in the sight of God, who said the bed is undefiled in marriage, just do your thing anyway. Your marriage doesn't really count, regardless of the Supreme Court or the law of man. And maybe gays really don't care as long as they get the government benefits for married couples and temporary victories, and get to disrupt and destroy things that are good in God's sight.

A larger issue with the actions of the Supreme Court is their disobedience to God, who said that what He has joined together, let no man put asunder (separate into parts and pieces)—Mark 10:9; Matthew 19:6. God put the male and female factor into play together. A man shall leave his father and mother, and the two (man and wife) shall be one. God has always been about oneness and wholeness. The Father, Son, and Holy Ghost are one in the Godhead. God took a rib from Adam to form the woman and presented her to him. "Bone of my bone, flesh of my flesh." God's design was for the two to come together as man and wife and be one again in marriage. "The two shall be made one." The oneness or wholeness, with each supplying the correct amount of chromosomes, can produce a whole human being—a child, the fruit of the womb, God's inherence.This marriage status is designed for production. God designed everything to be in a productive state; everything produces after its own kind. The very fact that the homosexuals' defiant nature toward God is unproductive, puts it in an abominable status. See Mark 10:6–8; Matthew 19:4–5; Genesis 1:27–31; 2:24. God also warns judges not to cause His people to sin.

A little leaven leavens the whole lump; to be guilty in one point is to be guilty in all points. To tamper with, mess with, or make changes disannuls the God-instituted institution and makes it null and void. Either you are right or wrong. Scriptural marriage falls under the freedom of religion, so that's not going anywhere. Calling man with man and woman with woman a marriage—well, people on this planet can do that too. But we are fooling ourselves if we think Satan is going to stop there. At some point, someone will want to have his or her animal recognized as his or her spouse or child if this identification helps with social security benefits, inheritance taxes, and so forth. After gay marriage, bestiality isn't far behind on the Supreme Court's roster for some sort of recognition in society, an issue against cultural norms. It is in people's hearts to continue to do evil.

In a live debate on Piers Morgan Show, March 15, 2013, Suze Orman attacked and/or looked down on Ryan Anderson [Heritage Foundation][101].

---

[101] Anderson, Ryan T., Marriage, the Court, and the Future (May 1, 2017). Harvard Journal of Law and Public Policy, Vol. 40, No. 2, 2017. Available at SSRN: https://ssrn.com/abstract=3113593 ; https://creativecatholicworks.org/wp-content/uploads/2014/07/What-Is-Marriage-Ryan-T.-Anderson.pdf

"Let no man despise your youth; but be an example of the believers, in word, in conversation, in charity, in spirit, in faith, in purity" (1 Timothy 4:12). Ms. Orman taunted Mr. Anderson like a Goliath, but he certainly had his stone or rock ready for her. He may have been young, but look at what 1 Samuel 17:32 has to say. "And David said to Saul, Let no man's heart fail because of him; your servant will go and fight with this Philistine." The exchange was something to witness live on Piers Morgan. Ms. Orman couldn't stand up against the wisdom of the youth this young man brought to the debate. She attacked him by calling him unintelligent, saying no one was interested in what his age-group had to say, alluding to some poll taken on people in his age-group. Appallingly, Ms. Orman pulled the mob mentality of the audience to her side. Mr. Anderson never did, even after she did it to him. He stuck with the issue of the definition of marriage not being redefined by the Supreme Court, which would have a federal impact on the nation. He was opposed to the Supreme Court not allowing each individual state's citizens to decide the matter on a state-by-state level.

Piers Stefan Pughe- Morgan a British journalist and television host in one of his statements on his show: Marriage Is Marriage on March 15, 2013 alluded to and tried to equate the Bible and the U.S. Constitution. While listening to this Brit, the only thing I could think of was the Boston Tea Party, religious freedom, and war; but I digress. What I will impart at this moment is Genesis 2. One doesn't have to look far; just turn a few pages from the front of his or her Bible. "And the rib, which the Lord God had taken from man, made He a woman, and brought her to the man. And Adam said this is now bone of my bones, and flesh of my flesh; she shall be called Woman, because she was taken out of Man. Therefore shall a man leave his father and his mother, and shall cling to his wife; and they shall be one flesh" (Genesis 2:22–24). Marriage is a God thing. God created it! And through this union of the man and woman, children are born. Now just open the Bible to the first chapter. "So God created man in His own image, in the image of God created He him: man and female created He them. And God blessed them, and God said to them, Be fruitful, and multiply, and replenish the earth, and subdue it; and have dominion over the fish of the sea, and over the fowl of the air, and over every living thing that moves upon the earth" (Genesis 1:27–28).

It's quite interesting that there are Americans (on this show) having another conversation with a Brit about religious freedom or the Bible's definition of marriage. America left British rule, and we are a nation under God. Yes, Mr. Morgan, it is a nation under God, capital *G*, and a government of the people, by the people, and for the people; it isn't a monarchy. Mr. Anderson had a legitimate argument. People of each state should've decided on the marriage issue, not the Supreme Court for *these* United States. People should have the freedom to live in the states they choose; the ones who honor the Bible or the ones who don't by creating their own definition of marriage in those states. Abraham Lincoln talked about a new birth of freedom. We fought for it and won it as a nation under God; it shall not perish, and it shouldn't be taken away from us. The people of each state should decide.

Amazingly, gays demand equal rights in like manner, or the same fashion, as the man and woman God put together. After God put them together, He asked them to replenish the earth. Gays want to destroy and pervert the institution God built, and rob and steal God's heritage and His gift of that union. They can't give God anything back with their unions. They are busy about destroying the union of man and woman. Satan is at his job, going to and fro and seeking whom he can destroy. "Lo, children are a heritage of the Lord: and the fruit of the womb His reward" (Psalm 127:3). Before we as a nation start adopting out our children and subjecting them to an environment God calls an abomination to support the gay or lesbian agenda for legal marriage and the coveted federal benefits that come with the marriage union, we should honestly consider the following: "But whoso shall offend one of these little ones which believe in Me, it were better for him that a millstone were hanged about his neck, and that he were drowned in the depth of the sea" (Matthew 18:6). To live in abomination to God and then teach the child that the lifestyle he or she is reared in is scripturally wrong won't happen in these family environments. A kingdom divided against itself cannot stand. The situation will cause the child to lose faith. Faith produces obedience in God. This scripture supports children, be it new converts in Christ or children reared in an environment preventing the basic foundation of the family, the union of man and woman and their offspring, set forth by God in creation. Why toy with our children in this manner? We are no better than pagan worshippers and barbaric tribes, who offered up their children or infants in the fires to idols and false gods.

We must be wise and vigilant, as Satan keeps hammering at institutions of Christian morals and values. "For the weapons of our warfare are not carnal, but mighty through God to the pulling down of strong holds; Casting down imaginations, and every high thing that exalts itself against the knowledge of God, and bringing into captivity every thought to be obedience of Christ" (2 Corinthians 10:4–5).

Georgia, a Bible Belt state, is the original home of Chick-fil-A. Its owner, S. Truett Cathy, (who died September 8, 2014, reportedly in his nineties), observed Sunday as a day for worship to God. Store policy allowed its restaurants to close and give employees the opportunity as a day to rest and attend services. This practice didn't hinder the chain's financial success in the fast-food industry. "Dan Cathy [Truett Cathy's son] told the Baptist Press in 2012 that the company was "'guilty as charged' for backing 'the biblical definition of a family.'"[102] Gay rights groups and other called for boycotts and kiss-ins at Cathy's restaurants. The Jim Henson Company pulled its Muppet toys from kids' meals, while politicians in Boston and Chicago told the chain it wasn't welcome there. I mean, really, the best chicken sandwich resturant in the universe with a moral compass that allows employees off on Sundays to worship, and still it outperforms its open-seven-days-a-week business competition.

Suze Orman on Piers Morgan's Show

Piers Morgan and Suze Orman tried to justify their stance with opinion polls and others of the gay persuasion. "For we dare not make ourselves of the number, or compare ourselves with some that commend themselves: but they measuring themselves among themselves, are not wise" (2 Corinthians 10:12).

Orman, a renowned finance guru, whom Morgan described as an American business icon, was out of her league—already defeated when she tried to attack marriage, whether it was a debate with Mr. Ryan Anderson from the Heritage Foundation or not. But for the sake of the debate, traditionally marriage has always been defined as the union between a man and a woman. Mr. Anderson stated it wasn't until the year 2000 that communities started to shift in their opinions (according to polls) that marriage was a male and female relationship. If one took the time to search a little farther back into the history of marriage, he or she would recognize that it was God who created marriage and that the first couple in the union was Adam and Eve. God made it clear what His expectations for this union were; a man should leave his mother and father and cleave to his wife; and the two should be one in the eyes of God, with the bed undefiled. And they should be fruitful and multiply.

It was visible that Ms. Orman didn't have a solid foundation for her argument, and she panicked and lashed out at Mr. Anderson, calling him uneducated. Her attempt to defend why the federal government needed to get involved with gay marriages offered nothing other than the money aspect. Orman's argument was about social security benefits, widow benefits, health

---

[102] K. Allen Blume, ed. Biblical Reporter. " 'Guilty as Charged' backing Biblical definition of a family" Baptist Press in 2012

benefits, income tax, estate taxes or death taxes, the economic benefits of children in this union, and the economic disadvantage of not being considered a "married" couple in a gay or lesbian union. I thought, *How uneducated she is about her soul.* Ms. Orman is interested only in finances. What would a man give in exchange for his soul? Her very words would judge her in the end. She said she felt compassion for Mr. Anderson. It is Mr. Anderson who showed compassion and didn't revile her when she showed hostility toward him. Piers Morgan found God's way, which Mr. Anderson defended, offensive because he believed God should change His word to fit America in the "modern era." Now, this is the God who says He can't lie and that His word will never change. Mr. Morgan wants God to lie to accommodate the openly gay guest panelists like Elton John and Suze Orman. How many angels do you think were laughing or cracking up at him when he made that statement? Let's see if E. John and S. Orman will be around for the next hundred years. They die like all other human beings before and after them. God, the Alpha and Omega, lives forever. God isn't tolerant of anyone who sins against Him. "Repent," He says.

In the CNN interview, it was stated that forty-one states were against same-sex marriage. Nine states supported same-sex marriage, and one hundred twenty thousand same-sex marriages were on the books, so to speak. Anderson's stand wasn't to talk about gay or lesbian activities, taxes, and economic reasons; he chose to discuss the courts. The Supreme Court shouldn't redefine marriage (a union between a man and woman) for the people of the United States. What I found most interesting was those desiring gay or lesbian unions wanted the same benefits of people who can populate the earth. They cannot produce anything as far as continuing life, but they want everything it has to offer. They want your children and the benefits that come along with the God-created union of marriage.

The joke is on America. Place a male and female in one state, just the two of them. In a hundred years, the probability of finding at least one hundred people is likely. Now place a same-sex couple in another state, just the two of them. In a hundred years, you will find two skeletons and at best only one or two, one-hundred year-old person(s). Yet they have convinced America that they deserve every benefit a married couple has as well as their children, because, they claim, a gay or lesbian parent is better than no home or parent. This is God's inheritance, which we are sacrificing to an abominable home environment. Give to Caesar what is Caesar and to God what is God. He is a jealous God! He wants what is His! *Children need a family, we are told, even if it's a gay family.* Someone needed to touch the *Ark of the Covenant* to keep it from falling (it didn't matter who); these situations sounded like two good ideas. There is a way that seems right unto a man, but the end thereof is death. Children are a gift from God; they shouldn't be sacrificed to evil and caused to turn away from their Maker. Parents are commanded to bring them up in the nurture and admonition of the Lord. What gay or lesbian couple is going to teach the child what the Bible calls an abomination? A kingdom divided against itself cannot stand.

As Far as Me and My House, Joshua 24:15

As mentioned earlier, Republican Senator Rob Portman of Ohio, once considered antigay, had a change of mind after his son announced he was gay. CNN interviewed him. His record in Washington demonstrates that he:

1. supported a constitutional amendment to ban gay marriage;
2. voted for the Defense of Marriage Act (DOMA); and
3. voted for a bill to prohibit gay couples from adopting babies.

In April 2013, Earvin Magic Johnson III (EJ), son of Earvin Magic Johnson Jr., NBA Hall of Framer, told the world he was gay—he was "coming out." Mr. Johnson said he couldn't be prouder of his son and was behind his son one million percent. This news was great for him and the gay community. Mr. Johnson has deemed himself a spokesperson for the gay community and has suggested that other young black men should come out, too. Take a good look at the fathers of these gay men. Remember Joshua? Joshua's attitude was that he was the leader of his household. He didn't bow down to his children, who had gone astray. He remained with God and said he and his household were going to follow God. He didn't once say, "I will go along with my children in my household."

Thoughts and Imaginations of Men's Heart Were Evil Continually (Genesis 6:5; Mark 7:20-23)

Where do we go from here? Bestiality? Will we hear parents say, "I'm proud of my child who decided to sleep with his animal, put it on their taxes and health insurance plan, and so forth"? Will America legalize the activity with a document, joining the two in a union or partnership arrangement?

If you think that after you allow Satan a ride he won't want to drive, you are mistaken. One step in: a little leaven leavenes the whole lump.

And Such Were Some of You–1 Corinthians 6:9-11

"Know you not that the unrighteous shall not inherit the kingdom of God? Be not deceived, neither shall," the following:

- Fornicators
- Idolaters
- Adulterers
- Effeminate
- Abusers of themselves with mankind (homosexuals)
- Thieves
- Covetous
- Drunkards
- Revilers
- Extortioners

The list of sins above is what ignited the desire and provided the impetus, to write this book. It is the very fact that no other group on "the list" except for the effeminate or abusers of themselves with mankind demand to be recognized as a political group or sect. Here we are back at Sodom and Gomorrah all over again. Interestingly, they were the only group on "the list" God condemned as abominable.

In my researching and writing this book, I came across an article on the Internet titled "The Williams-Asher Debate on Homosexuality."[103] When I read this transcript on the debate, it was obvious Mr. Williams wasn't familiar with the Holy Scriptures. He presented a few scriptures in his defense, but his take on them was nonsensical and not logical. His personal interjections to what was written in scripture were completely foolish. The debate is from *Out of the Closet* (Faith And Facts Press).

The acceptance of homosexuality has made inroads into our twenty-first-century society. Many have become accepting and acclimated to the behavior due to the fact that TV programs, sport figures, political figures and even

---

[103] Jeff Asher, "The Williams-Asher Debate on Homosexuality," *Out of the Closet* (Indianapolis, IN: Faith And Facts Press, 1997).

so-called ministers of the word have come out of the closets and are openly defending their choice of a lifestyle that is contrary to the will of God.

Some find themselves so bewildered and don't know what to make of the gay *pandemonium* that's penetrating every aspect of our lives in these United States, including issues relating to what's the definition of a spouse, medical benefits, adoption of our children, alternate lifestyles of our political leaders, sports figures, entertainment (actors), educators, and religious leaders. We are so inundated and overwhelmed now by the gay inroads into our everyday lives. We are made to feel that if we say something that isn't agreeable with the movement, we are against another human being's civil rights. Not wanting to repeat the 1950s and 1960s and earlier struggles black people endured at the hands of this society in America, we put on our tolerance hats and in some cases our approval hats, not really knowing what to expect or where this will lead our country and civilization as we know it. What we do know from the Holy Scriptures is that a little leaven leavens the whole lump. Sin is contagious. Remember, Adam's sin put mankind in a state of sin. "By one man, Adam, sin and death; and by one man, Christ, freedom from sin and death and the gift of eternal life."

I wasn't aware before reading this transcript from the debate that a Gay Atheist Association existed. The article stated that while there are many homosexuals who are militantly atheistic, quite a few believe in God and practice Christianity. *How can that be done if God calls the homosexual lifestyle an abomination?.* If homosexuals are Christians, then Satan is a Christian. No gay person can be a Christian—just like no liar, thief, murder, fornicator, adulterer, and so forth can be a Christian—unless he or she repents and walks in the Light (Christ), the Light of the world.

> And such were some you. (1 Corinthians 6:11)
> For the word of God is quick, and powerful, and sharper than any two-edged sword, piercing even to the dividing asunder of soul and spirit, and of the joints and marrow, and is a discerner of the thoughts and intents of the heart. (Hebrews 4:12)

There are gays who advocate that they are seeking places that will accept them in worship. There is no debate in the Lord's church. He died and shed His blood for the sinner, and we all have sinned and come short of the glory of God. If one took the time to read the word of God, he or she would know that only Christ can *add* one to "The" church, His body. It is man who can vote you out or allow you to *join* "a" church, the one he established and built.

Man-made churches can spend their time debating whether to accept gays or not. God has already spoken—debate over. If the truth, the word of God, is being spoken without addition or subtraction, it will either draw or drive you away. And I say, again, I've heard the platitude or truism that a hit dog will holler.

> For outside are dogs, and sorcerers, and whoremongers, and murderers, and idolaters, and whosoever loves and makes a lie. (Revelations 22:15)
> I Jesus have sent Mine angel to testify to you these things in the churches [individual congregations of the body of Christ]. (Revelation 15:16)

If you love the truth, you will stay and be obedient to it. If you hate the truth, you will leave or stay and continuously kick, mummer, fight against it, and cause derision with the ones who are trying to obey the truth.

The gays seem to be disingenuous in their attitude toward churches. It isn't the church they are seeking to accept them; they are interested in any institution, from the Boy Scouts to whatever, that represents what is good, moral, and perceived to be holy in God's sight. They want to destroy God-friendly institutions: church, marriage, and His gift to the married union, children. They are after anything they see as good, holy, and belonging to God. What better place to launch an attack against civilization (God's creation) than in the most powerful nation in the world, whose motto is "In God We Trust"?

When it comes to obeying God, the debate ends. Create your gay churches or worship in the mainstream denominations that accept openly gay roles in their "vain" worship to God, with gay priests, ministers, and clergymen. Religious denominations' preachers are unlike the apostle Paul, who didn't fail to preach the whole council of God and wasn't concerned about the word of God offending others or losing membership. "Many will say to me in that day, Lord, Lord, have we not prophesied in thy name? And in thy name cast out devils? And in thy name done many wonderful works? And then will I profess unto them I never knew you: depart from me, ye that work iniquity" (Matthew 7:22–23). Any man, gay or straight, who is deliberately disobedient to God's will should have a ball on this time side of life. It will be his only time.

> If in this life only we have hope in Christ, we are all men most miserable. (1 Corinthians 15:19)

If after the manner of men I have fought with beasts at
Ephesus, what advantage it me, if the dead rise not? Let us
eat and drink; for tomorrow we die. (1 Corinthians 15:32)

Rest assured that there is a Judgment Day, and you will be there. The
question is, Who are you gonna call—ghost busters? The only ghost showing
up is the Holy Ghost, and you spent your time on this time side of life denying
Him (God) the Holy Spirit, the Father (God), and Jesus Christ (God) the Son.

The article said that on December 16, 1989, Mr. Williams became the
first practicing homosexual ordained into the priesthood of the Episcopal
Church since that denomination barred homosexuals from ordination in
1978 by resolution A-53. The Internet article said Mr. Williams is regarded
as one of the most outspoken advocates of the position that the homosexual
lifestyle is compatible with Christianity and acceptable unto God.

Ground Zero, the Garden of Eden

Now isn't that just what Satan told Eve? God had said eating of the tree wasn't
acceptable and would bring death. Satan said to Eve that she would surely
not die. Mr. Williams said being effeminate (homosexual) was acceptable to
God, and God said that the effeminate lifestyle was abominable unto Him. It
seems that when it comes to obeying God, man has never left ground zero. It
has become even more commonplace in this century for many to put words
in God's mouth. It was clear what God told Eve, and Satan comes along to
put words in God's mouth—something God didn't say. Satan tried to tempt
Jesus with his quoting the scriptures, and Jesus knew what the Father had said
was able to defeat Satan with "It is written." Until we search the scriptures,
we will allow Satan and his angels to put words in God's mouth—something
He never said.

God is the one who called homosexual acts, men having sex with men,
an abomination in His sight. Please tell me why we are debating and arguing
about the word of God. No one is trying to make you serve God. You are given
an opportunity to choose to serve God. "And if it seem evil unto you to serve
the Lord, choose you this day whom ye will serve; whether the gods which
your fathers served that were on the other side of the flood, or the gods of the
Amorites, in whose land ye dwell; but as for me and my house, we will serve
the Lord" (Joshua 24:15). Are we willing to make the Joshua call? It really is
our choice. The debate is over. If you want to do right and live with God—just

do it. If you want to serve sin and live eternally without God in hell, which is prepared for Satan and his angels, just do it. Honestly, debate is over.

God says individuals who commit such acts cannot enter heaven and that those who commit such acts are looking to be accepted into the kingdom of God. The Bible says, "Let God be true and every man a lie." C'mon, stay with me. Who are you going to believe? Who are you going to trust? God? Are you going to believe Satan and his servants (anyone who isn't of God) or Mr. Williams, who, like Satan, lies on God and says the opposite of what is written in scripture?

And Such Were Some of You

"And such were some of you. But you were washed, you were sanctified, you were justified in the name of the Lord Jesus Christ and by the Spirit of our God" (1 Corinthians 6:11).

Gay and lesbian activities have been around since biblical times, and these scriptures certainly support that fact. And so has sin, and there are scriptures to support that fact. Christ came to set the straight man and the gay man free from sin, and that is a biblical fact, too. But guess what? The invitation to come out (from the world and sin) hasn't changed. God is the same today, yesterday, and forever. Man is eternal, based on the fact that God breathed into his nostrils, and he became a living soul—a part of God. It's man and only man (not animals, birds, fish, or insects) that has this ability to choose. Man can choose his eternal home, heaven or hell. But rest assured that God won't put up with nonsense. "And the times of this ignorance God winked [overlooked] at; but now commands all men everywhere to repent: Because He has appointed a day in the which He will judge the world in righteousness by that Man whom He has ordained; whereof He has given assurance to all men, in that He has raised Him from the dead" (Acts 17:30–31). He hates sin so much that He had Jesus be a go-between (not the pope) while man worked out his soul salvation, aligning himself back to God through Jesus Christ. God doesn't want to talk to you. You talk to Jesus. When God said, "Come out," that call was for the straight and the gay. But what a detour the gays decided to take!

Satan is like a roaring lion, seeking whom he shall devour; he wants to take down mankind (1 Peter 5:8). A soul is very valuable. "And when Jesus had called the people to Him with His disciples also, He said to them, Whosoever will come after Me, let him deny himself, and take up his cross, and follow Me. For whosoever will save his life shall lose it; but whosoever shall lose his life for My sake and the gospel's the same shall save it. For what shall it profit a man, if he shall gain the whole world, and lose his own soul? Or what shall a man give in exchange for his soul?" (Mark 8:34–37).

Let's stop here. What if homosexuality takes over the whole earth? Have we forgotten who built this place? It was certainly not the gays and lesbians. How long do you think God will put up with it? Do you think He has no more Sodom and Gomorrah fire left in His back pocket? What if He is just letting you who are nongay, tolerant, and accepting see who you are and what you would do? In other words, He is measuring your faithfulness. "I am come to send fire on the earth; and what will I, if it be already kindled?" (Luke 12:49). I say, What if wildfires, volcanoes eruptions, and nuclear bombs have the earth already kindled when the time comes? Will God not answer the prayers of the faithful, His own elect, which pray to Him day and night, though He bears long with them? God will answer the righteous prayers. Nevertheless, when the Son of Man comes, shall He find faith on the earth? See Luke 18:8.

How valuable is a soul? God wants yours; after all, He created it. Satan wants yours because he wants to hurt God; he desires to get back at Him for kicking him out of heaven. Satan does a fantastic job at transforming into an angel of light (2 Corinthians 11:14.) It's no great thing that denominational ministers (those who fail to preach the whole counsel of God) also present themselves as ministers of righteousness, whose end shall be according to their works (2 Corinthians 11:15). There is no way of getting around it; all will have to obey God, from the pulpit to the pews. We have God's word thanks to Jesus's apostles, men who wrote the inspired word of God through the guidance of the Holy Ghost. We can say to Satan, like our spiritual Brother, Jesus, "It is written ... Get thee hence ... Get behind me Satan." Satan is so good at what he does that he has led man to believe that man is one of the major players.

> Thou believest that there is one God; thou doest well; the devil also believe, and tremble. (James 2:19)
>
> To open their eyes, and to turn them from darkness to light, and from the power of Satan to God, that they may receive forgiveness of sins, and inheritance among them which are sanctified by faith that is in Me. (Acts 26:18)

War in Heaven

> Therefore rejoice you heavens, and you that dwell in them. Woe to the inhabiters of the earth and of the sea! For the devil is come down to you, having great wrath, because he knows that he has but a short time. (Revelation 12:12)
>
> And the devil that deceived them was cast into the lake of fire and brimstone, where the beast and the false prophet are and shall be tormented day and night forever and ever. (Revelation 20:10)
>
> For the weapons of our warfare are not carnal, but mighty through God to the pulling down of strong holds; Casting down imaginations, and every high thing that exalts itself against the knowledge of God, bringing into captivity every thought to the obedience of Christ. (2 Corinthians 10:4–5)
>
> For we wrestle not against flesh and blood, but against principalities, against powers, against the rulers of the darkness of this world, against spiritual wickedness in high places. (Ephesians 6:12)

How should you approach this battle between the powers and influences over your life, which will determine where you spend eternity? You should come suited with the proper amour. There is the attitude that God can't tell me what to do and Satan can't tell me what to do; it's my life. That's what Satan wants your rationalization to be, like you've really got some power here. Man, you better be suited up! You need to be prepared to withstand the tricks of Satan. You must have your loins girt about with truth. You must put on the breastplate of righteousness, have your feet shod with the preparation of the gospel of peace, and above all, take the shield of faith so that you shall quench all the fiery darts of the wicked with the helmet of salvation and the sword of the Spirit, which is the word of God (Ephesians 6:13–17).

> For though we walk in the flesh, we do not war after the flesh. (2 Corinthians 10:3–5)
>
> Put on the whole armour of God, that ye may be able to stand against the wiles of the devil. (Ephesians 6:11)

We aren't the major players. The players are good and evil: God and Satan. The only power we have is the ability to choose the side of the board we want to be on—that's it. Satan has convinced people (mankind) that they really don't have to do anything—just bench it out or sit it out—if they like to. Man doesn't have to do anything, we are told. He is okay one way or the other. When he dies, there is no hell or heaven. He is just dead. How crafty! Indecision is a decision, and unfortunately, you lose, because faith involves work. Game over. Satan has won your soul. To be on Christ's side of the board, one has to do something—obey. There are others Satan has persuaded to his side of the board, individuals who have little or no knowledge of the instructions and rules of the game—God's will for man and His plan of salvation. Those are the will worshippers who have gone about to establish their own righteousness but not according to knowledge and the righteousness of God. Satan is a wise opponent and very crafty. When making your choice, choose wisely. Seek out your soul's salvation with trembling and fear; take this matter seriously.

Mr. Williams said there are a vast majority of lesbians and gays who are deeply spiritual and are searching for a place where they can *practice* their deep-seated religious longings. But denominations have turned their backs on them. The apostle Paul told a group of people that they ignorantly worshipped God, but he wanted to make God known to them (Acts 17: 23). God isn't hiding from you. You don't need to search for a place to worship. You *do* need to search the scriptures, and there you'll find the acceptable worship of God with obedient and faithful Christians. You will find some who were once as you but have obeyed the gospel of our Lord Jesus Christ.

📖 Book Corner Excerpt

(Transcript of *Radio Debate between Robert Williams and Jeff Asher— January 20, 1990) Adobe Acrobat Version prepared by David Padfield (http:// www.padfield.com)*

Jeff Asher–Robert Williams Debate on Homosexuality (debate excerpted from *Out of the Closet* [Faith And Facts Press, 1997]).[104] The use of copyrighted material appears by permission of the author.

---

[104] Jeff Asher, "The Williams-Asher Debate on Homosexuality," *Out of the Closet* (Indianapolis, IN: Faith And Facts Press, 1997).

The Williams—Asher Debate On Homosexuality

[On December 16, 1989, Robert Williams was ordained by John Shelby Spong, Bishop of the Dioceses of Newark, New Jersey, into the priesthood of the Episcopal Church. This action immediately ignited heated controversy across the country. Feeling there would be general interest in a discussion of homosexuality from a biblical perspective. I sought and arranged this with Mr. Williams. The discussion took place January 20, 1990, via telephone on <u>BibleTalk</u> *the weekly call-in-program of the Dumas Drive Church of Christ in Amarillo, Texas. What follows is a transcript of the program taken from tape.]*

Jeff Asher: A very pleasant good morning and welcome to "BibleTalk." I am Jeff Asher, your host this morning and the evangelist for the Dumas Drive Church of Christ. Today we have a very special guest with us. For the last twenty years there has been in the United States an emergence of homosexuality as a prevalent behavior pattern. In certain quarters homosexuality is not only tolerated but approved. This change in attitude has occurred because some of our most prominent citizens: actors, politicians, athletes, and even clergymen, have openly declared their homosexual lifestyle and publicly defended it.

Many homosexuals are militantly atheistic as is proven by the existence of the Gay Atheist Association. Yet a large group of homosexuals profess to be Christians. Since 1968 the Universal Fellowship of Metropolitan Community Churches has ministered almost exclusively in the homosexual community, advocating the compatibility of the homosexual lifestyle with Christianity. Since 1968 the question of whether or not homosexuality is a compatible and acceptable behavior has gradually moved to the top of the list of major religious issues to be debated in the coming decade. The mainline denominations are all troubled not only by homosexual memberships but by the ordination of practicing homosexuals into the various ministries. This fact is demonstrated by the ordination today in San Francisco of three gay Lutheran Clergymen.

On December 16, 1989, Robert Williams became the first practicing homosexual ordained into the priesthood of the Episcopal Church since that denomination barred homosexuals from ordination in 1979 by resolution A-53. He is regarded as one of the most outspoken advocates of the position that a homosexual lifestyle is compatible with Christianity and acceptable unto God. Mr. Williams is currently involved in a homosexual relationship with James Skelly, a divorced father of two teen-aged daughters.

Robert Williams is our guest today on BibleTalk. He and I will discuss this issue from its Biblical perspectives, examining, hopefully, all of the pertinent Bible passages and arguments made to support the position that Mr. Williams and numerous other homosexuals and non-homosexuals make regarding this practice. Mr. Williams understands that I am not sympathetic to his position and will be making observations and arguments intended to convince him and others of the falsity of their position. In order that we can focus on the issue and get the homosexual position clearly and accurately stated we are going to give Mr. Williams an opportunity to make some opening remarks. Mr. Williams, good morning and welcome to "Bible Talk."

Robert Williams: Good morning, thank you, nice to be on your show. Let me start by responding to a couple of things you said in your introduction. Just sort of correcting them from my viewpoint.

The major one is, you described an emergence of homosexuality in the last 20 years. I don't believe that's true. I believe that the gay and lesbian people have been a part of the culture of every society and every time, including the Biblical society, and the only thing that's different in the past twenty years is that we have been in the position politically to be more open and more visible. I don't believe that there are any more or less lesbian and gay people today than there were 100 years ago or 2,000 years ago. I think that we have always been approximately the same percentage of the general population, which is somewhere between 10 and 20 percent.

Secondly, just to correct the perception about a large number of gay people being militantly atheistic. In fact, the Gay Atheist League of America is a very small group, a very small minority, and my experience has been that the majority of lesbian and gay people, although they may have turned their backs on the established church because it has not been friendly to them, the vast majority of lesbian and gay people are deeply spiritual people who are searching for a place in which they can practice their deep seated religious longings. And, in fact, those who have chosen to go in a militantly atheistic way are a tiny minority of the lesbian and gay community.

And this, just about my own ordination, the press has somewhat misunderstood the significance of the ordination, I think. I'm certainly not the first openly gay Episcopal priest. There are in fact other Episcopal priests who have even written books about being gay priests. So, there are a large number of openly gay Episcopal priests. What was different and significant about my ordination was, first of all, that my being gay was a fact, a published fact, before the ordination occurred. In other words, I didn't come out publicly after I was ordained, but rather before it happened. Thus, my ordination itself was a more public and political event than any of the ordinations of gay people that have happened since 1979. But there have been dozens of gay and lesbian priests ordained in the Episcopal church since that 1979 resolution. I'm only one among many.

Another thing that is perhaps different is the ministry to which I feel called is a ministry specifically to and among the lesbian and gay community, and that sort of put it in a different category and got some attention. But there are plenty of lesbian and gay priests who are just working in regular parish ministries and in every diocese in the country.

Do you want to go ahead into the approach to the Bible or do you have a question?

A: Well, Robert, if you'd like to go on and give us your Biblical perspective, then that will give me an opportunity to ask some questions and to direct our course this morning. I'd appreciate it.

W: OK, the first thing I want to say is that I grew up in West Texas, Abilene, Texas, and I'm quite familiar with the Church of Christ. Abilene, Texas, as you probably know, is where there is a very large Church of Christ university, Abilene Christian. So I'm pretty familiar with your church, and the first thing I want to say about dealing with the Bible and this sort of program is that it is almost impossible for us to do anything along the lines of a debate, because, as you know, one of the first principles of debate is that you have to be arguing from the same premise, and I don't think we are. My approach to Scripture, as an Episcopalian, is fundamentally different from the approach to Scripture that the Church of Christ takes. So, from the beginning we are sort of starting out on completely different footing. I just don't deal with the Bible in the same way that members of the Church of Christ would deal with the Bible.

Episcopalians, Anglicans, since the beginning of the Anglican Church at the time of the Reformation have always held up what we call the three legged stool. There are three factors that have to be taken under consideration in making any kind of decision in the church. All three of these are equally important. And those are Scripture, tradition, and reason. It's like a stool with three legs, and when you remove any one of those three legs it will fall. So Scripture is part of the equation, but it is only one third of the equation, and reason is equally a third of the equation. Reason includes listening to the data from the sciences, both the natural sciences and the social sciences. And in the Anglican tradition that is as important as the Scripture itself. And in fact the two inform each other and have to be held in tension.

So, if in fact a biologist or a psychologist tells us that homosexuality is in fact a natural phenomenon that occurs among approximately 20% of the population, then as Episcopalians we have to take that very seriously. And say, "OK, here's some factual data, what do we do with it." We factor it in as one third of that equation and we weigh it over against the Bible.

What we most certainly are not is Biblical fundamentalists. We approach the Bible reverently and carefully. But carefully includes approaching it with a very careful scholarship and putting it through the rigorous process of Biblical exegesis, which includes putting it in its historical and cultural context, doing linguistic studies, doing textual studies. We just don't take as given that, just because something is in the Bible, it necessarily has anything to do with our lives today.

In fact there are some Biblical scholars, some of them Episcopalian, some of them not, but Biblical scholars whose work I follow very closely, particularly among feminist scholars who are dealing with the whole question of canon. How do we in fact decide which books or which parts of books ought to be in the Bible? Just because a decision was made several centuries ago by the Catholic Church doesn't mean that they made the right decision. As you know, Martin Luther thought that the book of James should not be included in the canon of Scripture. There are scholars today who are questioning in a similar way, "Should this book even have been included, or should this passage be included?" How do we decide, what is our criterion for deciding, what in fact is the Scripture, the canon of Scripture, that the Christian Church should be using? And coming down on the side of saying if it brings life to people, if it brings people into an encounter with the living Christ, then its Scripture. If it brings death to people, it is used in a way to label people, to harm people, if it's used as a club with which to beat people over the head, which most of the passages about homosexuality are, then we can't in good conscience call it the word of God. We can't read it in a worship service and afterward say, "This is the word of the Lord." If it's a harmful and negative passage, it's not the word of the Lord of love.

A: Robert, let's stop right there. This is a good place for me to begin to respond in some way. First of all, I think that our audience needs to be made aware of the fact that Robert and I are certainly not adversaries in the sense that we are enemies of one another. I have a great deal of respect for him as a person, and, though I sincerely believe he is wrong, I would hope that today I could convince him of that.

Now, your opening statements, or your reply to the introductory material clarified some points, and really I have no desire to delve into that any further other than to suggest that we do recognize that they are substantially correct and that we are agreed that we have a climate in which homosexuality has become, if not more prevalent in the sense of numbers, at least more prevalent in the sense of being exposed or being held in regard by some in my lifetime. I know I'm not very old. I'm not much younger than you and the fact remains that I can remember the time when a subject like this wouldn't even be discussed in a pulpit, let alone on a religious radio program. So some prevalence does exist now, that hasn't existed in the past.

The fact that you make the statement that we are not arguing from the same Biblical perspective I believe is a good place to start. We are not coming from the same perspective because, as Robert indicated, we do not have the same attitude toward the Scriptures. He does not regard the word of God as the plenary, verbally inspired revelation of the mind of God. Therefore he says he is not fundamentalist. So we have a vast difference of perspectives with regard to that. But the fact of the matter is the Bible is inspired, and the Bible is the word of God. And, we would challenge, that if there are errors, if there are mistakes, that this be proven. To just simply disparage the Bible is not proof. A great many people have used it as a standard of morality and a code of faith for centuries. And the contention we make is that the Bible is the inspired word of God.

Now with regard to the three legged stool. We are not opposed to reason. Certainly reason is a means by which we are to come to the Scriptures, or to interpret the Bible. You cannot handle the Bible contrary to reason. You cannot array Scripture against Scripture. You cannot make the Bible say one thing one time and make it say something else at another time. So reason is certainly a part of any hermeneutic that we bring to the Scriptures. But to suggest that tradition (which has no authority higher than man) is to be a part of this equation is faulty. We are talking about a divine book, and to suggest that these traditions are on equal standing with the Scripture certainly does not harmonize with what the Bible would reveal.

Now, to the point with regard to "reason" that Robert made. He uses a different concept of "reason" than I do. When I talk about "reason" I mean taking the passages, studying them, drawing the proper conclusions, harmonizing, taking all the facts together. Some of these things he mentioned. But simply because some psychologist or psychiatrist tells us that there are significant numbers of people in the population that are homosexual does not negate what the Bible says about homosexuality.

There are a significant number of people in the population who are alcoholics. That does not negate what the Bible says about drunkenness. There are a significant number of people in our society who are given to incest, pederasty, and other things that are immoral. But that doesn't negate what the Bible says of those sins.

This idea that a passage of Scripture is to be rejected if it brings harm to people, or if it is a negative passage, or if it is a passage of Scripture which is used as a club to label someone, therefore, it ought to be rejected could be used by any group that had some moral perversion that they wish to substantiate. The alcoholic would say, "Well, the Bible condemns drunkenness, therefore all the passages in the Bible that relate to drunkenness are not Scripture." The same thing could be said of the person who is involved in incest. "The Bible condemns incest therefore, all the passages that talk about incest, that's negative to me. Lest someone label me as one guilty of incest, let's take those out of the Bible."

Now we do not approve of nor are we guilty of using Scripture to label people in the sense that we want to pigeonhole them and make them into a minority and segregate them. If the Bible calls something a sin, then that is what it is. If it is lying, do we label people because the Bible condemns lying? A man is a liar, is that a label? Is that negative? Should we just disregard that passage of Scripture because someone is called a liar? Or, as far as the

Bible is concerned, someone is called a thief. A thief might think that's rather negative terminology. How could I get up and preach from Ephesians chapter four that a man is to work, to give of his means, and to stop stealing without calling a man a thief in the process? We believe that we ought to preach the truth in love. So we have no animosity toward people who are guilty of sin. Homosexual sin is not any different than heterosexual sin or any other kind of sin. They are all sin before God. And if the Bible condemns it, then it is a practice which needs to be repented of. And it is a practice that a man must quit in order to be saved in eternity.

Robert, at this point I am interested, in that you have suggested this idea of "negative passages," in considering some of these, and you give me either an explanation or just tell me whether or not they belong in the Bible. Would you be willing to do that?

W: Certainly.

A: Alright, let's just begin in the beginning, and that is in the book of Genesis. The case of Sodom, which is Genesis chapter nineteen and verse four, where Moses tells us that the men of Sodom, from the understanding that I have, came out to commit the sin of homosexuality against these men who had come there, who we know by the Scriptures to have been angels. This is the basis of the term "sodomy," which appears in some passages of Scripture in the Bible and has come into the English language in our law statutes. But there in the nineteenth chapter and verse four, it says: "The men of the city, before they laid down, the men of the city, even the men of Sodom encompassed the house around both old and young, all the people of every quarter, and they called unto Lot and said unto him, 'Where are the men which came into thee this night? Bring them out unto us that we may know them.' And Lot went out at the door unto them and shut the door after them and said, 'I pray thee brethren do not so wickedly, behold now I have two daughters which have not known man. Let me now I pray you bring them out unto you and do ye to them what is good in your eyes. Only unto these men do nothing, for therefore came they under the shadow of My roof.'"

We know here they then threatened Lot, and the angels smote the men of the city blind and then pronounced that they were going to destroy the city of Sodom. How do you deal with that passage?

W: Well, my first question is, why do you see this as a passage that has anything to do with homosexuality? Will you read to me the part that indicates, to you, that it has anything to do with homosexuality?

A: I would suggest that verse five is the verse that does that. "And they called unto Lot and they said unto him, where are the men which came unto thee this night? bring them out unto us that we may know them."

W: And so you are taking that word "know" as being something about sex?

A: Yes.

W: Well, in fact the use of that word in the Scripture in most places has absolutely no sexual context. It means simply "know." One possible interpretation is that the men of Sodom had an almost Ku Klux Klan type distrust of foreigners, and here are foreigners in their midst who are being housed and protected by Lot. And they come to him to say we do not want these people here at least until we know who they are. Send them out to us. Also, the indication of whether it includes a sexual component or not is not there. Clearly the intention of the men is violent, to do violence to these men, to those angels whom they think are men.

I have no problem in saying that the Scriptures certainly condemn violence against anyone, whether or not a sexual component is included as part of that violence. And in fact that would be the sin of Sodom. It is the sin of "sodomy" to do violence against people who were strangers in their midst. And elsewhere in Scripture, including in the New Testament, when Jesus refers back to Sodom, or in other places in the Old Testament when Sodom is referred to, this is the sin of Sodom.

Not one of those instances mentions anything sexual about Sodom. It says the sin of Sodom is the sin of essentially what we might call "inhospitality," the sin of not responding kindly to the stranger in the midst, which in the desert society is a matter of life and death. If you did not put up strangers, they could die in the desert over night, so part of the code of the Hebrew people was to take care of the stranger and sojourner.

Rather than taking care of them, the men of Sodom were wanting to do violence to them. Well, certainly that is condemned, but it is only since about the eighteenth century that Christians have read anything sexual into the Sodom story. Up until that point they saw it simply as being about doing violence to strangers.

A: Let me reply to this in some way. I would encourage all of our listeners to get their Bibles and turn to Genesis nineteen, and I will show you the truth of this passage by what we can show from the context. In verse five they do demand, "Bring them out that we may know them."

Now, Mr. Williams is correct in suggesting that in the majority of the passages the word "Yadah" does simply indicate "become acquainted with." But there are 12 passages in the Old Testament that have this sexual connotation. Four of those uses are associated with this sin of homosexuality. In Genesis 19 you have the word "know" and its derivative "known" used twice. Likewise the book of Judges chapter 19 where you have the men of Gibeah. You have the same thing again. Now, in verse five they ask the question or make the demand, "Bring them out that we may know them." Lot went out at the door unto them and shut the door after them. We would first observe that if it just simply means bring them out that we may get acquainted with them, Lot in refusing to bring them out, is the one who is guilty of inhospitality. That doesn't make any sense.

Secondly, we would point out that in verse seven he says, "I pray ye brethren, do not so wickedly." If all they wanted to do was to get acquainted with these men in order to overcome their distrust of foreigners, why would Lot suggest that what they wanted to do was wicked? Then in verse eight, the statement is made, "Behold now I have two daughters which have not known man. Let me I pray bring them out unto you." This is the use that would govern our understanding that this has a sexual connotation. And he uses the same word to refer to his daughters, don't know these men, don't have sexual relations with these men, but rather, and Lot had really slipped here, and I'm not justifying what Lot did, but he simply uses the word to suggest that he offers these men an opportunity to have sexual relations with his daughters instead. So it is obvious that the context is talking about sexual relations. Furthermore, you made the statement that there were no sexual overtones in the sin of Sodom. But Jude seven says, "Even as Sodom and Gomorrah and the cities about them in like manner, giving themselves over to fornication and going after strange flesh are set forth for an example, suffering the vengeance of eternal fire."

Alright, here Jude says the sin that Sodom was guilty of was fornication, sexual immorality. They went after strange flesh. We can develop this more, I hope, in the course of the discussion. But, "strange flesh" will include the sin of homosexuality. The only flesh that God authorized that any man know was the flesh of his wife and that from Genesis two, where Adam said, "Now this is bone of my bone, and flesh of my flesh." So "strange flesh" would be flesh other than my flesh, and the only flesh that is my flesh or a man's flesh is the flesh of his wife. And so here we have a definite New Testament passage that condemns the sin of Sodom as having a sexual nature.

Now when we go back to the context of Genesis 19 we see that it is obviously a homosexual act.

W: The notion of "strange" flesh in the Jude passage, I think, is really stretching it to say that it refers to homosexuality. In fact, I think, for the writer of Jude, it refers to the notion of human beings having sex with angels, which is what, if there is a sexual connotation in the Genesis passage, seems to be indicated. The idea of the whole term, "strange flesh," there is a reference to the fact that the adults, human beings with angelic beings, and that to have any sort of sexual activities there is off limits. Again there is no reason to assume that the passage refers to homosexuality. It is only to take a prejudice that the interpreter already has in her or his mind and read it back into a passage that, in fact, doesn't deal with that at all.

A: But, we made it very clear that in Genesis 19:5 the question is asked, "Where are the men which came in to thee this night?" They had no knowledge that these were angels. They came seeking men. The same thing is true in Judges nineteen. The same word "know" is used in Judges 19 with regard to the sin of Gibeah. And there are no angels involved. What they desired was to have sexual relations with a man.

To strengthen the point on "strange flesh," I call everyone's attention to Genesis chapter two, because in Genesis two Adam clearly says, in verse 23: "This is now bone of my bones, and flesh of my flesh. She shall be called woman because she was taken out of man. Therefore, shall a man leave his father and his mother and shall cleave unto his wife and they shall be one flesh."

The Bible clearly teaches from the beginning that this was a one flesh union, and that this was the only flesh that man has a right to, whether it is heterosexual fornication or homosexual fornication doesn't make any difference. We are not going to elevate homosexual fornication above heterosexual fornication and say all you heterosexual fornicators can go home, God approves of that. The Bible does not teach that. It is one man and one woman for one lifetime and that in the union of marriage.

W: When did Adam and Eve marry?

A: Right there in Genesis two, that is when they married, when God brought them together.

W: I just wondered. There is nothing in the entire book of Genesis that indicates that there is a marriage there.

A: Well, Robert, I'm not going to ask you to define marriage, because we know that your relationship hasn't been sanctioned by the Episcopal Church as yet, even though there seems to be plans for that. But Ephesians chapter five, when talking about the relationship between a husband and his wife being parallel to that of Christ and the church, obviously indicates the marriage relationship.

W: I understand that.

A: And this very passage, Genesis two, is quoted in connection with that. This idea of the one flesh union has always, and your own church recognized that, that the one flesh union described in Genesis two is the marriage relationship. I'm not talking about a certificate given by a judge or a justice of the peace. I'm talking about a God ordained, God recognized marriage.

W: Well, in fact, that is what a lot of unmarried heterosexual couples would say they have, because they have not had a ceremony or certificate but they consider themselves to be married. I was just reacting to your speaking of Adam and Eve and their being married.

A: Well, it is definitely a marriage. There is no disputing that point. Jesus in the nineteenth chapter of the book of Matthew quotes the very words of Moses there and applies that to the marriage relationship. Let's be turning there to read that. "The Pharisee's also came unto him tempting him and saying unto him. Is it lawful for a man to put away his wife for every cause?" That's the context of marriage.

"And he answered and said unto them, have you not read that he which made them at the beginning made them male and female and said for this cause shall a man leave father and mother and shall cleave to his wife and they twain shall be one flesh, what therefore God hath joined together let not man put asunder." There is no denying that. And from the beginning we have the God ordained pattern: one man, one woman, for one lifetime, and this being the only flesh union that God recognizes.

W: Who performed their marriage do you think?

A: Well, you have a sacramental concept. There is nothing in the Bible that teaches a preacher has to unite two people. I'm satisfied with the fact that God brought her to him and gave her to him.

W: In the case of my marriage I'm satisfied with the fact that God brought us together. It's being sanctioned by a particular body (church) is beside the point. We are kind of off the subject, but I think it's sort of fascinating because I would say that this Genesis passage gives precedent for that.

A: The point of the Genesis passage, and you haven't addressed this point, the only flesh union sanctioned in the Bible is the union between a man and a woman. You made the statement earlier that the passages in the New Testament where Jesus spoke with regard to Sodom and Gomorrah didn't say anything about their being guilty of homosexuality. In each of those passages though, he used Sodom and Gomorrah as an example of a nation that was guilty of sin and was condemned of God. Those were the applications that he made. Let's look at what Jesus said.

W: I said that I accept that, but the sin was about violence against strangers. It was not, as you were saying a few minutes ago, the intention was not wasn't simply wanting to get to know these strangers. The intention was to essentially lynch these strangers, which, in fact, may have included a sexual element. They may have intended to rape them also. But obviously we could say that the burden of Scripture condemns rape, heterosexual or homosexual. And obviously the burden of Scripture condemns violence against anyone. In that point we are in agreement. We're saying Sodom is condemned throughout the entire canon of Scripture, Old and New Testament. I'm just saying it's not about homosexuality, its about violence.

A: Well, you can't have it both ways, Robert. It can't mean get acquainted with, then have a sexual overtone. So you've got to admit that the Genesis passage has the sexual overtone.

W: I don't have to admit that. I'm saying I'm not even talking about sex. I'm talking about violence. That obviously these men of Sodom intended to do harm to the strangers who were Lot's house guests.

A: Well does it condemn fornication then? Does the passage condemn fornication?

W: I don't think the passage has any connection to fornication.

A: Alright, so you're just going to say there are no sexual overtones at all in the passage. It may or may not be talking about rape.

W: I'm saying that's one possible interpretation of it. The bottom line, back to my introductory remark, is I just don't really care as much as you do about what this passage says.

A: Alright, let's go back to what Jesus did say then. That seems to be something that you do care about.

W: Let me make one more comment about the Genesis passage because you had asked about the types of things I would say do not belong in the canon of Scripture. I'm not sure I would say that about the Sodom story in general, but the part, the unspeakable act of domestic violence that is implied by Lot's wanting to throw out his two virgin daughters to a mob of men, that's clearly not a passage that I can read in a church service and say this is the word of the Lord. That's a passage that's wrong. Just plain wrong. It is evil and twisted and contributes to the treating of women as property. It contributes to the high incidence of domestic violence in our society, which is almost always done to women by adult male relatives. This sort of passage, holding this up as the word of God, helps create that situation. So that's an example of a passage I would say by that test does not belong in the canon of Scripture.

A: Alright, let me make this final note and then we'll go back to Matthew nineteen. Certainly every one in the audience can see that there is nothing in Genesis nineteen that would suggest that God approved of what Sodom did or what Lot did. The fact that it is in the word of God and is an example of gross immorality is by implication a disapproval of what Lot did. To suggest that it needs to be removed because it speaks of something that is unspeakable is ridiculous. It is simply a passage of Scripture that shows that that is not how anyone should treat a woman. And that passage is no basis at all for condoning that kind of behavior.

W: There is no indication in the passage that Lot's suggestion is condemned by God or by anyone. It was sort of a matter of course. And there is no reaction to it at all.

A: It is an historical narrative Robert, and it just simply states what happened. So you can't take the passage and say that it approves of anything. Now, I want to get back to Matthew nineteen, because you had made the statement earlier that Jesus did not condemn the sin of Sodom and Gomorrah as being homosexuality. Then we made some remarks about marriage. Does Matthew nineteen not clearly teach what God authorizes with regard to sexual relationships between a man and anyone? Jesus said in Matthew nineteen, going all the way back to the beginning, "For this cause shall a man leave father and mother and cleave to his wife and they twain shall be one flesh." Now, that is going to exclude incest, polyandry, polygamy, and bestiality. And that's going to exclude homosexuality. Jesus said a man shall cleave unto his wife. On what basis do you find any scriptural approval of a man/man sexual relationship, in light of that passage?

W: Well, would you like me to suggest a passage in which I think I do see that?

A: Yes, if you would.

W: Luke chapter seven, beginning around verse two. This is the story of Jesus' healing the centurion's "pais." In this particular place the word "pais," which is transliterated from the Greek "pais," is translated in English as "slave".

Elsewhere, when the same story is told in other gospels, it is obviously the same story but the word "slave" is not used. It is rather the word "boy." So there seems to be some confusion about what the identity of this young man is. Is he a servant in the centurion's household, or is he a son of the centurion? I would suggest that the confusion is because he is in fact neither, but is romantically linked, he is the lover we might say, of the centurion. Which in fact would not be at all uncommon in the Roman culture, in particular in the Roman army, for a somewhat older man, particularly in the army, to take a somewhat younger man as a lover. This was a fairly common thing. The word "pais" by the way, is almost never translated "slave," either in Scripture or contemporary writings of the same time. It almost always means "boy," the same word that a parent might call their son. It's always a word of affection and endearment. It never just means "servant." So, if in fact this was a servant in this centurion's household, he was a servant with a highly unusual relationship, a relationship of affection to the centurion. At any rate, he's fallen ill, and the centurion had heard of Jesus. This man has had a relationship with the Jews in the area, and in fact he was probably sort of over them as magistrate. So he sent some of the elders whom he knew to send word to Jesus and say, "Please come and heal my 'pais.'" And they came to him and said, "This man deserves this, because he is a good man and has done good things for us." And Jesus goes with them, and He's on his way to the house. The centurion seems to be troubled, which is instructive here. He runs out and says: "Lord you don't have to come under my roof. I'm not worthy of you, to have you under my roof, and I know that it is not even necessary. You can just say the word and the 'pais' will be healed."

Now, if in fact this man is a Roman soldier living in a homosexual relationship, and yet, he is very informed about the religion of the Jews, then he would have suspected that Jesus might have condemned this relationship. So he seems to be a little troubled here and says, "You don't have to come into the house." It is kind of odd that he would say that, so at any point, Jesus turns to the crowd, to his disciples, who are Jews behind him, and says, "Not even in Israel have I found such great faith; you know, this man's faith is better than yours." Then, in fact, the boy is healed.

Now, it seems to me that Jesus is encountering here a homosexual relationship, a relationship between an army officer and his male lover. There is some indication in the passage that the man is a little nervous about how Jesus would react. So, he does not want Him to come into his house. Yet, what he gets from Jesus is no condemnation, but in fact praise, by His saying, "You know this man has more faith than you, my followers," to whom he is speaking. So I see this as a passage in which Jesus encounters a committed homosexual relationship, not batting an eye and not offering any condemnation.

A: I think you have made your point on that. Now let me reply. First of all, while you were talking I did a little checking here in my concordances and lexicons. The word "slave" in this passage is not translated anywhere else in the Scripture by the word "boy." Now that's just not so. It's not in the New Testament.

W: I'm not talking about just Scripture. I'm talking about in contemporary writing.

A: You made the statement in the beginning that we take things in their context; we look at the words, we do the hermeneutical and linguistic studies.

Lexicography by itself does not prove anything. I can go to the lexicons and find many different meanings for different words and then come back and impose that on something. I'm telling you, and I'm sticking with it, that the word that you've cited in Luke 7:2 is not translated anywhere in the Scripture by the word "boy." Now there is nothing, then, to suggest by that lexical argument that has any merit here in this context.

Secondly, the point of this passage is that this centurion is used as an example of faith. He is held up in contrast to the faith of the Israelites or the Jews. His faith is great because he believes Christ can do what he came and asked Him to do. There is not a thing in the context anywhere other than the one word, "servant," which you picked out, and have assigned a meaning of "boy," based upon Roman behavior. You don't know if this man was a homosexual. You don't know if this man had a slave or servant that he used in a homosexual fashion and engaged in that kind of practice. You have nothing at all from the context to argue that. And so that is completely unfounded. The point of the whole illustration is that it is a comparison of the faith of Israel with that of the centurion, and Jesus calls it great faith. Now that's all there is to that. Your argument on "pais" is incorrect and is not in the Scripture.

W: When you use the word "context," you are meaning a very different thing than when I use the word "context." When you use the word "context," you seem to be limiting it to the printed word on the pages themselves, and that is your concept. When I say the word "context," I'm talking about the entire setting. I mean let's look at the story, when it happened, look at what we know about the Roman culture, from history, from anthropology.

A: Fine Robert, but you began your remarks by saying you didn't think there were any more homosexuals now than there were then as a part of society. Then I'll give you the big number, 20%. Are you going to take here an example where 8 out of 10 centurions that might have come to Jesus were not homosexuals and then argue that he was? You have nothing from the passage.

W: But what I am saying is that what we know about the Roman military is that, in fact, the percentages would have been probably higher there, because homosexuality was not only not condemned but encouraged in the Roman army.

A: Let me read something to you here. This comes from the book Counseling Homosexuals, by Bill Flatt, Dowell Flatt, and Jack Lewis, and Bill Flatt is quoting Plutarch. And, he says, Plutarch in the "Dialogue On Love" illustrates, and he quotes: "There is only one genuine love, the love of boys. You will see it in the schools of philosophy or perhaps in the gymnasiums and the palaestrae. Making love to a slave boy, however, is not gentlemanly or urbane, such is mere copulation, like the love of women." To many Greeks, Flatt says, the ideal sexual experience for a man was to love a lad in the flower of his youth. Here you have said he was a servant or slave, and this is a quotation of Plutarch, which says that wasn't even regarded among the Romans as being gentlemanly.

W: Well, it wasn't regarded by Plutarch.

A: Well, you're trying to make an argument on Roman culture and I'm showing you that Roman culture ...

W: Yeah, but you're talking about one particular Roman writer.

A: Well, I'm talking about one particular Roman writer that extols what you would call the homosexual condition. I'm talking about one particular Roman writer who would say that the love of boys was a good thing, and yet, the very thing that you use as your proof in the New Testament is the very thing that he condemns. You are inconsistent.

W: No, I'm not inconsistent. I'm just saying I can point to other Roman writers, particularly Aristotle, who go into long passages of tracing such relationships. I also think it's interesting that you're quoting Plutarch from a secondary source, instead of reading Plutarch. You're reading what somebody says Plutarch said, taking his word for it, which is very shoddy scholarship.

A: Well, I think that I can have pretty good confidence in Jack Lewis, Dowell Flatt, and Bill Flatt, who are recognized scholars. Jack Lewis is recognized as one of the leading Hebrew scholars in the United States.

W: I don't know who any of those people are.

A: You said you were from Abilene, and you're supposed to be familiar with my brethren. You ought to know these things if you make that kind of statement. Jack Lewis is a leading Hebrew scholar in the United States, he served on the translating committee for the New International Version.

W: I'm not questioning the …

A: You questioned the source. I'm giving you the facts, and we're not going to let you impugn the integrity of the source.

W: No, I'm questioning the method. If you are going to quote Plutarch, you read from Plutarch; you don't read from a contemporary writer who quotes from Plutarch.

A: The best you can do is Luke chapter seven, and you have made a statement yourself ambiguously referring to Greek and Roman sources which you haven't produced. If we're going to talk about "shoddy scholarship," you haven't produced any of those, and you haven't made your case on the word. This is the only argument you have made from Scripture, Luke 7 verse 2, where you have one word which is never, I've already shown, never translated "boy," as you suggested, in the standard versions. And you have made your whole argument based on an assumption about a Roman centurion for which there is nothing in the Scriptures whatsoever to make any contention. Now, is there another passage of Scripture that you would like to suggest here?

W: So, what you are charging that I am doing with the Luke passage is what I am charging you are doing with the Genesis passage. And in both cases we are taking our own experience and finding the Scripture to support that experience. And I would be willing to grant that is what I am doing, and that is what you are doing with the Genesis passage. You are taking a passage that has nothing do with homosexuality and finding it. And your charging that I am taking a passage that has nothing to do with …

A: We have just a few minutes left Robert, and we have got to get back to Matthew nineteen, because you have not dealt with that passage, which is how we came to this any way. And I want you to explain how you are going to harmonize the statement of Jesus that a man shall leave father and mother and cleave only unto his wife. How are you going to harmonize that statement with your practice of homosexuality?

W: First of all, I would say that according to the traditional interpretation that Jesus himself did not obey that. You know there is no evidence that Jesus married.

A: Well, Jesus did not say all men had to marry. That is not the point of Matthew nineteen. There are only two options in Matthew nineteen, either marriage or celibacy. Now that is what you have.

W: I have chosen the option of marriage.

A: But the marriage that Jesus authorized in Matthew nineteen is one man and one woman. "A man shall leave father and mother and cleave unto his wife." And that cannot mean anything but a woman.

W: You are making a big assumption, that, because he quoted from Genesis, he is therefore saying this is the only model in which you can have a marriage. In fact, I am saying that here he is looking at a same sex marriage, saying this is a good thing.

A: But you have not produced Scripture for anything else.

W: I do not use Scripture like you do.

A: So your whole point, I want to make this clear because I do not want to misrepresent you, is that you believe you can engage in your homosexual activity simply because you want to, whether or not Jesus said you could, or Paul said you could, or anybody said you could.

W: No, I believe that what Jesus said is terribly important, but it is not what is printed in that book. That book is not the Word of God. The living Christ is the Word of God, and it is my encounter with the risen Christ in worship, in prayer, in meditation, in community with other Christians that is my source of authority. Not words printed on a page.

A: You cannot encounter Christ apart from the Scripture. That is the only place we know about Christ. If it were not for the Scriptures we would have no knowledge of Christ whatsoever.

W: I disagree absolutely. I would say you would not encounter Christ apart from the worship community. And that, in fact, the worship community is prior to the Scripture. The whole question of canon is that the worshipping community chose which books were to be canon. So that suggests that the community is prior to the book.

A: Let me suggest to you that the living Christ, as you refer to Him, is encountered in the living Word. Hebrews four verse twelve: "For the word of the Lord ...

W: I don't agree with that ...

A: ... is quick and powerful," or living and active, "and sharper than any two-edged sword, piercing even to the dividing asunder of soul and spirit and joints and marrows and is a discerner of the thoughts and intents of the heart."

W: I am just saying I do not agree with that. I see it as the Bible is the church's book rather than the church being the people of the Bible. The Bible is the property of the church to interpret and to deal with, and the primary place of encounter with Christ for me is within a community of other Christians, specifically within the eucharist.

A: So you're telling me that you do not encounter Christ, or have any authority for your man to man relationship in the Scripture, but you find your authority for that in the church.

W: I think that is fairly accurate. I do not think there is any authority for anything in a person reading Scripture alone.

A: So, the church, then, is your source of authority. Whatever your church recognizes is authority.

W: Whatever my worship community recognizes.

A: Well, I guess so, because your church certainly does not recognize your relationship.

W: My worship community recognizes my relationship.

A: Yes, your "Oasis" in Hoboken, New Jersey.

W: No, I'm talking about my Parish in Hoboken, New Jersey.

A: Well, we're at the top of the hour and out of time. Ladies and gentlemen we thank you for listening this morning.

Every Man a Liar: Is Where a Legitimate Debate Starts and Ends

"Let every man be a liar, but God be true."

On the day of Pentecost, AD 33, the apostle Peter and other apostles preached the first gospel sermon. Over three thousand souls were saved and added to the Lord's church—the church of Christ, the body of Christ, the kingdom of God. This was the beginning of the New Testament church, which Christ promised to establish upon His death. His bride, the church, has the responsibility and duty to produce spiritual births of His children (Christians). Christ established this in the first century.

> Now the Spirit speaks expressly, that in the latter times some shall depart from the faith, giving heed to seducing spirits, and doctrines of devils; speaking lies in hypocrisy; having their conscience seared with a hot iron; forbidding to marry, and commanding to abstain from meats, which God has created to be received with thanksgiving of them which believe and know the truth. For every creature of God is good, and nothing to be refused, if it be received with thanksgiving. For it is sanctified by the word of God and prayer. If you put the brethren in remembrance of these things; you shall be a good minister of Jesus Christ, nourished up in the words of faith and of good doctrine, whereto you have attained. (1 Timothy 4:1–6)

TRADITIONS OF MEN AND GATE TROUBLES

Tradition of Man Verses the Word of God

Alvin Jenkins wrote that men who elevated themselves as successors of the apostles and wanted high-ranking roles and offices in the churches sought to change how the New Testament church was governed, which is by doctrine, the inspired word of God. (See chapter one about *Roman Catholicism* [part one] in Alvin Jenkins, *Tradition of Men versus The Word of*

God).[105] They departed from the faith and in AD 325 established the Council of Nicaea, the official law-making organization for church rules. Constantine approved this organization and made Christianity the national religion of the Roman Empire. Constantine stopped the persecution of Christians. By 608, Boniface declared himself to be "universal bishop/papa." In 1870, the Vatican council declared the doctrine of papal (another doctrine or another gospel, according to scripture) to be infallible. This act or proclamation set the stage for tradition and hierarchy in the Roman Catholic Church or Catholicism.

"You hypocrites, well did Isaiah prophesy of you, saying, This person draw near to Me with their mouth and honor Me with their lips; but their heart is far from Me" (Matthew 15:7–8).

Christ vs. Catholicism

In the New Testament church, the overseers and shepherd are elders; those who serve in leadership roles are deacons and ministers. Christ is the High Priest, and saints are individual Christians, who are priests and part of the priesthood. Confess your faults one to another. It is Christ who hears our prayers and forgives us of our sins. This first-century New Testament church of Christ doctrine teaches that Christians should confess their sins or faults to each other. Sins were confessed to each other, and prayers were made for each other. "Confess your faults one to another, and pray one for another, that you may be healed. The effectual fervent prayer of a righteous man avails much" (James 5:16).

What happened to the Ten Commandments and the Law of Moses? Upon Christ's death, He became the new testate, and a new law or covenant came into existence. The Law of Moses condemned to death. Under the New Covenant, the New Testament, one can find grace and mercy. There was no more animal blood sacrifice for the sins of the people. Christ became the blood sacrifice for man's sins. There was no need for a priest, bishop, or pope; Christ became our High Priest. Tradition can jack you up at the gate! But if you fail to study God's word, be honest, who can you blame?

If you want to claim salvation (Law of Moses) before Christ died, you are too early. If you want to claim salvation in denominational churches established after Christ ascended into heaven and Pentecost, the beginning of the New Testament church in AD 33 (Acts 2:1–47), you are too late. You

---

[105] Alvin Jennings, *Tradition of Men versus The Word of God* (Fort Worth, TX: Star Bible Publications, 1973), p 9.

don't have the authority. You do have the power to start a new doctrine, teaching, denomination after AD 33, but you have no authority. You just don't have the authority to build on Christ's foundation, to add or subtract from His word. There is no changing with the times. Well, looking at what's going on in America today, I guess you can change, but where you are going with it—to heaven? You'll get upset if someone tells you, "Straight to hell." So I won't say it. But let me be clear: God says to warn the wicked so His blood won't be on your head. You can consider yourself warned.

"Beware of the scribes, which desire to walk in long robes, and love greetings in the markets, and the highest seats in the synagogues, and the chief rooms at feasts; Which devour widows' houses, and for show make long prayers; the same shall receive greater damnation" (Luke 20:46). There are those who forbid marrying (1Timothy 4:3). In studying biblical history, one can see that even the priest God appointed had wives. What is this with the man-made tradition and denomination that is held up as Christ's church doing? Why are they acting as the mediator between God and man when the scriptures say it is Christ? What's with the kissing of rings and hands? This tradition of forbidding priests to marry allowed Satan inroads to homosexuality and homosexual activities among man-made priests in the Catholic Church. In my research of Internet articles when writing this book, I found an article about priests and pedophiles. An Italian newspaper reported Pope Francis as saying, "About two percent of Roman Catholic clerics are sexual pedophiles."[106] Another news article is "Seattle Archdiocese to pay $12 million to settle child sex abuse claims.[107] This story describes thirty men who allegedly were sexually abused as children and teens at two Seattle-area schools from the 1950s until 1984.

CBC News World Reports investigated a report from a United Nations (UN) human rights committee, dated Wednesday, February 5, 2014; it said that the Vatican "systematically" adopted policies that allowed priests to rape and molest tens of thousands of children over decades.[108] This story was all over the news and Internet on Wednesday, February 5, 2014. The UN committee

[106] Phillip Pullella, "Pope Francis Says about Two Percent of Priests Are Pedo philes: Paper," *Reuters*, July 13, 2014, http://www.reuters.com/article/2014/07/13/us-pope-abuse-idUSKBN0FI0R020140713.

[107] Eric M. Johnson, "Seattle Archdiocese to Pay $12 million to Settle Child Sex Abuse Claims," *Reuters*, June 25, 2014, http://www.reuters.com/article/2014/06/25/us-usa-seattle-church-idUSKBN0F015I20140625.

[108] " https://www.cbc.ca/news/world/vatican-slammed-by-un-human-rights-committee-over-sex-abuse-1.2523737

was urging the organization of Catholic priest overseers or earthly rulers to open its files on pedophiles and bishops who had conceal their crimes. This news really begs one to ask, "Is a man more righteous than God?" It is God who said, "Let every man have his own wife and every woman her own husband." No priests in the Bible, certainly not Moses, Aaron, or other priests from the Levitical line of priesthood, were asked to abstain from marriage.

In my research and reading this article from the Associated Press and Canadian Press, I discovered something called the UN Convention on the Rights of the Child. The key UN treaty on child protection, which the high-ranking officials (referring to themselves as something "holy") of this denomination (Catholic Church), was ratified in 1990. These sadists, pedophiles, and homosexuals have had plenty of time to repent, but they aren't trying to do right; this is an activity or lifestyle that is enjoyed and hidden behind a code of silence. What I found so disturbing in this article was the reference to the Vatican, as the supreme power of the Catholic Church, making decisions about how men should live. What happened? What about the supreme power of the almighty, holy, and righteous God of the heavens, the Creator of man? Does He get a say-so here? Is He worthy to be heard in this matter? The article repeatedly references the Holy See. Pray tell me: what is the Holy See? Did this Holy See die or shed his blood of atonement for your sins? Does this Holy See have a hell or heaven to put you in? Did he tell you he was going away and would return? Has he promised you a mansion in heaven? Can this Holy See forgive you of your sins—I mean, for real while being in sin himself? Will this Holy See raise you from the dead and give you eternal life?

The article states that the Vatican has never sanctioned a Catholic bishop for sheltering an abusive priest. Vatican officials have acknowledged that bishop accountability remains a major problem and have suggested that under Francis, things might begin to change. The only change Pope Francis can do is obey the gospel of our Lord Jesus Christ and help the Catholic Church do the same. And because of the issue of sexual child abuse and homosexuality among the priests or clergy, they need to teach what the Bible teaches about marriage, which has nothing to do with the Catholic tradition of priests abstaining from marriage. It has to do with abstaining from placing their sexual desires and fulfillment in the little, innocent children within their care. "Now the Spirit speaks expressly, that in the latter times some shall depart from the faith, giving heed to deducing spirits, and doctrines

The Associated Press · Posted: Feb 05, 2014 5:50 AM ET | Last Updated: February 5, 2014 *CBC News, February* 5, 2014. UN Report: Priest Rape and Molest Tens of Thousands of Children over Decades," *CBC News, February* 5, 2014.

of devils; speaking lies in hypocrisy; having their conscience seared with an hot iron; *forbidding to marry*, and commanding to abstain from meats, which God has created to be received with thanksgiving of them which believe and know the truth" (1 Timothy 4:1–3, emphasis added).

The New Testament tells Christians they are priests. "But you are a chosen generation, a royal priesthood, an holy nation, a peculiar people; that you should show forth the praises of Him who has called you out of darkness into His marvelous light. Which in time past were not a people, but are now the people of God which had not obtained mercy, but now have obtained mercy. Dearly beloved, I beseech you as strangers and pilgrims abstain from fleshly lust, which war against the soul" (1 Peter 2:9–11).

First Peter 2: 25 says Christ is the Shepherd and Bishop of your souls. That would mean no earthly bishop, pope, or priest.

First Timothy 2:5 says, "For there is one God, and one mediator between God and men, the man Christ Jesus." In the New Testament church, body of Christ, church of Christ, there is no confession box. James 5:16 says to confess your faults one to another and pray one for another so you may be healed. The effectual, fervent prayer of a righteous man avails much. "For the grace of God that brings salvation has appeared to all men, teaching us that, denying ungodliness and worldly lusts, we should live soberly, righteously, and godly, in this present world; looking for that blessed hope, and the glorious appearing of the great God and our Savior Jesus Christ; Who gave Himself for us, that He might redeem us from all iniquity, and purify to Himself a peculiar people, zealous of good works" (Titus 2:11–14).

Nearly half a year later, after I wrote the paragraph above on the UN Convention on the Rights of the Child, MSN posted two articles on the Internet. The Argentine pope met with victims whom priests had sexually abused. "He vowed zero tolerance for abusers and said bishops would be held accountable if they covered up crimes by priests in their dioceses."[109]

The following statement is from the plaintiffs' attorney: "The Archdioceses of Seattle has agreed to pay about $12.125 million to 30 men who alleged they were sexually abused as children and teens at two Seattle-area schools from the 1950s until 1984." The writer of this article reports, "The agreement comes weeks after Pope Francis said the Roman Catholic Church had to take a stronger stand on a sexual abuse crisis that has disgraced it for more than two decades."[110]

---

[109] Ibid.
[110] Sofina Mirza-Reid, ed., MSN, June 25, 2014, http://news.msn.com/us/seattle-archidioceses-to-pay-dollar12-million-to-settle-child-sex-abuse-claims.

Saints

One who belongs to the body of Christ is a child of God—a saint. No one can make you or come up with some elaborate ceremony to make you or officially deem you a saint—well, at least a saint scripturally. There is no authority in scripture for praying to saints or apostles. Better yet; no saints asked you to pray to them for anything. There are many situations in scripture where prayer was offered to God; let that sink in. All prayers to God have to go through His Son, Jesus Christ (John 14:13–14). "And He that searches the hearts knows what is the mind of the Spirit, because He makes intercession for the saints according to the will of God" (Romans 8:27). "Dare any of you go to law before the unjust, and not before the saints? Do you not know that the saints shall judge the world? and if the world shall be judged by you, are you unworthy to judge the smallest matters? Know you not that we shall judge angels? How much more things that pertain to this life?" (1 Corinthians 6:1–3). There are many scriptures that reference saints (1 Thessalonians 3:13; Jude 1:14–15; 1 Samuel 2:9; Matthew 27:52–53; Psalm 34:9; 37:28).

First Corinthians 14:33 says, "For God is not the author of confusion, but of peace, as in all churches [congregations] of the saints."

Holy Father

In Matthew 13, being called Rabbi, Father, or Master and elevating oneself over others in the church were condemned. Walking around while adorned in robes and jewelry (ring or hand kissing) to make one self-important or seen as high spiritual leaders or scribes and Pharisees was looked on in scripture as sinners and hypocrites. All of us, Christians and non-Christians alike, have heard this statement: "If the blind leave the blind, they both fall in the ditch." Why is it hard for us to see the truth when it comes to something we are set on and have made up our minds to do anyway?

> And call no man your father [nonbiological] upon the earth: for One is your Father, which is in heaven, neither be you called masters; for One is your Master, even Christ. (Matthew 23:9–10)
> But woe to you, scribes and Pharisees, hypocrites, for you shut up the kingdom of heaven against men; for you

neither go in yourselves, neither allow you them that are entering to go in. (Matthew 23:13)

For Moses truly said to the fathers, A prophet shall the Lord your God raise up to you of your brethren like to me; Him shall you hear in all things whatsoever He shall say to you. (Acts 3:22)

Communion

The early church communed on the first day of the week.

For as often as you do this, you do it in remembrance of Me. (Acts 20:7)

For I have received of the Lord that which also I delivered to you, That the Lord Jesus the same night in which He was betrayed took bread: And when He had given thanks, He broke it, and said, Take, eat: this is My body, which is broken for you: this do in remembrance of me. After the same manner also He took the cup, when He had supped, saying, This cup is the new testament in My blood: this do you, as oft as you drink it, in remembrance of Me. For as often as you eat this bread, and drink this cup, you do show the Lord's death till He come. (1 Corinthians 11:23–26; also see Luke 22:14–20)

Baptism

John (the Baptist or baptizer), Jesus's cousin, baptized him, and the apostles baptized the first Christians in Acts 2 (AD 33) in the beginning and infancy of *The Church*. All who were added to the Lord's body, church, or kingdom were immersed, buried in water. Sprinkling wasn't a practice and therefore not authorized in scripture as a spiritual burial (liquid grave) of water baptism, thus rising up to walk in the newness of life. All New Testament scriptural or Bible baptisms involved a burial (liquid grave) and rising up out of the liquid grave. Man's obedience to Christ connects Him to the Savior's atoning blood. This is a death to sin, a burial (water), and a rising up out of the liquid grave (resurrection) to a new life in Christ; out came blood and water. Sprinkling wasn't authorized then and doesn't save now: obedience is better than sacrifice.

Pope Francis

Viewing the *Piers Morgan Live* show on September 18, 2013, and following viewers' and guests' comments about their feelings on Pope Francis's remarks on gays. I believe the Catholic Church has been a breeding ground for homosexual activities due to its strength in this world and its connection in high places. Now I am observing its bold stand, in particular, in building a platform for lobbying for a once-held position of power in the likes of Sodom and Gomorrah.

I have to agree that Pope Francis made some very powerful statements that are scripturally true, whether he knew they were profound or not. No one can argue with him over what he said, and many were happy to hear he considered himself a sinner. As far as scripture is concerned, that is the first step toward salvation—knowing that you stand a guilty distance from God, that you are a sinner, and that you understand the need to obey the will of God in baptism. It's my hope that before Pope Francis leaves this life, he will no longer consider himself a hyphenated Christian (Catholic Christian) but a Christian only; this position is in line with the holy word of God. "And the disciples were called Christians first in Antioch" (Acts 11:26).

Pope Francis said he won't "judge" gays and lesbians, including gay priests. Well, he spoke well; it's not his call to judge the world. God shall judge the righteous and the wicked (Ecclesiastes 3:17).

> God judges the righteous, and God is angry with the wicked every day. (Psalm 7:11)
>
> And if any man hears My words, and believes not, I judge him not: for I came not to judge the world, but to save the world. He that rejects Me and receives not My words, has one that judges him; the word that I have spoken, the same shall judge him in the last day. (John 12:47–48)

There is nothing marginal about the souls of men, and no group of people who stand a guilty distance from God should be marginalized. Christians everywhere should seek and save the lost (Matthew 28:19–20).

Pope Francis said that "if someone is gay and he searches for the Lord and has good will who am I to judge?" Again he spoke well. "Ask, and it shall be given you; seek, and you shall find; knock, and it shall be opened to you. For every one that asks receives; and he that seeks finds; and to him that knocks it shall be opened" (Matthew 7:7–8). Seek God with your heart and all your soul (Deuteronomy 4:29).

Good People Don't Go to Heaven

Many people have been led to believe by religious organizations and spiritual leaders that their goodness and good deeds save them. And Lord forbid, there are those who are led to believe they can buy their way into heaven by making large donations and charitable contributions to the worship service. Hello, what you have isn't yours anyway. It's on loan to you just to see how you will behave: for the best or the worst. Will what you have save or condemn you? Go to the graveyard; no, someone has already retrieved that off the deceased. Just follow the hearse. Who do you see carrying their bank accounts, luxury cars, and million-dollar mansions with them? Nothing is really yours— nothing. "And Jesus said to him, why call you Me good? There is none good but one, that is God" (Mark 10:18; also see Luke 18:19). *Heaven is a prepared place for prepared people.* You don't stumble your way into heaven and are all surprised about how you got there.

"Many will say to Me in that day, Lord, Lord, have we not prophesied in Your name? and in Your name have cast out devils? and in Your name done many wonderful works? And then I will profess to them, I never knew you: depart from Me you that work iniquity" (Matthew 7:21–23). It's a hard lesson for many to swallow that Jesus asks only for obedience to His will, not their will. Anything that isn't of God, that isn't authorized by God is sin. It doesn't matter how grand and great you think it is and what you are doing to please Him. If it isn't authorized in scripture, it is done in vain.

> For they being ignorant of God's righteousness, and going about to establish their own righteousness, have not submitted themselves to the righteousness of God. (Romans 10:3)
>
> There is a way that seems right to a man, but the end thereof are the ways of death. (Proverbs 16:25; 14:12)
>
> Take a look back at Aaron's two sons, Nadab and Abihu (Leviticus 10:1–2).

Jesus Learned Obedience

"Though He were a Son, yet learned He obedience by the things which He suffered: And being made perfect, He became the author of eternal salvation to all them that obey Him" (Hebrews 5:8–9). Jesus came down from heaven and obeyed God. "O My Father, if it be possible, let this cup pass from Me: nevertheless not as I will, but as you will" (Matthew 26:39).

Now let's start a legitimate debate. "Then said He, Lo, I come to do Your will, O God" (Hebrews 10:7, 9; Psalm 40:7). If Jesus Christ obeyed God the Father, suffering and dying on the cross to redeem man's soul, and didn't deviate or change the plan of salvation, where would man fit on the totem pole (hierarchy) as far as having to obey God, too? Let's have a serious debate about this. And before you say anything, no, Mr. Morgan, God won't change and amend His word like the U.S. Constitution to fit the times or culture, whether it's gays, straights, or whatever issue you find interesting to debate.

FOR I AM THE LORD, I CHANGE NOT. (Malachi 3:6)
But the word of the Lord endures forever. And this is the
word which by the gospel I preached to you. (1 Peter 1:25)

Message to the Debaters of This World

If God said—well, not if –because we know the scriptures clearly and plainly say God called effeminate men (homosexuality) or men having sex with men an abomination. With this being noted in scripture, tell me who is going to debate this fact with God? Go ahead and be an idiot, full of words and no knowledge. "Where were you when I laid the foundations of the earth? declare, if you have understanding" (Job 38:4). The holy word of God posed the question: "Shall mortal man be more just than God? Shall a man be more pure than his maker?" (Job 4:17). Man, please. Just because we don't like what the scripture has to say about our sinful lifestyles, that doesn't give us any rights—yes, rights, freedoms, constitutions, laws, and all that earthly perishable stuff we cling to in an attempt to challenge and defy our Maker. God said it—debate over!

Now what you can do is take advantage of the liberty your Maker, the Savior, Christ Jesus, has extended to you. Joshua posed, "And if it seem evil to you to serve the Lord, choose you this day whom you will serve" (Joshua 24:15). And be advised (once again) that no one is going to drag you kicking and screaming into heaven. Make your choice now, on this side of the grave (life), to be there! And by God's rules, not yours. Remember— Lord, Lord, didn't I do many wonderful works in your name? But you will hear, "Depart from me I never knew you." I know Frank Sinatra made the world feel good with the lyrics "I did it my way." But that's not how we get to heaven. Seek

God's plan of salvation. *His* will for man. It's God's way—God's way only. I know, I know; we want to debate that, too.

Debate the fact that man is a servant and that each and every day is one heartbeat from the grave. One heartbeat from life eternally in hell or heaven, that's all. You are either a servant of righteousness or a servant of sin. There is no in between. The God–man relationship isn't democratic; it's God, the Creator (Maker, Master) and man the creature or servant made from the dust of the ground.

In March 2013, I started writing this book, following the news media, Supreme Court decisions, and Internet articles on the issue of gay marriage. In my introductory statement of this chapter, I made a comment that Piers Morgan made the most ridiculous comment I have ever heard. I was mistaken. A year later, in March 2014, Reverend Troy Mendez from the Episcopal faith tried (in support of homosexual activity) to interpret the scriptures on love. First thing: holy and reverend is God's name (Psalm 111:9). His presentation was so irrational that I couldn't believe what I was hearing. He sat there, adorned in a white collar, while Anderson Cooper, gay news reporter for CNN, interviewed him. Listening to the ridiculousness of his statement about how God wants us to love our neighbors, I saw his artfulness in crafting his message, in adding some truth in with his lie. Satan is wise and crafty. He mixes a little truth with a little lie. Unfortunately, that cocktail is never safe to drink. It reminds me of the apostle Paul in Acts 20:27–30. "For I have not shunned to declare to you all [the whole] counsel [word] of God. Take heed therefore to yourselves, and to all the flock, over the which the Holy Ghost has made you overseers, to feed the church of God, which He has purchased with His own blood. For I know this that after my departing [death] shall grievous wolves enter in among you, not sparing the flock. Also of your own selves shall men arise, speaking perverse things, to draw away disciples after them."

A tall, cold glass of ice water laced with cyanide consumed on a hot, summer day will go down just as tasty, good, and refreshing as an untainted tall glass of ice water; nevertheless, it contains deadly properties. Satan is here to steal and kill by any means necessary, even appearing as an angel of light (priest). Mr. Troy Mendez is no more a priest in God's kingdom than the devil is. "And no marvel; for Satan himself is transformed into an angel of light" (2 Corinthians 11:14).

Mr. Mendez tried to interpret Luke 10:27 and Mark 12:30–31. He expressed that it is wrong to speak out against homosexuality; to do so, he said, doesn't express the love Jesus taught about loving our neighbors as ourselves. Well, let us examine the scriptures. God rebukes and chastens whom He loves. "And you have forgotten the exhortation which speaks to you as to children, My son, despise not you the chastening of the Lord, nor faint when you are rebuked by Him: For whom the Lord loves He chastens, and scourges every son whom He receives. If you endure chastening, God deals with you as with sons; for what son is he whom the father chastens not? But if you be without chastisement, whereof all are partakers, then you are bastards, and not sons" (Hebrews 12:5–7; also see Proverbs 3:11–12).

The first part of the scriptural text Mr. Mendez referenced says, "Love the Lord your God with all your heart, and with all your soul, and with all your strength, and with all your mind." This should be interpreted as the following:

> If you love Me, keep My commandments. (John 14:15)
> You shall not lie with mankind as with womankind; it is abomination. (Leviticus 18:22)
> Know you not that the unrighteous shall not inherit the kingdom of God? Be not deceived: neither fornicators, nor idolaters, nor adulterers, nor effeminate (homosexuals) nor abusers of themselves with mankind, nor thieves, nor covetous, nor drunkards, nor revilers, nor extortioners, shall inherit the kingdom of God. (1 Corinthians 6:9–10)

The second half of the same scriptural text Mr. Mendez referenced says to love your neighbor as yourself. Let's not get this twisted. God is first and foremost; obey God rather than man! The scripture asks, "How can two walk together unless they agree?" Jesus says to come out of sin. You cannot walk with Jesus and be a liar, fornicator, thief, or homosexual. 1 Corinthians addressed this issue and says, "And such were some of you, but now you have been washed and sanctified and justified by Jesus by the Spirit of God." This means you are no longer participating in those activities. Yes, God loves you so much that He won't allow you to continue in sin, but He saves you based on your obedience. Yes, Christians should love gays, and that is by telling them what the scripture says about how to come to Christ, escape the wrath to come, and leave the homosexual lifestyle. Look at Mark 9:47 and Matthew 18:9. It's better to enter heaven with one eye than to go to hell with both eyes. Some things we will have to let go of so we can take up the cross and follow Christ. Some have become eunuchs for the kingdom of God (Matthew 19:11–12). The question to ask Mr. Mendez and the gay community is, Do you hate me because I tell you the truth? (Galatian 4:16; John 8:45). God chastens whom He loves. The thing is, gays don't want any chastisement. To tell the gay population what thus saith the Lord means you hate them. Is this the message (safety net) Mr. Mendez (priest) wants to leave the gay community? Two people sinned. Adam and Eve jacked it up for the rest of the world; even the ground was cursed. If gays are allowed to permeate this century and jack us up in America, what will happen to the rest of societies around the globe? Once again, Jesus saves. But in the twentieth-first century, who will stand in the gap? Who will speak up and out for the old path that pleased God?

Mr. Mendez has made a stand against the will of God, to speak against Christians who warn the wicked (disobedient ones) so their blood won't be on their hands. "Preach the word; be instant in season, out of season; reprove, rebuke, exhort with all longsuffering and doctrine. For the time will come when they will not endure sound doctrine, but after their own lusts shall they heap to themselves teachers, having itching ears; and they shall turn away their ears from the truth, and shall be turned to fables" (2 Timothy 4:2–4).

If you aren't reading your Bible, you will fall for Mr. Mendez's interpretation of scripture and his utter nonsense. What you need to do is what Jesus did to Satan: "It is written." Know that you love your neighbor as yourself; don't supersede the first part of the same verse, which is to love God first. And to do that, you must obey His commandments: warn the wicked.

Civil Rights Trump Religious Wrongs

"You give your mouth to evil, and your tongue frames deceit" (Psalm 50:19). Being forced to disobey God is how many hold the argument of religious rights to refuse to participate in the propagation of the gay agenda. It must feel very strange to think our forefathers left Europe, seeking religious freedom, only to realize it is slowly being taken away in the twenty-first century. When the Supreme Courts decided *all* states will have to recognize gay marriages, the American-born idea of "we the people, by the people, for the people" was over. Consider the opinion of Justice Alito in his dissenting statement: "Unless the Court is willing to allow this to occur [state-by-state decision], the whiffs of federalism in the today's opinion of the Court will soon be scattered to the wind." [111] (*United States v. Windsor.* 570 U.S. ___ (2013) (Alito, Samuel. dissenting opinion).

When civil rights (men's rules) triumph over God's laws and commandments, let's see what happens. It has never been a good outcome for man until he decides to repent and turn toward righteousness, back to

---

[111] *United States v. Windsor.* 570 U.S. ___(2013)

God. We need God. He doesn't need us. "If I were hungry, I would not tell you; for the world is Mine, and the fullness thereof" (Psalm 50:12). Yes, we need God's rain and sun; we depend on them just to plant and eat the crops of food God allows to grow. God can turn this land of opportunity into a wasteland. "He turns rivers into a wilderness, and the watersprings into dry ground; a fruitful land into barrenness, for the wickedness of them that dwell therein" (Psalm 107:33–34). Know this: America was founded and exists because of the providence of God. We shouldn't lose our station on these shores of time as a lighthouse and beacon for the almighty God. We should influence other nations and counties to obey and trust in God.

Washington Week, the *New York Times*, *Huffington Post*, CNN, other newspapers and the Internet have had to continue to have something to say on the subject daily. But the only thing that matters is what God has to say. So what if judges, politicians, presidents, and priests strike down all the bans on gay marriages all over the world; check in with the people left on the outside of the ark and get their advice. Maybe it's time for another cleansing—who knows? There are nations and terrorist cells (including sleeper cells) that stand ready to launch an attack on America's soil. We know it won't be water this time. It could easily be some deathly plague, virus, and/ or chemical. Way to go, Mr. Todd Staples. "I will change my definition of marriage when God changes His." It couldn't have been better put.

There is no end to books. Lots and lots of things can be said, and many more studies from other authors and authorities on matters related to this research can be noted, but my goal is to conclude with what is most important. "Let us hear the conclusion of the whole matter: Fear God and keep his commandments for this is the whole duty of man. For God shall bring every work into judgment, with every secret thing, whether it be good, or whether it be evil" (Ecclesiastes 12:12–14).

📖 Book Corner (A Critique)

The Bible and Human Sexuality—Marriage in the Old Testament [112] by J. Andrew Dearman

"'Rights' are first privileges of membership rather than the means of self-fulfillment or keys to personal autonomy. If this is, broadly speaking, the

---

[112] J. Andrew Dearman. "Marriage in the Old Testament", in *Biblical Ethics & Homosexuality: Listening to Scripture* edited by Robert Bradley (Louisville, KY: Westminster John Knox Press, 1996), 64

biblical perspective on social institutions, it differs markedly from a dominant perspective of modernity. The option to return to preindustrial, patriarchal societal norms is neither viable nor desirable for modern communities of faith; what is required in the task of faithful biblical interpretation is recognition that modern cultural assumption may hinder as well as help with theological understanding." (pg. 64)

In my research on the subject of homosexual marriage, Dearman's philosophy expressed in the above paragraph, along with the views of many other writers or authors crowding bookshelves support the idea that the Bible has little to no influence on the twenty-first century's man and culture and most notably the LGBT community. Modern man's faith and biblical interpretation are left up to him—autonomy. By his own actions, man forfeits his "rights" to eternal life and privileges as a Christian (saved child of God) and a home in heaven, everlasting life with God through the only mediator for his sins, Jesus Christ. He loses his rights to membership in God's family because he failed to deny himself (self-fulfillment) and keep to the old path (don't remove the landmarks)—to live for God.

It Is Not All about Procreation—It's about Obedience

Although I don't agree (based on my knowledge of scripture) with a great portion of Mr. Mauser's interpretations of scripture in this book, on page 13 of *Biblical Ethics & Homosexuality*, edited by Robert L. Brawley (Louisville, KY: Westminster John Knox Press) under the subtitle "Creation and Human Sexuality in the New Testament," Ulrich W. Mauser writes that the New Testament reference to Old Testament text in Genesis 1 and 2 describes the sexual relationship sanctioned by God between the man and his wife (woman), to which I agree. Out of all the gay persuasion books and their attempts to rewrite scripture I have read on the subject, his summation was on point: Mauser writes, "The New Testament has resolutely chosen to make the revelation in Geneses 1 and 2 of human sexuality as God's good creation the measure and judge of our conduct, not the other way around."[113] God measures and judges our conduct, not the other way around. I couldn't have said it any better.

God is about productivity. His instructions were to be fruitful and

[113] Ulrich W. Mauser, "Creation and Human Sexuality in the New Testament," in *Biblical Ethics & Homosexuality: Listening to Scripture*, ed. Robert L. Brawley (Louisville, KY: Westminster John Knox Press, 1996), p.13

multiply. God gave Adam instructions to till the garden. The sex act in labor (work) of corporeality is about productivity. Childbirth is labor in bringing a child into the world and is about increase and productivity. If you are defiant in planting seeds where God won't act outside of His design of "good" and His framework of productivity to give the increase, it is a sin, you are defiant, and that in itself is the abomination. Let's consider the act of spilling seeds in the rectum; outside of the framework of productivity. Onan (Genesis 38:8–10), spilling his seed upon the ground was the very same act of defiance against God . God was displeased and destroyed Onan. The argument about couples and individuals who don't or can't have children is irrelevant because one can have sex every day and for many years and not conceive until God allows or gives the increase; ask Sarah and Abraham about that or talk to their son, Isaac. Corn and wheat seeds that are planted or falls onto soil won't germinate or product unless God gives the increase. There are couples who have endured many expensive procedures to conceive, and as soon as they had a child from those procedures, they were able to conceive the second child naturally. There wouldn't have been an increase in Abraham's family by God's will and design if Abraham had decided to use his body parts in an unauthorized manner or outside the framework of productivity to impregnate Sarah. This issue is about homosexuality being an abomination and defiant act. Now the question is, Who said that? The same One who told Adam and Eve they were naked. If you are determined to be defiant, wouldn't it just be better to be defiant and leave off rewriting or reinterpreting scriptures, which comes with an additional punishment? "If an angel brings any other gospel than we have preached, let him be a curse." Not even the homosexuals set on fire in Sodom and Gomorrah were accused of trying to rewrite scripture.

Be honest and say you will love whom you want to love and behave how you want to behave, no matter what the scripture says. The heart of men (people) is set in them to continue to do evil. Stop trying to fight with God and Christians, followers of Christ. What's the fight about? All that isn't of God will come to naught anyway. God tests and tries man, so the real issue is with those who allow this lewdness and abominable behavior to permeate this society. Will God find ten righteous (obedient believers) in America?

This is certainly a generation that will go down in history for calling good, evil and evil, good. "Woe to them that call evil good, and good evil; that put darkness for light, and light for darkness; that put bitter for sweet, and sweet for bitter! Woe to them that are wise in their own eyes, and prudent in their own sight! ... Which justify the wicked for reward, and take away the righteousness of the righteous from him!" (Isaiah 5:20–21, 23).

It's a few days after Tuesday, November 4, 2014, the statewide elections. I have always voted the Democratic ticket. I followed everyone running for office. Because of a recent move to the "hanging chad" state, I refused to get involved with any politics or local elections. I voted in this state only for the president in both terms: 2008 and 2012. If there hadn't been a presidential election when I relocated to Florida, I wouldn't have voted during those last two terms. I closed my eyes, just went down the ballot, and checked all Florida's Democrats. I wasn't going to vote at all in the November 4, 2014 election, but I decided at the last minutes to vote for Charlie Chris only because the First Lady, Michelle Obama, had campaigned for him. So I went to the Internet, pulled up candidates and qualified politicians and party affiliation, and saved them in an Excel file. I then deleted every candidate except the Democrats. I went to each one's bio and looked at his or her districts; all of them were governors, attorney generals, chief financial officers, county commissioners, and so forth. I crossed out those who supported (or whose support was inferred) what the Bible condemns (effeminate). I confess that I didn't make it down the whole list; it was obvious that the gavel landed in one direction. I didn't vote in this election. I didn't have time to research the Republican candidates. I know for sure that if they didn't take the same stand on this issue, it would have been my time to switch parties—well at least this election.

In the 2016 presidential election, I watched the coverage of the election that evening. The commentators danced around the issue of homosexual marriage and federal benefits on the ballots and just smoothed it over (lower voter turnout), stating that many people were challenged by the moral debates and decided not to participate in the November 4 election. Here is a debate: Did the Democratic Party lose voters because of its support for the proliferation of the homosexual agenda in America? The half-clad, butt-shaking, crotch-grabbing rap songs didn't help persuade the "deplorable" Trump-based voters or the Electoral College votes either. Now that was a thin veneer between winning and not winning. Months before considering submitting this manuscript to the publisher, there were individuals discussing and talking about a thin veneer between peace and chaos or civil and uncivil society.

In the 2016 presidential debates, there was an opportunity for Hillary Clinton to take a step higher on their slogan "They go low. We go high." By going much higher and carrying her torch instead of Obama's torch. It is my guess that she would have sent a stronger message and at least persuaded more of the Electoral College votes. She allowed a smaller percentage of the population with the help of the Electoral College to put the Bramble Bush in office. No one running for the U.S. president's office wanted to take a stand for right in the sight of God for fear of losing voters or being on the unpopular side: what some are calling the wrong side of history, as far as tolerance of the homosexual issue in this country. A country that is existing only because of the providence of God. Presidential candidates were looking at the gay influence or worthiness in the polls. Most candidates had an opportunity to stand "in the gap" and chose the old path (not depart from righteousness in the sight of God) by being the olive tree, fig tree, or grapevine. The 2016 voters' outcome allowed the thorny and revengeful Bramble Bush to take office—rule over the office of the president. See Judges 9:6–16. Many voters were uncomfortable dealing with the gay issue and how the Supreme Court had ruled, which reflected in the low turnout in the polls.

Then candidate Trump knew and observed the winds of the tides, and he made them work for him [Alt-Right, Birther and Tea Party movements, and democrat-supported gay marriage], even though he lived a life of questionable personal, business, and ethical standards. His transgressions weren't an in-your-face or shoved down-your-throat issue, so it was easier to swallow than the homosexual issue the courts had forced on America. Hillary Clinton was overqualified for the position, but the less qualified and less presidential won because she was afraid to trust what was right. Mrs. Clinton (overqualified) didn't lose the election, and Mr. Trump (underqualified) didn't win the election. It was God's hands in this election, because of America's disobedience. Check biblical history. God put the unlikely in power to bring about repentance or, should I say, a cleansing. When Israel sinned, God caused them to be led into captivity to suffer at the hands of their enemies, and when they repented, God restored them to a peaceful existence. There is nothing new under the sun—know that. And know this; there are no competing goods when it comes to holy matrimony verses gay marriage.

Many will agree with me on the fact that Mr. Trump "technically" won due to the Electoral College votes. I would argue that God allowed this to be so. Many have questioned themselves about if Mr. Trump knows what he is doing, and he has probably questioned himself on how he really got there—this office in the White House. Not realizing that God is using him as a vessel. God uses good vessels and bad vessels to bring about a change. America has forgotten God and needs to repent. God is allowing America to take a good look at itself and decide on what side of history it wants to show up on in His book..

Chapter 8
DOMA: Justice Alito Dissenting

"TO THE EXTENT that the Court takes the position that the question of same-sex marriage should be resolved primarily at the state level, I wholeheartedly agree. I hope that the Court will ultimately permit the people of each State to decide this question for themselves. Unless the Court is willing to allow this to occur, the whiffs of federalism in the today's opinion of the Court will soon be scattered *to the wind.*"[114] *(United States v. Windsor, 570 U.S. ___, (2013) (Alito, J., dissenting).*

DOMA is public law 104-199—Defense of Marriage Act. President Bill Clinton signed it into law in 1996. On July 11, 2012, it was considered and passed the House on September 10; then it was considered and passed in the Senate.

Biblical Definition of Marriage

> Male and female created He them; and blessed them, and called their name Adam, in the day when they were created. (Genesis 5:2)
> But from the beginning of the creation God made them male and female, for this cause shall a man leave his father and mother, and cleave to his wife; and they two shall be one flesh; so then they are no more two, but one flesh. What

---

[114] *United States* v. *Windsor,* 570 U.S. ___(2013)

therefore God has joined together, let not man put asunder. (Mark 10:6–9)

What "we the people" of the United States in the twenty-first century need to ask ourselves in this whole marriage debate is, Are we putting asunder holy matrimony itself by separating and creating a new *unauthorized* relationship in the unions of male and female—in other words, male with male and female with female?

> So God created man in His own image [*knowledge of good and evil; not with beast, bird, or fish brains types of minds*] in the image of God created He him, male and female created He them. And God blessed them, and God said to them, be fruitful, and multiply and replenish the earth. (Genesis 1:27–28)
>
> And the Lord God said, behold the man is become as one of Us, to know good and evil; and now, less he put forth his hand and take also of the tree of life and eat, and live forever; therefore God sends him forth from the garden of Eden to till the ground from where he was taken. (Genesis 3:22)

Make no mistake about it, God has always given man the freedom to choose right from wrong: eternal life or eternal damnation. Do not eat of the tree in the midst of the Garden of Eden. People who try to force others to believe in God and live a God-fearing and/or Christian life don't understand the kingdom of God. It isn't by force and never will be or has been. Bloodthirsty Christian crusaders aren't following the authorized or inspired word of God found in the New Testament or followers of Christ (Christianity). Bloodthirsty, modern-day religions that are beheading their fellowman in the name of God because they don't share their religious views aren't practicing Christianity; they are not followers of Christ, the Son of God.

God didn't force Adam and Eve to do right. They chose to disobey, and mankind suffered the consequences. God *will not* force a gay person to live straight or heterosexual, even though He has created man upright; ability to choose good over evil. But rest assured, like the ground was cursed to bring forth thrones and thistles, this generation will be left hanging in the balance, leaving one to reconsider views on *climate change* and the statement of Jeremiah Wright, "God Damn America." After Adam and Eve sinned, the whole earth was cursed. It is the law of nature: for every action, there is a reaction. It was their actions that started the chain of sin and death in the course of mankind's journey on earth. Jesus's invitation has always been "Whosoever will, let him come." No matter what you feel or believe, you don't get a say so in opposition of what God has put in place (marriage, home, children, family, or church) without suffering the consequences.

Joe Biden says, "Prejudice is prejudice." God says, "Sin is sin." That would be heterosexual sin and homosexual sin. God is no respecter of persons. You don't even get to stay here on earth. You didn't build this, and you have no control over it. Talk to the ice storms, the lightning storms, the wildfires, the mudslides, the volcanoes, the typhoons, the earthquakes, and the whirlwinds, hurricanes or tornadoes. Find a human solution to the mass killings of the innocent ones, whom we have lost and who leave us in disarray and feelings of helplessness, and then consider that the earth is trying to spew us out. Unfortunately, many suffer for sins or unlawful acts committed by one or two people: Adam and Eve and the fall of mankind. Jesus suffered the death of the cross to bring man back into a proper relationship with God, the Creator.

After Adam sinned, the earth delivered up thrones and thistles, and man has to labor by the sweat of the brow to eat. It repented God that He had made man (Genesis 6:6–7)—hear that. He can't stand the sight of us anymore. Are we trying to return to that condemnation? The thoughts of man's heart are to do evil continually. Remember, God got so angry *that He wiped man off the face of the earth, leaving righteous Noah and his family. Remember* what God did to the people of Sodom and Gomorrah?

The earth (call it "global warming" or whatever label you care or want) is giving the twenty-first century enough signs that once again God is angry with the wicked every day and that man (his disobedience) makes Him sick. God spews him out, and the earth can't stand him. So what if the fire is already kindled when He comes? "I am come to send fire on the earth; and what will I, if it be already kindled?" (Luke 12:49).

There are many news reports of how cold America's winters could get. The visits of arctic temperatures are putting the fear of the revival of the ice age in people. "The unpleasant assessment [climate changes] comes from an international group of scientists who released a study examining the past and the future of the jet stream. Working with lake-sediment cores and climate models, they discovered that the stream's pattern shifted about 4,000 years ago into a 'positive' or curvy phase—the same dynamic responsible for the ongoing hot/cold divide in America."[115] "A University of Utah-led study shows that pattern became more pronounced 4,000 years ago, and suggests it may worsen as Earth's climate warms."[116]

Federal Definition of Marriage

Congress and the DOMA (Defense of Marriage Act [28 U.S.C. §1738]) federal statutes' use of the term *spouse* reads, "In determining the meaning of any Act of Congress, or of any ruling, regulation, or interpretation of the various administrative bureaus and agencies of the United States, the word 'marriage' means only a legal union between one man and one woman as husband and wife, and the word 'spouse' refers only to a person of the opposite sex who is a husband or a wife" (1 U.S.C.§7). [117] 570 U. S. ____ (2013) (Alito, J., dissenting).

Federal Marriage Amendment (FMA)

Supporters of the amendment feel it protects the institute of marriage in the States. In other words, the U.S. Constitution acknowledges only the union between opposite sexes. This amendment opposes judges from giving homosexuals the right to marry. Each state (autonomous entity) in the United States regulates civil unions and their legality or validity for that individual state's constitution: requirements for legitimacy.

Background and Current Laws (before 2015 Supreme Court ruling)

State law governs civil marriage. The federal government didn't define the legal issue of marriage. The state determined it. Before 1996 the federal

---

[115] John Metcalfe, "Earth Climate Warms," *Atlantic Cities*, April 16, 2014, https://www.citylab.com/life/2014/04/america-could-get-more-and-more-super-freezing-winters/8901/; https://phys.org/news/2014-04-west-cold-east-year-pattern.html

[116] https://archive.unews.utah.edu/news_releases/warm-u-s-west-cold-east-a-4000-year-pattern/

[117] 570 U.S. ___(2013).

government didn't define marriage and recognize any state law on marriage, even if not recognized by another (sister state), although this wasn't the situation with interracial marriage, which some states banned by statute.

In 1934, the amendment that allowed states to issue marriage licenses was the First Restatement of Conflicts on Marriage and Legitimacy, s.121.1934. Each state was free to set the conditions for a valid marriage, subject to limits set by the state's own constitution and the U.S. Constitution.[118] A sister state can refuse to recognize a marriage if the marriage violates a strong public policy of the state, even if the marriage is legal in the state where it took place. A strong public policy would be against underage marriages, incestuous marriages, polygamous marriages, and at one point in the history of the United States, interracial marriages. In the history of marriage in the United States, Congress has regulated certain aspect; for example, the 1862 Morrill Anti-Bigamy Act, which made bigamy a punishable federal offense in US territories and federal laws, was designed to end the practice of polygamy.

Section 3 of DOMA defined marriage as a legal union of one man and one woman for the purpose of interpreting federal law. The federal government didn't recognize same-sex marriages, even if state law recognized those unions. In 1996, Congress passed the Defense of Marriage Act (DOMA) in reaction to a state-level judicial ruling prohibiting same-sex marriage, which may violate Hawaii's constitutional equal protection clause (*Baehr v. Mike*, 80 Hawaii 341). The US Supreme Court struck down DOMA section 3 in *U.S. v. Windsor* on June 26, 2013.

God commanded the Jews not to marry into other nations of people because He didn't want other nations' pagan gods to turn Israel's hearts away from the true God. God never called a people an abomination. This country (USA) was more willing and eager to embrace an abominable act or lifestyle in 2015 (*twenty-first century-Supreme Court ruling on gay marriage*) than it was another human being, made in the image of God, when it involves interracial marriage in the 1960s. This act of calling evil, good and good, evil will certainly go down in history as a testament against this century and the history of this country. The twenty-first century is widely accepting of the gay lifestyle, and recent public opinions and polls demonstrate support for this way of life, which the Holy Bible calls an abomination in the sight of God.

Prior to 2004, same-sex marriage wasn't performed in any U.S. jurisdiction. Before the rulings in June 2014, most courts held the traditional

---

[118] "Conflicts on Marriage and Legitimacy." https://en.wikipedia.org/wiki/U.S._state_constitutional_amendments_banning_same-sex_unions last edited on 17 September 2017, at 09:26

(Christian) view, defining marriage as a union between a man and a woman. Same-sex marriage wasn't recognized, even if it was performed elsewhere in the United States, Canada, and so forth. In 2006, the Senate Judiciary Committee approved FMA—*Federal Marriage Act*, which attempted to stop states from recognizing same-sex marriage on a party-line vote. The full Senate debated it, but it was defeated in both houses of Congress. On April 2, 2014, the Alabama State House adopted a resolution calling for a constitutional convent to propose an amendment to ban same-sex marriage nationwide. An article written by Andy Towle, entitled, "Alabama House Passes Call to Put Same-Sex Marriage Ban in U.S. Constitution," *Montgomery Advertiser*, April 2, 2014."[119]

The situation in (2014) was that the US federal government recognizes same-sex marriages, and thirty-five states have granted them. In February 2014, the Justice Department expanded recognition of same-sex marriages in federal legal matters, including bankruptcies, prison visits, survivor benefits, and the legal rights to refuse to testify to incriminate a spouse.

---

[119] Andy Towle, the *Montgomery Advertiser*, April 3, 2014" https://www.towleroad.com/2014/04/alabama-house-passes-resolution-calling-for-gay-marriage-ban-in-the-us-constitution/
https://www.montgomeryadvertiser.com/story/news/2014/04/02/alabama-house-approves-call-to-put-same-sex-marriage-ban-in-us-constitution/72 22115/

State Law 2014

Recognizes same-sex marriages	Jurisdictions that do not license or recognize same-sex marriages	Litigation seeking to reverse court decisions to legalize same-sex union continues … Courts cite bans on same-sex marriages unconstitutional
As of November 20, 2014, thirty-five states including the District of Columbia issued marriage licenses to same-sex couples and recognized same-sex marriages from other jurisdictions.	Alabama, Arkansas, Florida, Georgia, Kentucky, Louisiana, Michigan, Mississippi, Nebraska, North Dakota, Ohio, South Dakota, Tennessee, Texas, Puerto Rico, and the Virgin Islands	As of October 2014, the following states' autonomous power was taken away to accommodate an abominable lifestyle in the sight of God: Alaska, Arizona, Idaho, Kansas, Missouri, Montana, Nevada, North Carolina, Oregon, and South Carolina. The US. Supreme Court, on October 6, 2014, declined to hear appeals from Indiana, Oklahoma, Utah, Virginia, and Wisconsin. Bans are being invalidated by the courts, which affect Idaho, Nevada, Alaska, Arizona, and Montana. Other states forced to legalize same-sex unions are Colorado, Kansas, North Carolina, South Carolina, West Virginia, and Wyoming.
Alaska, Arizona, California, Colorado, Connecticut, Delaware, Hawaii, Idaho, Illinois, Indiana, Iowa, Kansas, Maine, Maryland, Massachusetts, Minnesota, Montana, Nevada, New Hampshire, New Jersey, New Mexico, New York, North Carolina, Oklahoma, Oregon, Pennsylvania, Rhode Island, South Carolina, Utah, Vermont, Virginia, Washington, West Virginia, Wisconsin, and Wyoming	American Samoa, Guam, and the Northern Mariana Islands do not have any law prohibiting or recognizing same-sex marriage. Even with no prohibition, none of these territories recognize same-sex marriage.	

It seems that morals and ethics have no bearing on the conduct of our affairs before God Almighty. "Judge Vaughn Walker states in his ruling that moral opposition to same-sex marriage is not sufficient reason to make a law valid."[120]

According to an article in Wikipedia, FMA has been introduced in the United States ten different times: 2002–2006, 2008 and 2013. Marilyn Musgrave, former Republican Colorado legislator, lost her bid for the fourth congressional district seat. She had an unsuccessful run for office during her fourth term in 2008. She was an unsuccessful sponsor of a constitutional amendment to bar same-sex couples from marrying. Musgrave is the first Republican woman elected to Congress from Colorado. In June 2006, Musgrave sponsored a resolution in Congress to declare 2007 as the "National Year of the Bible." The resolution text requested that President Bush issue a proclamation calling on all citizens to "rediscover and apply the priceless and timeless message of the Bible," and encourage them to join the US federal government in celebrating the year with Bible "programs, ceremonies, and activities."[121] The resolution died in committee.

Ms. Musgrave is quoted concerning her statement related to the bill in 2003, countering a statement made by Rep. Barney Frank (D-Mass.) on FMA. She felt that the Massachusetts marriages were court ordered. She said, "If we're going to redefine marriage, let's let the American people, through their elected representative, decide—not activist judges. Let the people of Massachusetts decide."[122]

Sodomy and Laws against Nature

In some states, there are still laws on the books that criminalized the act of both oral *and* anal sex. Under the state of Michigan's sodomy laws, engaging in this type of abominable activity can lead to fifteen years' imprisonment. The law is called the Abominable and Detestable Crime Against Nature statute. There is also a separate law called "gross indecency." Those engaged in the act must register as sex offenders. Laws that consider sodomy a crime remain on

---

[120] Wikipedia, "Moral Opposition to Same-Sex Marriage Is Not Sufficient Reason," http://en.wikipedia.org/wiki/Federal_Marriage_Amendment.

[121] Wikipedia, s.v. "Marilyn Musgrave," http://en.wikipedia.org/wiki/Marilyn_Musgrave.

[122] Wikipedia, s.v. "Federal Marriage Amendment." http://en.wikipedia.org/wiki/Federal_Marriage_Amendment.

the books in seventeen states and continue to be enforced in several states, even though the US Supreme Court declared the laws unconstitutional. Rudy Serra, a Michigan gay rights attorney, said that "*Lawrence v. Texas* decision renders these laws unconstitutional."[123]

The Equality Matters report notes, however, that police and prosecutors in some states, including Michigan and Texas, have continued to enforce sodomy laws despite the fact that state courts have joined the US Supreme Court in invalidating those laws.

The Lawrence loophole: Some attorneys believe judges and prosecutors are claiming passage in the Lawrence decision written by Justice Anthony Kennedy (now retired), who wrote the majority opinion in the case. He provided a broad loophole that gives them authority to continue enforcing their state sodomy laws in cases involving public sex, sex with minors, or prostitution-related sex.

The Center for Constitutional Rights defends people charged under Louisiana's crime against nature law. They say their clients have to register as sex offenders because [if convicted] under provisions of a *200-year-old statute*: non-procreative or acts traditionally associated with homosexuality activities are viewed morally wrong by society.[124] "You shall not lie with mankind, as with womankind: it is an abomination. Neither shall you lie with any beast to defile yourself therewith: neither shall any woman stand before a beast to lie down thereto: it is confusion" (Leviticus 18:22–23; 20:13). When the Center for Constitutional Rights can date this law, then let's start to talk about what _rights_ man has, homosexual or heterosexual. "Lo, this only have I found, that God has made man upright; but they have sought out many inventions" (Ecclesiastes 7:29).

Text appearing in italics below indicates the states' sodomy law applies only to gay sex: Alabama, Florida, Georgia, Idaho, *Kansas*, Louisiana, Maryland, Massachusetts, Michigan, Minnesota, Mississippi, *Montana*, North Carolina, *Oklahoma*, South Carolina, *Texas*, Utah, and Virginia.[125]

---

[123] https://www.washingtonblade.com/2013/04/17/sodomy-laws-remain-on-books-in-17-states-including-md-and-va-/

[124] https://en.wikipedia.org/wiki/Center_for_Constitutional_Rights

[125] Lou Chibbaro Jr., "Sodomy Laws Remain on Books in 17 States, including Md. and Va.," *Washington Blade*, April 17, 2013, http://www.washingtonblade.com/2013/04/17/sodomy-laws-remain-on-books-in-17-states-including-md-and-va-/#sthash.cwVFRfM1.spuf.

Do Not Cause My People to Sin

It behooves judges and rulers of nations to understand and know that God deals, and has dealt, with a nation based on its attitude toward God and His moral laws. The biblical history of the Jews and nation of Israel merits our twenty-first century's consideration. After Joshua, the Lord raised up judges to deliver the Israelites from their adversaries. When Israel sinned, they were taken captive and brought into exile, and when the nation of Israel repented, the blessings of the nation were restored. It's important that judges don't cause the people of America to sin against God. Not all adversaries are outside. Many nations have crumbled because of what's happening *inside* the gates of the city—lack of morals and disrespect toward God. There is a history of over two thousand years to ponder how God dealt with nations that forgot God.

> Let every soul be subject to the higher powers. For there is no power but of God: the powers that be are ordained of God. Whosoever, therefore, resist the power, resists the ordinance of God: and they that resist shall receive to themselves damnation. For rulers are not a terror to good works, but to the evil. Will you then not be afraid of the power? Do that which is good, and you shall have praise of the same: For he is the minister of God to you for good. But if you do that which is evil, be afraid; for he bears not the sword in vain: for he is the minister of God, a revenger to execute wrath upon him that does evil (Romans 13:1–4). See Isaiah 5:20-23; Isaiah 9:16, and Isaiah 10.

This is God's world, and it's God who orders the steps of man. By the providence of God, judges and rulers are in place to rule and direct the lives of the people. This is a heavy or weighty responsibility, even if one who finds himself or herself in the position of judge or ruler doesn't totally understand how the position relates to the order of things: God and the universe. One in this position of power should fear causing the people to sin or make laws that would cause the people to sin or turn their hearts away from God. Judges shouldn't make doing right in the sight of God an uphill battle for states that respect God and lead people's hearts away from God and His laws. The gays say they are right, and the Bible (the word of God) is right, but the two *do not* agree. God settled this issue when He said, "Let every man be a liar, but God be true." The Bible says God cannot lie. Gays aren't even trying to make the claim that they aren't liars or cannot lie; that very fact alone in a court of law would cause them to lose (throw out) their case. If they can prove that their claim (I was born this way; God made me this way) is true for having anal sex or sodomy and that man marrying man should have some merit with God, then they have a case. Jesus will take their case. The thing is, Satan wouldn't even attempt a senseless argument with God.

Satan, liar and deceiver, continues to deceive the hearts of men to do the opposite of what God demands of him. Just like the original sin, God said, "Don't eat of the tree in the midst of the Garden." Satan added his two cents, changing the course of nature in the God-man relationship. God said a man should leave father and mother and cleave to his wife; and the two shall be one in the union (the bed undefiled). Satan once again added his two cents; the states have sovereign prerogative to define marriage. Really, riddle me this; do states have a heaven or a hell to put people in throughout eternity?

Here we go again, back to ground zero, and messing with what God has commanded us not to touch. Don't touch the tree, don't put the man-woman relationship asunder, and man shouldn't lie with man as with womankind. Do we really want to mess with the man-woman, husband- wife relationship thing God put in place? Just like the tree of life, which God put (in place) in the Garden of Eden, it was a very bad thing to get cut off and lose access to eternal life because of disobedience. Will man ever learn (centuries on top of centuries)? Will he ever learn? The thorns, thistles, and sweat of the brow curse versus paradise (Eden; Genesis 3:18–19) can easily become a twenty-first century's four seasons (spring, summer, fall, and winter) versus earth in Arctic (below freezing) climate/weather for the entire planet overnight for forty or four hundred years. This generation experiencing frozen arctic wilderness until it is wiped out—like the generations wiped out in the wilderness under Moses or the inhabitants of earth wiped out by the flood.

> He gives snow like wool: He scatters the hoarfrost like ashes. He casts forth His ice like morsels: who can stand before His cold? (Psalm 147:16–17)
>
> Fire, and hail; snow, and vapor; stormy wind fulfilling His word. (Psalm 148:8)
>
> Whatsoever the Lord pleased, that did He in heaven, and in earth, in the seas, and all deep places. He causes the vapors to ascend from the ends of the earth; He makes lightnings for the rain; He brings the wind out of His treasuries. (Psalm 135:6–7)

We cannot fathom the massive weapons of destruction God holds in His Treasures (warehouse); an arsenal of weaponry and artillery. "By the blast of God they perish, and by the breath of His nostrils are they consumed" (Job 4:9).

February 2014, I saw the following headline news in newspapers and Internet websites: "By the Numbers: Wicked Ice Storm Takes Massive Toll on South." "Whiteout: Monster Snowstorm Wipes Out Power for Half Million." The news media described the ice storm as ferocious, deadly, catastrophic, wreaking havoc; and at one point, sixty percent of the United States was sheeted in snow, and over three hundred and fifty-thousand were without electrical power. At some point during the freezing, arctic snowstorm that hit the South, the storm progress brought reports of six hundred and eighty-nine thousand power outages across the United States, affecting twenty-two states. Atlanta (Bible belt state), which normally enjoys mild and short-lived winter weather, is known for its heavy gay and lesbian activity.

God always looks out for those who are praying and doing His will. Abraham asked God whether He would destroy the good with the bad. "That be far from You to do after this manner, to slay the righteous with the wicked: and that the righteous should be as the wicked, that be far from you: Shall not the Judge of all the earth do right?" (Genesis 18:25). The first warning was a blessing in disguise. The old cliché "God works in mysterious ways" certainly was in play here in Atlanta, Georgia. God knew what was in store: the second and more treacherous ice storm to follow. Many heeded the order and stayed off the roads when the second warning came. They avoided dire consequences of being on the roads or stuck in places other than their personal homes, and no doubt saving many lives.

I have always heard that man's arms are too short to box with God. We try, but we try to no avail, bringing destructions on ourselves and the ground we stand on. But God's invitation remains the same. "Come out." The scripture still reads, "Who is man that God is mindful of him?" God suffers long with mankind, not wanting any to perish. But many feel it is safe to squander the few days they have here on earth, because they feel no imminent threat of Judgment Day or simply choose not to believe there is a day of judgment.

When it comes to anyone defining marriage, that was in the beginning and established and instituted by God in the first male and female relationship on earth, this person is well over thousands of years too late with the definition; some would say, "A day late and a dollar short." And it's equally too late to try to lay the ground rules. The scriptures say, "Let God be true and every man a liar." The scriptures say, "Obey God rather than man." God's word is true.

Truth has always been and has never changed. God cannot lie. The scripture says that God, who made man, fathered us (Christians) with the word of truth, and in Him (God) is no variableness (James 1:17–18). A lie (unlike a constant—truth) is a variable that changes with the winds of the times, the current century, the popular vote, polling of beliefs, situational ethics, and concepts of morality in a particular cultural setting.

All our plans, if not God approved, would fail. The last thing Christians should be alarmed about are evildoers, whose plans will come to naught. The battle has already been won. To be saved, it was about getting on the boat with Noah and his family, and saving the animals as God had instructed. To be saved now, it's about getting in the church or kingdom of God for Christians, and bringing someone else with you, a faithful and fruitful servant as God has instructed. The ranting and raging over writing another Bible that doesn't illuminate the homosexual lifestyle and abominable deeds or persecuting the church for preaching the gospel when it comes to being effeminate, will come to naught. After all, is man more righteous than God? This is God's world. There is nothing to win here in opposition to God's will for man, His creation. If you don't believe me, ask the residents of Sodom and Gomorrah. Check out the places where Sodom and Gomorrah once existed in history.

A nation is only as strong as its ability to learn from the past. The problem or portend concerning the Supreme Court's ruling on gay marriage is that we have never left ground zero. We didn't learn the lesson. The problem became the crafty words of Satan (presenting himself to be the voice of reasoning—an angel of light, if you will) in the Garden of Eden. The U.S. Supreme Court presents itself as the voice of reasoning (an angel of light, if you will) in crafty words to persuade the people of these United States that not only is holy marriage "good" but so is homosexual marriage—*competing views*. It was God who said, "Do not eat of the tree," and it was God who said that it is sin for a man to have sex with a man. This wasn't a decision for the court to make; this matter belongs to God.

What example will the USA leave to generations to come? Will archeologists and historians tell the story of a once land of opportunity left in ruins because of its disobedient act toward God? Will the USA be nuked or reduced to ashes like Sodom and Gomorrah, never to be inhabited again? Who will suffer this time around? Will it be the tolerant and those afraid to speak out against such sinful and evil acts?

Alito expressed concerns that the majority's opinion would be used to attack the beliefs of those who disagree with same-sex marriage, who "will risk being labeled as bigots and treated as such by governments, employers, and schools," leading to "bitter and lasting wounds." Expressing concern for judicial abuse, Alito concluded, "Most Americans—understandably—will cheer or lament today's decision because of their views on the issue of same-sex marriage. But all Americans, whatever their thinking on that issue, should worry about what the majority's claim of power portends." [126]

Once again, let us consider scripture in these words of Judge Alito's statement, "majority's claim of power portends." In Daniel 5, King Belshazzar took and defiled what was God (belonged to God). And we are tempting God by defiling the sanctity of marriage, the church, and children (His heritage). Is it possible to be staring at the same message? "MENE MENE TEKEL U-PHARSIN." For America, the handwriting "is on the wall" if we fail to repent of our course.

The Defense of Marriage Act (Public Law 104-199,101; Statute 2419), enacted September 21, 1999 (1USC§7 and 28 USC§1738L) is a US federal law that allows states to refuse to recognize same-sex marriage granted under the laws of other states. DOMA (28 U.S.C. §1738b) allows each state to refuse to recognize same-sex marriage and to deny any rights and/or privileges and federal benefits allowed to traditional married couples. The Supreme Court ruled in June 2013 that section 3 of the act was unconstitutional.

Attorney General Eric H. Holder Jr. (Politics)

"In every courthouse, in every proceeding and in every place where a member of the Department of Justice stands on behalf of the United States, they will strive to ensure that same-sex [anal/sodomy sex] marriage receive the same privileges, protections, and rights as opposite-sex [God-approved sex] marriages," says Mr. Holder. While Holder rants on like Ramses, the Egyptian king, or pharaoh against Moses in his proclamations, let him consider what the Lord says. "Know you not that the unrighteous shall not inherit the kingdom of God? Be not deceived: neither fornicators, nor idolaters, nor adulterers, nor effeminate, nor abuser of themselves with mankind, nor thieves, nor covetous, nor drunkards, nor revilers, nor extortioners, shall inherit the kingdom of God," says God. Stop, think, and examine these words. Was there any discrimination on the part of God and His holy word in the above scriptures (1 Corinthians 6:9–10)? Did the scripture (God's holy word) not call out the fornicator, adulterer, drunkard, thief, and others in the same way it called out the effeminate (homosexuals: gay and lesbian)?

---

[126] Obergefell, 135 S. Ct. at 2643.

If a man also lies with mankind as he lies with a woman, both of them have committed an abomination. (Leviticus: 20:13)

Ye shall not lie with mankind, as with womankind: it is an abomination. (Leviticus 18:22)

The thing is, we are hypocrites. We arrest and jail the prostitute, brothel owner, call girl, madam, thief, reviler, rioter, extortioner, and drunkard. We jail a liar for perjury and penalize the guilty party in divorce court, but we make up separate rules for the effeminate. Who is discriminating here? The effeminate isn't on a separate list, so there shouldn't be any confusion. If God didn't treat someone differently for wrongful acts or transgressions, we shouldn't reward effeminate behavior over the other wrongdoers on "the list." Jail the thief and those who engage in lewd, unnatural acts. If offenders don't want to be judged, then hide their sin like the thief? Thieves don't flaunt themselves or their thievery in public and expect that lifestyle to be accepted. Can the thief come out of the homeowner's closet and say, "I'm a thief, and I got rights. Don't treat me like a thief. I should have the same access to your things that you have or worked and labored for." Absurd? Yes!

The child kidnapper wants to take what you labored in copulation to achieve. The gays say they should have the rights to adopt your children. Their abominable unions leave them void of producing fruit from a fruitless act, labor, or work. They hunger after, covet, and lust to have the same dignity as a union of *holy* matrimony, undefiled before God. Well, God is the only one who can truly grant blessings and dignity to a marriage union—not man (court or state). After all, God started the whole marriage thing. Man has been capitalizing on the tradition of marriage in many aspects, especially monetarily. Today, because of greed (estate tax) and other monetary reasons, man wants to capitalize on this ungodly union under the disguise of a marriage.

Mr. Holder seems to be the black champion for gays' civil rights. In 2013, the Supreme Court declared it unconstitutional to refuse federal benefits to married same-sex couples. Since the June 2013 ruling from the Supreme Court, many of the federal rules relating to same-sex couples have been rewritten. Same-sex couples can now file taxes together and receive Medicare benefits from their gay partners. Criminal investigation would be covered under spousal privileges (they can't testify against each other). The Bureau of Prisons (federal institute) will allow same-sex conjugal visits. *Webster's New*

World Dictionary defines *conjugal*[127] (kän´jə gəl) this way: *"adj.* [[<L *conjunx*, spouse]] of marriage or the relation between husband and wife—con´ju-gal-ly adv." What hypocrites; the courts jail many offenders or sinful acts from "the list" (1 Corinthians 6) and allow unchallenged passage of rights to the sinful abdominal act from the same scripture verses—book, chapter, and verse. In the context of a moral gauge, how can one act be discriminated against the other? Man can never be more righteous and wiser than God. Oh, he wants to be; he tries to act like it—this got the devil or Satan kicked out of heaven, along with his angels, and doomed for the fires of hell. God asked Adam, "Who told you that you were naked?" Adam no longer was veiled from the fact that he was naked once he had eaten of the tree of knowledge. It's our knowledge of God's word that tells us we are liars, thieves, murderers, and even effeminate (homosexual). The question is, Who told gays they are effeminate or behaving unnaturally toward the same sex? Was it the public in opposition to the gay lifestyle, politicians, and judges? Was it God and ministers of the gospel? Whom are you: homosexuals and lesbians angry with? Is it with God? Psalm 2:1:Why do heathen rage? Well, before you put your pants on all wrong and get all upset with people who don't accept the gay lifestyle, know it was God who told homosexuals they were behaving unnaturally—that their actions or activities were an abomination—that they were effeminate (gay).

Now, to be fair to Mr. Holder and the former president, Mr. Obama, at the time this paragraph was written, they both held offices that put them in positions to uphold the laws and protect the rights of citizens in the United States. So here again, it was time for the people of these United States to stand up and fight for their constitutional rights to be heard as a people and not let one, two, or a couple of individuals speak for them. The following paragraph is from an article published by Voice of America (VOA) News:

"During the Wednesday session, conservative justices Anthony Kennedy (now retired), Antonin Scalia (now deceased), and Chief Justice John Roberts said they were troubled by President Barack Obama's decision not to defend in court the law Congress had approved. They said it called into question his willingness to defend other laws passed by Congress and challenged in court."[128]

Citizens (we, the people) are responsible for the laws of this country as

---

[127] *Webster's New World Dictionary*, s.v. "conjugal" (Wiley Publishing, 2003), 141.
[128] "US Supreme Court Considers Federal Definition of Marriage," Voice of America, March 27, 2013, http://www.voanews.com/content/us-supreme-court-considers-federal-definition-of-marriage/1629747.html

much as the ones our votes elect to uphold the laws. Consider this: is it the politicians or the Supreme Courts that decide for the people of the States, or is it the people who put politicians in office (who pick judges) who will represent their values system while in office? Is it unconstitutional for the Supreme Court to dictate to the states on the issue of gay marriage, which is in opposition to the people's beliefs in America—a God-fearing country? This view wasn't foreign to this country's forefathers on the issue of the *autonomous* position of each state. The issue of gay marriage wasn't on the minds of the founding fathers of this country. They were all married, except for two or three, and 90 percent or more of the men who signed the U.S. Constitution fathered children. We, the people, must save our states, save our nation from the pending second coming of Sodom and Gomorrah—in other words, of history repeating itself. Did Sodom and Gomorrah know what was coming down the pipeline? I don't know, but we do. Things written before were written for our learning. "For whatsoever things were written aforetime were written for our learning, that we through patience and comfort of the scriptures might have hope" (Romans 15:4).

State Laws' Saving Grace?

The federal rules have no effect on state laws. This is where "for the people, of the people, and by the people" should step in and take back the United States, the one our forefathers envisioned for a people who trusted in God: "In God We Trust." At the time I wrote this in the manuscript, there were challenges to pulling bans on same-sex marriage. Many states were holding out and fighting the Supreme Court rulings.

Challenging the Supreme Court ruling would focus on what the court believed they were acting on: the question of two competing goods. Really? Upon reading Justice Alito's dissent, legislatures believe they have no other choice but to legislate between the two views on marriage. The political branches of state and federal government shouldn't remain neutral with what is viewed as competing versions of the good, provided that the version of good they adopt isn't *countermanded* by the Constitution. "Government 'may make a value judgment favoring childbirth over abortion.'" "Accordingly, both Congress and the States are entitled to enact laws recognizing either of the two understandings of marriage. And given the size of government and the degree of which it now regulates daily life, it seems unlikely that either

Congress or the States could maintain in complete neutrality even if they tried assiduously to do so."[129]

I believe that may be the case for Congress and the States, but the people of these United States should have a say-so, too. After all, it is unconstitutional that the people are denied their rights. If the people go down with the next version or type of fire and brimstone, it should be their choice to make. Wrong the people and their blood will be on your hands. Let the people of each state decide whether they want their state to recognize unions God deems abominable. After all, the politicians aren't the only ones asking God to bless America.

Again, hello out there, world. News flash: No one is good but God! "And Jesus said to him, why call you Me good? There is none good but one, that is God" (Mark 10:18). For one to be good, he or she would pretty much be God. Was Jesus good? Yes. Was Jesus God? Yes. Did the rich young ruler understand what he was saying to Jesus in his salutation: "Good" Master? Maybe yes, maybe no. Perhaps from his response to Jesus, he thought he was pretty much a good guy already. He felt it was his deeds that made him good, and if there were any other good deeds he could personally do to *merit* salvation (eternal life), he wanted Jesus to let him in on it so he could live forever. Did this young man recognize Jesus as God, or did he see him as a prophet and preacher, a messenger of God? He certainly saw Jesus as someone who could tell him what to do to be saved eternally. Do we as Americans trust that Jesus can show us the way of salvation as we shout out "God Bless America"? When he was shown that he lacked total commitment to God (despite his personal achievement of wealth and his idea of goodness), and that what he sought was found in total submission to God, he left—not fully understanding the good Jesus (deity) and good God (deity). He failed to understand the obedience of walking in Christ, not ourselves or our idea of righteousness or idea of good.

We are commanded to do good works, but what really makes this work good?

> For we are His workmanship, created in Christ Jesus to good works; which God has before ordained that we should walk in them. (Ephesians 2:10)
> But we are all as an unclean thing, and all our righteousness are as filthy rags; and we all do fade as a

---

[129] *United States v. Windsor*, 570 U.S. 744 (2013).

leaf; and our iniquities, like the wind, have taken us away. (Isaiah 64:6)

This then is the message which we have heard of Him, and declare to you, that God is light, and in Him is no darkness at all. If we say that we have fellowship with Him, and walk in darkness, we lie, and do not the truth: But if we walk in the light, as He is in the light, we have fellowship one with another and the blood of Jesus Christ His Son cleanses us from all sin. If we say that we have no sin, we deceive ourselves, and the truth is not in us. If we confess our sins, He is faithful and just to forgive us our sins, and to cleanse us from all unrighteousness. If we say that we have not sinned, we make Him a liar, and His word is not in us. (1 John 1:5–10)

When looking at the competing versions of good (marriage is good be it heterosexual or homosexual), one has to question who has the final say-so on what is good. Is it God or man? If you aren't walking in the light of God's word, Jesus Christ, can anything you do be good? "And no marvel; for Satan himself is transformed into an angel of light" (2 Corinthians 11:14). Don't be fooled; even Satan can parade around disguised in so-called good deeds. It's good when God approves. Homosexual marriage is not God-approved marriage, and no version of it is good.

Mr. Holder is a black guy fighting for the civil rights of gays and lesbians to behave unnaturally and abominable in the sight of God. Martin Luther King Jr., the most recognizable face of the civil rights movement, led the struggles of the black man to be treated like a man God created—Upright. Race, ethnicity, and nationality have never been a sin.

And the sons of Noah that went forth of the ark were Shem, Ham, and Japheth. These are the three sons of Noah and of them was the whole earth overspread. (Genesis 9:18–19)

And the whole earth was of one language and of one speech. (Genesis 11:1)

So the Lord scattered them abroad from there upon the face of all the earth. (Genesis 11:7–8)

Listen: Shem, Ham, and Japheth weren't homosexuals, okay! From them was the whole world repopulated.

The homosexual civil rights movement (sodomy and unnatural affections in the sight of God) cannot be compared to the black civil rights movement. Black people wanted to be treated like a human being, not three-fifths of a man (God-given inalienable rights). Dr. King led God-fearing people in marches—crying, praying, and carrying the Bible. The civil rights movement called on God to intervene in their struggles. Is the civil rights movement for gays and lesbians calling on God to intervene in their struggles to be accepted in their alternative lifestyle? Are they fearlessly making demands on God-fearing people in a Christian nation?

Gay Civil Rights vs. Black Civil Rights

The civil rights movement for the black people wasn't going against anything that was against God. The civil rights movement was about humanity and many Christians and God-fearing people (blacks, whites, and Jews) marched, fought, suffered, and died for future generations of people and for the souls of their oppressors and for this country.

> "But let none of you suffer as a murderer, or as a thief, or an *evildoer*" (1 Peter 4:15, emphasis added).

The homosexual movement is disingenuous in its attempt to create (by deception) a parallel cause, using landmark cases in African American's struggles. To the homosexual, God's message would be the same one He gave Cain. "If you do well, shall you not be accepted?" (Genesis 4:7).

My question to the homosexual is, What exactly do you want other than to destroy all that is good and holy in the sight of God? Is it marriage, church, and family (father, mother, and children—the inheritance of God)?

Full Faith and Credit Clause

Is found in the Articles of Confederation, and serves to maintain order between states, meaning states should be obliged to honor sister states (states of the Union) judgments without the need to relitigate the entire cause of the case. However, it's important to note that the desire of the framers of this Constitution was to unify the states in the United States and at the same time preserve the autonomy of the states and allow them the freedom to govern themselves. The clause guaranteed that judgments rendered by the courts of one state wouldn't be ignored by the courts of another state.

The Supreme Courts use the Full Faith and Credit Clause to police states, proceeding in the following matters:

1. To determine when a state can take jurisdiction over claims that arise in other states
2. To limit application of one state law over another state law in multistate disputes
3. To enforce judgments rendered in sister-state courts

How does this clause affect same-sex marriage from state to state? The Full Faith and Credit Clause is used to enforce judgment and recognize the validity of a marriage. For example, a judgment rendered by a court in one state (marriage license issued to gay or lesbian couple) requires that this judgment (the issuing of a marriage license) receive the same credence and legitimacy or merit in other states. The Supreme Court makes it difficult for any lower court to categorically refuse to hear claims from another state's legal system, especially when like laws on the claims or issues exist in that state's legal system. And the Supreme Court has restricted lower courts from being in control of their own state laws on multistate disputes.

From these two instances cited above, same-sex couples have gained a foothold with legal backing from state to state in these United States in their agenda to destroy *holy* matrimony or anything that represents the will of God, as it pertains to the home and family. This is a victory for the gay or lesbian agenda and/or plight. But the ultimate question is, Is this a victory in Jesus? If not, it's not eternal. It's yet another example of gaining the world and losing your soul. "If in this life only we have hope in Christ, we are of all men most miserable" 1 Corinthians 15:19.

"In 1993, the Hawaii Supreme Court held that Hawaii's statute restricting legal marriage to parties of the opposite sex establishes a sex-based classification, which is subject to Strict Scrutiny if challenged on Equal Protection grounds (Baehr v. Lewin, 852 P.2d 44, 74 Haw. 530). Although the court did not recognize a constitutional right to same-sex marriage, it raised the possibility that a successful equal protection challenge to the state's marriage laws could eventually lead to state-sanctioned same-sex marriage. In response to the Baehr case, Congress in 1996 passed the Defense of Marriage Act (110 Stat. § 2419), which defines marriage as a union of a man and woman for federal purposes and expressly grants states the right to refuse to recognize a same-sex marriage performed in another state." [130]

> —Hamilton, Heather, 1988. "The Defense of Marriage Act: A Critical Analysis of Its Constitutionality Under the Full Faith and Credit Clause." DePaul Law Review 47 (summer). Hasegawa, Kaleen S. 1999. "Re-Evaluating the Limits of the Full Faith and Credit Claus." University of Hawaii Law Review 21 (winter).[131]

Is It about the Money (Economics) or about Destroying Bible-Based Traditional Marriage?

Some argue that banning same-sex marriage and denying same-sex married couples who have identical benefits or federally recognized benefits as those granted to heterosexual couples are at the heart of the same-sex controversy and are unconstitutional. In other words, it's just the economics they are fighting to gain. Another argument is that the federal government's definition of *spouse*, a man or woman for an opposite-sex union, is the only recognition of marriage. In other words, destroying the concept of traditional marriage and family based on biblical principles is the underlying fight. With this

---

[130] https://en.wikipedia.org/wiki/Baehr_v._Miike

[131] Heather Hamilton, *The Defense of Marriage Act: A Critical Analysis of Its Constitutionality under the Full Faith and Credit Clause*, 47 DePaul L. Rev. 943 (1998) Available at: https://via.library.depaul.edu/law-review/vol47/iss4/5

definition and my search of federal laws related to marriage and spouse and family or children benefits, I pulled up over 12,272 links to codes, statutes, and laws between these two sites—http://uscode.house.gov and http://www.gpo.gov—on marriage, spouse, and family benefits.

The federal benefits granted to heterosexual couples, which gay couples now covet *in their arrangements*, where they are incapable of giving back to society or continuing the existence of government—any form of government—manned by another human being, demand such things as social security benefits for the surviving spouse, income tax deductions, survivor benefits for military service, bankruptcy codes, and so forth. The gay or lesbian rights activists are challenging the *constitutionality* of the 1996 federal law definition of marriage, which is part of the DOMA.

What is under consideration for the courts—not God? He had His say on the matter already. Now man (the creature) will consider in his or her courts the matter over which God had the say from the beginning of the world. Simply put, what man will debate and make a decision about are the following:

1. Will the gay or lesbian unions (marriages) be unfairly represented by federal laws?
2. Or will they be discriminated against if they are denied or deprived of the rights to enjoy the same privileges and equal protection under the federal marriage laws guaranteed to the *holy* matrimony—God-sanctioned unions?

They want to destroy what God-fearing couples have—it represents God. "Husbands, love your wives, even as Christ also loved the church and gave Himself for it … So ought men to love their wives as their own bodies. He who loves his wife loves himself. For no man ever yet hated his own flesh; but nourishes and cherishes it, even as the Lord the church" (Ephesians 5:25, 28–29). The gay agenda aims at picking the traditional marriage, Bible-based union apart. They want to dismantle what God put together: déjà vu. Satan told Adam and Eve they would be like God, and they got kicked out of Eden. Satan wanted to be like God and got kicked out of heaven. We want to be like God and will get kicked off this continent—North America. People dreaming of coming to America could possibly see a place that is no longer habitable, and the USA kicked out of this garden of the land of opportunity.

Windsor v. United States

The situation with *United States v. Windsor* is about two women, Edith Schlain Windsor and Thea Clara Spyer. Their same-sex union under the definition of *spouse* was made invalid by US code in the federal law.

When Satan (the devil) got kicked out of heaven, God's presence, he went after man, seeking to destroy him and hurt God. When gay unions were denied coveted federal benefits and recognition as legitimate marriages, gays set out to destroy the whole concept of the traditional, holy matrimony institute of God and all its core values: husband, wife, and children—the building block of a family and society and the continuation of civilization. These were the first words God said to Adam and Eve: "Be fruitful and multiply." The gays in defiance cannot multiply in same-sex unions, but they will use your children to push their agenda on unsuspecting man.

The gay community and activists challenged DOMA because it would not accept states' definitions of marriage or it allowed states to refuse to recognize same-sex marriage granted by laws of other states. They pretty much believe this will lead to stigmatizing gay or lesbian (same-sex) unions and place them in a separate status; then the authority of the Supreme Courts won't recognize such a status as a legal union. The position is held by DOMA. Another concern for the gay community is that DOMA, by not recognizing their unions, will create two contradictory marriage regimes within the same state. This will defeat enjoying benefits granted to traditional unions if only the states recognize the unions and not the federal laws, which support the union only between a male and female.

What gays don't get is that when they are in opposition to God, they create the contradiction by their own hands. The gay community seeks *equal dignity*; in other words, they want what's *unnatural* (with origins outside God's command for His creature, man) to equate to the dignity God bestows on holy matrimony. There shouldn't be bestiality or male-with-male or female-with-female sex to be accepted as equal to the God-sanctioned union of male and female, which is respected as divine in nature.

Alito wrote, "The family is an ancient and universal human institution. Family structure reflects the characteristics of a civilization, and changes in family structure and in the popular understanding of marriage and the family can have profound effects."[132]

---

[132] 570 U.S. at _____(2013); *Obergefell*, 135 S. Ct. 2584,2642 (2015)

What Is the Meaning of Situation Ethics?

Luke 9:54–56 says, "And when his disciples James and John saw this, they said, Lord, wilt thou that we command fire to come down from heaven, and consume them, even as Elias did?" Christians shouldn't go around cursing and condemning sinners to hell. A Christian's duty is to share the gospel in love, hoping to save someone's soul from eternal damnation. In Luke 9:56, Jesus told James and John, "For the Son of man is not come to destroy men's lives, but to save them." The scriptures instruct Christians to teach in love. No true Christian will condemn, harass, prosecute, or gay bash, perhaps remembering that "such were some of you." Knowing what Jesus was and is about, Christians will share the gospel. And that is as far as they have been commanded to go—along with being an example in words, deeds, and thoughts. So with that thought in mind, being dogmatic in correcting someone isn't the solution. Yet at the same time, sugarcoating a situation to make the offended party not feel bad and accepting the individual in his or her undone condition isn't the solution either. No liar will enter heaven; that will be the little liar, big liar, black liar, white liar, and any and all other kind of liars.

📖 Book Corner Excerpt (copied by permission from Getwellchurchofchrist.org)

The Spiritual Sword, Theme: A Handy Guide to Biblical Morality-July 2010
What Is the Meaning of Situation Ethics? by Winford Claiborne[133]

Is it wrong to lie? It all depends. "If a lie is told unlovingly it is wrong, evil; if it is told in love it is good, right?" "The situationist holds that whatever is the most loving thing in the situation is the right and good thing" (Fletcher, 65). "Is it wrong to commit adultery? It all depends. "But if people do not believe it is wrong to have sex outside marriage, it isn't unless they hurt themselves, their partners, or others" (Fletcher, 140). "For the situationist there are no rules—none at all" (Fletcher, 55). "Could the one rule be that there are no rules?"

In February 1971 San Diego State College's Cultural Arts Board

---

[133] Winford Claiborne, "What Is the Meaning of Situation Ethics?", *The Spiritual Sword ed., Highers, Alan E.*41 (July 2010), no. 4; 11–17.

sponsored a debate on situation ethics. Joseph Fletcher, the leading proponent of situation ethics in the United States, and John Warwick Montgomery, an internationally known scholar from the Lutheran Church-Missouri Synod, were the disputants. Fletcher asserted: "I think there are no normative moral principles whatsoever which are intrinsically valid or universally obliging . ... Whether we ought to follow a moral principle or not would, I contend, always depend on the situation." Fletcher readily admits that his view involves "ethical relativity" (Fletcher and Montgomery, 15). Montgomery responded: "The insurmountable difficulty is simply this: there is no way, short of sodium pentothal, of knowing when the situationist is actually endeavoring to set forth genuine facts and true opinions, and when he is lying like a trooper" (Fletcher and Montgomery, 31). Even though Fletcher was an Episcopal priest (and later medical ethicist at the University of Virginia Medical School), he did not accept Jesus Christ as the standard for Christian conduct. "Jesus was a simple Jewish peasant. He had no more philosophical sophistication than a guinea pig, and I don't turn to Jesus for philosophical sophistication"(Fletcher and Montgomery, 55). Fletcher argued that Jesus "was in rebellion against the Torah" (Fletcher and Montgomery, 59). Montgomery replied: "He is not against the Torah. . . . Jesus is trying to peel away the traditions of the Jews that obscured the original teaching given to them" (Fletcher and Montgomery, 60-61).

Humanist Ethical Views

Humanist Manifesto I was published in 1933. Its chief architects were Paul Kurtz and John Dewey. Humanist Manifesto II was published in 1973. The combined publication was endorsed by leading philosophers, scientists, and theologians, such as, Francis Crick, co-discoverer of the double helix in DNA; Antony Flew, one of England's most aggressive atheists; Lester Mondale, former vice president Walter Mondale's older brother; B.F. Skinner, a behaviorist psychologist from Harvard; Joseph Fletcher; Betty Friedan, a radical feminist; and others. The humanist's Bible—Humanist Manifestos I and II—outlines the ethical views of secular humanists. "Without countenancing mindless permissiveness and unbridled promiscuity, a civilized society should be a tolerant one. Short of harming others or compelling them to do likewise, individuals should be permitted to express their sexual proclivities and pursue their lifestyles as they desire" (*Humanist Manifestos I and II, 18*).

"Situational" means that nothing is wrong or right
within itself. It all depends on the situation.

Humanist cannot avoid—nor can anyone else—employing words like "should," "ought" and "must"—words that logically imply a standard. In this excerpt from the *Humanist Manifestos I and II*, the authors use the word "should" two times. How do the humanists decide what it means to be tolerant? What standard do humanists use to determine what it means to harm others? Russell Vannoy is a secular humanist. His book, *Sex without Love*, applies the radical views of situation ethicists to human sexual behavior. "Terms like *unnatural, abnormal,* and sick are merely expressions of society's distaste for certain sexual preferences, and do not refer to anything objectively present in the desire itself" (Vannoy, 43). Vannoy insists: "In an unselfish society, everyone should be sexually available to everyone else, so that no one—men or women—would be sexually unfulfilled" (Vannoy, 54). If Vannoy were correct, there would be no logical way situationists could condemn anyone's sexual conduct.

Humanists believe that "moral values derive their source from human experience. Ethics is autonomous and situational" (*Humanist Manifestos I and II, 17*). Whose experience should serve as the norm for our behavior? Should it be the experience of the Marquis de Sade, Pol Pot, Adolf Hitler, or Mao tse Tung? The word "autonomous" means self-rule or self-law. The book of Judges describes conditions during one of the darkest periods in the history of the Israelite people. "In those days there was no king in Israel, but every man did that which was right in his own eyes" (Jdgs. 17:6). That attitude almost destroyed the nation of Israel. "Situational" means that nothing is wrong or right within itself. It all depends on the situation.

Do situation ethicists deny the sacredness of all human life? Is human life valuable to them only in some situations and not in others? Humanists demand the "recognition of an individual's right to die with dignity, euthanasia, and the right to suicide" (*Humanist Manifestos I and II, 19*). Could all of these so-called "rights" become a reality if we ration healthcare for severely handicapped babies and nonproductive old people? The State of Oregon has already legalized physician-assisted suicide

Some situation ethicists recognize the difficulty, if not the impossibility, of discovering or inventing a solid foundation for ethics. Will Durant, the distinguished American historian of philosophy and an atheist, believes that humanists "will find it no easy task to mold a natural ethic strong enough to maintain moral restraint and social order without the support of supernatural consolations, hopes and fears" (Storer, 8). Alastair Hannay,

Professor of Philosophy at the University of Trondheim, Norway, affirms: "Humanists naturally want to believe that we have more obligations, duties, in some virtually legalistic sense but not the product of arbitrary legislation, to one another. But on what can the belief be based? The divine legislator and guarantor of human value has gone by the board, but the human legislator does not have the credentials" (Storer, 187).

Theological Situationism

Wesley Baker served for a number of years on the faculty of San Francisco Theological Seminary and the "pastor" of Frist Presbyterian Church in Rafael, California. He enthusiastically endorses "the new morality"—situationism. He says "there is a historic suspicion that Jesus saw society as morally open-ended" (Baker, 16). Is that the same Jesus who said: "But out of the heart proceed evil thoughts, murders, adulteries, fornications, thefts, false witness, blasphemies: these are the things that defile the man; but to eat with unwashen hands does not defile the man" (Mt. 15:19-20)?

Baker denies there is any such thing "as a morally defensible position" (Baker, 29). Does that include the positions he defends in his irrational book? He says he agrees with Joseph Fletcher "that love and justice are the same, always." He then dogmatically states: "There are not absolutes, no unbreakable ground rules, no qualifying principles" (Baker, 59). Does he believe he is absolutely right? He asks: "Is it ever right to be involved in extramarital sexual intercourse? Should a person lie to protect job or family? Is moral compromise ever justifiable?" His equivocal answer: "Quite possibly" (Baker, 60). He accuses the people in various religious groups of having" missed seeing the crux of the Sermon on the Mount" (Baker, 170). If he thinks "there is a historical suspicion that Jesus saw society as morally open-ended" he is the one who has missed "the crux of the Sermon on the Mount."

Ethical Relativism

James Q. Wilson is James Collins Professor of Management and Public Policy at UCLA and one of the most respected criminologists in the United States. Wilson says some parents "have persuaded themselves that children will be harmed if they are told right from wrong." If we do not teach our children to distinguish between right and wrong, it will lead to barbarism. "People who have persuaded themselves to embrace non-moral standards should not be surprised if young people who have heard these ideas grow up taking drugs, cheating on tests, and shooting their enemies" (Wilson, ix-x). Relativism permeates many classrooms in colleges and universities in the United States. "When asked why people should be tolerant, act fairly, or respect liberty, many students will look at me as if I were merely engaging in professional cleverness, while a few will attempt to construct intellectual defenses of these notions, defenses typically based on utility: for example, society is better off if everybody behaves that way" (Wilson, 7). Wilson discovered that many of the young people in his classes could not consistently show why the people who perpetrated the Holocaust "were guilty of a moral horror" (Wilson, 8).

Francis Beckwith and Gregory Koukl provided a powerful argument that "moral relativism . . . is the unofficial creed of American culture, especially in education, law, and public policy" (Beckwith and Koukl, 13). These authors quote one graduate who delivered a Harvard commencement address: "The freedom of our day is the freedom to devote ourselves to any values we please, on the mere condition that we do not believe them to be true" (Beckwith and Koukl, 20). Beckwith tells of some questions he asked an assistant in a physician's office. "Do you believe that morality is absolute, or do all people decide for themselves?" She replied, "What do you mean by morality?" He then asked: "Is murder wrong? Is it wrong to take an innocent person's life?" She waffled, "Well . . ." Beckwith asked, "Well . . .. what?" She finally responded, "Well, I'm thinking." Beckwith further asked, "Can we say that taking innocent human life is acceptable?" She answered, "I guess it depends." "Depends on what?" "It depends on what other people thin or decide" (Beckwith and Koukl, 34).

Fletcher's Indebtedness to Others

The expression "situation ethics" is almost synonymous with the name Joseph Fletcher. But Fletcher was indebted to many predecessors for his ethical views. John Jefferson Davis, Professor of Theology at Gordon-Conwell Seminary, traces Fletcher's beliefs to Emil Brunner's *The Divine Imperative*. Brunner's observations sound very much like those of Fletcher. "We are united by the Command of love, which excludes legalistic rules and every attempt to stereotype human relationships" (Davis, 13). David Lipe lists a number of other to whom Fletcher was almost certainly indebted: Karl Barth, Dietrich Bonhoeffer, John A. T. Robinson, and Rudolph Bultmann (Lipe, 177).

The Bible and Situation Ethics

Those who accept the Bible as the word of God understand the place of love in the scheme of human redemption. Our motivation for serving God and our fellowmen is love" "Let all that you do be done in love" (I Cor. 16:15). "In this the children of God are manifest and the children of the devil: whosoever does not righteousness is not of God, neither he who does not love his brother" (I Jn. 3:10). Fletcher has argued that the only absolute is love. But he does not provide any content to love. "In situation ethics even the most revered principles may be thrown aside if they conflict with love." He says Karl Barth strongly believed in absolute wrong but allows that love in a particular situation might override the absolute. "The instant he gives is abortion" (Fletcher, 33). The greatest blunder of situation ethicists is ignoring or discounting the authority of Jesus Christ and of his apostles.

Conclusion

If Joseph Fletcher and other situation ethicists were right, there would be no possibility of knowing what to do in any given situation. There would be no principles to guide either young or old people in making decisions about their relationships to others. Has situationism led to the deaths of 45,000,000 babies in their mothers' wombs, the enormous increase in crime in many of our communities, the confusion about sexual identify, and other destructive elements in our nation?

References

Baker, Wesley C. (1968), *The Open End of Christian Morals* (Philadelphia, PA: The Westminster Press).

Beckwith, Francis J., and Gregory Koukl (1998), *Relativism: Feet Firmly Planted in Mid-Air* (Grand Rapids, MI: Baker Books).

Davis, John Jefferson (1985), *Evangelical Ethics: Issues Facing the Church Today* (Philadelphia, PA: Presbyterian and Reformed Publishing Company).

Fletcher, Joseph (1966), *Situation Ethics: The New Morality* (Philadelphia, PA: The Westminster Press).

Fletcher, Joseph, and John Warwick Montgomery (1972), *Situation Ethics* (Minneapolis, MN: Bethany Fellowship).

Humanist Ethics (1980), Edited Morris B. Storer (Buffalo, NY: Prometheus Books).

Humanist Manifesto I and II (1973), Edited Paul Kurtz (Buffalo, NY: Prometheus Books).

Lipe, David (1986), "Situation Ethics" in *Ethics for Daily Living*, Edited Winford Claiborne (Henderson, TN: Freed-Hardeman University).

Vannoy, Russell (1980), *Sex without Love: A Philosophical Exploration* (Buffalo, NY: Prometheus Books).

Wilson, James Q. (1993). *The Moral Sense* (New York, NY: The Free Press).

Winford Claiborne is speaker on the International Gospel Hour, sponsored by the West Fayettevill (TN) Church of Christ.

Acceptance of Gay Marriage Debate

This is from an article published on November 5, 1989, in the *New York Times*, written by Philip S. Gutis. When this article in IDEAS & TRENDS: *Small Steps Toward Acceptance Renew Debate on Gay Marriage* (*NYT* section 4, page 24) was written, twenty-five states still had sodomy laws, though they were seldom enforced, and no state permitted same-sex marriages. But the issue was rekindled by moves in San Francisco, Seattle, New York, and several other cities toward laws that give fringe benefits to the unmarried partners of city employees. In this article, Thomas F. Coleman, the codirector of the Family Diversity Project in Los Angeles, argues that[gays] aren't seeking to redefine the idea of marriage or spouse. The article stated that in 1987 the bishop of the Newark Diocese of the Episcopal Church in New Jersey urged that the national episcopal organization support the blessing of the couples of the same sex. The bishop wanted to offer his Kool-Aid and go all Jim Jones (religious leader, Jonestown Massacre) or David Koresh (religious leader, Waco, TX) on people who accept the Bible on the words of a preacher without actually opening, studying, and reading it for themselves. "And they took him and brought him to Areopagus, saying, May we know that this new doctrine, whereof you speak, is? For you bring certain strange things to our ears: we would know therefore what these things mean" (Acts 17:19–20). The apostle Paul spoke of the Bereans as being more noble than those he had met in Thessalonica because they received the word (not some bishop or pope misquoting or not quoting the scriptures) and searched the scriptures daily to see whether what he said was in the scriptures (Acts 17:11). The Reverend Robert Williams, executive director of the Oasis, will perform the ceremonies. He said he would like to see the church's canon changed to allow same-sex marriage. "If we learned anything from the 60's," he said, "separate but equal is unequal."[134]

What should have been learned from the sixties is that black people didn't break any laws of God, and they fought, bled, and died to be treated like human beings. To equate the black man's struggles in these United States with the homosexual plight is an insult to decency and all that is pure, good, and holy.

Does God Condone Situation Ethics?

The situation with *United States vs. Winsor* is about two women, Edith Schlain Windsor and Thea Clara Spyer. Their same-sex union under the definition of *spouse* was made invalid by US code in the federal law. *A strong argument for the gay community is that section 3 of DOMA or the definitional provision does forbid states from permitting same-sex marriage or from providing state benefits to gay or lesbians' civil unions and domestic partners.*

This situation brings to my memory the following scripture: "For what shall it profit a man, if he gained the whole world, and lose his own soul?" (Mark 8:36). What did Windsor win—money? Suze Orman, a renowned financial guru, and the gay or lesbian community may see it as a victory. But when it is time for God to call and Windsor to answer, will she find victory in Christ Jesus? "But thanks be to God which give us the victory through our Lord Jesus Christ" (1 Corinthians 15:57).

In 2 Samuel 6, Uzzah had good intentions when he reached out to help keep the ark of God sturdy while going over rough terrain. Unfortunately, it cost him his life; only specified individuals of the Levite tribe were instructed to handle (touch or approach) the ark. See Numbers 3–4. Jews were knowledgeable of this fact as well as individuals today of the New Testament scriptures prohibiting one from being effeminate. Yet we tempt God with our personal, political, and popular views of rights, wrongs, morals, and worship. Worship is about following God's instructions on how He

---

[134] Philip S. Gutis. *"Small Steps Toward Acceptance Renew Debate on Gay Marriage ."* The New York Times Nov. 5, 1989. https://www.nytimes.com/1989/11/05/weekinreview/ideas-trends-small-steps-toward-acceptance-renew-debate-on-gay-marriage.html

should be worshipped. Our thoughts and ways about worship aren't God approved and will bring the same result, spiritual death or separation, where God says to us that we cannot come.

Nowhere in scripture does God compromise right for wrong. Even our versions of what is "good," those that aren't God approved, are evil in His sight. Remember the conversation Jesus had with the apostle Peter. "Get behind me, Satan." And because God is the only true and "just" judge, it is His favor we should seek in conduct for our lives. It is in His court where we have our final ruling on the Judgment Day. God expelled Satan out of heaven.

We bargain with Satan when we compromise our children (God's inheritance or fruit of the womb) to live in situations God condemns as abominable in His sight. Satan has deceived us into thinking any home is better than no home, so we compromise and bargain with Satan regarding our children. Perhaps Uzzah felt any help in keeping the ark from falling was better than no help at all—only to realize it wasn't his call to make. See 1 Chronicles 13:1–14. Uzzah ended up on the wrong side of history with his version of what was the right thing to do, because that right or helpful thing wasn't God approved.

In his dissent, was it Justice Alito's attempt to declare that the unholy union of homosexuals in marriage wasn't the Supreme Court's call to make?

📖 Book Corner Excerpt (copied by permission from Defender: http://www.bellviewcoc.com

The following document was written by Michael Hatcher, editor of *Defender* (2008 lectureship article republished in the February 2019 *Defender*[135]).

The Effects of Liberalism and Humanism on the Home

Introduction

The home is the foundation of society. The very fabric of an orderly, meaningful society is woven within the home and marriage unit. President James A. Garfield stated, "the

---

[135] Michael Hatcher, ed., "The Effects of Liberalism and Humanism on the Home," *Defender* 48, no. 2 (February 2019). http://www.bellviewcoc.com/defender.html

sanctity of marriage and the family relation makes the cornerstone of our American society and civilization." The reason is that society is made up of people, and people are built in homes. When the home is threatened or destroyed, then people will not be built as God wants them with the result that society as a whole will suffer.

Our nation is in trouble. This is evidenced by the rising crime rate. People are literally afraid of leaving their homes for fear of being accosted, beaten, robbed, raped, killed, etc. Often there is no reason for this except they were walking on someone's *turf*. Daily we read of drive-by murders (someone out to avenge themselves of some supposed wrong and killing anyone around). Then there is another type of murder that has become legalized in our nation—abortion. Some viciously rip, tear, and destroy humans who cannot defend themselves and should be protected because they are in a place that should be safe—the womb—but is now one of the most dangerous places in the world, and others love and insist to have it so. The homosexual community has continued to make inroads into America. They have convinced many Americans that this wicked perversion is simply an alternate lifestyle into which they were born. They continue to cry for their rights (see Rom. 1:26–27, 31–32) and have become one of the most influential groups in our nation. This list of evils within our nation could go on and on (drunkenness, fornication and adultery, witchcraft, hatred, disrespect for authority and those in authority, materialism, etc.)

Just about everything begins in the home including respect for authority and lawlessness. As the saying goes, "As the twig is bent, so grows the tree." The Bible recognizes this principle in the commands of parents and specifically fathers to train up their children in the "nurture and admonition of the Lord" (Eph. 6:4). When one is disobedient to the parents it will lead to all types of evil within the individual. "Backbiters, haters of God, despiteful, proud, boasters, inventors of evil things, disobedient to parents" (Rom. 1:30). "For men shall be lovers of their own selves, covetous, boasters, proud, blasphemers, disobedient to parents, unthankful, unholy" (2 Tim. 3:2). When children are not brought up with the proper teaching, then what the wise man wrote is true: *"There is* a generation *that* curseth their father, and doth not bless their mother"* (Pro. 30:11). That truly is the situation in America today.

The home is under attack today in America. Brother Winford Claiborne correctly observed: Attacks against the home are so numerous and so vicious that it appears a conspiracy to destroy the home exist in our society. Some of those attacks against the home are theological; others are social, political and academic. Secular humanism has had a detrimental impact on every one of those attacks against the home. It has provided the inspiration for sociologists, psychologists, anthropologists, media personnel, liberal politicians and theologians (86–87).

Nations cannot long exist when they leave God. "Righteousness exalteth a nation: but sin *is* a reproach to any people" (Pro. 14:34). While God is long-suffering to people and nations, there comes a time when that patience comes to an end and God chastises that nation (Heb. 12:5–11).

At what instant I shall speak concerning a nation, and concerning a kingdom, to pluck up, and to pull down, and to destroy *it*; If that nation, against whom I have pronounced, turn from their evil, I will repent of the evil that I thought to do unto them. And *at what* instant I shall speak concerning a nation, and concerning a kingdom, to build and to plant *it*; If it do evil in my sight, that it obey not my voice, then I will repent of the good, wherewith I said I would benefit them (Jer. 18:7-10). We begin wondering how long God will put up with this nation that has turned against God. Since it begins in the home and the home is under attack, it is profitable for us to consider and study how these things (humanism and liberalism) affects the home.

Humanism

Sadly, many do not know and understand *Humanism.* Many will confuse Humanism with Humanitarianism. We should all be humanitarian—that is, we should do good to others, show compassion, be kind, and merciful. Humanism is not humanitarianism. The effects of Humanism will destroy the humanitarian attitude in people. If Humanism is not Humanitarianism, what is it?

Humanism is best defined by the two manifestos written by the Humanists to explain their doctrine. The first was written in 1933 and the second (a revision and update) in 1973. Let us consider some of the doctrines found within the two manifestos. The first and beginning point of both documents is the denial of the existence of God. Denying God's existence, they then deny the divinity of Jesus Christ, the inspiration of the Bible, the existence of the soul and thus life after death with heaven and hell. Notice some quotes from the Manifestos.

We find insufficient evidence for belief in the existence of a supernatural. As nontheists, we begin with humans, not God, nature not deity.

As in 1933, humanists still believe that traditional theism, especially faith in the prayer-hearing God, assumed to love and care for persons, to hear and understand their prayers, and to be able to do something about them, is an unproven and outmoded faith. Salvationism, based on mere affirmation, still appears as harmful, diverting people with false hopes of heaven hereafter. Reasonable minds look to other means for survival.

Modern science discredits such historic concepts as the "ghost in the machine" and the "separable soul." They not only disbelieve in an afterlife, they think it is damaging: Promises of immortal salvation or fear of eternal damnation are both illusory and harmful. With the elimination of God, there is also the elimination of a purpose or value of life.

But we can discover no divine purpose or providence for the human species. While there is much that we do not know, humans are responsible for what we are or will become. No deity will save us; we must save ourselves.

The Humanist Manifesto 2 recognized this problem in the Preface referring to events since the first:

> Events since then make the earlier statements seem far too optimistic. Nazism has shown the depths of brutality

of which humanity is capable. Other totalitarian regimes have suppressed human rights without ending poverty. Science has sometimes brought evil as well as good. ... In the choice between despair and home, humanist respond in this *Humanist Manifesto ll* with a positive declaration for times of uncertainty.

Since God does not exist, to the Humanist, there can be no absolutes, no right and no wrong. Morals are self-determined and situational (do your own thing as long as it does not harm anyone else). With this view they desire the removal of any distinctive roles between males and females. If there are no absolutes, then there can be no limits regarding sexual freedom between consenting individuals (regardless of age). They, therefore, advocate premarital sex, homo sexuality and lesbianism, and incest.

They also demand the right to abortion, because there is no respect of life and for those who grow old and a "burden on society" they affirm the need for euthanasia (mercy killing) and suicide.

In the area of sexuality, we believe that intolerant attitudes, often cultivated by orthodox religions and puritanical cultures, unduly repress sexual conduct. The right to birth control, abortion, and divorce should be recognized. While we do not approve of exploitative, denigrating forms of sexual expression, neither do we wish to prohibit, by law or social sanction, sexual behavior between consenting adults. The many varieties of sexual exploration should not in themselves be considered "evil." Without countenancing mindless permissiveness or unbridled promiscuity, a civilized society should be a *tolerant* one. Short of harming others or compelling them to do likewise, individuals should be permitted to express their sexual proclivities and pursue their lifestyles as they desire.

The reason they view sexual expression in such a way is because they have rejected God's standard of morals. We affirm that moral values derive their source from human experience. Ethics is autonomous and situational, needing no theological or ideological sanction. Ethics stem from human need and interest. To deny this distorts the whole basis of life.

If this is true, then we are faced with some moral questions with the main question being: How can any act be considered wrong? If one discusses murder, euthanasia (mercy killing, or murdering the aged and infirmed), abortion (murdering babies in the womb), infanticide (murdering newborn babies), upon what basis would one consider any of these actions wrong. In the sexual realm there could not be anything wrong with incest, bestiality, or rape (while many would not place this within the subject no one can deny that there is a sexual aspect of rape). Discrimination of any form whether sexual, racial, social, or any other type, could not be considered wrong or evil.

If morals are from human experience, as Humanists claim, then whose human experience should we go by? Should we live according to the human experience of Hitler, Mussolini, or a Stalin or Khrushchev, or a Ted Bundy or some other mass murderer? They also say that morals are situational and autonomous, however this is a contradiction. Morals cannot be both situational and at the same time be autonomous. *Autonomous* means self-law; thus, one does what he feels is best—he is a law unto himself. In this case every man is his own law, and no one can impose their law on anyone else. If you believe it is wrong to rape and murder but I want to do it, you cannot say it is wrong, and I am under obligation to rape and murder.

If, however, morals are situational, then nothing is right or wrong on its own basis, it all depends on the situation. If the situation is of such a nature that rape and murder appears to be best, then I am under obligation to perform this action.

Liberalism

Modernistic and liberal theology is basically and essentially Humanist. One of the more renown liberals or modernists of our day is John Shelby Spong. Spong was the bishop of the Newark, New Jersey, Diocese of the Episcopal Church (now retired). Spong is a good illustration of what liberal theology is doing to the home and to morals in our nation. He wrote a book titled *Living In Sin?* in which he sets forth his views (and the views of those who are modernists and liberals). In noticing what Mister Spong advocates, we begin seeing a parallel between the modernist (liberal) and the Humanist. While the Humanist rejects the idea of God (they are non-theist), Spong does believe that God exists. Though he believes God is, he rejects the Bible as the inerrent, infallible, verbally inspired Word of God.

A word of caution is in order here concerning the use of semantics in dealing with the Modernists and liberals. They will often speak of the same things we speak of and use the same terms we use. However, they do not mean what we mean by the terms. They will speak of the inspiration of the Bible, but they do not mean what we mean. They do not believe the Bible is verbally (word by word) inspired of God. What they might mean is that the Bible is inspired just like any good writing was inspired, or they mean that the overall teachings of the Bible are inspired but not the actual words and details. The writers wrote out of their own knowledge, feelings, and background. They will, thus, speak of the Bible's mistakes and contradictions.

For example, they will speak of the resurrection of Christ, but they do not believe that the body of Jesus that was laid in the tomb was physically and actually raised from the dead. When they speak of the resurrection of Christ, they might mean that His ideas and teachings were brought back to people's thinking or were being taught again. Spong, like all Modernists and Liberals, affirms that the Bible is full of contradictions, anachronisms, and prejudices.

If the Bible is simply written from the writers own thinking, feelings, and background, then we cannot state that what is found in the Bible concerning morals and ethics can be applied to our lifestyles. Thus, Spong ridicules those who obtain their sexual norms from Scripture. Spong affirms that marriage is not the only relationship where the sexual privileges may be enjoyed, there is nothing wrong with premarital or extramarital sexual relations. He states that churches must have an encouraging word to those who are unmarried, divorced, and the post-married whether through death or desertion and any sexual relations they might want to engage in. He believes that those churches who condemn such actions are going to die out because they cannot relate to people of our society. Regarding homosexuality, Spong believes that churches cannot expect them to change in anyway. We must accept them for what they are and that they are simply living an alternate lifestyle. He wants churches to embrace practicing homosexuals and even develop some ritualistic ceremony for homosexual unions. He states that our society has produced prejudice toward homosexuality and those committing such and it is the churches responsibility to bring about change in society to learn to accept such and recognize the positive good of such a lifestyle in some people's lives. He affirms the same thing concerning women and divorce. Ethically speaking there is no difference between John Shelby Spong and a Humanist, and he would probably agree completely with the Humanist on every point except the existence of God.

Some might ask at this point: Why talk about Spong? He is not of us, he is a part of a liberal denomination, why use him. The main reason is that the only difference between Spong and some of our liberal brethren like Rubel Shelly, Marvin Philips, Jim Woodroof, Steve Flatt, Andre Resner, Max Lucado, Joe Beam, Buddy Bell, Jeff Walling, Mike Cope, Terry Rush, and a host of others is simply a matter of degree. The underlying principle is the same: a rejection of the Bible as the infallible, inerrant, plenary (in its totality) verbally (word by word) inspired Word of God, which is also the basis for what Spong believes and what Humanism affirms. A single example of this would be the article written by Andre Resner (a former Bible professor at Abilene Christian University) titled "Christmas at Matthew's House" and published in *Wineskins* edited by Rubel Shelly and Mike Cope. In this article Resner denies the virgin birth of Jesus by opining that Mary (the mother of Jesus) was another sexually questionable woman, the exact same view as held by Spong and the Humanist.

This principle is also the basis for every denomination in existence. They will deny some aspect of God's Word. Read 1 Peter 3:21 or the first part of Mark 16:16 and see if they believe it. There is no difference (at least in principle) in rejecting these verses (or other verses) and in rejecting the Bible's ethic—its laws concerning morals and the home. To see how this affects the home, consider the statement the Southern Baptists made recently that said the wife was to lovingly submit to the authority of her husband and the furor that resulted. Yet, this is what the Bible has always stated. "Wives, submit yourselves unto your own husbands, as unto the Lord" (Eph. 5:22). Yet, the majority of people and denominations today (including our liberal brethren) refuse to accept such clear plain statements of the Bible.

Effects on the Home

It should be obvious to all that both Humanism and Liberalism affect the home as God has instituted and arranged. For homes to prosper, they must be built on God and His Word. The Psalmist wrote, "Except the LORD build the house, they labour in vain that build it: except the LORD keep the city, the watchman waketh *but* in vain" (Psa. 127:1). God gave the principles of successful homes and marriages with His Word. He also gave principles that will lead to successful relationships between people (including husbands and wives). However, Humanism denies the existence of God and advances the idea that God's Word is detrimental to society and the home in particular. Thus, it will lead to unhappiness and unfulfilled homes.

The basic idea of Humanism is self. Self is god to the Humanist. (Eventually the same is true of Liberalism. They dethrone God for self and selfish desires.) However, for marriages to be successful, each mate needs to be putting the will and wishes of the other above self.

Marriage has never been a 50-50 proposition, it is a complete giving of self to satisfy one's marriage partner. It is none of self and all of mate. (We must understand that God comes first within our lives. Jesus said to "seek ye first the kingdom of God, and his righteousness" in Mat.

6:33. However, when we are seeking God first—living and abiding by His principles revealed within the pages of the New Testament—we will be doing what is here advocated.) When one in the marriage relationship is more concerned with self than with their mate, it will lead to disaster within the marriage.

Humanists are determined to destroy the home as God intended. They realize that to destroy religion and have everyone yield to the Humanist Philosophy, they must destroy the home. To accomplish their goal, they use sex and undermine sexual fidelity within the marriage relationship. They begin in the school systems to accomplish their goals. Consider what James Dobson wrote:

Secular humanists, particularly the more radical activists, have a specific objective in mind for the future. They hope to accomplish that goal primarily by isolating children from their parents ... It will then be relatively easy to "reorient" and indoctrinate the next generation of Americans. This strategy explains why their most bitter campaigns are being waged over school curricula and other issues that involve our kids. Children are the key to the future (Bauer and Dobson 35). Sister Rita Rhodes Ward adds: When the Christian mother leads her 6-year-old to the first grade room or her 5-year-old to kindergarten, she leads him from the sheltered environment of the home into the cold, pagan environment of secular humanism. From that day on, the child will be taught two contradictory religions (520).

Lest some think that this is simply overreacting consider what Humanist Charles Pierce said:

> Every child in America entering school at the age of five is mentally ill, because he comes to schools with certain allegiances toward our founding fathers, toward our elected officials, toward his parents, toward a belief in a supernatural Being, toward the sovereignty of this nation as a separate entity. It's up to you teachers to make all of these sick children well by

creating the international children of the future (Thompson 24).

One of the major means Humanists use in the school systems to accomplish their goals is sex education.

> Schools across the country are implementing liberal sex education courses into their curricula. They have tried to justify this by arguing that such courses will help reduce the dangers of teen pregnancy and AIDS. But these reasons only mask their true agenda. By opening the classrooms to frank discussions about sexuality, humanistic educators know they can subvert the values systems parents have tried to impress upon their children. Dobson lists three reasons that humanists have chosen child and adolescent sexuality as a battleground: (1) By teaching a different sexual ethic, they can drive a wedge between parents and children; (2) By undermining sexual fidelity on which marriage is based, the family can be destroyed; (3) By destroying religious values concerning sex, they can destroy children's faith (Beard 184).

Conclusion: We are in a war—not fought with guns and physical armaments, but a battle for the mind of man. This battle has eternal consequences. It also has consequences for the nation. If we lose, then our homes as God intended will be destroyed. In many respects we are losing this battle—many do not even know we are in this battle. What constitutes a family? It is variously defined today to include homosexuals, pedophiles, and any other type of perversion. The biblical standard of the family has almost disappeared because of the inroads of humanism and the loosing of liberalism. We must beware of these false standards and return to God's Word as our standard. What God has given us is for our good. "And the LORD commanded us to do all these statutes, to fear the LORD our God, **for our good always**, that he might preserve us alive, as *it is* at this day" (Deu. 6:24).

Works Cited:

Bauer, Gary L. and James Dobson. *Children at Risk: The Battle for the Hearts and Minds of our Kids.* Dallas, TX: Word, 1990.

Beard, Kevin. "Humanism." *Dangerous 'Isms.* ed. B. J. Clarke. Southaven, MS: Southaven Church of Christ, 1977.

Claiborn, Winford. "How Humanism Destroys The Home And The Family." *Embattled Christianity: A Call to Alarm the Church to Humanism.* ed. Terry M. Hightower. San Antonio, TX; Shenandoah Church of Christ, 1989.

Spong, John Shelby. *Living in Sin?* San Francisco, CA: Harper & Row, 1988.

Thompson, Bert. "Why are We Losing Our Children?" *Reason and Revelation.* 1993.

citing Chester Pierce, lecture presented at Denver Colorado seminar on childhood education, 1973, quoted in Johanna Michaelsen, *Like Lambs to the Slaughter.* Eugene OR: Harvest, 1989.

Ward, Rita Rhodes. "Educating Children in an Anti-Christian Environment." *Gospel Advocate.* 4 September, 1986.
MH

You Did Not Build It—Marriage

In Genesis 1 we read, "In the beginning God created the heaven and the earth." Earth isn't ours; we don't get a say-so in its beginning or ending. And God formed man and the woman, and He blessed the union to be fruitful and multiply, and replenish and subdue the earth.

Satan, the Father of Lies, will try to convince man that recognition of same-sex marriage will fortify a now-shaky institution. This source is referenced in 540 U.S. (2013).[136],[137]

Now, don't get this "thang" twisted either; these are men who believe man is more righteous and more knowledgeable than God. These are men who believe they can improve on what God personally created. He made male and female with instructions on how to behave in this union, leaving father and mother, and cleaving to each other. Notice in both writings that neither author mentions that God invited them to the table of discussion with God (Father, Son, and Holy Ghost) about their thoughts or what direction He (God) should take on this issue. If they did, it would be like they at least tried to make some validity to their opinion on this matter. They come across the scene (this very late date after creation) in time for a brief moment and try to convenience America that they have the better answers and solutions to man (people's) problems in marriage. Check with Mr. Rauch on his three hundredth birthday and see whether he still holds the same opinion. He has only a few days on this earth, and this is what he wants to come out of his mouth before he meets God, the Creator of marriage and the husband-wife union.

The scripture concludes that they have NO LOT IN THIS MATTER. "You have neither part nor lot in this matter: for your heart is not right in the sight of God" (Acts 8:21). They have a few days and like a vapor are gone tomorrow, but God is eternal.

> Whereas you know not what shall be on the morrow. For what is your life? It is even as a vapor, that appears for a little time, and then vanishes away. (James 4:14)
>
> For My thoughts are not your thoughts, neither are your ways My ways, says the Lord. For as the heavens are higher than the earth, so are My ways higher than your ways, and My thoughts than your thoughts. (Isaiah 55:8–9)

Where are we when we would rather hear man than God? Compared to God, man hasn't been around long enough to have an opinion about anything. He isn't capable of getting a heaven's view of the whole matter

---

[136] A. Sullivan, *Virtually Normal: An Argument About Homosexuality* (1996), 202–203.

[137] J. Rauch, *Gay Marriage: Why It is Good for Gays, Good for Straights, and Good for America* (2004), 94.

from the ground or earth. We are limited in our time, space, and view of things on earth.

Alito wrote, "At present, no one—including social scientists, philosophers, and historians—can predict with any certainty what the long-term ramifications of widespread acceptance of same-sex marriage will be."[138] *United States* v. *Windsor*, 570 U.S. ___, ___, 570 U.S. 744, 133 S. Ct. 2675, 186 L. Ed. 2d 808, 830 (2013) (Alito, J., dissenting).

I can give a prediction in four words: Sodom and Gomorrah again. And we all know the outcome—never more inhabited. Is America on its way back to ground zero like the predicament of Sodom and Gomorrah? If we fail to turn from our course, we will become a place where in the past many sought to come to America, only to see it as an uninhabitable place where no one dares to come or rebuild. Nothing has been built in Sodom and Gomorrah after the God-sent fire. Check with the historians, theologians, philosophers, and scientists.

Alito wrote, "While modern cultural changes have weakened the link between marriage and procreation in the popular mind, there is no doubt that throughout human history and across many cultures marriage has been viewed as an exclusively opposite-sex institution and as one inextricably linked to procreation and biological kinship."[139] (*United States v. Windsor*, 570 U.S. 744 (2013) (Alito, J., dissenting).

Try to wrap your mind around the ideology of why gays and lesbians feel that DOMA and federal laws on "marriage" and "spouse" are discriminatory. They argue gender differentiation isn't relevant because traditional marriage is about couples in committed relationships marked by emotional attachment and sexual attractions between two people. What I find interesting is that this definition or view of what constitutes a marriage isn't codified in the Constitution.

Alito wrote, "The Constitution does not codify either of these views of marriage (although I suspect it would have been hard at the time of the adoption of the Constitution or the Fifth Amendment to find Americans who did not take the traditional view for granted). The silence of the Constitution on this question should be enough to end the matter as far as the judiciary is concerned. Yet, Windsor and the United States implicitly ask us to endorse the consent-based view of marriage and to reject the traditional view, thereby arrogating to ourselves the power to decide a question that philosophers, historians, social scientists, and theologians are better qualified to explore.

---

138 Obergefell v. Hodges, 135 S.Ct. 2584, 2642 (2015)
139 570 U. S. ___, a defense, at 23–28. (2013)

Because our constitutional order assigns the resolution of questions of this nature to the people, would not presume to enshrine either version of marriage in our constitutional jurisprudence."[140] *Windsor*, 570 U.S., at ___, 133 S. Ct. 2675, 186 L. Ed. 2d at 852 (Alito, J., dissenting).

Alito continued in this language...although those in the legislative branch of government feel they have very little choice but to decide the constitutionality of what is equal and fair between the two views of marriage (two individuals coming together to form a union of commitment based on emotional attachment and sexual attraction in a *consent-based version* of marriage versus the *traditional-based version* of marriage of two individuals of the opposite sex forming a union of commitment from emotional attachment and sexual attraction), it has been the Supreme Court's opinion that the politics in branches of federal and state government should *not* be neutral in what they believe to be "competing versions of good." 570 U. S. ____ (2013) ALITO, J., dissenting.

The Supreme Court views marriage as a *good* thing, so traditional marriage is good, and any other form of marriage is good, except (for now) marriage between men and animals, which at this point in man's history on the earth would be considered disallowed by the Constitution. But for how long? For now, both Congress and the states feel they are entitled (not remaining neutral) to enact laws recognizing both heterosexual and homosexual unions as good. I can hear the words of Jesus to the rich young ruler ringing in my ears: "Call no man good." God is good. America, listen to a good and just God.

---

[140] 570 U.S. 744 (2013)

US Constitution

The US Constitution is the supreme law of the USA. It is to the governing of US citizens as the Bible is to the governing of Christians. Because of its founding fathers' religious beliefs, it reflects many biblical principles. The individuals who constructed and put their signatures to the Constitution, because of their Christian and religious principles, took the traditional or Bible-based view of marriage, and no other view was entertained. If there were some, they should have stepped up then. Consider the following:

Who Signed the US Constitution?	Which State Was Represented?	Name of Wife or Second Wife	How Many Were Procreated or Fathered?
William Samuel Johnson	Connecticut	Anne Beach and her cousin, Mary Brewster Beach	11
Roger Sherman	Connecticut	Elizabeth Hartwell or Rebecca Prescott	7+8=15
Richard Bassett	Delaware	Ann Ennals, second wife named Bruff	Several
Gunning Bedford Jr.	Delaware	Jane B. Parker	1
Jacob Broom	Delaware	Rachel Pierce	8
John Dickinson	Delaware	Mary Norris	1
Georgia Reed	Delaware	Gertrude Ross Till	5
Abraham Baldwin	Georgia	Never married	

William Few	Georgia	Catherine Nicholson	3
Daniel Carroll	Maryland	Eleanor Carroll	
Daniel of St. Thomas Jenifer	Maryland	Never Married	
James McHenry	Maryland	Margaret Allison Caldwell	3
Nathaniel Gorham	Massachusetts	Rebecca Call	9
Rufus King	Massachusetts	Mary Alsop	Several
Nicholas Gilman	New Hampshire	A bachelor when he signed US Constitution	
John Langdon	New Hampshire	Elizabeth Sherburne	1
David Brearly	New Jersey	Elizabeth Mullen or Elizabeth Higbee	
Jonathan Dayton	New Jersey	Sarah Williamson	2
William Livingston	New Jersey	Susanna French	13
William Paterson	New Jersey	Cornelia Bell or second wife, Euphemia White	3+0
Alexander Hamilton	New York	Elizabeth Schuyler	8
William Blount	North Carolina	Mary Grainger (Granger)	6
Richard Dobbs Spaight Sr.	North Carolina	Mary Leach	3
Hugh Williamson	North Carolina	Maria Apthorpe	2
George Clymer	Pennsylvania	Elizabeth (Merediths?)	yes
Thomas FitzSimons	Pennsylvania	Catherine Meade	
Benjamin Franklin	Pennsylvania	Deborah Read	2–3
Jared Ingersoll	Pennsylvania	Elizabeth Petti (Petit)	3
Thomas Mifflin	Pennsylvania	Sarah Morris	
Gouverneur Morris	Pennsylvania	Anne Cary (Carey) Randolph	1
Robert Morris	Pennsylvania	Mary White	7
James Wilson	Pennsylvania	Hannah Gray (second wife)	6+0
Pierce Butler	South Carolina	Mary Middleton	1
Charles Cotesworth Pinckney	South Carolina	Sarah Middleton and second wife, Mary Stead	3
Charles Pinckney	South Carolina	Mary Eleanor Laurens	3
John Rutledge	South Carolina	Elizabeth Grimke	10
John Blair	Virginia	Jean Balfour	
James Madison	Virginia	Dolly Payne Todd	1 stepchild
George Washington	Virginia	Martha Dandridge Custis	2 stepchildren

William Jackson Secretary to the US Constitution		Elizabeth Willing	

141

Moral Dilemmas

The movement to chip away at the moral fiber of the family, marriage, and religious and Christian-based institutions bit by bit is the work of a master, Satan. Satan is good at his job. He goes about like a roaring lion, seeking whom he can devour. Unfortunately, man believes he is in the driver's seat. But in actuality, he is being taken for a ride. And like little children, he falls asleep in the "quiet noise," arriving at destinations without a clue how he got there. I watched the movie *Jurassic Park (1993)* a few years back and remembered how the dinosaur, the T. rex, was depicted as smart and cleaver—seeking weak spots in the electric fence. This movement has been waiting for its chance to escape from the dark closet with no fear of God—shaking its fist in His face. It has spent years (quiet noise) softening up the conscience of America through situation comedies, soap operas, and movies establishing bleeding hearts for tolerance and acceptance as a sect of people who wanted love, happiness, and freedom to be seen as normal just like you and me in their unnatural/alternative lifestyles. And for the most part, America has bought into the agenda and defends the LGBT movement. They have been lobbying and becoming poll worthy in political campaigns, silently working their way into key positions while most of America slept and many still sleep—unaware of what is happening in the USA today, morally speaking.

> Rather than fully embracing the arguments made by Windsor and the United States, the Supreme Courts strikes down section 3 of DOMA as a classification not properly supported by its objective. This is because the Supreme Court believes that section 3 encroaches upon the States' sovereign prerogative to define marriage. And since their view of section 3 of DOMA is about encouraging states not to accept same-sex marriage and states recognizing

---

141 Signers of the Constitution," National Park Service, accessed April 17, 2014 "https://www.nps.gov/parkhistory/online_books/constitution/bio2.htm (lasted updated 29-Jul-2004)

marriages of same-sex couples from other states and keeping
the federal law definition of marriage between a male and
female of the opposite sex, where the word, "spouse" means
such, thus making federal benefits unattainable for same-
sex unions, this congressional action to strike down section
3 of DOMA puts states in the driver's seat, constitutionally.
DOMA will be unable to influence the decision-making
process in the matter on a state-base. The Supreme Count
explanation for this—in their view—DOMA was in
violation of the Fifth Amendment stating it, "singles out a
class of persons deemed by a State entitled to recognition
and protection to enhance their own liberty," and "imposes
a disability on the class by refusing to acknowledge a status
the State finds to be dignified and proper."[142] 17 Cite as: 570
U.S._____ (2013) Alito, J., dissenting.

Justice Samuel Alito (Dissenting)

"In any event, §3 of DOMA, in my view, does not encroach
on the prerogatives of the States, assuming of course
that the many federal statutes affected by DOMA have
not already done so. Section 3 does not prevent any State
from recognizing same-sex marriage or from extending to
same-sex couples any right, privilege, benefit, or obligation
stemming from state law. All that §3 does is to define a class
of persons to whom federal laws extend certain special
benefits and upon whom federal law imposes certain special
burdens. In these provisions, Congress used marital status
as a way of defining this class—in part, I assume, because it
viewed marriage as a valuable institution to be fostered and
in part because it viewed married couples as comprising a
unique type of economic unit that merits special regulatory
treatment. Assuming that Congress has the power under
the Constitution to enact the laws affected by §3, Congress
has the power to define the category of persons to whom
those laws apply.

---

[142] *Windsor*, 570 U.S., ___(2013)

For these reasons, I would hold that [section 3] §3 of DOMA does not violate the Fifth Amendment."[143] Justice Alito authored dissenting opinions, which were joined by Antonin Scalia, Clarence Thomas, and Chief Justice John Roberts.

All Men Are Created Equal

How true—all have sinned and have come short of the glory of God. And all will have to repent and obey God. Yes, all men are equal. In the news article by Adam Liptak in the February issue of the *New York Times*, a correction was made in attributing the phrase "'all men are created equal' to the Constitution, though it is in the Declaration of Independence."[144] In June 2013, the Supreme Court ruled that same-sex married couples should be recognized as legal unions and that federal benefits be extended as in heterosexual unions between a man and women. Since this time, June 2013, federal judges in Oklahoma, Utah, and Virginia, where same-sex unions were barred, now honor same-sex marriages. The article mentioned that supporters of same-sex marriages have been winning in their fight or plight in state courts and in state legislatures. The article by Liptak quoted a law professor at Northwestern, who in his opinion believes that rapid changes in public opinion are playing a part in the momentum and winning streak the gay movement is experiencing in America, and the professor feels that if judges rule against same-sex marriages, their grandchildren will see them as bigots. Really? Wouldn't it be better if their grandchildren saw them as men fearing and loving God? Better yet, does the law professor at Northwestern believe that God, who made man *upright* and tells man how to live and walk before Him, is a bigot? He can look that up in his law books or try looking it up in the Bible, the law of God. You can bet that not any of his law books are as old or binding on man as the Bible, the word (law) of God.

Mr. Liptak wrote, "The judge who struck down Virginia's ban on same-sex marriage, Judge Arenda L. Wright Allen of Federal District Court in Norfolk, relied heavily on the Supreme Court's decision in June in *United*

---

[143] Id., 570 U.S., at ___,

[144] Adam Liptak, "A Steady Path to Supreme Court as Gay Marriage Gains Momentum in States," *New York Times*, February 14, 2014, https://www.nytimes.com/2014/02/15/us/politics/a-steady-path-to-justices-as-gay-marriage-gains-momentum-in-states.html.

States v. Windsor, which ruled that the federal government must provide benefits to same-sex couples married in states that allow such unions."

The article mentioned that Supreme Court Judge Scalia, who dissented in Windsor, declared that anyone opposing same-sex marriage was an enemy of human decency. The Supreme Ruler and Creator of man says in His Holy Word that those who fail to speak out against sin is an enemy of God. The scriptures warn against calling good, evil and evil, good. See Isaiah 5: 20–23. Consider anal or anus (where the stool passes out the body) sex and lewd acts; did we miss something here? Is there a second definition to decency we haven't been made aware of? There is no life in defecation or feces and the human waste area; the area that voids toxic and potentially disease prone matter. God gave life, reproduction, and fruitfulness upfront, upright; it's a commandment. Science has discovered that from the upfront stuff, man can use the stem cells from the embryonic cord to help save lives. Has science discovered any life-giving properties from the anus and what is expelled? Any decent stuff to use? Agricultural crops contaminated by human and animal waste (bacteria in the intestines of humans and animals) can cause outbreaks of food-borne illness, such as E. coli (*Escherichia Coli*). HIV/AIDS gripped this country and helped spread internationally from homosexual activities.

Judge Arenda L. Wright Allen of Virginia quoted Justice Anthony M. Kennedy's opinion about states' roles in defining marriage. "Notwithstanding the wisdom usually residing within proper deference to state authorities regarding domestic relationships," Judge Wright Allen wrote that prompt action from the courts was required. "When core civil rights are at stake," she said, "the judiciary must act."

She drew on other parts of Justice Kennedy's opinion, and she had plenty to work with. Treating same-sex marriages differently from others, he wrote, "demeans the couple, whose moral and sexual choices the Constitution protects, and whose relationship the state has sought to dignify. ... and it humiliates tens of thousands of children now being raised by same-sex couples."(*Windsor, supra*, at __, 133 S. Ct.2675, 186 L.Ed. 2d at 828)

What a Pickle We Get Ourselves in When We Think We Are More Righteous Than God!

An article written by Adam Liptak February 2014 brought to light a very interesting gauge of man's morality. "Public opinion in 1967 was strongly against interracial marriage, while most polls show that a rapidly growing majority of Americans support same-sex marriage."[145] It only goes to show how far man has moved away from God. Removing the ancient landmark of decency and morals and being defiant toward God's commands will only bring wrath on America. "The princes of Judah were like them that remove the bound: therefore I will pour out My wrath upon them like water" (Hosea 5:10). Interracial marriage isn't an abomination, but the practice of men lying with men as with womankind is. One thing God didn't want was Jews marrying nations that didn't know or honor God and would take their hearts away from Him. It makes one wonder who these Americans in the polls are. Are they recent to America, new Americans who know nothing of our forefathers and the founders/framers of our Constitution? Are they naturalized citizens from countries where God isn't whom they trust? If one would search history, he or she would find that dynasties and kingdoms fell from trouble within and not so much from enemies without. While we shake our fists in God's face from within, who is watching the city? Is it the military? "Except the Lord keep the city the watchman watches in vain" (Psalm 127:1). How far will we move away from the boundaries God set in place? When the enemies are at the gate, will God hear us when we call on Him to bless America? Have we gone too far? What is left is just the handwriting on the wall for America. That is pride before destruction. America, turn your course.

There are many lesser factions (less militarily prepared in our "intelligent" view) and countries ready to take on America. They could very well be our version (twenty-first century) of fire and brimstone. Our strength is in the One who keeps the city, not the watchmen or military might. Let's keep ourselves in a position to call on God. "God, bless America!" And He will hear. What military arm of government was watching the Pentagon, the twin towers, and the airspace over New York on 9/11? Within a twinkling of an eye, what we know as America can change. Trust God to keep America from ultimate annihilation. Despite its ("hellrific") beginnings for many, America didn't happen by accident. It was the providence of God that set America up as a beacon to the world to look to the God of heaven. Many missionaries have gone out from America, spreading the gospel of the New Testament, Christ, the Son of God, to nations plagued by pagans and idol worshippers. In many times and instances, Christ isn't the center of faith and practice. Women, girls, and children are treated poorly. Now that we have come to trust in our own military might and intellectual thinking above and beyond God, we have

---

[145] Adam Lipak https://www.nytimes.com/2014/02/15/us/politics/a-steady-path-to-justices-as-gay-marriage-gains-momentum-in-states.html

fixed ourselves to be more righteous in judgment than God. It's foreigners or nationalized American citizens who dictate to America whether they want to pledge allegiance to the USA flag and trust in God, for which we, the people, stand or pray to God in our pastime sporting events and in our schools. Take away our God; take away our America.

We need only to look to the Tower of Babel and see how God broke that little party up. Men were scattered throughout the world, basically starting from scratch to rebuild; communication was brought to a halt. See Genesis 11:1–9. Joseph was placed in a pit (a "hellrific" position) by his brothers, but it was due to the providence of God that he rose to greatness and saved Israel. America should be, because of its blessings, an example to the rest of the world to follow almighty God in morals and conduct, but it has made a turn down a dark past after the likes of Sodom and Gomorrah. After the Supreme Court's ruling or tampering with God's marriage plan for man, the portal /wormhole was opened. Darkness (evil spirits) was allowed to enter this hemisphere, causing Americans to be in an uproar in our civilized duty toward each other. It shows its ugly head/ side again, from the lewd and baser sort all the way up to the White House. "Righteousness exalts a nation: but sin is a reproach to any people" (Proverbs 14:34). Spirits are darker than before; when in history has America lost so many children (innocents) to school shootings? Were the kids led in prayer that morning? Were they allowed to place their hands over their hearts and pledge allegiance to the flag of the USA? And acknowledge that we are one nation under God, and in God we trust?

Marrying and Given into Marriage (Twenty-First-Century Homosexual Marriage)

"For as in the days that were before the flood they were eating and drinking, marrying and giving in marriage, until the day that Noah entered into the ark, and knew not until the flood came, and took them all away; so shall also the coming of the Son of man be" (Matthew 24:38–39).

"At present, no one—including social scientist, philosophers, and historians—can predict with any certainty what the long-term ramifications of widespread acceptance of same-sex marriage will be" (Judge Alito, dissenting).[146] James Obergefell v. Richard Hodges. 576 U.S. _____ (2015) (Alito, J., dissenting).

---

[146] Obergefell v. Hodges, 576 U.S. ___(2015)

The scriptures tell us what the long-term ramification will be for same-sex marriage. The Old Testament was written for our learning (Romans 15:4). The question is, Did we learn anything from the account of Sodom and Gomorrah? Are we willing to take God out of America and see what the ramifications will be? Will God find twenty, ten, five, or only one righteous person and spare the city, country, and nation? While we are focusing on the gays, God is looking at the one who declares himself to be righteous to step up or speak up and stand in the gap. If it's not homosexuality, then it's bestiality or something else. Will God find one person in America to speak out against harm to the church, family, and His blessings to the marriage union—children (His heritage or reward)? See Psalm 127:3, Proverbs 22:6, and Ephesians 6:4.

The most high God rules in the kingdom of men. Our pride has lifted itself against the God of Heaven. Like Belshazzar, son of Nebuchadnezzar, who took and used the vessel from the temple of Jerusalem (belong and sacred to God) for his own cause, gays are using the fruit of the womb (God's heritage—what belong to God) for their own cause. Will America stand tolerantly by and see the writing on the wall: MENE, MENE, TEKEL, UPHARIS? Are our days as a nation numbered? America, let's not find ourselves weighed in the balance and found wanting toward God. Repent. See Daniel 5.

Conclusion

If you feel that the temporal relationships of homosexual (effeminate, lesbian, gay) or heterosexual (adulterous or fornicator) on earth with your partner or nonbiblical spouse are better than an eternal relationship in heaven with God, Joshua would say to "choose you *this day* whom you will serve" (emphasis added). Make a stand, be clear about it, and understand the consequences; for every action, there is a reaction. On this side of the cross, you have the freedom to go all Al Green on God: "If loving you is wrong, I don't wanna be right." But when you cross over to the other side, upon your departure from this world, this life, what will be your stance? "God, You made me this way"?

Stop! The blame game didn't work with Adam or Eve, so just stop. There will be no polls to take of popular opinions, no political persuasions or lobbyists, and no judicial debates and rulings on propositions or rights (civil or non-civil) to present to your Maker. The Constitution is no longer valid to you—only to those in the world you just left behind. Once you reach the other side, the question God will pose to you (just you) is, Do I know you? Meaning, do we (you and I) have a *relationship*? It's time for you to answer the question, now. This attitude toward God and His word and where am I going with this decision I've made: the goats on the left hand or the sheep on the right hand? One should work out his or her own soul salvation with fear and trembling (Philippians 2:12). When the parades, marches, and waving of rainbow flags are over; when lobbying for rights that your abominable lifestyle in the sight of God is accepted in a Christian nation; and when your individual curtain is called, will you be "coming out" on the right side of God? Your concerns won't be on the right side of the *history* of man (in this generations) at this point, because once you leave this world, the only thing that matters is, Are you "coming out" on the right side of God (sheep) or on the left side (goat)? What rights will you petition God for? Oh, by the way, man's relationship with God isn't democratic—work through that, if you will. Heads up, if you haven't figured it out already, it's a clay-potter relationship somewhat and much more, depending on the clay's response to the kneading of the potter. Yield to the potter's hands and become a vessel fit for a room in a mansion in heaven.

Of course, the choice has always been yours. "Whosoever will, let him come." It's a personal decision, not a majority vote. If none of this means anything to you, it won't make God's word of none effect. Yet there is another invitation from God: "Eat, drink, and be merry." But on a cautionary note, if you haven't made preparations to meet God, He considers you a fool. C'mon, do you want God to see you as a fool? See Ecclesiastes 8:15; Psalm 14:1; Psalm 53:1; Luke 12:19–21.

We are quick to say we are all equal in the sight of God. If we really believe that, why are we doing everything sinful and abominable that is possible to live beneath the level and standard of righteousness He calls us into? If we really believe we are all equal in God's sight when our choices are contrary to His will, then whomever God calls in judgment to stand on the side of the sheep will be okay with standing on the opposite side with the goats, too. One thing we are right about is that we are equal in God's sight as far as having equal opportunity to heed the call of the gospel and be obedient to His will. "Whosoever will, let him come." The scriptures tell us that God is angry with the wicked every day and that He saves the upright in heart (Psalm 7:10–11).

God has given man a soul. God regards the soul of man as more valuable than anything on earth. The question the word of God poses is, "What would a man give in exchange for his soul?" This is a piece of work God breathed into, and man became a living soul.

When Esau sold his birthright to Jacob, he wanted it back and wept bitterly after it, but it was a done deal. The soul is something angels in heaven rejoice over when a man who once went astray from God returns, repents, and reconciles his relationship with God. Not only that, but God values His creation, man, to the extent that He allowed His own Son to bear the sins of man. Christ suffered on the cross, experiencing death just to make sure man had a lifeline back to God. That is man's rightful state and initial relationship from the beginning.

What does this tell you about the value of man? Remember the precious stones found in Eden. Nothing is a match for the soul of man. There is nothing on earth in the sight of God that comes anywhere near the value of the soul of man—any man. This would be whether he or she is rich, poor, homeless, educated, uneducated, or drunkard (sot); any man or woman who is a thief, fornicator, adulterer, or effeminate. And there is someone else who knows the value of the soul far more than man; that would be Satan, who seeks to claim you as his own. Like Esau, who squandered and took his birthright lightly for the temporary pleasure of a few delectable and mouth-watering morsels, will we repeat in like fashion as to take lightly our eternal inheritance for a few moments or days on earth due to temporary sexual pleasures and allow Satan to take our souls to hell with him? He won't give them back though we will weep bitterly (weeping and gnashing of teeth) to have another opportunity to make the right choice. Again, "Chose you *this day* whom you will serve" (Joshua 24:15).

"What is man that God is mindful of him?" In six days God created the heavens and the earth. He spoke things into existence. But when it came to man, God made it a hands-on event. He shaped and molded man and breathed into man a part of Him. Man became a living soul; someone just like God, someone that will never die. The soul can never die; only the flesh will return to the dust from whence it came. One interesting thing worth noting, if you have never considered it on your own, is that God spoke of all His creation as "good," and when it came to man, God said, "It was *very* good" (Genesis 1:31). God took the glory of man not from the ground, the dirt, but from the man's side or rib, the part Christ used as a vessel to come to earth and walk among men. Christ comes in the fashion of a man through the woman.

What is a soul? "sōl) *n.* **1.** The rational, emotional, and volitional faculties in man, conceived of as forming an entity distinct from the body. **2.** *Theol.* **a** The divine principle of life in man. **b** The moral or spiritual part of man as related to God, considered as surviving death and liable to joy or misery in a future state..."[147]

One thing you should know about a soul; it is more valuable than earth itself. No one can purchase the soul other than the blood of Jesus Christ. We spend so much time trying to live in the right neighborhood when a mansion is waiting for us in heaven. We spend so much time trying to make friends with the right people when we have a heavenly host of friends. We spend so much time trying to get a degree from a man-made institution when all knowledge is from God. We spend so much time trying to add years to our lives when God has already promised eternal life. This striving to be successful is in vain because what we are trying to obtain is perishable. The whole duty of man is to fear God and keep His commandments. You are here because God put you here. You didn't die in childbirth, and God has fixed it

---

[147] "What Is a Soul?" *Reader's Digest Great Encyclopedic Dictionary, Funck & Wagnalls Standard College Dictionary*, 10th ed., 1280. Publisher, Reader's Digest Association, Inc.,: New York (1966).

that the earth spins on its axis and the gravitational pull—well, you can't even accidentally walk to the end of the earth and fall off. There's no hiding on the moon. It will turn to blood, and the sea will give up her dead.

Take a look at the face of a homeless person, someone eating out of the garbage, and someone you may dislike for any reason. Take a good, long, and hard look; you are looking at someone who is more valuable than earth itself. Now look in the mirror at yourself and note that you are that valuable, too. When it comes to the gay or lesbian issue (homosexuality) and straight, we have all sinned and come short of the glory of God. We will all need to repent of our sins and obey God. We are sinners in need of a savior. Making your sinful and abominable lifestyle a political issue could score some temporal gain or victory in some parts of this earth, but where are you going with it? You cannot stay here. *You did not build it or create earth or heaven!* Again, where do you plan to go with this agenda? For too many, the vast majority of people on earth live far, far beneath their true station in life. It is because of the lack of knowledge and disobedience to God that we all find ourselves in this state: deceiving ourselves and others, and being deceived by Satan.

Pundits Say No One Knows What Is Happening–God Does

God allows the rise and fall of everything, and through His providence, He allows things to come about to test the hearts of men. It's not that He doesn't know what is in the hearts of men, but He allows man to see himself more closely—to examine himself to see whether he is walking with God. The very fact that the homosexual phenomenon of pandemic proportion around the globe has made a comeback in history as in the days of Sodom and Gomorrah, brazenly and fearlessly attacking what belongs to God, is a test to this generation of the twenty-first century. And once again, the conversation isn't about homosexuals and their attack on angels in the days of Lot (nephew of Abraham) or God's institution of marriage, family (husband, wife, children), and His church in the twenty-first century, but it's the same as in the conversation between Abraham and God. "And the Lord said, If I find in Sodom fifty righteous within the city, then I will spare all the place for their sakes." (Genesis 18:26). God isn't confused about the fact that the wicked will continue to do wickedly. His question is, Who will be willing to stand in the gap when Satan rears his ugly head in whatever century?

It appears that being effeminate wasn't the only offense named in 1

Corinthians 6 ("the list"). But take note here that it also appears that some who were gay (effeminate: men with men; and like manner behavior in the case of women with women) were no longer living in such an abominable lifestyle. "For such were some of you." The problem of disobedience (homosexuality or abominable lifestyles) was solved in obedience to the gospel.

Men (young and old) gathered from all parts of the city to attempt an assault on Lot's houseguests (Genesis 19:4–7). Where were the protestors in light of their behavior? There were none found, not even five. The LGBT movement is gathering momentum against God's institutions of marriage, family, and the church. Again, this book isn't about homosexuals; it's about those who allow the behavior to permeate this society. The judgment is against you. Now know this: the battle has already been won. God won't allow the behavior to continue, just like He didn't in Sodom and Gomorrah. But take note of the number of people (more than likely those who refused to speak out against this activity) who went down in the flames. If it isn't homosexuality, then it is bestiality or something even more unimaginable. It is set in man to continue to do evil (Genesis 6:5). Man isn't going to stop sinning until the day Christ returns; this is in like fashion to the people in Noah's day who kept sinning until the day the rain came. Will America stand by and allow a few to ignite the flames again—history repeating itself? Don't think for a moment that God used up all the fire; there is more where that came from.

One comforting fact is that the battle has already been won over evil due to Jesus's death on the cross and His resurrection from the dead. God knows the hearts of men yet patiently gives all an opportunity to repent. All that is evil and contrary to God won't stand. The gay movement will run its course in this generation as it did before in Sodom and Gomorrah. Who is going down with it? Will it be the tolerant, the indifferent, those fearful to speak out, and those ashamed to preach the gospel? The question today, Since it is God's way to try and test the hearts of men to see who is faithful, will He find five righteous to spare the city (nation)? The USA, by legalizing an abominable act and forcing those who oppose unscriptural behavior to accept it, is found weighing in the balance.

Let God Be True and every man a liar. God won't be mocked. "Whatever a man soweth, that shall he reap."

Jesus's Invitation to You

Come out on the side of righteousness. What will be your response to His invitation? Do you really want to come out? Well, it's not coming out from the closet, where shameful deeds are done under the cover of darkness, to gain some constitutional victories and flaunt them in the sight of God; it's coming out from among evildoers and living an obedient life worthy of repentance in the sight of God.

Coming Out

The Lord says, "Therefore *come out* from them and be separated, having nothing to do with evildoers and He will receive you" (2 Corinthians 6:17, emphasis added). The very fact that you are called by the gospel to come out from among them (evildoers) makes "coming out" a good thing. Unfortunately, the fashionable "coming out" means coming out of the closet of darkness to flaunt your unholy deeds, shake your unholy fists in the face of God, establish your own house of worship (church), and call for rewriting the Holy Bible, which would omit passages that reference men with men and women with women. Don't take a penknife to God's word, or you will get a double portion of His word (Jeremiah 36:23).

Why Do the Heathen Rage?–Psalm 2

"Why do the heathen rage, and the people imagine a vain thing? The kings of the earth set themselves, and the rulers take counsel together, against the Lord, and against His anointed, saying, Let us break their bands asunder, and cast away their cords from us. He that sits in the heavens shall laugh: the Lord shall have them in derision. Be wise now, therefore, O you kings: be instructed, you judges of the earth" (Psalm 2:1–3 ... 10).

Satan, liar and deceiver, continues to deceive the hearts of men to do the opposite, just like the original sin. God said, "Don't eat." Satan adds his two cents, changing the course of nature in the God-man relationship. God said He has made man upright. Satan, like he did with Eve, delivers this message to the gays that God made them that way. God says, "Come out from sin—from among evildoers." Satan says, "Come out in your sins, flaunt your pride or sins, and make demands on God's institutions: marriage (husband, wife, and children) and church." But God's invitation remains the same, "Come out." The scripture still says, "Who is man that God is mindful of him?" God is still pleading for you to come out from among them and be separated— in other words, be sanctified. God is long-suffering, not willing that any should perish. Please don't get "sanctified," *set apart from the world*, confused with being a Holy Roller, speaking in tongues, foaming at the mouth, shouting or dancing for the Holy Ghost, and so forth.

Fathers Know How to Give Good Gifts to Their Children

Magic Johnson revealed to the media that his son, Earvin "EJ" Johnson III, is gay. This father had the audacity to extend an invitation to other young African Americans to come out. Be for real. This isn't like an invitation to come out to a Magic Johnson theater. This is your life, man! A life eternally with or without God. And, might I add, it's the only one you will get on this side of the grave, so be wise and chose whom you will obey.

Jesus is the only example to follow. That would be God's Son, not Michael Earvin Jr., Magic Johnson's son. Mr. Johnson said he is proud of his son and stands behinds him one million percent. God said Jesus is His beloved Son, in whom He is well pleased. And God didn't stop there; he said to man, "Hear ye Him." Where am I going with this? What God has to offer is beyond any calculation of millions, billions, and trillions of percentage. It's infinite—it's eternal. I would encourage Mr. Johnson to search the scriptures and learn what it means when it says, "Pride comes before destruction." This is being proud of what God calls abominable. Are you willing to be on the wrong side of God? Are you really ready to meet Him with that attitude? Pride has no place, only contrite hearts. "It is appointed unto man once to die and after death, the judgment where every knee shall bow before Him." Every knee— that's 100 percent of knees—will bow before God. My deductive reasoning, based on scripture, would suggest not millions of knees but innumerable knees bowing before God's Son.

Here's another example from scripture: "Let every man be a liar, but let God be true." Jeff Chu, author of *Does Jesus Really Love Me?*, talks about being disturbed due to the fact that so many churches deny gays a place to worship. He talks about his faith in God being secure. From his statement, it's apparent that not even God or gospel ministers can tell him whom he should love.

Faith is demonstrated in obedience. God has already demonstrated His love for man by sending His Son, Jesus Christ, to die for the sins of man. Here is the memo or scripture from Jesus Christ Mr. Chu missed: "If you love me you will keep my commandments." It's not so rare, from the look at mankind, that many others missed that memo or letter, too. Many have gone about to establish their own religions and righteousness; for example, gay Christians and gay houses of worship/sanctuaries.

Unfortunately, everyone who believes there is a God and in Jesus Christ declares himself or herself to be a Christian. Satan believed and trembled, but he didn't obey; and within that fact alone, he isn't a follower of Christ and therefore isn't a Christian. One thing Mr. Chu isn't aware of is that only Christ can add one to His church (Acts 2:41, 47). Christ added the first three thousand souls and continues to add all who are obedient to the gospel: Jesus's death, burial, and resurrection. And this occurs when one hears, believes, confesses, repents, and is baptized. This step begins a new creature and new walk with Christ until death—departure from this life on earth. Mr. Chu alludes to man-made religious institutions he says won't allow the solace of a place for his vain worship. Mr. Chu is being disingenuous and deceptive with a hidden agenda. What Mr. Chu needs is to obey God and allow Christ to add him to His church, body, or kingdom (Acts 2:38). It seems to me that Mr. Chu is looking for a place to be accepted as he is (old sinful man and lifestyle) and not to be obedient to God by putting off the old man and walking as a new creature in Christ. And such were some of you: effeminate.

No End to Books

I have heard many times that there are as many opinions as there are noses; everybody has one. Although I'm sure many will disagree with me, it isn't my intention that this book comes across as preachy. There are preachers and evangelists who are capable of presenting scripturally detailed sermons on the subject of homosexuality. There are many books, articles, and even Supreme Court rulings in favor of gays; other times they are against gays; and there are even more books and articles on gay genes and on and on.

I was motivated to write this book because I found it fascinating to note that being effeminate is listed with other sinful acts, and of all on "the list," it is the effeminate (man with man as with womankind) who demanded not to be viewed as sinners like the other sinners on the list, although the only sin deemed abominable by God, steps forth to infiltrate and dismember and dismantle God's institutions of marriage and church—the family structures. God has always been about relationships: the family—God, our Father; we, His children; and Jesus, our elder Brother. So His church and His institution of marriage are dear to Him. The church is the bride of Christ, and when the church goes out to reach lost souls and brings them to Christ, He adds souls, who become children of God in His kingdom to His family.

The idea of effeminate unions creates death—not life; the idea is an oxymoron and ostensible. Such unions produce nothing. Consider the fig tree Jesus cursed. Consider the man with one talent who hid it. God wants us to produce, not take and destroy or be parasites on the fruits of the living. I would like the reader to be honest with himself or herself on what he or she has been exposed to in these few pages and to be of noble character, to examine the scripture, and to measure himself or herself thereby, not according to public polls, political agendas, and judicial rulings of the day. It was over two thousand years ago when the Bible recorded, "The Bereans [Jews], these were more noble-minded than those in Thessalonica, in that they received the word with all readiness and eagerness of mind, and searched and examined the scriptures daily, to see whether those things the apostle Paul said were true" (Acts 17:11).

Consider this a lengthy letter to stir the consciences of the learned and unlearned about what thus says the Lord on the subject of being effeminate: gay and lesbian matters. "And further, by these, my son be admonished: of making many books there is no end; and much study is a weariness of the flesh. Let us hear the conclusion of the whole matter: Fear God, and keep His commandments; for this is the whole duty of man. For God shall bring every work into judgment, with every secret thing, whether it be good, or whether it be evil" (Ecclesiastes 12:12–14).

So What if You Don't Believe?

Know this one thing: your unbelief doesn't make the word of God of no effect. Let those who hear come to the knowledge of truth. "For this cause also thank we God without ceasing, because, when you received the word of God which you heard of us, you received it not as the word of men, but as it is in truth, the word of God, which effectually works also in you that believe" (1 Thessalonians 2:13).

Gay: Turn the Meaning Around, Turn the Word and World Around

Satan comes only to steal and destroy. What was once a beautiful word to describe happiness has been taken away. Every God-fearing institute of religious values is being attacked: the home, the husband, the wife, the children (God's heritage), the marriage, and the church. Sadness has come or returned to the face of the earth once again as in the days of Sodom and Gomorrah. The word *gay* has been taken, and no one has tried to reclaim it; it has been marred. Who would ever have thought that *GAY* could represent "Godless Are You?" These people are godlessly and fearlessly shaking their fists and waving their flags at God in defiance while engaging in vile anal intercourse.

This is an area of the body God designed to eliminate potential disease-causing, toxic waste from the body, and the medical research community agrees. It is an activity that is grossly unnatural, unhealthy, and an abomination in the sight of God; it is messing [no pun intended] with His purpose in man of being fruitful, multiplying, and replenishing the earth—not mankind with mankind as with womankind. It is a godless and fruitless behavior and a destroyer of what is good in the sight of God. This shows defiance in God's request to propel the existence of man, but it demands all the benefits offered those couples or individuals (obedient to the command) who make the sacrifice and make it possible for civilization to continue. And this movement has successfully persuaded man (Supreme Court) that God is wrong and they are right. The Supreme Court feels they are dealing with two "goods," biblical marriage and gay marriage. Woe unto them that call evil good, and good evil . . . (Isaiah 5:20). Call no man "good" and let God be true and every man a liar (Mark 10:18, Luke 18:19, Romans 3:4).

Those making old movies classics like *Breakfast at Tiffany's* and others in that genre could have never imagined that the expression *gay* (happy) would ever mean the sad display of ungodly pride of mankind toward God and the destruction of one of the happiest stations in life God gave to man, marriage. The man is to leave father and mother and cleave to his wife. The two become one in God's sight in *holy* matrimony. Can you imagine? Just like that, *gay* is gone from our lexicon for happiness. It is marred, and no one wants to use it other than "Godless Are You" individuals.

A little over two years ago, I came around a book at a thrift shop titled *JFK: A Complete Biography 1917–1963*[148] by William H. A. Carr. In the first chapter, page 7, first paragraph, the author said John Fitzgerald Kennedy, the nation's thirty-fifth president, was described by a British prime minister as a "young, gay, and brave statesman." I can only imagine that fifty-plus years ago, no one could have thought *gay* wasn't a good word to use to describe a decent family man and leader of the free world.

---

[148] William H. A. Carr, *JFK: A Complete Biography 1917–1963. New York: Lancer Books, Inc., Magnum Easy Eye Books. 1962*

The Four Fingers Pointing Back at You

Jesus didn't come to condemn man. But as human beings, we are quick to point fingers at others' sins. It was Jesus who said, "He that is without sin, cast the first stone." It was Jesus who said that *"all* have sinned and come short of the glory of God" (Romans 3:23, emphasis added). We have a grave situation in our society and nation today—not unlike the situation the first century faced with sodomy. We are back to square one—ground zero—with the gay, lesbians, and transvestites and the immorality issue that brought fire down from heaven. There is no doubt in my mind that God has some more fire left in His back pocket, if you will; it's not all used up, by no means. He said He will destroy this world by fire, so He has some more.

Don't count God's delay as slackness. He is only waiting and giving us a chance to make ourselves right with Him. What an awesome God!

It is continually set in man's heart to do evil. Remember, before the earth was fully populated, Cain killed Abel, his own brother. There will be some saved and some not saved. There were few saved souls on the ark. And like in the days of Noah, few will be saved when Christ returns. This world will continue on as it was in the days of Noah. People married and were given in marriage. They did as they did and we do as we do. They did what they did and didn't heed Noah just as people in the twenty-first century won't heed the ministers of the gospel.

So here is the real challenge to the non-gay population; we need not point one finger at the gays, lesbians, and transvestites because we may very well be condemning ourselves with the three or four fingers pointing back at us.

Look back at the conversation God had with Lot, Abraham's nephew. Observe closely. God, who cannot lie, agreed to spare Sodom and Gomorrah if there were five righteous found in the city. God is testing the so-called righteous individuals. He knows the sinners and that they will continue to sin. If it isn't homosexuality, then it will eventually be bestiality—they are waiting in the wings. God wants to find the faithful, who won't shut up at the opposition but speak out against evil when it shows its ugly head. Will the faithful allow the proliferation of this lewdness to permeate our society and be silenced to do little to nothing? The faithful can cause the city, the nation, the USA, to be spared.

There are basically two types of sins. The sin of commission is going against what God *forbids*, and the sin of omission is failing to do what God *commands*. While we remain quiet and tolerant toward those who are going against what God forbids, let's examine ourselves so we aren't failing to speak out against evil—in other words, doing what God commands. Knowing to do good and not doing it is sin (James 4:17). If you are guilty in one, you are guilty of all. No sinner will enter heaven. If you speak out against sin and warn the wicked, his or her blood won't be on your hands. You could very well save a soul, and it could be yours. What I appreciate about the four judges who gave their dissenting comments was their attempt to save a country, to save a nation. Now let the people speak: "We the people, for the people, by the people." Let's save our country, the USA. We will trust that God will have no reason *not* to bless this nation.

And in the words of Todd Staples,[149] a former Republican lawmaker, who ran for lieutenant governor in 2014, "I will change my definition of marriage when God changes His."

"So shall My word be that goes forth out of My mouth: it shall not return to Me void, but it shall accomplish that which I please, and it shall prosper in the thing whereto I sent it" (Isaiah 55:11). Although all won't be saved, as in the days of Noah, it's my desire that this book will reach honest hearts and prosper someone in his or her decision to choose good over evil in his or her lifestyle. I pray that God's word won't go out void.

Come out and be ye separated from evildoers,
Thus says the Lord.
Come out, turn right, and keep straight.

"Because strait is the gate, and narrow is the way, which leads to life, and few there be that find it" (Matthew 7:14).

---

[149] "Federal Judge Strikes Down Texas Ban on Same-Sex Marriage," *New York Times*, February 27, 2014, A14.

Bibliography

BOOKS/PUBLICATIONS

Brawley, Robert L. (Editor) <u>Biblical Ethics & Homosexuality</u>: *Listening to Scripture* Louisville, KY: Westminster John Knox Press, 1996.

Carr, William H. A. *<u>JFK: A Complete Biography 1917-1963</u>* New York, Lancer Books, Inc. Magnum Easy Eye Books, 1962.

Claiborne, Winford. "What Is the Meaning of Situation Ethics?" *"in The Spiritual Sword," Alan E. Highers, editor.* Memphis, TN: Published by Getwell Church. 41, no. 4 (July 2010): 11-17.

Dearman, J. Andrew. <u>The Bible and Human Sexuality--Marriage in the Old Testament,</u>

*in Biblical Ethics & Homosexuality: Listening to Scripture. Editor Robert L. Brawley.*Louisville, KY: Westminster John Knox Press. (1996). Part 2, #4.

Fagan, Kate. "The Reappearing Act: Coming Out as Gay on a College Basketball Team Led by Born-Again Christians" NY: Skyhorse Publishing, 2014.

Jennings, Alvin. *Traditions of Men verse The Word of God.* Fort Worth, TX: Star Bible Publications, 1973.

Hatcher, Michael, ed. "The Effect of Liberalism and Humanism on The Home." *Defender*, 48, no. 2 (February 2019).

Mauser, Ulrich W. "<u>Creation and Human Sexuality in the New Testament</u>," *in Biblical Ethics & Homosexuality: Listening to Scripture. Editor Robert L. Brawley.* Louisville, KY: Westminster John Knox Press (1996). Part 1, #1.

Rahman, Oazi and Glenn Wilson. <u>Born Gay</u>: <u>The Psychobiology of Sex Orientation</u> London, England: Peter Owen Publishers (2008)

Rauch, J. <u>"Gay Marriage: Why It is Good for Gays, Good for Straights, and Good for America."</u> New York: Times Books (2004) p. 94- *hardcover*

Seow, Choon-Leong. *Textual Orientation. In* Biblical Ethics & Homosexuality: *Listening to Scripture* Louisville, KY: Westminster John Knox Press (1996)— Part 1, # 2

Sullivan, Andrew. <u>Virtually Normal</u>: <u>An Argument About Homosexuality</u>, Pp.202-203; Random House Inc.,: NY, Vintage Books (1996)

Thompson, Bert. "Rock-Solid Faith" (part I, 2 & 3), pp. 123-181. Apologetics Press, Inc.

Thompson, Bert. "Rock-Solid Faith: How to Build It," pg. 238. Apologetics Press. Inc.

Wilson, L. R. The New Testament Church. In *Traditions of Men verse The Word of God*: Fort Worth, TX: Star Bible Publications, 1973.

U.S. SUPREME COURT
Opinion of the Court—Cite as 576 U.S. _____(2015)

Obergefell v. Hodges: Same-Sex Marriage argued April 28, 2015—Decided June 26, 2015. Dissenting Statements of Chief Justice John Roberts and Justices Clarence Thomas, Antonin Scalia and Justice Samuel Alito

Nexus Lexis (slip opinion): Obergefell v. Hodges, 576 U.S. _____, 135 S. Ct. 2584,192 L. Ed. 2d 609 (2015)

Obergefell v. Hodges (Appendix B to opinion of the Court) State Legislation and Judicial Decisions Legalizing Same-Sex Marriage As a philosophical matter, liberty is only freedom **from governmental** actions, not an entitlement **to governmental** benefits. Pg 13 Cite as: 576 U.S. _____ (2015) Thomas, J., dissenting.

OPINION OF THE U.S. SUPREME COURTS—JUNE 26, 2015
https://en.wikipedia.org/wiki/Obergefell_v._Hodges
www.supremecourt.gov/opinions/boundvolumes.aspx.

ARTICLES/INTERVIEWS

Asher, Jeff. "The Williams—Asher Debate On Homosexuality." *A radio debate between Robert Williams and Jeff Asher, (Jan. 20, 1990).*

Debate is excerpted from *Out of the Closet.* Publisher Faith And Facts Press. Adobe Acrobat Version prepared by David Padfield. Http://www.padfield.com; https://www.padfield.com/acrobat/asher/homo.pdf

Article originally appeared in print in Out of the Closet by Jeff Asher published by Faith and Facts Press of Indianapolis, IN, and online at www.Padfield.com.

Cameron, Paul. PhD in Psychology, Chairman of Family Research Institute. http://www.familyresearchinst.org/2009/02/medical-consequences-of-what-homosexuals-do/

Jackson, Wayne. The Bible Always Passes the Test
http://www.apologeticspress.org

Warren, Tony. "What are Eunuchs?" http://www.mountainretreatorg.net/fag/what_are_eunuchs.shtml (Accessed 6/5/13). *"What are Eunuchs?"* by Tony Warren, the biblical distinction was clearly drawn between what the Bible defines as a eunuch, looking at Acts 8: 27 and Ester 2:14, 2:3.

NEWS/WEBSITES

A. P. Scientists and Auxiliary Writers "About A.P.— ApologeticsPress.org" http://espanol.apologeticspress.org/apinfo/writers (Accessed May 5, 2014)

"Alabama House Passes Call to Put Same-Sex Marriage Ban in U.S. Constitution." *Montgomery Advertiser*, April 2, 2014. https://www.towleroad.com/2014/04/alabama-house-passes-resolution-calling-for-gay-marriage-ban-in-the-us-constitution/

Chibbaro Jr., Lou. "Sodomy Laws Remain on Books in 17 States, including Md. and Va." *Washington Blade*, April 17, 2013.

http://www.washingtonblade.com/2013/04/17/sodomy-laws-remain-o n-books-in-17-states-including-md-and-va-/#sthash.cwVFRfM1.spuf

Sodomy laws written by Lou Chibbaro, Jr, Senior News Reporter, Washington Blade. (18, April, 2013) http://www.washingtonblade.com/2013/04/17/sodomy-laws-remain-o n-books-in-17-states-including-md-and-va-/#sthash.cwVFRfM1.spuf

Chu, Jeff. "Does Jesus Really Love Me?" Harper (imprint of HarperCollins) Publisher, New York (2013).https://www.nytimes.com/2013/04/14/books/ review/does-jesus-really-love-me-by-jeff-chu.html

Jeff Chu, *"Does Jesus Really Love Me? A Gay Christian's Pilgrimage in Search of God in America"* Dan Savage, https://www.nytimes.com/2013/04/14/ books/review/does-jesus-reallylove-me-by-jeff-chu.html

Fernandez, Manny. "A Judge in Texas Struck Down the Ban on Same-Sex Marriage." *New York Times*, February 27, 2014, https://www.nytimes. com/2014/02/27/us/texas-judge-strikes-down-state-ban-on-same-sex-marriage. html

Food and Drug Administration, MSM *–men who have sex with men,* "have HIV prevalence 60 times higher than the general population, 800 times higher than first-time blood donors and 8,000 times higher than repeat blood donors. http://www.wnd.com/2008/04/61856/#iR0CuGqiqTu8hFDO.99

Hernandez, Greg. http://greginhollywood.com/president-obama-publicl y-supports-gay-marriage-67958; https://abcnews.go.com/GMA/video/obam a-supreme-court-ruling-sex-marriage-victory-america-32051016 http://www.gaystarnews.com/article/obama-us-supreme-courts-ga y-marraige-ruling-real-change-possible260615#sthash.YIX4Ix56.dpuf;http:// www.gaystarnews.com/article/obama-us-supreme-courts-gay-marriage-ruling-real-change-possible260615/print

International Journal of Epidemiology, Volume 26, Issue 3, Jun 1997, Pages 657–661. R S Hogg, S A Strathdee, K J Craib, M V O'Shaughnessy, J S Montaner, M T Schechter, Modelling the impact of HIV disease on mortality in gay and bisexual men https://doi.org/10.1093/ije/26.3.657

Italian newspaper reported Pope Francis saying, "About two percent of Roman Catholic clerics are sexual pedophiles." http://www.reuters.com/article/2014/07/13/us-pope-abuse-idUSKBN0FI0R020140713.

Johnson, Eric M. "Seattle Archdiocese to Pay $12 Million to Settle Child Sex Abuse Claims." *Reuters*, June 25, 2014. http://www.reuters.com/article/2014/06/25/us-usa-seattle-church-idUSKBN0F015I20140625

Kamisar, Ben. "Scalia: Gay Marriage Decision Shows Court Is America's 'Ruler,'" *The Hill*, June 26, 2015, https://thehill.com/blogs/blog-briefing-room/new s/246249-scalia-gay-marriage-decision-shows-americas-ruler-is-supreme

Kuhnhenn, Jim and Lisa Lerer. https://www.ksl.com/article/35257808/fo r-obama-and-clinton-twisty-paths-to-yes-on-gay-marriage (modified Dec. 22, 2019); https://oklahoman.com/article/feed/856956/for-obama-and-clinton-twisty-paths-to-yes-on-gay-marriage

"On May 9, 2012, Barack Obama became the first sitting U. S. president to publicly declare support for legalizing of same-sex marriage." http://en.wikipedia.org/wiki/Same-sex_marriage_in_the_United_States ABC 25 WPBF News. "Obama Affirms Support for Same-Sex Marriage." It is reported that the President says his position on marriage has evolved.

LifeSiteNews.Com. *"President Bush Stresses Sanctity of Marriage in State of the Union Address* https://www.lifesitenews.com/news/president-bus h-stresses-sanctity-of-marriage-in-state-of-the-union-address LifeSiteNews.com, January 21, 2004

LifeSiteNews.Com: Life, Family and Culture News written by A. Dean Byrd, Ph.D., MBA, MPH entitled, "Homosexuality Is Not Hardwired." https://www.lifesitenews.com/news/homosexuality-is-not-hardwired-concludes-head-of-the-human-genome-project

Liptak, Adam. "A Steady Path to Supreme Court as Gay Marriage Gains Momentum in States." *New York Times*, February 14, 2014. https://www.nytimes.com/2014/02/15/us/politics/a-steady-path-to-justices-as-gay-marriage-gains-momentum-in-states.html

MacDonald Dzirutwe, "Before Obama Trip, U.S. Gay Ruling Inspires Hope and Revulsion in Africa," *Reuters*, July 1, 2015, https://www.reuters.com/article/

us-africa-gaymarriage/before-obama-trip-u-s-gay-ruling-inspires-hope-and-revulsion-in-africa-idUSKCN0PB4OY20150701

US Same-Sex Marriage Ruling Revulsion in Africa." *Reuters*, July 1, 2015 Additional reporting by Elias Biryabarema in Kampala, David Clarke and Alexis Akwagyiram in Lagos, Edith Honan in Nairobi and James Giahyue in Monrovia; Editing by Mark Trevelyan.

Max Weber, Economy and Society (1992) [online] Available: http://en.wikipedia.org/wiki/Authority [cited 2 July 2013] https://en.wikipedia.org/wiki/Authority_(sociology)

Metcalfe, John. "A University of Utah-Led Study Shows That Pattern Became More Pronounced 4,000 Years Ago, and Suggests It May Worsen as Earth's Climate Warms." *Atlantic Cities*, April 16, 2014. https://archive.unews.utah.edu/news_releases/warm-u-s-west-cold-east-a-4000-year-pattern/ https://www.citylab.com/life/2014/04/america-could-get-more-and-more-super-freezing-winters/8901/ https://www.citylab.com/environment/2014/12/2014-an-epic-year-for-clima te-change-and-other-weather-related-disasters/383879/

Mirza-Reid,Sofina. (http://news.msn.com/us/seattle-archidioceses-to-pay-doll ar12-million-to-settle-child-sex-abuse-claims...); Edited by Sonfina Mirza-Reid, June 25, 2014.

Musgrave, Marilyn. http://en.wikipedia.org/wiki/Federal_Marriage_Amendment "If we're going to redefine marriage, let's let the American people, through their elected representative, decide—not activist judges. Let the people of Massachusetts decide."
U.S. Federal government in celebrating the year with Bible "programs, ceremonies, and activities." The resolution died in committee. http://en.wikipedia.org/wiki/Marilyn_Musgrave

Padfield, David. 2001 Homosexuality: What Does The Bible Say? [online]. Available from: http://www.padfield.com; https://www.padfield.com/acrobat/asher/homo.pdf

"Prejudice Is Prejudice: Biden Says Gay Rights Trump Culture." First reported by Associated Press; Https://www.nbcnews.com/news/prejudice-prejudice-biden-says-gay-rights-trump-culture-n140121

Pullella, Phillip. "Pope Says about Two Percent of Priests Are Pedophiles: paper." *Reuters*, July 13, 2014. https://www.reuters.com/article/us-pope-abuse/pope-says-about-two-percent-of-priests-are-pedophiles-paper-idUSK BN0FI0R020140713
Reporting By Philip Pullella; Editing by Rosalind Russell

Santos, Fernanda. "Arizona Governor Vetoes Bill on Refusal of Service to Gays." *The New York Times* (27, February 2014): the New York edition: Pg.(A1). http://nyti.ms/1jBufq0. http://www.nytimes.com/2014/02/27.us/ Brewer-arizona-gay-service-bill.html?emc=edit_na_2014

"Signers of the Constitution." National Park Service. Last Update: 29-Jul-2004. https://www.nps.gov/parkhistory/online_books/constitution/bio23.htm

"Small Steps Toward Acceptance Renew Debate on Gay Marriage." *New York Times*. https://www.nytimes.com/1989/11/05/weekinreview/ideas-trends-smal l-steps-toward-acceptance-renew-debate-on-gay-marriage.html

Smith, Jean Edward, and Herbert M. Levine. Civil Liberties and Civil Rights Debated. Englewood Cliffs, NJ: Prentice Hall, 1988. [online] Available: http:// en.wikipedia.org/wiki/Civil_liberties [cited 30 April 2013]

University of Calgary. "'Poop pill' capsule research paves the way for simpler C. difficile treatment: Fecal pill effectiveness is similar to more invasive treatment for stubborn intestinal infection." ScienceDaily. www.sciencedaily. com/releases/2017/12/171201091026.htm (accessed January 3, 2020).

"US Supreme Court Considers Federal Definition of Marriage." Voice of America News, March 27, 2013. http://www.voanews.com/content/us-suprem e-court-considers-federal-definition-of-marriage/1629747.html
They question Obama's willingness to defend other laws passed by Congress and challenged in court." *http://www.voanews.com/content/us-supreme-cour t-considers-federal-definition-of-marriage/1629747.html*

Wheeler, Lydia. "Chief Justice Decries Decision That Does Not 'Celebrate Constitution.'" *The Hill*, June 26, 2015. https://thehill.com/regulation/othe r/246256-chief-justice-decries-decision-that-does-not-celebrate-constitution

Index

239, 241, 242, 244, 245, 277,
278, 279, 297, 308, 309, 311,
315, 317, 327, 342, 344, 347,
348, 356, 358, 360

Children 81, 162, 168, 195, 241, 275,
286, 349, 350

Christian xvii, xviii, xix, 26, 62, 79,
80, 86, 91, 105, 117, 118, 122,
124, 126, 127, 128, 144, 145,
146, 147, 148, 156, 157, 159,
168, 169, 177, 178, 186, 188,
192, 193, 202, 203, 217, 222,
228, 239, 244, 282, 296, 300,
314, 319, 342, 344, 351, 358

Chu, 127

church v, ix, xviii, 6, 7, 11, 46, 48,
51, 52, 64, 117, 128, 135, 145,
146, 147, 159, 170, 209, 213,
216, 244, 245, 275, 276, 277,
280, 281, 285, 297, 308, 315,
317, 326, 350, 356, 358, 360

civil rights xxi, 66, 88, 89, 92, 101,
102, 103, 104, 107, 110, 177,
235, 244, 309, 313, 347

climate 141, 181, 235, 298, 368

COME OUT 362

COMING OUT 208

Commandments 18, 21, 39, 48, 55,
127, 152, 218, 286, 287, 288,
353, 357, 359

Condemn 28, 33, 79, 127, 151, 155,
156, 177, 216, 217, 220, 222,
226, 283, 319, 361

confess 20, 146, 156, 166, 168, 225,
276, 279, 291, 313

Congress xxiv, xxv, 90, 104, 298,
299, 300, 302, 310, 311, 312,
316, 341, 345

congressmen 183

Constitutionality 317, 341

Constitutional Rights 303

Contradictory 318

Covet 309, 317

D

Daniel xvii, 45, 53, 64, 191,
308, 343

Dearman
J. Andrew Dearman 288

Declaration xv, xxiii, xxvii,
118, 346

Denominations
Will Worship 51, 128, 144, 159,
216, 245, 250

Deuteronomy xxii, 55, 110, 282

Dignity 101, 102, 104, 124, 125, 177,
309, 318

discrimination xxvi, 101, 122, 123,
124, 154, 177, 178, 235, 308

disingenuous 123, 154, 216, 245,
309, 314, 358

dogmatic 209, 319

DOMA 122, 242, 295, 298, 299, 317,
318, 340, 344, 345
Defense of Marriage Act 122

drunkard xxii, 308, 352

Drunkards xv, xx, xxii, 85, 286, 308

E

Ecclesiastes 18, 34, 39, 57, 210, 282,
288, 303, 352, 359

effeminate xv, xxii, 25, 57, 68, 80,
81, 86, 127, 128, 129, 130, 134,
138, 155, 176, 178, 179, 181,
192, 208, 210, 213, 218, 246,
284, 286, 291, 307, 308, 310,
326, 351, 352, 358, 359

Emancipation xvi, xxvi

126, 128, 129, 132, 135, 146,
154, 179, 187, 213, 216, 220,
223, 227, 245, 277, 285, 287,
317, 319, 357
Luke xx, 3, 50, 53, 56, 64, 79, 116,
128, 129, 144, 146, 157, 165,
179, 228, 248, 277, 283, 285,
297, 319, 352

M

Malachi 228, 284
Man
 God is mindful of him xvi,
   xvii, xviii, xxi, xxii, xxvi,
   3, 4, 5, 6, 7, 8, 9, 11, 12,
   13, 14, 15, 16, 17, 18, 19,
   20, 21, 22, 23, 25, 26, 27,
   28, 29, 30, 32, 33, 34, 35,
   36, 37, 38, 39, 40, 41, 42,
   43, 44, 45, 46, 47, 48, 49,
   50, 51, 53, 55, 56, 58, 61,
   62, 63, 64, 67, 68, 79, 81,
   82, 83, 84, 85, 87, 89, 93,
   100, 102, 104, 105, 107,
   108, 109, 110, 114, 115,
   116, 122, 123, 124, 125,
   127, 128, 129, 130, 131,
   132, 138, 139, 140, 142,
   144, 145, 146, 147, 148,
   150, 151, 152, 153, 155,
   156, 157, 158, 161, 163,
   164, 165, 166, 168, 169,
   170, 173, 177, 178, 180,
   181, 182, 183, 184, 187,
   188, 192, 197, 198, 200,
   201, 202, 203, 207, 210,
   211, 212, 213, 214, 215,
   216, 217, 218, 220, 223,
   224, 225, 226, 227, 228,
   229, 230, 233, 234, 235,

236, 237, 238, 239, 240,
241, 242, 244, 245, 246,
247, 248, 275, 276, 277,
278, 279, 280, 282, 283,
284, 285, 286, 287, 288,
295, 296, 297, 298, 299,
300, 303, 304, 305, 306,
307, 309, 312, 313, 314,
316, 317, 318, 319, 326,
338, 339, 341, 344, 346,
347, 348, 349, 351, 352,
353, 356, 357, 358, 359,
360, 361
Mark 3, 35, 40, 50, 55, 56, 113, 114,
130, 145, 146, 157, 161, 179,
207, 211, 242, 248, 283, 285,
296, 312, 326
marriage xviii, 30, 38, 64, 65, 66,
90, 93, 102, 103, 104, 105,
110, 115, 116, 118, 119, 123,
125, 134, 135, 146, 177, 182,
183, 186, 192, 193, 200, 209,
212, 229, 233, 236, 237, 238,
239, 240, 241, 242, 245, 278,
285, 288, 291, 295, 296, 297,
298, 299, 301, 302, 305, 306,
308, 310, 311, 313, 315, 316,
317, 318, 325, 327, 339, 340,
341, 342, 344, 345, 346, 347,
349, 350, 356, 358, 360, 362
Marriage 194, 195, 196, 197, 198,
199, 200, 210, 237, 299, 307,
308, 310, 369
matrimony 82, 124, 309, 315,
317, 360
Matthew xx, 1, 3, 4, 6, 14, 18, 25,
35, 36, 38, 50, 53, 54, 55, 56,
86, 113, 114, 117, 130, 131,
134, 144, 159, 160, 161, 164,
178, 179, 211, 215, 225, 228,

Printed in the United States
By Bookmasters